WITHDR
UTSA Libraries
D0949824
RENEWALS 458-4574

THE SECRET LIVES OF TREBITSCH LINCOLN

1 Trebitsch Lincoln in 1912

THE SECRET LIVES of TREBITSCH LINCOLN

Bernard Wasserstein

Yale University Press
New Haven and London 1988

TO JANET

Copyright © 1988 by Bernard Wasserstein

All rights reserved. This book may not be reproduced, in whole or in part, in any form (beyond that copying permitted by Sections 107 and 108 of the US Copyright Law and except by reviewers for the public press), without written permission from the publishers.

Set in Linotron Bembo by Best-set Typesetter Limited, Hong Kong, and printed and bound in Great Britain at The Bath Press, Avon.

Designed by Ann Grindrod.

Library of Congress Cataloging-in-Publication Data

Wasserstein, Bernard
The secret lives of Trebitsch Lincoln/Bernard Wasserstein.
p. cm.
Bibliography: p.
Includes index.
ISBN 0300040768
1. Trebitsch-Lincoln, Ignatius Timothy, 1879–1943. 2. Adventure and adventurers — Biography. 3. Jews — Hungary — Biography.
I. Title.
D413.T68W37 1988
909.8′092′4—dc 19 87-22494
CIP

LIBRARY
The University of Texas
At San Antonio

CONTENTS

LIST OF ILLUSTRATIONS

ACKNOWLEDGEMENTS

I enjoyed the privilege, while working on this book, of staying as a Visiting Fellow, first at the elegant Jacobean manor house at Yarnton which serves as the headquarters of the Oxford Centre for Postgraduate Hebrew Studies, and then at the Institute for Advanced Studies of the Hebrew University of Jerusalem. What the authorities of these academic institutions will think of this book I shudder to imagine, since in neither case was the invitation originally extended for the purpose of facilitating a study so far removed from their primary purposes. But both provided me with an ideal environment for research, free from the distractions of my normal occupation, and for this I am deeply grateful. I wish also to thank Brandeis University for granting me leave in the academic year 1984–5. I acknowledge my debt to the owners of copyright material quoted in this book.

I owe most to members of my family, notably my mother, father, and brother, each of whom put in long hours of volunteer labour on my behalf. I thank the many correspondents who responded to letters of inquiry, the libraries and archives which supplied me with copies of published materials, all those mentioned in the foreword and in the essay on sources who enabled me to gain access to unpublished documents, and above all the members of Trebitsch Lincoln's family who were most generous with help and information. During my stay in England the Institute of Historical Research allowed me to make free of its wonderful research facilities. Dr Daniel Szechi of the University of Sheffield did valuable research for me in London after my departure, and Dr Elazar Barkan, Dr John Hill and Mr David Soule of Brandeis University did the same in Boston. For grants towards the costs of research I am grateful to Brandeis University and to the National Endowment for the Humanities.

For help in other ways I am grateful to: Professor Chimen Abramsky, Professor Eugene C. Black, Professor Steven Schuker, Professor Morton Keller, Herr Wolfgang Waldner, Senator Edward Kennedy, Miss Z. Nagy, Mr Burt Taylor, Mr Daniel P. Simon, Dr Ludwig Biewer, Dr Regina Mahlke, Messrs. Blyth Dutton, M. Louis Sabourin, Miss S. Carmen, Mr Lee S. Strickland, Mr Erik Petersen, Mr Hans Berggreen, Dr Gabriel Brenka, Sister Jotaka, Mr J.R. Edgington, Mr Roger Krondon, Mr J.C. Runyon, Pastor

Pawlitzki, Mr Victor Polgar, Mr Béla Juszel, General B. Pierluigi Bertinaria, Archivdirektor Dr Heyl, Archivdirektor Dr Morenz, Mlle. Rosine Cleyet-Michaud, General Delmas, M. Bernard Garnier, Mrs Susan Stanley Rice, Revd. K.R. McLean, Mr Thomas F. Conley, Messrs W.T. Walton & Son, Mr Harry Brunger, Ms Andrea Hinding, Dr Robert Baldock, Dr Jonathan Mandelbaum, Miss Ruth Ben-Ghiat, Miss Eleanor Sparagana, the Ven. Myoko-ni, Sir John Winnifrith, Ms Ingrid Eriksson Karth, Professor Rudolph Binion, Dr Albrecht Tyrell, Mr Steven Schlesinger, the Jewish Public Library of Montreal, Professor Richard Menkis, Ms Sharon Uno, Mr D.J. Blackwood and Miss White (of the Home Office), Mrs Paula Tao An Sirander, Ms Dagmar Getz, Dr Zsófia Benke, Ms Alice M. Neary, Professor Leonidas E. Hill, Mr Ed Trebitsch, Mrs Bryony Heap, Mr Tim Lincoln, the late Mr Alexander Krausz, Mrs Rennie Rudas, Mrs Martha Vandor, Miss Elsie Tarcai, Ms Margaret J. Cox, Mr and Mrs Ian Darby, Mrs Ina Malaguti, Dr Michael Silber, the late Dr John Mendelsohn, Mr George Wagner, Mr C.R.N. Swamy, Mr John E. Taylor, Revd. Walter Barker, Mrs J. Campbell, Mrs C.I. Constantinides, Archivrat Dr Weber, Dr István Kollega Tarsoly, Dr R. Neck, Professor Israel Guttman, Professor Hillel Kieval, Ms Dorothy Kealey, the Ven. H. St. C. Hilchey, Mrs G. Lebans, Hofrat Dr Anna Benna, Dr Maria Keipert, Revd. Paul Gerhardt Buttler, Pastor Martin Pörksen, Ms Marianne Wagner, Ms Paulette Dozois, Mr J. Kenneth McDonald, Mr Bennett McCardle, Mr John H. Wright, Mr Martin Gilbert, Miss Livia Gollancz, Professor John Grenville, Ms Arnona Rudavsky, Ms Elena Danielson, Mr János Buzási, Mr Martin Moir, Dr Werner Röder, Professor Eberhard Jäckel, Dr Robert Kapp, Mr E.G.W. Bill, M. Sven Welander, Dr Sybil Milton, Dr R. Cohen, Mr Dan Shute, Professor Dietrich Orlow, Dr H.J.O. Pogge von Strandmann, Mr Nicholas Pointer, Dr J.B. Post, Mr Robin Guthrie, Ms R. Campbell, Professor M. Marrus, Mr J.E.O. Screen, the late Professor Hugh Seton-Watson, Professor Jonathan Spence, President Hui-sen Chu, Miss Sabina Sutherland, Mr Robert Wolfe, Ms Amy Schmidt, Ms Cynthia G. Fox, Mr J. Dane Hartgrove, Ms Barbara Valle, Dr W.J. Sheils, Professor I. Getzler, Dr A. Shai, Revd. C. Glenn Lucas, Mr Timothy D. Dube, Ms Marianne Loenartz, Mr Bruce Hunter, Mr Peter Shepherd, Ms S. Gereau, and Mr Stanley G. Triggs.

My wife disapproved of this project from the outset and has never quite reconciled herself to the fact that Trebitsch Lincoln's ghost set up residence in our household for many months. I nevertheless dedicate this book to her — whether she likes it or not.

FOREWORD

On The Trail of Trebitsch Lincoln

This book is likely to be regarded as something of an affront to the austere canons of my profession. It may therefore be prudent to begin with some personal words in extenuation of my conduct in writing it. The life of a person who left barely any footprints in political history, whose literary relics are without enduring value, and whose fame, such as it is, resides chiefly in his execution of a series of extraordinary contortions in religious and political allegiance, is unlikely to be regarded by my academic colleagues as a significant contribution to the advancement of historical understanding. Realizing that, I wrote this book anyway. Let me try to explain why.

I cannot say quite when I first heard of Trebitsch Lincoln. He is one of those types, notorious in their own day, who sink rapidly into obscurity after their deaths, sometimes hovering briefly in the footnotes of history. Most modern historians have heard of them vaguely, but would be hard put to pinpoint them precisely. I believe that the outlines of Trebitsch Lincoln's story were told to me some years ago in Jerusalem by Dr Geoffrey Wigoder, whose veritably encyclopaedic knowledge of such historical byways is unrivalled. From him I heard, with incredulity, of Trebitsch's successive conversions from Judaism to various sects of Christianity and then to Buddhism, of his wanderings from his native Hungary to China, of his election to the British House of Commons, and of his activity as a German spy in both world wars. but in spite of the fantastic nature of the tale little remained in my memory save a dim recollection that the man was somehow mixed up in something scandalous.

Late one Friday afternoon in August I was imprisoned in the Bodleian Library in Oxford — as so often in Oxford in August — by heavy rain. Having no work by me, and it being too late to order up further books from the stacks, I took to browsing among the supremely boring items which Bodley's Librarian chooses to make available to readers on open access. My eye fell on the hundred or so red-and-green volumes of the *Index to the General Correspondence of the Foreign Office* — enthralling reading matter, at any rate for a historian on a wet afternoon. For reasons the psychological mechanics of which are still not clear to me, I decided out of the blue to look up the name Trebitsch Lincoln. I started to read while waiting for the storm to pass. That was more than a year ago, and the tempest has not yet abated.

The entries in the *Index* comprise the date, reference number and cover title of each file. Searching at random I came across entries for Trebitsch in almost every year between 1921 and 1938. These were frequently of a piquant nature, tantalising by reason of their brevity. Thus the entry for 1923:

> LINCOLN, Trebitsch (alias Patrick Keelan)
> Activities in connection with Chinese deputation to General Ludendorff respecting Sino-German relations C19697/19545/18

or for 1924:

> LINCOLN, Trebitsch (alias Trautwein)
> Activities in connection with alleged sale of bogus German military plans to French authorities C10301/10301/18

As I moved to the volumes dealing with the 1930s the arena of activity appeared to shift:

1931:

> LINCOLN, Trebitsch
> Request for facilities to return to UK refused; Foreign Office minute on career of; initiated as Buddhist priest F4266/4266/10

1937:

> LINCOLN, Trebitsch
> Japanese propaganda activity F10871/480/10

and 1938:

> LINCOLN, Trebitsch
> Activity in Tibet; movements F11794/44/10

At seven o'clock the library closed and I was thrust out into the rain. While cycling away I pondered the meaning of the frequent changes of name, the apparent movement from Europe to the Far East, and the seeming combination of religious and political intrigue.

As I considered the matter further during that dank weekend it seemed wise to dismiss the man as a colourful but unimportant confidence trickster or adventurer. But the following week I found myself drawn back to the Bodleian, where I ordered up everything I could find relating to Trebitsch Lincoln. I read his two autobiographies, which struck me as highly unreliable and full of tall stories, as well as a tract which he published in Shanghai in the 1930s. Investigating a little further, I discovered that there existed a quite large literature on Trebitsch Lincoln, most of it published in his lifetime, and generally of a sensational or journalistic nature. The most recent work on him, *The Self-Made Villain* by David Lampe and Laszlo Szenasi, appeared to be more serious in character. But even that book, published in 1961, was based to a large degree on newspaper cuttings and other published works, including those of Trebitsch himself, which could not be regarded as altogether satisfactory sources given the subject's admitted propensity to exaggeration and lying. On the final page of the book the authors noted: 'We have been assured that the complete Foreign Office dossier on Trebitsch-Lincoln — if one exists — will be opened to the public in 1993.'

At this point it should be explained that in 1961 there prevailed in Britain what was known as the 'fifty-year rule'. This meant that official records were, in general, closed to historians until half a century had elapsed from the date of their production. Whatever the merits of the regulation in protecting the reputations, during their lifetimes, of politicians and civil servants, the rule had the effect of virtually preventing contemporary historians of Britain from writing any documented political history, since what should have been their chief sources, namely government papers, were barred from view. The election of Harold Wilson's Labour Government in 1964 changed all this. Perhaps the only lasting achievement of his first two governments between 1964 and 1970 (at any rate from the unprejudiced historian's point of view) was the shortening of the period of embargo from fifty to thirty years. This suddenly opened the greater part of the inter-war period to professional historical research, and, by a further concession in 1972, almost the entire range of records for the Second World War was made available. One consequence of all this was that the Foreign Office records concerning Trebitsch Lincoln, of whose very existence Lampe and Szenasi had been uncertain, but which were listed in the published indexes I had seen, must now have been released for inspection at the Public Record Office in Kew.

I set off on the train from Oxford down the Thames to Kew in order to satisfy my growing curiosity. Would these official papers corroborate the outrageous account of his life given by Trebitsch himself, or even the somewhat more reserved version accepted by Lampe and Szenasi in their pioneering study? I was still highly sceptical as to whether I would find the answer at Kew. I knew from experience that not all files listed in the *Index* actually reached the Public Record Office. Most unimportant or repetitive papers are 'weeded' out and destroyed in Whitehall before dispatch to the great repository. The volume of public business these days is such that only documents deemed likely to be of historical importance can possibly be stored for posterity — a tiny fraction of the miles of paper spewed forth each year by government departments. Trebitsch Lincoln did not seem, from my researches thus far, to have been a person of any great weight or significance, and it was therefore entirely possible that the files listed in the *Index* would have been destroyed long ago by a zealous Whitehall 'weeder'. Moreover, even if the files, or some of them, existed, disappointing experiences in the past had taught me that files with what appear to be the most sensational titles often contain the most dreary and unilluminating material; occasionally they are altogether empty. I did not, therefore, hold any great expectations, and even rationalised my conduct by persuading myself that I was travelling to Kew not on the trail of Trebitsch Lincoln at all but in pursuit of another more respectable research project on which I was at that time engaged. I thought, however, that I might amuse myself, perhaps during part of my lunch break, by checking a few of the Trebitsch Lincoln references.

I took no lunch that day — nor on several subsequent visits to the archive. For I found that my scepticism, at any rate as to the existence of the files, was unjustified. Nearly all were there. Nor were they empty; indeed, some were bulging with telegrams, letters and reports. As I dug further I found that the series of Foreign Office files on Trebitsch Lincoln had in fact begun as early as 1906 and that other government departments too had kept records of their dealings with him. But the contents of the files did not quench my curiosity. If anything they increased my perplexity. For they opened a window into a world of such bizarre and complex conspiratorial activity that it seemed impossible to disentangle truth from rumour, propaganda stunts, or psychological warfare, let alone downright lies. I returned to Oxford more puzzled than ever, bemused as to why the British Government had involved itself with this man for more than three decades, and wondering whether it was really worth my while to take the trouble to try to find out.

I had half-resolved to extrude Trebitsch Lincoln from my mind altogether when a second chance discovery embroiled me deeper in his affairs. Once again it occurred in the Bodleian Library where I had returned with the intention of devoting myself to my more conventional scholarly avocations. Passing one day through Duke Humphrey's reading room, the ancient heart of the library, I happened to notice a large set of filing drawers. These were familiar to me as containing the catalogue of the Bodleian's massive holdings of unpublished private papers of individuals over several centuries. I checked the catalogue on the off-chance that some document concerning Trebitsch Lincoln might have found its way to Oxford — which seemed unlikely since he had apparently spent the last years of his life in China. The catalogue did not carry his name. I was about to give up the matter entirely when I recalled that I had noted somewhere that the Bodleian had recently acquired the archives of some missionary society. I linked this with a fact I had already learnt from the published sources, that Trebitsch had briefly served as a missionary in Canada around the turn of the century. I made inquiries and was directed across the road to that hideously ugly pile, known as the New Bodleian, where modern historical papers are kept. It was a long shot, and I hesitated before walking across. There had existed, after all, hundreds of missionary societies, and the chance of any documentation about an individual missionary, and a thoroughly undistinguished one at that, who had worked for only a short time in Montreal more than eight decades ago, turning up in the university library at Oxford seemed quite remote.

In the New Bodleian I discovered that my memory had not deceived me. The papers of the Church's Ministry among the Jews (formerly known as the London Society for the Promotion of Christianity among the Jews) had recently been deposited in the Bodleian and were open to readers. The society had maintained a Canadian section, of which a few bundles of papers were still extant, and it was to these letters and reports that I first directed my attention. To my astonishment I found that they included a detailed and highly circumstantial account of the short career as an employee of the society of the Revd. I.T. Trebitsch. These contemporary papers gave a vivid picture of his spiritual wrestlings as well as of certain financial irregularities in his early life. They form the main basis of chapter two of this book.

For the first time I felt that I had begun to penetrate beyond the curtain of bluff and bombast behind which Trebitsch had concealed himself from scrutiny. True, these papers by themselves were not the key to the mystery of his personality. But they persuaded me that there existed here a problem in historical psychology which it would be worthwhile and, with some further luck, also possible to unravel. My initial curiosity had by now grown into genuine interest; eventually, I must confess, it was to develop into a virtual obsession as I stripped away veil after veil shrouding the truth about Trebitsch Lincoln.

During the next few weeks I dispatched more than a hundred letters to archives, libraries, and individuals in a dozen or more countries, inquiring as to the whereabouts of any relevant unpublished documentation. Some sent back negative replies, but a surprisingly large number either sent me copies of documents or invited me to call and inspect their holdings. With the aid of these primary sources it was now possible to prepare an outline of the bare facts of Trebitsch Lincoln's life. As a result, this book presents for the first time in print an authentic and *verifiable* account of his doings.

But beyond that, as pieces of the jigsaw slowly came together, it became plain to me that I must investigate not just the pattern of his movements and activities, but a cluster of questions in social, political, and diplomatic history. How had a complete outsider succeeded in burrowing his way through to the core of three quite separate national élites, all highly exclusive, xenophobic and mutually antagonistic: the British, the German, and the Chinese? What had been the real nature of Trebitsch's political role in each of these three countries and in the murky waters of international intrigue in which he seemed to fish? What exactly had been the function of the web of relationships he had apparently spun with the intelligence organizations of half a dozen states? How had it come about that a man repeatedly dismissed as a crank or a madman had kept bouncing back, forcing himself on the attention of statesmen and officials and popping up time after time in a new trouble-making capacity?

Above all, there was the enigma of Trebitsch's inner life. Gradually it dawned on me that the psychological dimension was crucial to an understanding of the entire phenomenon. Trebitsch had evidently suffered from a psychosis which, towards the end of his life, completely took control of his personality and without some closer diagnosis of which I could not arrive at an explanation of his actions or an appreciation of the meaning of his life as a whole. At this point I was greatly assisted by discussions with my friend Dr Roland Littlewood of the Department of Psychiatric Medicine at University College, London, who pointed me towards the interpretation of Trebitsch's personality offered in this book. I should add immediately that he would no doubt disapprove of much of the crude layman's language in which my argument is couched. Nor, in the end, do I present this to the reader as an exercise in psychohistory. What I have simply tried to do is to portray all the facets of a unique and many-sided life, both internally as an exploration of one highly disturbed mind, and externally as a no less disturbing influence on the lives of others.

One major difficulty which confronted me as soon as I began to organize my heterogeneous materials was what value to place on Trebitsch's own writings, notably his two autobiographical works,

Revelations of an International Spy (1916) and *Autobiography of an Adventurer* (1932). On many points these gave a completely distorted picture, but for some periods they seemed to provide the only available source for Trebitsch's whereabouts and activities. Here, happily, I had the example before me of two classic biographies (whose sujects bear a frequently uncanny resemblance to — and on one occasion* may even directly impinge on — the life of Trebitsch Lincoln): A.J.A. Symons' brilliant 'experiment in biography', *The Quest for Corvo*, and Hugh Trevor-Roper's subtle study of Sir Edmund Backhouse, *Hermit of Peking*. In both cases, as in that of Trebitsch Lincoln, the subject was a combination of exhibitionist and recluse whose word simply could not be trusted. Having received my first instruction in history at Oxford from the lectures on Edward Gibbon of the then Regius Professor, Hugh Trevor-Roper, I decided to follow his method as set forth in the prologue to his account of Backhouse, and to build up Trebitsch Lincoln's history 'as far as possible, solely from external sources, without any reference to his memoirs, even as a starting point.'[1] Apart from instances, therefore, where Trebitsch's own words are quoted as evidence of what he wished the world to believe about himself or (more rarely and with caution) as clues towards his mental state, this book is based entirely on primary sources drawn from persons other than the subject himself.

Once that decision had been taken I was able to proceed to erect scaffolding for much of the story. But one fundamental aspect continued to elude me. Apart from a few snippets of information garnered from such places as the archives of the Budapest Drama Academy and the police records of various countries, I possessed little authentic information about Trebitsch's childhood. How would it be possible for me to explain his later development without some examination of the formative influences on his character of his family and early surroundings? For a time I ignored the problem, comforting myself with Evelyn Waugh's airy dismissal (in the early pages of his own autobiography, *A Little Learning*) of the common notion that the events of early childhood determine the patterns of adult life. Would it really be helpful, after all, to know whether Freud was toilet-trained at the age of one, Einstein moonstruck at two, or little Niccolò Machiavelli unscrupulously manipulating the affairs of his playmates at three? Even if such information were available, does not such an approach risk falling into the trap of hindsight — of seeing a false significance and reference point in events, in themselves trivial, merely because of their superficial connexion with adult characteristics? Nevertheless, this gap in my

* See below p. 198.

evidence bothered me and I was at a loss as to how to deal with it.

It was at this point that two further chance events, occurring almost simultaneously, came to my rescue. It so happened that I had been corresponding for some time with Professor John Greppin, an expert in Armenian linguistics at Cleveland State University in Ohio. The subject of our correspondence was the ethnography of Palestinian gypsies. When, therefore, the following October I moved on temporary assignment to Jerusalem, I wrote to Professor Greppin with some further trivial information which had come my way on the gypsies. Meanwhile, I had found out, in the course of my researches, that a younger brother of Trebitsch Lincoln had emigrated around 1910 from Hungary to the USA and had settled in Cleveland, where he had established a Hungarian socialist newspaper. Beyond that I had next to no information about him. But I thought it worth adding, in my letter to Professor Greppin, a query as to whether it might be possible, some three quarters of a century later, to trace any descendants of this man who might, I surmised, still live in Cleveland.

What Professor Greppin (whom I have never had an opportunity of meeting) made of such a strange request I do not know. But he is evidently a person of tolerant spirit and rare resource. For by return of post I heard that he had indeed located a lady, now in her late eighties, still resident in Cleveland, who was Trebitsch Lincoln's niece. She not only responded kindly to my many questions, but also very generously sent me a copy of a manuscript about her father, her uncle, and the Trebitsch family, which she had set to paper when a college student in the late 1920s.

A little later a no less miraculous conjunction brought me further help. One evening at a concert in the Jerusalem Theatre, I happened to meet my old friend, Dr Elizabeth Eppler, a noted authority on the history of the Jews in Hungary, who had recently settled in Jerusalem. When I mentioned to her that I was writing a book about Trebitsch Lincoln, she responded by telling me that one of her greatest friends was a great-niece of Trebitsch Lincoln, and she fished out of her handbag the address and those of another niece and a nephew of Trebitsch Lincoln, both now in their nineties and living in London. Within a short time I was on a plane back to England, where I had the pleasure of meeting these relatives of my subject. In spite of their advanced years, they could both remember their uncle with remarkable precision and lucidity, and since they had known him well (and in the case of the nephew had even worked closely with him*) their testimony was invaluable. Moreover, through them I was introduced to one of Trebitsch Lincoln's

* See chapter 5.

granddaughters, who, over lunch in the charming restaurant which she and her husband ran in Greenwich, provided me with further vital information for my story.

By combining the new evidence given me by Trebitsch Lincoln's surviving relations with what I already knew from other sources, I was now in a position to attempt to draw at any rate the outlines of an account of his childhood and adolescence — and of the relationship of his early experiences to the wayward odyssey of his adult life.

My quest for materials carried me far from my usual beat and along a number of rarely frequented avenues. I little expected on that first rainy day in Oxford that a year or so later I should be immersed in the records of the Special Branch of the Shanghai Municipal Police, let alone that these documents would furnish me with the last crucial set of clues that would enable me finally to unravel the mystery of Trebitsch Lincoln.

Trebitsch retains, even in death, a capacity to astound, and it is, I suppose, possible that he may yet rise from the grave, in the form of a posthumous *cache* of documents, in order to contradict everything that I say about him in this book. Notwithstanding that faint possibility, I feel for the time being sufficiently confident in the authenticity and amplitude of the evidence at my disposal to claim that what follows is the closest accessible approach to the true history of a false messiah.

London
August 1987

CHAPTER 1

The Early Life of Ignácz Trebitsch

In 1726 the Emperor Charles VI of the Holy Roman Empire promulgated a law known as the *Familiantengesetz*. The object of this decree was to restrict the population of Jews living in the Czech crown lands of Bohemia, Moravia and Silesia, which formed part of the Emperor's dominions. To this end a limit was set on the number of Jewish households permitted in these areas. The law was reaffirmed by Charles VI's daughter, the Empress Maria Theresa, and remained in force, with some modifications, until 1848. Its practical effect was that only the eldest son in each Jewish family was permitted to marry and establish his domicile in the Czech lands.[1] A pattern therefore developed of younger sons delaying marriage and then being compelled to move away from their places of origin in order to set up their own households. The result was a considerable Jewish migration flowing both eastwards into Poland and south into Hungary.

Among these involuntary emigrants were probably (we have no written record) the ancestors of the subject of this book, Ignácz Trebitsch, later known as Trebitsch Lincoln. When, under the rule of Maria Theresa's son, Joseph II, it was laid down that Jews must take on surnames (hitherto not usual among them), many of these emigrants naturally took on the name of their place of origin. The Trebitsch family, if they conformed to the usual pattern, thus in all likelihood derived their name from the little Moravian town of Třebič.

Ignácz Trebitsch was born on 4 April 1879 at Paks, a small town on the bank of the Danube south of Budapest in central Hungary.[2] His father, Nathan Trebitsch, was a prosperous Jewish merchant, the owner of a fleet of barges which transported grain supplies on the river. Ignácz's mother, Julia, née Freund, came of a wealthy Jewish family who some time after her marriage were raised to the Hungarian nobility.

In their economic and social advance the Trebitsch and Freund families were typical representatives of the upper crust of the Hungarian Jewish bourgeoisie in this period. One of the first acts of independent Hungary after the establishment of the Dual Monarchy in 1867 had been to complete the emancipation of the Jews, a process begun but not fully achieved under Joseph II. The half-century after 1867 was, in many ways, the golden age of Hungarian Jewry, clouded only a little by the rise of political anti-Semitism towards the end of the nineteenth century. Many Jews moved into the professions, particularly in Budapest, where they formed a large part of the population. Among the rich some, like the Freunds, became landowners and sought to merge into the aristocracy; others, like Nathan Trebitsch, were wholesale transporters, particularly of grain, or moved into high finance.

Of the personal characteristics of Ignácz Trebitsch's parents little is known. Nathan Trebitsch, however, differed from others of his class in that he neither converted to Christianity nor modified his religious habits after the manner of the reformist *Neolog* Jews; he hewed instead to the strict path of orthodoxy and enjoined this on his family in a dictatorial fashion. Julia Trebitsch too was traditionally minded in her religious practices and, by extension, in her conception of her role as a woman. She bore her husband fourteen (by another account, sixteen) children, several of whom died in infancy.[3]

Of the survivors six were boys. Ignácz was the second son. His elder brother, Vilmos, gained a reputation for brilliance at school and entered banking; he subsequently went mad. The third son, Lajos, was also academically gifted and became a progressive educationalist; later he went into politics and emerged as a leader of the nascent Hungarian Social Democratic Party in the early years of the twentieth century; we shall meet him again at a later stage. We shall also encounter the fourth son, József, and the sixth, Simon, both of whom emigrated to the USA. The fifth, Sándor, remained in Hungary, where he was murdered by the Nazis in World War II. This, in outline, was a fairly typical family history for middle-class Hungarian Jews in this period — with the exception of the strain of mental illness.

The competitive struggle for parental attention among this large brood seems to have scarred several of the children, though probably none more than Ignácz. The domineering father, the mother who (according to one granddaughter's account) 'served the men with hand and foot',[4] the gifted but unstable elder brother who was the cynosure of parental admiration and ambition, the ever-increasing phalanx of younger children clamouring for favour — these family circumstances may perhaps help explain the tendency, noticeable in Ignácz Trebitsch throughout his life, always to try almost compulsively to call attention to himself. As we shall see, this characteristic was evident even in circumstances where a wiser policy would have been to shut up.

The education of Ignácz, like that of his brothers, was imbued with the father's religious convictions and reflected his ascending social status. Although the Jewish community of Paks numbered in the 1880s only just over a thousand the town boasted a *yeshiva* (talmudical college), and orthodoxy remained strong. The Trebitsch boys received an orthodox religious education at the Paks Jewish elementary school. According to the school register Ignácz completed the fourth grade successfully in 1889. But perhaps the most important formative influence on him in these years was a period he spent staying with a family in Pressburg (Bratislava).[5] Why he was sent to this distant city we do not know, although Pressburg was regarded as the capital of central European Jewish orthodoxy, and there were strong links with other orthodox communities of eastern Hungary. The significance of the episode for Ignácz was twofold: first, it accustomed him in early youth to living away from home; secondly, since the language of the household was German, he attained a ready fluency in this second language — presaging his later outstanding linguistic achievements.*

A little later the Trebitsch family moved to Budapest, where Nathan Trebitsch was drawn away from his solid barge transportation business into a heady whirlpool of high finance and stock-market speculation. For the early adolescent the change from a sleepy provincial backwater to the glittering royal capital was evidently an exciting and unsettling experience. Ignácz was dazzled by the glamour of the great city — again, one can detect throughout his life a similar stirring of the blood whenever he encountered the cosmopolitanism and bustle of a large metropolis. Perhaps for this reason he performed miserably in his studies and seems to have been overshadowed by his elder brother, Vilmos. He played truant, and failed the examinations in the sixth form of the local secondary school.[6] In fact, in spite of his undoubted gift for languages, his insubordinate and restless temperament rendered him an impossible pupil — with the result that his knowledge, although often impressively broad, was that of a snapper-up of unconsidered trifles rather than the product of profound or systematic learning.

Soon after they moved to Budapest, Ignácz decided, rather than follow his elder brother into banking, to indulge his predilection for bright lights and public attention by becoming an actor. On 5

* Although his German was excellent it was not quite perfect: he always spoke it with a slight accent and could be readily identified as non-German. His German writings, while fluent and idiomatic, are marked by minor but persistent errors.

September 1895 he enrolled as a student at the Royal Hungarian Academy of Dramatic Art. He was still only sixteen and appears to have lied about his age, since the register of the academy gives his date of birth as '1877 or 1878'. His record of achievement at the academy was minimal, indeed virtually non-existent. He left in the course of the first year without taking any examinations or appearing in any public performances. In October 1896 he was permitted to enter again as a first-year student, but dropped out a second time in the course of the year, never to return.[7]

In the spring of 1897 Ignácz Trebitsch was eighteen years old. Of medium height and stocky build, he had black hair, a moustache, and (his most striking feature) piercing dark eyes. Superficially precocious and worldly in some ways, he remained naive, provincial and immature in others. Indeed, emotionally he probably never fully matured. All his life he was prone to childish outbreaks of rage; he was unable to concentrate on any one thing for very long; he was given to flagrant exhibitionism, always trying to outshine his fellows whatever the company; he would harp on trivial grievances, standing on his pride with an infant's petulance; he was capable of bursts of sentimentality but not of love; a show-off in society, he had no real friends. And yet he possessed an unusual capacity to charm those with whom he came into contact: more than that, he often left an indelible and overwhelming initial impression on people he met. He could talk entertainingly and with apparent profundity on a variety of subjects. His knowledge of languages, his voluble conversation, and his nervous excitability suggested a sensitive temperament and a high, if ill-disciplined intelligence. If he never succeeded in taming his temper or mending his other defects, he did exploit to the full his few assets — characteristics essential in each of his successive careers.

Meanwhile the Trebitsch family had suffered a sudden reversal of fortunes. Nathan Trebitsch lost heavily in a stock-market crash, went out on a limb in an effort to save what remained — then lost that too.[8] The family was reduced to penury — a bitter blow most particularly for Ignácz's mother, who had grown up used to a life of ease. The family's finances never recovered and in later years their interrelationships were to degenerate into pathetic squabbles about paltry sums of money.

This drastic alteration in circumstances, upsetting to economic, social, and emotional security, had lasting effects on the impressionable teenager. In the conduct of financial affairs he plainly concluded (although in a different way from his socialist brother, Lajos) that the bourgeois morality that had first enriched and then destroyed his father served no purpose, save to cloak an amoral capitalist jungle. For most of the rest of his life he evinced a strange mixture of unscrupulous determination in the acquisition of money and carefree irresponsibility in its spending.

A Budapest police report in 1897 stated that Ignácz Trebitsch had been accused, some time before, of the theft of a gold watch worth two hundred crowns.[9] Around the same time the police in the port city of Trieste requested information about him, since he had been accused of theft there too. In these early essays in juvenile petty thievery we may recognize (with the benefit of hindsight) the first inklings of one of the great (or at any rate one of the most bizarre) criminal careers of modern times.

In neither case could proceedings be taken against him, because the bird had flown. A fugitive from the law, Trebitsch now embarked on what was to be a lifetime of wanderings. According to his own account his travels at this period took him as far afield as North and South America.[10] It is possible that he did indeed cross the Atlantic, although we have no independent corroboration of this story. But he certainly went as far as England, apparently attracted there by the forthcoming celebration of Queen Victoria's Diamond Jubilee.[11] This journey was the harbinger of many more: for most of his life he rarely stayed in one place for more than a few months (or weeks or days) unless obliged to do so by some compelling external force (such as imprisonment or lack of a passport). Travel for Trebitsch was not a source of amusement or of intellectual enrichment; it was a disease. It was as if some nomadic genie were inside him always urging him to move on in search of new stimulations, new opportunities, and new people to impress. It was an illness for which there was no cure, although on this first visit to England an attempt was made to rein in his irredeemable restlessness of spirit.

In England Trebitsch fell among missionaries. Down and out in the east end of London, he was taken in by the Revd. Lypshytz of the Barbican mission to the Jews. This was a branch of the London Society for the Promotion of Christianity among the Jews, an old and well-established missionary organization with outposts in various parts of the world. Operating under the aegis of the Church of England, the London Society made particular efforts to proselytise among the masses of poor Jewish immigrants from eastern and central Europe who crowded into Whitechapel and neighbouring areas in the east end of London. Like many agents of the society Revd. Lypshytz was himself a convert from Judaism. The missionaries in the immigrant areas found their task a hard one since most of their potential proselytes were either orthodox Jews, immune to their ministrations, or radicals and atheists who had thrown off the shackles of religion altogether. Occasionally, however, they encountered a readier response among young single men, socially and spiritually disoriented by their new surroundings. It was to this group among the immigrants that the London Society's agents especially directed their gospel in the form of tracts and street-corner sermons, often delivered in Yiddish. But it must be admitted that the rescue of such potential converts (or, as the missionaries' opponents put it, the entrapment of bewildered youths) was often facilitated by more tangible inducements — a bed for the night, a free meal, or even a chair in a heated reading room.

Trebitsch's attraction towards the mission was probably a compound of spiritual and material elements. He had already abandoned the orthodox faith of his father. Conversion to Christianity among Hungarian Jews in this period was frequent, particularly among the middle class, and was not regarded with quite the horror felt by more traditional east European Jews towards those they felt to be renegades and traitors. But while Trebitsch had lost interest in Judaism, he by no means jettisoned religion altogether; indeed, as we shall see, spiritual enthusiasm fulfilled vital psychological needs for him throughout his life. Tramping around friendless in the east end he undoubtedly appreciated the warmth of Revd. Lypshytz's hospitality. Although the evangelist was to be cruelly disappointed in his young protégé, and although Trebitsch rewarded kindness with criminality, it would be wrong for us to take a completely cynical view of his motives in accepting the missionary's generosity (which was, after all, itself, from one point of view, by no means wholly disinterested).

After briefly inducting Trebitsch into the aims and purposes of the society, Lypshytz decided to send him to stay at a hostel in Bristol which had been established for the specific purpose of providing a refuge for immigrant youths who were potential converts. The Wanderers' Home, as it was called, had been established in London in the 1850s, but in 1894 it was moved to Bristol, probably because the inmates would there be much less susceptible to the anti-missionary influences rampant in the areas of large immigrant Jewish concentration. The administrator of the home at the time of Trebitsch's sojourn was the Revd. John Moses Epstein, another 'Hebrew Christian'. Epstein was a much respected missionary for the London Society, with a long string of successful baptisms to his credit. But even in Bristol he encountered bitter Jewish hostility to his work.

A contemporary leaflet, entitled *Propagating the Gospel Among the Jews*, fiercely denounced the London Society as the 'Society for turning bad Jews into worse Christians'. The Wanderers' Home was reviled with peculiar venom, the pamphlet declaring that it catered to wandering *schnorrers* who were given three months' free board and lodging plus sixpence a week pocket money. The attack continued: 'Those who, after having done "time", declare their willingness to be baptised, receive the assurance of either a free passage to Canada, or a promise of a few pounds to start something for a living here.'[12] No doubt in response to such attacks, Revd. Epstein had a statement printed which was issued to all would-be inmates, including, presumably, Trebitsch. This announced, somewhat defensively:

> *All applicants for admission to the Wanderers' Home are hereby informed what the Home is not, and what it is.*
> 1. It is *not* a place for poor Jews to be fed, lodged and clothed, in order that, merely because they have no other means of subsistence, they may be instructed in the Christian religion, and even baptized.
> 2. It is *not* a school, or a college, nor is it an establishment to induce or bribe Jews to be baptized.
> 3. It is a shelter where, for a limited time, honest and sincere inquirers, who are often obliged to leave home, kindred and friends, may study God's Word unmolested, enjoy the benefits of daily religious instruction, and have the advantages of a well-regulated Christian home.[13]

Such a hostel might be thought to have been ideally suited to the needs of one such as Trebitsch, providing him with a peaceful arbour for contemplation while he determined the future direction of his life. In fact, the contrary was the case. We have already noted Trebitsch's lack of self-discipline and insubordinate temper. It is hard, indeed, to imagine a type less likely to fit into what was (as the 'Wanderers' Home Rules and Regulations', issued in 1897, demonstrate) a severe regimen:

> 1. At the ringing of the first bell, everyone must rise AT ONCE, wash and dress himself, do the work assigned to him, make his bed, and get down to the Lecture Room in time for prayers. This must be strictly observed . . .
> 4. In the afternoon the inmates are allowed to go out for walks for one or two hours, and when they return they may employ their time in secular studies or reading. At six o'clock there will be tea, when all are expected to be present.
> 5. Evening prayers are at nine o'clock, and every inmate is expected to be present. After prayers no one is allowed to leave the home. . . .
> 9. All low, unseemly or immoral remarks, teazing, nagging, and practical jokes are strictly forbidden. . . .
> 16. Visits to Jews, and all seeking of temporary relief from them, or anyone else, are strictly prohibited.
> 17. Inmates are expected to go at least twice to church every Sunday and to be very attentive and devout during the service and sermon.

> 18. It is required of all inmates to learn the Messianic passages by heart, to acquaint themselves with the history, miracles, and parables of our Lord, to study carefully the Acts of the Apostles, the Epistles of the Hebrews and the Romans, and to learn the Church Catechism by heart, in any language they choose.[14]

Trebitsch did not long endure this regime. The importance of his stay in Bristol was indirect: it furnished a model of how *not* to run a missionary enterprise — one which would be of use to Trebitsch later in his own work as a missionary for Christianity, Buddhism, and other causes. Moreover, the episode marked the start of the alternating pattern of the ascetic and the voluptuary that was to characterise most of Trebitsch's adult life.

Returning to London Trebitsch was again afforded lodging by the Revd. Lypshytz. Perhaps the cleric hoped that the unruly youth might respond better to a system less harsh than the muscular Christianity of the Wanderers' Home. If so he was disillusioned, for Trebitsch disappeared soon afterwards. Simultaneously there vanished a watch and chain, the property of Revd. Lypshytz's wife, and a passport belonging to another Jewish immigrant youth who had also taken shelter with the London Society.[15] (Since passports were not generally needed for international travel at this period it is not clear why Trebitsch stole this document — if, as, alas, one must assume, he was the thief. Perhaps he took it to conceal his identity. Whatever the reason, the incident serves as a foretaste of his later obsessional preoccupation with travel documents of all varieties, of which, as we shall see, he was to form an impressive collection.) Fortunately for Trebitsch his former host, now victim, seems not to have reported the theft to the police. At any rate Trebitsch returned unapprehended to Hungary.

Back home he cast around for some means of making a living. But his failure at the Drama Academy had already demonstrated his inability to concentrate his mind and focus his energies sufficiently to train for a profession. With his parents preoccupied by the problems of maintaining their large family in sadly reduced circumstances, there was little to be expected by way of help or guidance from home. Unable to settle down to a steady job, Trebitsch drifted into occasional journalism and, according to one account, combined this with an interest in esoteric religion by becoming editor of a spiritualist paper.[16] Soon after his return to Budapest, however, the police received yet another complaint that he had stolen a gold watch.[17] In late 1898 he left home, this time for ever. He went first to Hamburg where he once again found refuge in a mission house. This was the 'Jerusalem' house, the Irish Presbyterian mission in Hamburg, presided over by another converted Hungarian Jew, the

Revd. Arnold Frank. In a report written about two years afterwards, Trebitsch recalled:

> I left my fatherland, my family, my relations, and went to Germany. God rewarded this my step. On the 26th of November 1898, I arrived in Hamburg, and four days later I could say, 'My Lord, and my God'.[18]

Trebitsch spent the following year in Hamburg studying under the direction of Revd. Frank, in preparation for conversion to Christianity.

Given his tendency, already apparent, to become restive if he remained for any length of time in one place, Trebitsch's repose in Hamburg even for as long as a year may seem surprising. But he had another motive, beyond his spiritual interests, for stopping. Trebitsch had met his future wife.

Margarethe Kahlor, a Lutheran, the daughter of a retired ship's captain, Johann Kahlor, was two years older than Trebitsch. A simple, unworldly, impressionable, sentimental, rather plain and in every way ordinary girl, she was overwhelmed and dazzled by the glib and boastful conversation of the young Hebrew Christian. She later recalled her first meeting with him, one Sunday afternoon, when a friend of her parents brought Trebitsch to their home in Hamburg:

> Our new acquaintance, Herr Trebitsch, looked so harmless with his beautiful brown eyes, full of expression and sympathy. He was then nineteen years old, tall and slim, his hair a mass of black curls. He was altogether different to the young people I was acquainted with, and I admired his rather sad, but arresting, personality.... He told me he was a journalist; that his father preferred him to continue his studies with a view to becoming a doctor and gaining a prominent position in life. He had resisted and decided to travel round the world to gain experience.

He became a regular caller at the Kahlor home, the visits always ending in prayer led by Trebitsch:

> We were prepared for his request: 'Now let us pray'. We would kneel down. While his prayer lasted, my parents seemed transported into another world. I watched him as he prayed. It was an interesting demonstration. His eyes were tightly closed, his arms raised, and his hands clenched. Raising his voice he would cry fervently: 'Deliver us from all sins, purify our hearts, take possession of our lives.... Enter now to monopolise our souls.'[19]

Captain Kahlor was a respectable man, apparently of some means; his behaviour in allowing a penniless young foreigner, and a Jew to boot, thus to gain an ascendancy over his daughter was perhaps unconventional. But the father was conscious of one flaw which must dim her attractiveness in the eyes of most suitors: she was not alone. An illegitimate child, Julius Robert, had been born to her in October 1897, apparently of an Alsatian father from whom he took the surname Tut.[20] The child's father had decamped, leaving Margarethe and her family to care for the baby. In these circumstances the Kahlors probably could not afford to be too particular about the social standing of their young visitor.

Meanwhile Trebitsch's instruction in the Christian faith, in its Irish Presbyterian mode, proceeded apace, and after a little over a year he was judged ready to be received into the church. The death of his father in July 1899 no doubt made it easier for him to contemplate the great step. On Christmas Day 1899 in the Jerusalem chapel in Hamburg he was baptised by Revd. Frank as Ignatius Timotheus Trebitsch, and became a Christian.[21] Frank was so impressed by the potentialities of his new proselyte that he recommended him for admission to the Lutheran theological seminary at Breklum in Schleswig-Holstein. This institution had been established in 1879 by Pastor Christian Jensen, who served as its first rector. The Breklum seminary specialised in the training of Lutheran pastors for congre gations in America as well as missionaries for service in Asia, Africa, and other parts of the world. At the time of Trebitsch's admission Jensen was ill and dying and the effective head of the establishment was his son, also called Christian Jensen. None of the parties concerned seems to have given a moment's thought to the minor doctrinal and ritual distinctions between the Presbyterian and Lutheran sects. Thus it was that when Trebitsch arrived at Breklum on 8 January 1900, after just thirteen days in the Presbyterian fold, he crossed into the embrace of the Lutheran church.[22]

If the Bristol Wanderers' Home had about it something of the air of Dotheboys Hall, Breklum was certainly a far more serious academic institution. But here too, it seems, there was little room for those unwilling to buckle down to hard work, both mental and physical. According to the plan formulated by the elder Jensen at the time of the seminary's foundation, the official timetable was to begin each day at six a.m. and continue until ten in the evening. Apart from a lunch break the seminarians were given no time to themselves. Two hours each morning were to be devoted to outdoor work such as gardening and the afternoon was occupied with practical activity such as shoe-making. The evening hours were reserved for the preparation of lessons.[23]

Such a routine, alternating cobbling and catechism, had proved itself a pedagogic success during the previous two decades, but, all too predictably, it held little attraction for the refractory young

Hungarian. The move from Hamburg, a great international port, to Breklum, a sleepy provincial backwater near the Danish frontier, scarcely enthused a young man whose instincts impelled him so relentlessly towards metropolitan excitement. Moreover, as we have noted, Trebitsch had a special reason for regretting the move from Hamburg, and he continued to correspond with Margarethe Kahlor throughout their separation.[24] A succinct notation in the hand of the younger Pastor Jensen, preserved among the archives of the Breklum seminary, records the ignominious outcome: 'Left middle May nervous headache.'[25]

Trebitsch returned to Hamburg. Pastor Frank, however, evidently felt that the Jerusalem mission could not provide a permanent home for the failed seminarian. Whether at Frank's recommendation (as Trebitsch's own account has it)[26] or on his own initiative, Trebitsch bade farewell to Margarethe, and embarked on a boat for the Americas.

Upon arrival in Canada he found his way to the Presbyterian mission to the Jews in Montreal, an ailing enterprise headed by a devoted but weary and disillusioned minister, the Revd. J. McCarter. 'In the summer of 1900 [McCarter later wrote] a young Hebrew Christian, Mr J.T. Trebitsch arrived from Germany, and called upon me. He impressed me most favourably and seemed to me one of the few of his class, whom I have chanced to meet, in whom one can feel like putting full confidence.'[27] Trebitsch appears to have hoped that he might be given shelter by the mission, but the parlous financial condition of the enterprise precluded any such hospitality. He thereupon made his way to New York. How he survived there for the next few months we do not know, but he remained in correspondence with both Margarethe and McCarter. Towards the end of 1900 he proposed to the missionary that he return to Montreal not as a charity case but as an employee. He undertook to assist McCarter in the work of the mission while completing his interrupted theological studies at the city's Presbyterian college.[28]

Trebitsch's application coincided with a crisis in the affairs of the Montreal Presbyterian mission, which, since its initiation in 1892, had suffered from a chronic shortage of funds and lack of support from the Presbytery. Revd. McCarter received no regular income from the church and was compelled to rely on voluntary offerings from a handful of supporters. 'We simply cast ourselves upon God, and upon the friends of Israel in any and every church', he recalled. McCarter had hoped for support not only from Presbyterians but also from Christians generally, but (as he noted wistfully) 'this was almost the only point in which I was out in my calculations'.[29] By the end of 1900 McCarter was almost in despair as to how he could maintain the mission, and he made a final appeal to his own church. According to the minutes of the Presbytery, its members 'listened with much interest to the details of the work among the Jews in Montreal, as carried on by Mr McCarter, and cordially recommend-[ed] this work to the practical sympathy of the Christian public, who are in a position to help in so important a cause'.[30]

This not quite ringing endorsement was unaccompanied by any contribution from the church's own coffers. But (and of this we shall shortly have further evidence) the missionary to the Jews, by the very nature of his calling, belongs to a breed among whom hope must spring, if not eternal, at least nearly so, immune to repeated buffetings of disappointment. So it was that in December 1900. McCarter decided to accept the Presbytery's 'kindly expressed recommendation' as an encouraging sign, and was emboldened to try to revive the mission by engaging as Missionary Co-Worker the young, apparently enthusiastic and linguistically versatile, even if academically under-qualified Hebrew Christian who volunteered his services from New York.[31]

There is reason to suspect that Trebitsch may have exaggerated his educational accomplishments more than a little in order to secure this, his first precarious step on the ladder of ecclesiastical preferment. Trebitsch's correspondence with McCarter seems no longer to exist, and we cannot know the precise extent of the claims made by Trebitsch in his application for employment. But we possess two biographical sketches of the young missionary, written soon after these events in celebration of his own conversion and his work to win others for Christ. Since the material for both must be presumed to originate with the subject himself we have some second-hand but persuasive evidence. The first such *curriculum vitae*, prepared in 1903 (in circumstances to be explained shortly) for the Canadian Auxiliary of the London Society for the Promotion of Christianity among the Jews, declared:

> The Reverend Ignatius Timotheus Trebitsch was born of Hebrew parents, in Paks, Hungary, in the year 1879. His father was a wealthy and zealous rabbi [*sic*], who brought up his son with great strictness in the Hebrew faith. His early education was received in Paks, after which he made a brilliant career through Pressburg and Budapesth Universities and the Royal Academy for Art and Literature. He at first adopted journalism as a profession. . . . Step by step he was led through many dark Experiences into the glorious light of the Truth. He then determined to proclaim the Gospel of Glad Tidings to his brethren. He spent some further

> years [*sic*] in the study of Theology in Hamburg and Breklüm; and then — his health giving way — he came over to Canada ... falling in with Mr McCarter.[32]

A second biography appeared, together with a photograph of Trebitsch, in an American missionary magazine, *The Glory of Israel*, at about the same time. While this did not allege any university qualifications it asserted that the youthful Trebitsch had pursued his academic studies 'with the greatest assiduity', and maintained somewhat incredibly: 'He often spent eighteen hours of every twenty-four in study.'[33] The latter detail appears also in Trebitsch's first autobiography, published in 1916,[34] reinforcing the suspicion that he himself was the original source of the entire gallimaufry of untruths thus (no doubt, innocently) propagated by his Christian admirers.

In December 1900 Trebitsch moved from New York to Montreal and took up employment as assistant to Revd. McCarter. With his arrival in Montreal at the age of twenty-one, in regular employment for the first time in his life and zealous to spread the doctrines of his new faith (or, to be more precise, of the Presbyterian sect which, after the brief Lutheran interval, he now rejoined), we leave behind a youth, still, regrettably for the historian, somewhat shadowy, and open a narrative of his adult life, for which the historical evidence is, with few exceptions, amply preserved.

CHAPTER 2

The Montreal Mission

Trebitsch began work for the Montreal mission under an auspicious star. Revd. McCarter rejoiced in the revivification of his efforts and offered praises to heaven for his good fortune: 'We have heart-felt cause to thank the Lord, who led the steps of this his youthful servant to Montreal, and for the much zealous and effective service which the mission has enjoyed through him'.[1] The superintendent's exultation was shared by his missionary co-worker:

> It is nearly one year since the Lord led me to Montreal, and, looking back to that time, my heart is overflowing with joy and gladness, because 'the Lord hath done great things for us'. Then, in spite of the fact that my father was a Pharisee, a member of the strongest existing sect among the Jews, a 'Chased', in spite of his having brought me up in the same spirit — here I am preaching the blessed Gospel of the Redemption to my brethren.[2]

McCarter's happiness was, however, tempered by continuing anxiety about the financial condition of the mission. Offerings remained low, and McCarter noted sadly that the 'kindly expressed recommendation' of the Presbytery had 'led to no practical results'.[3] The income of the mission in 1901 amounted to at most $1,200 — which meagre sum had to be stretched to cover the entire needs of the mission, including the salaries of McCarter and Trebitsch, the upkeep of the mission house, and the expenses incurred in missionary activity.[4]

The enthusiasm of the missionary co-worker was in no way impaired (at any rate initially) by the sparseness of available resources. Trebitsch threw himself into the proselytising effort with energy and zeal. He visited Jews in their homes; he argued with them in the streets; he instructed them in Bible classes; he distributed Yiddish scriptures: and above all he discovered in himself a singular talent for public speaking in several languages — German, Hungarian, Yiddish and English. He ventured beyond the cramped confines of Montreal's immigrant Jewish quarter, setting forth on lecturing tours to regions where the potential audience for his homilies was small indeed — little towns such as Cardinal, Iroquois and Ogdensburg, where only the occasional Jewish pedlar and wandering refugee normally set foot.

There is no evidence that in his work for the Presbyterian mission Trebitsch ever converted a single Jew. His task, it must be conceded, was a hard one. The Russian and Roumanian Jewish immigrants, nearly all recent arrivals in Canada, were stony soil in which to plant the seeds of redemption. The majority were strictly orthodox and rigid in their adherence to the laws and customs of their fathers; a minority were freethinking socialists. Canada at the turn of the century was, in its way, no less Christian a country than those from which the Jewish immigrants came. But the newcomers, freed from the constraints of anti-semitic laws and from the terror of pogroms and blood libels, felt little attraction to the gospel, particularly as expounded by a man regarded with the peculiar repugnance reserved for the apostate. In a society relatively open to the talents, conversion would unlock few doors that were not anyway already ajar. Trebitsch's faced an uphill struggle, in which even a greater spirit could justifiably have felt despair.

But Trebitsch was far from discouraged. On the contrary, fired by the attention, albeit generally hostile, which his sermons attracted, he evidently felt a surge of self-confidence. After the hectic wanderings and spiritual turbulence of his adolescence, his life now seemed more normal and settled. Side by side with his missionary work he enrolled for the academic year 1901–1902 at McGill University's Presbyterian College. He so impressed the college authorities that he was admitted direct into the final year, and the college awarded him a special scholarship of twenty-five dollars for an "Essay on the Evidences".[5] However sparse the fruits of his missionary labours, Trebitsch might thus look forward, after qualifying at McGill, to a lifelong career in the Presbyterian ministry.

By the summer of 1901 he felt sufficiently confident of his position in Canada to send a telegram to Margarethe Kahlor who had corresponded with him faithfully ever since his departure from Hamburg, asking her to marry him. Her parents, no doubt relieved to be rid of the girl, encumbered as she was with an illegitimate son, gave their consent within twenty-four hours, and Margarethe sailed almost immediately for America. Reunited with her betrothed she found it 'rather strange to see him in his clerical garb'. In the period since their last meeting in Germany he seemed to have 'matured far above the average young man'. The couple were married by Revd. McCarter in Montreal in July 1901. The bride, fresh off the boat,

2 Trebitsch Lincoln, 1901

knew so little English that when the time came for her to make her responses the groom was obliged to step in and answer on her behalf — a signal foretaste of his self-centred dominance of her personality throughout their marriage.[6]

Trebitsch's life seemed set fair. He could boast a new religion, a new country, a new job and now a new wife (also a new stepson —

but of the infant Julius Tut little was heard at this period). In a proud statement of his accomplishments in the autumn of 1901 Trebitsch quoted happily, if obscurely, from the Song of Songs: 'Take us the foxes, the little foxes that spoil the vine, for the vines have tender grapes.'[7] Yet threats soon arose to both his personal and his professional life. In what was to develop into a recurring pattern in Trebitsch's various existences, the immediate cause of trouble with both his wife and McCarter was the same: money. Captain Kahlor had provided for his daughter a dowry amounting to several hundred dollars. Trebitsch appears to have bargained for rather more substantial compensation. His wife later recalled: 'Evidently he had expected more. He never mentioned it to me, nor even hinted at his disappointment, but my great affection for him enabled me to divine his thoughts.'[8] There is an element of the pathetic, strangely touching, in the naively loyal construction thus placed by the wife on her husband's ill-concealed cupidity and chagrin — the more so when one reflects that these words were written years later after he had abandoned and betrayed her. The matter evidently soured the first few months of the marriage, but there could be no turning back now and Trebitsch immediately set about spending his modest benison.

At the same time as these financial troubles, his work at the mission received a sudden upset. In December 1901 Revd. McCarter decided to give up his mission. In an article a few months later in the *Dominion Presbyterian* McCarter explained that after forty years in the ministry and six in the mission he felt that it was 'perhaps the fittest for the interest of my work to offer it in its entirety to the church, and to the care of my young co-worker'. In the same article McCarter hinted at a more pressing reason for his decision:

> Financially it has been a heavy personal loss, for the voluntary gifts, generous on the part of many, still left a constant shortage which fell as an unequal burden on my family. But for this I have neither complaints nor regrets. It was a voluntary offering to God, and I will not mar the integrity of the sacrifice by any reflections.[9]

Privately McCarter betrayed a greater readiness to reflect — hardly marring the sacrifice, but blessing the historian with a clear view of the harsh economic pressures which compelled his withdrawal:

> Under God I have been . . . the occasion of bringing forward Mr Trebitsch as a missionary. I found him nearly two years ago freshly arrived from Europe, without friends, means or prospects and, had he been my own brother, I could not have done more for him. In ready cash he received from me $400.00. To him it was a meagre salary, and to a wealthy Society it would have been nothing, but for us I had to stint my family in the accessories of life to furnish it.[10]

The undertone of reproach in the Superintendent's references to his missionary co-worker is readily explained when one learns that the total income of the mission in the final year of McCarter's superintendence had dwindled to a mere $780.

The news of McCarter's retirement came as a blow to Trebitsch. True, McCarter had recommended that the Presbyterian church take over the mission with Trebitsch as its head, but the hitherto half-hearted attitude of the church did not suggest that they would take charge eagerly — particularly given the financial burdens that would be entailed. Already in his relations with the Presbyterian Board Trebitsch had encountered difficulties and what he viewed as petty obstruction. Even if he were retained at the mission there could be no certainty as to his future income. As the Board deliberated and a decision was delayed Trebitsch was plunged into gloom and even considered returning to Europe.

Providentially, at this low point, a saviour appeared in the form of Revd. A.F. Burt, an Anglican vicar from Shediac, New Brunswick. Burt had acted since 1899 as the organizing secretary for Canada of the London Society for the Promotion of Christianity among the Jews — that same organization whose agents had already, a few years earlier, rescued Trebitsch and offered him refuge in the Wanderers' Home in Bristol. The activities of the London Society in Canada had hitherto been limited mainly to the raising of funds for transmission to the parent body, but ever since his appointment Burt had been trying to breathe life into the society's evangelizing efforts in the Dominion. From his isolated rectory in New Brunswick Burt could not engage in missionary work himself. He therefore pressed repeatedly for the appointment of a permanent missionary to the Jews in Montreal under the auspices of the London Society. Predictably he encountered reluctance on the part of the Presbyterians to allow the fruits of McCarter's long labours to be snatched away by an interloper. In a letter to Burt in December 1900 on behalf of the Presbyterian mission, Revd. J.L. George explained that McCarter's work was just now (with the appointment of Trebitsch) being put 'on a more permanent basis'. George avowed that 'co-operation in such work was essentially needed', but gently suggested that it would be 'well to delay opening another mission at present'. Burt dismissed the recommendation with the reflection that 'Mr George was thinking more of his own organisation's immediate interests and prospects'. He continued to urge the appointment of a missionary in Montreal, adding that 'the choice should, *if in any way possible*, fall upon a *Jew*' [i.e. a convert].[11] By the early autumn of 1901 Burt's campaign was successful: the committee of the London Society consented to the appointment of a missionary in Montreal and a search was initiated for 'a man fully qualified to undertake this difficult and important task'.[12]

This was the background to Trebitsch's uncertain position. Deftly he now embarked on a manoeuvre to retrieve and indeed greatly enhance his professional standing. Over the previous months he had no doubt got wind of the Anglicans' interest in Jewish evangelization. Now, with the aid of Burt and others, Trebitsch engineered what amounted to an Anglican take-over bid for the Jewish mission in Montreal. One circumstance in particular must have rendered the scheme supremely attractive to Trebitsch: by contrast with the pauperized Presbyterian mission, the London Society possessed a secure capital base. The Canadian branch alone had collected in the previous year no less than $2,533.41 — more than three times the income of McCarter's mission. Moreover, if Trebitsch could secure appointment as head of the Anglican mission, he would presumably be master of the entire fund, no longer dependent on the self-sacrificing doles of his Superintendent.

As soon as he heard of McCarter's decision, Trebitsch communicated with the Diocesan Secretary of the Anglican Archbishopric in Montreal, Revd. G. Osborne Troop. He found in him a willing coadjutor, for Troop had long been a staunch supporter of the London Society. Troop immediately wrote to Burt:

> Have you any further word from the Society as to the appointment of an Agent in Montreal? You will perhaps have seen that Mr McCarter is before long to leave the city. He has offered his work to the Presbyterian Church; but they are as yet undecided about taking it over. Mr McCarter's chief Assistant, on the other hand, would prefer that the work should be undertaken by our Society. He thinks only *trained* Jewish missionaries can do the work as it ought to be done. I agree with him.[13]

Burt was excited and encouraged by Troop's letter and, after a period of consideration, applied to the committee of the London Society for authority to go to Montreal for discussions with 'the friends of Jewish Missionary work there'.[14]

After some delays Burt secured the desired permission. He set out on 8 April, but just before leaving Shediac he received a letter from Trebitsch (whom he had not yet met) with disappointing news. The Presbyterian Board of Missions, it appeared, had finally agreed to take over responsibility for McCarter's mission and had engaged Trebitsch as missionary. Consequently Trebitsch informed Burt that he thought it would be inadvisable for the London Society to start another mission just now. Evidently Trebitsch had reached the conclusion that a puny bird in hand was preferable to a plump one in the bush. Reporting to the London committee, Burt confessed that he was 'much discouraged' by Trebitsch's letter. But having undertaken to deliver several sermons and lectures on behalf of the society in Montreal he decided he could not now draw back and so proceeded on his journey.[15]

On arrival in Montreal on 10 April Burt began a round of calls which are best described in his own words. His first visit was to Revd. Troop:

> We discussed the situation and were led to the conviction that, without greater support & experience than they had had in their past efforts to reach the Jews, the presbyterian mission could not but fail, as it had failed twice already; and that it was wise for the London Society to go on; provided that the Presbyterians could be persuaded of our good faith and would agree to co-operate in the work.

Troop accompanied Burt to the house of the Anglican Archbishop of Montreal, William Bond, who promised his support for a mission 'charging only that there should be no rivalry with nor antagonism to the presbyterians.'

Burt's next call was on Trebitsch. His report to the London committee continued:

> I found that, although he recognized the fact that the London Society was better able to take up the work than the Presbyterians were, he had sought to discourage me, because he was of opinion that the establishment of a second mission — independently of his — might seem like division and rivalry; and, as such, would have a bad effect upon Hebrews and Christians alike. I pointed out that your Committee desired nothing but the fullest fraternity, good-will and co-operation; and that nothing would be done without it. He at once withdrew his objections; saying that in that case, the Society's mission would be a strength rather than a weakness to his work; that he would be glad if the Society would start; and, for his part, he would do all in his power to co-operate, and facilitate. He told me that he had a house in view for a mission house; and that the Presbyterian Board were already negotiating a lease of it. He asked me to go with him next morning, and inspect the premises; which I promised to do.

After leaving Trebitsch, Burt called on a senior member of the Anglican Synod and secured his support. Meanwhile Trebitsch pondered on the implications of his talk with Burt. It was evident that Burt's heart was set on the creation of an Anglican mission. Consequently the bird in the bush now appeared an attainable as well as an attractive prize. Dropping his momentary objections, Trebitsch accordingly reverted to his original scheme of a complete Anglican take-over of the Montreal Jewish mission with himself to be employed as missionary.

In his encounter with Burt the following day Trebitsch set about winning him for the idea of such a marriage. Not surprisingly Burt proved willing and eager to be wooed, as his own account demonstrates:

> On the next morning — April 11th — Mr Trebitsch called on me. We went together to the Jewish quarter. I found the proposed mission-house to be in a poor state of repair: but to be situated in a locality fairly good for the purpose; a stonesthrow from the old synagogue; with the open space of Dominion Square immediately in front — a convenience for open-air meetings. My chief objection to it is its immediate propinquity to the Synagogue: for, in case of riots — which are not unknown when a mission begins to succeed — the mob would naturally gather in the square fronting the Synagogue; and the mission-premises across the street would offer a great temptation to wreckers; and might immediately suffer damage before the authorities could interfere. The Presbyterians had not even considered the possibility of this: but Mr Trebitsch's experience acknowledged the force of the objection.

Burt invited Trebitsch to his lodgings and, as they walked, the young missionary began persuading his companion to fall in with his scheme, leading gradually up to his main point:

> On the way Mr Trebitsch began to open his heart to me. He recounted his struggles with the Presbyterian Board; described their utter ignorance of the needs of a mission to the Jews, and the way to go about it; the difficulties he had encountered in endeavouring to secure even the promise of the first necessaries of equipment. . . . For some months he had had heartsearchings about these things. He had prayed for God to do something to clear away the difficulties and to open up the way. . . . He had sacrificed a good deal for the Jews in Montreal — had spent four or five hundred dollars of his wife's dower on the work there; had used up the rest of it for his expenses in college and home; and was now absolutely in need, and dependent upon the small income promised him by the Presbyterian board. These statements he verified by showing me his savings-book and cheques. . . . Since speaking with me yesterday he and his wife had been much in prayer; and they had come to the conclusion that the intervention of the London Society at this critical juncture was of God. That he himself was a fruit of the London Society's work. He knew it: understood it: loved it. He had become identified with the Presbyterians through the sheer accident of being directed to Pastor Frank in Hamburg instead of to the Society's agent there. He had not believed in Christ that he might become a sectarian. He had not a desire to make converts to Presbyterianism or to any 'ism'. His

> one desire was to win his brethren to Christ, as he had been won; and he wanted to work under those who were best fitted to support and carry on the work. He had had other discouragements of a quite personal nature at the hands of the Presbyterian Board — but they alone were not worth considering, because they had to do with his own living — and not, except indirectly, with the work itself. Still they all pointed him to the one conclusion. He thought that if the London Society's Committee would allow him to work under them he would give up his connexion with the Presbyterians.

Trebitsch broached his proposal in a skilful if unorthodox manner, utilising to the full his months of experience in preaching to sceptical audiences. Happily for Trebitsch, Burt was far from sceptical: the missionary's words were music to the ears of the Anglican parson, for they coincided precisely with the direction of his own thoughts. A less credulous man than Burt might have raised an eyebrow at Trebitsch's reference to his bank book rather than the Good Book; and a stricter sectarian than the broad church episcopalian might have been astonished at Trebitsch's airy nonchalance in regard to such matters as the thirty-nine articles, bishops, ritual — the whole gamut of difference between the English and the Scottish rites which to the Hungarian Jew, imbued with pure ecumenical indifferentism, seemed of such slight import.

Although taken aback by the effrontery of Trebitsch's proposal, Burt was already more than half-converted. Yet he dimly perceived certain problems ahead. He pointed out to Trebitsch that 'misunderstandings and ill-feelings towards himself and the Society might result' from such an abrupt switch of employers as that proposed by the evangelist. Burt added:

> I felt also, that I might be charged, or suspected, of influencing him and causing him to change his colours — a thing which I had in nowise attempted to do. But he said that no one could think that; because he had already told his Board some weeks ago that unless they agreed to certain matters in the interests of the work, he would withdraw from them in any case: — and the Board had not agreed to them. That he was not indebted to them in any way, but rather the contrary [thus lightly were Revd. McCarter's sacrifices passed over!]; and that until the 1st of May he was at liberty to withdraw from his engagement.

This glimpse of Trebitsch's strained relations with his present patrons momentarily sobered Burt. He told Trebitsch that he did not know whether the London Society would engage him or not. And he encouraged him to pray and think: 'if it were God's will that he should become an agent of the Society, He would bring it to pass'. In his report to London Burt added: 'I was profoundly impressed, however, with his earnestness; his faith in God; and his desire to seek the true spiritual welfare of his people.'

Thus ended the second meeting of Burt and Trebitsch. It is plain that by the end of the third, Burt had fallen completely under Trebitsch's spell. The middle-aged priest appears from his own account to have been almost mesmerised by the youthful novitiate:

> The next morning — Saturday 12th — Mr Trebitsch came to me about noon. He said that he and his wife had been all night in prayer to God. They had considered everything; and felt that they had been led to make their decision: ... They had decided definitely that he would withdraw from the Presbyterians and trust in God. Beyond that, for themselves, it was now dark ... While he was telling me this I watched him keenly. His eyes were aglow, and his whole face was lit with enthusiasm. His words were modest and respectful; but his manner was manly, independent and determined. I confess that my heart went out to him. And, knowing that in deciding in this way he was throwing away a certainty for an uncertainty; and yet was confident in his trust in God alone, it was borne in upon me that God had indeed, of himself, called him to us; and that I dare not say no.[16]

The missionary had won a soul, and the matter was as good as settled. Burt cabled to London: 'Found splendidly qualified convert deeply spiritual seven languages shall I retain?'[17] Meanwhile he secured the approval of the committee of the Anglican Synod for the establishment of the mission; thus armed he proceeded in the company of McCarter, Troop, and Trebitsch to a meeting with the Presbyterian Board. The merger was now about to be consummated; in his report to London Burt confessed that he 'trembled lest some misword of ours should kindle their Presbyterian asperity or light the flames of their sectarian jealousy and pride. But God did not let us say the misword; and the conference throughout was perfectly friendly and harmonious.' After Burt had spoken, Trebitsch announced to the Board his intention to resign, giving his reasons, 'at which [Burt reported] they winced not a little'. After a brief retirement on the part of the Anglicans, McCarter and Trebitsch, the Board announced their approval of the scheme: the field would be left free to the London Society; Trebitsch would be released from his engagement to the Presbyterians; and the Board wished the Montreal Mission to the Jews good speed.

Delighted with the successful outcome of his trip to Montreal, Burt returned to Shediac. Just before his departure he received a call from McCarter, who came to express his thanks and his gladness that the Anglicans were taking over the mission. He related to Burt 'some most touching experiences of his difficulties'; how no one organization had been willing to support his work; how his whole means had been only sixteen or seventeen dollars a week; how, out of this, he had given Trebitsch seven dollars. 'With tears in his eyes [Burt reported] he told me that he felt it like the loss of his own child.' He expatiated on his financial sacrifices. And [as Burt further narrated] he intimated that if the London Committee 'saw fit to make him some small grant by way of recompense for "the goodwill of the business as it were", he would be grateful'.[18] In token whereof he handed over to Burt his subscription list. Back in Shediac on 21 April Burt compiled a massive report on his visit to Montreal, which he dispatched to London with ten enclosures, among them a 'confidential report of attainments and character of I.T. Trebitsch' (sadly no longer extant), certificates of baptism and of graduation from the Presbyterian College, and a formal letter of application from Trebitsch for employment under the society.

On 16 May 1902 the General Committee considered Burt's voluminous package of documents. It was resolved that 'the usual queries be sent to Mr Trebitsch', but that 'meanwhile, as the matter is urgent, Mr Burt be empowered as a temporary expedient to engage the services of Mr Trebitsch for six months.' Trebitsch was to receive a salary of £150 per annum.[19] A fortnight later the society's Correspondence Committee authorised the rental of a mission house, and expenditures on equipment required for the work of evangelization; twelve pounds was to be paid to McCarter in respect of furniture, Yiddish Bibles and so forth, which he had passed over to the Anglican mission, but the minutes stated that 'the Committee cannot grant him any remuneration for the "goodwill" referred to in Mr Burt's letter.'[20]

The establishment of the Montreal mission was announced in the July 1902 number of the London Society's organ, *Jewish Missionary Intelligence*. The announcement, however, carried a rider to the effect that the enterprise had been launched 'on the understanding that the entire outlay will be covered by increased subscriptions from Canadian sources'. A flier distributed with the journal contained a further indication of financial stringency: the society's accumulated deficit had reached the sum of £5,764. 6s. 3d. and funds were urgently needed to meet the arrears. If Trebitsch had hoped to solve his finanical problems, by transferring to the service of the London Society, there were thus clear signs to the contrary.

Any pleasure Trebitsch might have taken in his new appointment was in any case almost immediately shattered by a domestic tragedy. On 25 April a first son was born to Margarethe but Robert Johann Naphthali Trebitsch was sickly and not expected to survive.

Husband and wife fell into a black depression, as Burt reported to London on 5 June:

> It is with deep distress that I have to report that Mrs Trebitsch has suddenly been bereft of her reason, and is now in the Verdun Lunatic Asylum. I have no details of the attack; but I presume that it is the outcome of some irregularity following the birth of her little one; and I do hope and pray that it may be only of a temporary nature. Poor Trebitsch! He is of course in terrible trouble. We can only pray that a merciful God may comfort him and restore his wife. At his request I forwarded his first month's stipend out of the Canadian funds and charged it in my accounts which I now enclose. He will answer the questions [i.e. the 'usual queries' required by the committee when it sanctioned his appointment] as soon as he can quiet his mind sufficiently to enable him to do so.[21]

Soon afterwards the child died.[22]

Trebitsch was fortunate during these bleak months in enjoying the sympathy and solicitude of Burt and the patient understanding of the London Society. On 1 August the society's General Committee approved the continuation of Trebitsch's appointment for a further period of six months, 'subject to his Replies to Queries being satisfactory'.[23]

On 4 August 1902 Trebitsch moved into the newly established Mission House at 374 Lagauchetière Street, a three-storey structure in the immigrant Jewish quarter. The house had been amply fitted out for mission work, a signboard in Hebrew letters had been placed above the front door, and Trebitsch was assigned two upstairs rooms as living quarters for himself and his slowly recuperating wife.

The same week Trebitsch convened his first mission meeting and succeeded in attracting thirty-four Jews to hear him. Accompanied by Burt, Trebitsch also continued the outdoor evangelising that had already made him a familiar figure in the streets of the Jewish quarter. In an article in the *Jewish Missionary Intelligence* Burt gave a vivid account of one such foray:

> All around us is a bedlam of gesticulating volubility. Rude jests, laughter, sneers, catcalls, and discordant interruptions are heard on the outskirts of the crowd, the nucleus of which is formed by us and two or three particular Jews, arguing altogether, with one another and with us, simultaneously. Hard thrusts, not always polite, are given by the listeners, which Mr Trebitsch takes with the utmost good humour, and returns with equal vigour. Very soon the disputants begin to grow excited. They leave English and use several other tongues, as one speaker after another is met. . . . Words are bandied backwards and forwards. Some turn away,

visibly disgusted that the rest give any attention to the missionary; and others, more curious, take their places.... One savage-looking fellow, with a great bludgeon in his brown hand, looks anything but peaceful.

In the same issue of the *Intelligence* extracts from a report by Trebitsch himself were published, presenting the Missionary's exposition of his technique:

I do not teach Christian dogmatics as many missionaries do. I do not preach the Trinity, the two-fold nature of our LORD, and other Christian doctrines, although I am always ready to prove them if objected to. I do not attack Judaism, nor do I praise the Jews. They are self-conceited enough without making them more so.

Trebitsch's own self-promoting puff could not however report a single baptism — but then that was hardly to be expected at such an early stage in the life of the mission. Impressed, the editors of the *Intelligence* concluded: 'We bespeak the earnest prayers of our readers for this new work, thus auspiciously commenced among the Montreal Jews.'[24]

The autumn of 1902 marked the high point of Trebitsch's missionary career. Considerable publicity attended the formal opening of the mission house on 16 October 1902. Archbishop Bond presided; Revd. Professor Scrimger of the Presbyterian College praised Trebitsch, declaring 'that he had the utmost confidence in his integrity and ability'; the congregation (among whom were '30 to 40 Jews') sang hymns; and Trebitsch 'present[ed] the claims of Christ' in Yiddish, German and Hungarian. A collection yielded the sum of eight dollars and fifty cents.[25] The publicity occasioned by the ceremony aroused a flurry of interest in the Jewish quarter, much of it far from friendly. The *Intelligence* reported that on the following Sunday a large crowd of Jews gathered at the mission-house:

'Of course,' says Mr. Trebitsch 'they came to disturb the meeting. The opening is a thorn in their sides. I noticed at once their intention, and tried to prevent it by exceptionally kind words. They listened fairly attentively, although they disturbed my address'.

With the self-delusion characteristic of the style of the agents of the London Society, Trebitsch asserted: 'The opposition of the Jews in a drastic manner, shews clearly that we are moving forward.'[26]

These striking successes (in the eyes of the London Society) secured for Trebitsch rapid advancement. On 16 November he was confirmed by the Archbishop of Montreal, and on 21 December he was ordained a deacon in the Anglican cathedral of Christ Church.

The health of Margarethe had much improved, helped by the arrival of her mother on a visit from Hamburg. Mrs Trebitsch later recalled that one afternoon, while her husband was out, Archbishop Bond called and took tea with her. 'When leaving, he asked me to convey his heartiest congratulations to my husband, who, he said, was bound to achieve great things one day; in fact, he would not be in the least surprised to see him step into his shoes and become Archbishop of Montreal.'[27]*

In January 1903 Trebitsch travelled with Burt to Halifax, Nova Scotia, where he delivered a series of lectures and sermons in connexion with a 'Missionary Loan Exhibition' in the city.[29] The company of the admiring Burt, the astonishing prophecy of the Archbishop, and the favourable reception accorded his homiletic discourses now began to go to Trebitsch's head. He wrote a boastful report on his activities, replete with the statistics beloved of the authorities of the London Society. ('I distributed 40 Bibles, 86 New Testaments, and 247 tracts . . . I had 879 enquirers in my house . . . During the last nine months 382 visits were paid by Mrs Trebitsch or myself.') With nine months of missionary work behind him Trebitsch ventured the ambitious claim that one Jew had asked to be baptised, 'which request we hope to grant in February';[30] the baptismal registers of the London Society however contain no record of any such conversion.

Happily for Trebitsch the society did not remunerate its agents on the basis of results. The matter of salary was now returning to the forefront of his attention. The arrival of his mother-in-law meant that there was an additional mouth to feed without (so far as is known) any supplementary disbursements from Hamburg. Moreover, at about this time the household was further enlarged by the unexpected arrival of Trebitsch's younger brother, József. Apparently sharing something of Ignácz Trebitsch's wanderlust and taste for adventure, József had left home and stowed away on a ship bound for South Africa. Somehow he had then made his way across the Atlantic and (according to subsequent family legend) stumbled across his elder brother quite by chance in Montreal.[31] Burdened by these additional responsibilities and emboldened by his successes and rapid preferment, Trebitsch committed a fatal blunder. He told Burt that he would not continue as Missionary in Montreal unless he received a substantial increase in pay. The faithful Secretary for the

* Archbishop Bond, who was aged eighty-seven at the time of the alleged call on Mrs Trebitsch, had started his own career in the priesthood as a missionary, preaching from 1842 to 1853 in the area west of the Richelieu river — presumably to Indians. He is described by one ecclesiastical historian as an 'uncompromising champion of the Evangelical School.'[28]

Dominion relayed Trebitsch's claim to the London headquarters, and awaited its response.[32]

A few days later Trebitsch reached the pinnacle of his career in the Anglican Church of Canada. Invited to address the Synod of the Diocese of Montreal, presided over by Archbishop Bond, Trebitsch took the opportunity to try, with much daring, to effect a repetition of his successful manoeuvre of a year or so earlier. At that time he had masterminded a take-over bid by the London Society of the Presbyterian Church's mission to the Jews in Montreal. By now Trebitsch was highly dissatisfied with the relationship between the mission and the London Society. The strict control exercised by the parent body, the constant reference back to London about minor matters, not to mention the suppurating grievance concerning his salary — all this appeared a quite unnecessary and indefensible barrier to the success of the mission in the eyes of Missionary. He therefore proposed that the Montreal mission should, as it were, declare its independence of the London Society, henceforth running its own affairs without outside interference. Trebitsch must have been confident that, once the supervision of London were removed, Bond, Troop and Burt, who had all evinced such respect for him, would prove obliging in the matter of his salary.

His speech to the Synod was recorded in the columns of the *Canadian Churchman* in the following remarkable terms:

> One of the most notable addresses ever heard in the Synod of Montreal was that delivered by the Rev. J.T. Trebitsch, on the motion to transfer work among the Jews in Canada from the care of the London Society to that of the new Board of Missions. Mr Trebitsch is a Jew, born, we believe, in Hungary; he is quite a young man, was ordained deacon in this diocese last Advent, and has a high university record. That his speech moved the Synod as the Synod has seldom been moved, is to state the case very mildly; his eloquence, his pride of race (which he by no means hides), his transparent faith in the power of the Cross to break the heart of the stubborn Jew — all these combined to produce upon the minds of the members of the Synod an overwhelming impression, not only in favor of the motion, but in favor of the man himself. The Rev. G.O. Troop, who has much befriended Mr Trebitsch in the city, spoke with characteristic warmth of him and commended him with all confidence to the affection of the church.[33]

With this oratorical triumph still fresh in his mind, it came as a rude shock to Trebitsch a few days later to learn from Burt that the General Committee of the London Society, had resolved with 'much regret that they cannot increase Mr Trebitsch's salary at present'.[34] As to Trebitsch's scheme for a unilateral declaration of independence from London by the Montreal mission, it rapidly emerged that Trebitsch had won the hearts but not the minds of his audience at the Synod. No formal overture was, in fact, made by the Anglican Church in Canada to the London Society for a secession of the Montreal mission. For reasons lost in the mists of ecclesiastical politics Trebitsch failed to replicate his take-over of the previous year.

To this double blow was added a third: Margarethe Trebitsch's only sister died in Hamburg. Margarethe and her mother urgently wished to return to Germany, where the bereaved Captain Kahlor now lived alone. Trebitsch acquiesced and agreed to accompany them[35]

He therefore resigned his post as Missionary under the London Society. A laconic minute of the society's General Committee states that Burt reported 'serious difficulties in connexion with the Society's Mission in Montreal, namely Rev. J.T. Trebitsch's resignation, subsequent withdrawal of the same, and breakdown in his health.'[36] In the meantime Trebitsch and his family (with the exception of his brother József) had abruptly left Montreal, bound for Hamburg. After a short stay at his wife's family home. Trebitsch seems to have sobered down sufficiently to appreciate that he had rashly and impulsively thrown away his job, his future prospects, his home, and the respect of his colleagues. He decided to retrace his steps to England to try to retrieve something from the débris.

CHAPTER 3

From Canterbury to York

Trebitsch's return to England was that of the black sheep rather than the prodigal son. Upon his arrival, some time towards the end of March 1903, he seems to have hoped to reinstate himself in the good graces of the London Society, perhaps even to secure continued employment under its wing. He immediately tried to remove one potential obstacle by sending a letter to Revd. Lypshytz confessing to the theft of Mrs Lypshytz's jewellery and promising to buy a replacement watch and chain. Lypshytz later recollected that the promise was never fulfilled. Looking back on the incident many years afterwards, Lypshytz said of his former protégé: 'He is thoroughly bad, a genius, and very attractive, but taking the crooked way always for choice.'[1] Trebitsch purchased neither the watch nor his former protector's forgiveness, but his letter evidently bought him time, for its appears that Lypshytz did not at this stage inform his superiors in the London Society of the squalid treatment he had endured at Trebitsch's hands.

Trebitsch now turned to the directors of the society in an effort to repair the damage caused by his recent outrageous conduct. He appeared before the society's committee to express sorrow and plead for reinstatement. His contrition had some effect, but the minutes of the meeting suggest that his behaviour had rendered the position irretrievable. Moreover, the committee had by now received no fewer than six communications from Burt as well as two from Revd. Osborne Troop. From these it emerged Trebitsch had, at some stage during his mission work in Montreal, obtained from Troop the sum of three hundred dollars — whether as a loan or as a contribution is not clear. Troop now appears to have asked for this money back, if not from Trebitsch himself, then from the society.

In the circumstances the society treated their wayward agent with undeserved charity. Although his employment was terminated, Trebitsch was allowed a 'special Grant, *ex gratia*' of £37.10.00, equivalent to three months' salary, and the committee further agreed that 'the fixtures left in the Mission House at Montreal by Mr Trebitsch, belonging to him, be taken at valuation.' In the matter of the three hundred dollars given to Trebitsch by Troop, the society seems to have decided on a prudent neutrality: the minutes state merely 'that this Committee does not recognize their liability with ref. to 300 Dollars given to Mr Trebitsch by the Rev. G. Osborne Troop, as this donation was originally given towards his personal work and not for the Society'.[2] At the same time the society's General Committee passed a resolution expressing its 'desire to sympathize very sincerely with Mr Burt in the trouble and anxiety he has had in connexion with the Mission'.[3]

The generosity of these terms of disengagement between the society and its former missionary is defined in sharper relief by a sequel recorded in the society's minute book. On 17 July the committee read a letter from Burt reporting that one further week's salary was due to Trebitsch in respect of the period 24 to 31 March. The minutes do not make it clear whether this money was paid to Trebitsch — or, for that matter, why it should have been, given Trebitsch's absence from his post during that period. Burt's letter further stated that 'Mr Trebitsch's brother was in temporary charge' of the Montreal mission house — a reference to József Trebitsch, who had remained behind when the family quit Montreal. The letter also alluded to 'the three hundred dollars paid to Mr Trebitsch by Rev. J.M. Snowdon.' It is unclear if this was *another* three hundred dollar debt incurred by Trebitsch, or another reference to the 'donation' previously reported as having been given to him by Troop![4]

The society was not, however, even yet quite rid of Trebitsch. The committee minutes record that, following two more letters from Burt, it was agreed 'that the sum of 2¾ Dollars (say 11/–) be paid to Rev. I.T. Trebitsch in settlement of his claim for electric light fittings left in the Mission House at Montreal!'[5] The last entry concerning Trebitsch in the minute book records the distressing conclusion to the sorry tale: at the committee's meeting on 20 November yet another letter from Burt was read, whereupon it was resolved 'that on no account can the Committee pay any debts that the Rev. I.T. Trebitsch may have left behind him with the sole exception of 12.98 dollars (£2.13.0) to the Gas Lighting Company, and that only in case they threaten to cut off the supply of gas'. Finally, the committee resolved 'that it be noted that Mr Trebitsch's brother disappeared with the keys of the Mission House'.[6] Trebitsch should not of course be held responsible for the abscondence of his brother, but even disregarding this unfortunate coda it cannot be said that Trebitsch emerged with any credit (except in purely financial terms) from his short-lived career as a missionary in Canada.

Meanwhile, as the London Society slowly disentangled the web of indebtedness and disorder left behind in Montreal, Trebitsch had found alternative employment. *Crockford's Clerical Directory* for 1904 lists the Revd. Ignatius Timotheus Trebitsch, formerly Missionary to the Jews in the Diocese of Montreal, as having been appointed in 1903 curate in the parish of Appledore-with-Ebony in Kent. The memoirs of Mrs Trebitsch (as well as those of Trebitsch himself) allege that he obtained this preferment following an interview with the Archbishop of Canterbury, Dr Randall Davidson. The papers of Dr Davidson at Lambeth Palace do not substantiate this claim — although, as we shall shortly observe, they do provide evidence of a later interview between the Archbishop and Trebitsch. Something of a mystery remains, therefore, as to exactly how Trebitsch managed to secure this position. Our only clue is a later statement by Revd. Lypshytz to the effect that Trebitsch 'applied to the Archbishop of Canterbury for permission to officiate in England and the Primate gave him a temporary license to Appledore parish on condition that he come up for his examination, after passing which the Archbishop promised that he should be ordained as a priest. He failed ingloriously and that was the end of his spiritual pretensions.'[7]

Whatever the origins of the appointment, Lypshytz's testimony as to its outcome is corroborated by other evidence. Archbishop Davidson's Ordination Book contains a brief *curriculum vitae* of Trebitsch, listing his age, his education, his experience ('Mission work in Canada. 3 years'), his reading ('Considerable'), and his appointment as curate under the vicar of Appledore, the Revd. C.B. Hall. The entry continues: 'To come up for Priests Orders Trinity 1904 and to be examined in all the *Deacons* Subjects only'.[8] The Ordinands Examination Book for Trinity 1904, which gives the marks obtained by all those examined with a view to ordination, reveals the dismal nature of Trebitsch's performance. He came bottom out of the eight deacons examined: with the exception of Church History and General Bible, in which subjects he scraped by respectably, he disgraced himself in nearly every paper, receiving also the lowest mark for his viva voce examination. In the column reserved for examiners' comments we read: 'Some of his work very bad. Surely ought not to pass. No Greek, no Latin, his Hebrew bad even [*sic*] for a Jew.'

During the year or so prior to this disappointing dénouement Trebitsch had officiated under the supervision of Revd. Hall in the beautiful thirteenth-century church in Appledore. The work cannot have been very onerous. The village, really little more than a hamlet, situated on the edge of Romney Marsh, contained a mere 521 inhabitants. At first, the new curate lived alone, since his wife had remained in Hamburg, where, on 12 July 1903, she bore a son. The child was named after his father, Ignatius Emanuel: in view of the terrible fate which awaited this infant the historian is tempted to regard the name as a veritable mark of Cain. Margarethe Trebitsch, however, was happily ignorant of what lay in store for little Ignatius. After the tragedy of her loss of Robert Trebitsch in Montreal, she was naturally delighted that her newborn son was in good health. Soon afterwards Trebitsch came to Hamburg to fetch her and the baby. The family settled down in Appledore, which the curate's wife found pleasant, albeit damp. The villagers seemed 'very nice, though inquisitive', and Mrs Trebitsch took great pride in her husband's eloquent and dramatic sermons — most of them delivered virtually extempore since his only preparation consisted of looking up a text and giving it 'a few minutes' consideration.'[9]

But if Margarethe (now Margaret) Trebitsch relished the simple pleasures and sodden rusticity of Romney marsh, Trebitsch chafed at the bit. The position gave no outlet for his restless energy, nor for his self-aggrandisement, nor for his love of argument (not to speak of his quarrelsome nature). The villagers apparently asked questions, but they did not pose the sort of challenge he had faced from disputatious audiences in his Canadian missionary work. What the villagers made of his Hungarian-accented sermons we do not know, but they seem to have been docile country folk to whom it would never have occurred to complain. On 29 April 1904, during his examination with a view to ordination, Trebitsch was interviewed by his bishop: since Appledore lay in the Diocese of Canterbury, he thus met the Primate of the Anglican Communion. Dr Davidson entered the following handwritten notation in his Ordination Book after the interview:

> He shows a strange lack of knowledge on some of the pts on wh. one wd have expected him to be strongest. His Gk he has practically forgotten. He cant really read Gk text tho' he says he cd fit himself to do so quite easily in a few months! as he knew it thoroughly at one time & has only forgotten it. I promised to weigh everything before deciding as to Psthood.

When the examination results were announced, a further entry was placed in the book: 'Very bad Report on Examn. Bidden to postpone.'[10]

In view of his sorry performance Trebitsch was fortunate in winning a period of grace rather than being summarily defrocked. Margaret Trebitsch later recalled her husband's state of mind at this time:

> The life of a country curate did not satisfy his active brain and indefatigable ambition. The pace was too slow for him; he had no patience to wait. If he could have become a vicar within a short

time, with the prospects of further advancement in the Church, he would, perhaps, have continued, but he seemed to think there was very little chance.[11]

Meanwhile, the sudden death of Mrs Trebitsch's father provided, as it were, a heaven-sent opportunity for the dissatisfied curate. Captain Kahlor left his daughter some money; the exact amount is unknown, but it was sufficient at any rate to enable the bereaved Trebitsch to reach a decision.* He wrote to Archbishop Davidson saying that he had succeeded to money and proposed to give up clerical work altogether. A laconic final note in the Ordination Book, in the Archbishop's hand, reads: 'I dont think he is a gt loss.'

Liberated for the moment from both spiritual and temporal cares, Trebitsch moved his family in September 1904 from Appledore to the somewhat drier ground of Hampton-on-Thames, a semi-suburban town on the south-eastern fringe of London. Trebitsch now had four dependants, for, in addition to his wife, his step-son Julius Tut, and little Ignatius, they were joined permanently by Margaret Trebitsch's widowed mother-in-law. 'Trebitsch seemed very happy', his wife later wrote. 'He bought books to his heart's desire, principally on international politics and economics. His study looked more like a library. A tremendous bookcase along all four walls was not sufficient. Shelves were extended from floor to ceiling to install his books.'[12] Along with the new house Trebitsch took a new name. From October 1904 onwards he and his family (including Julius Tut) were known as 'Tribich Lincoln'.[13] Apart from the fact that the new name sounded more indigenous to England, no reason ever seems to have been given by Trebitsch for his choice of a new surname — unless it were a passing reference some years later to his admiration for President Abraham Lincoln.

Trebitsch (as we shall continue to know him, although to the world he now introduced himself as I.T.T. Lincoln) settled down to enjoy Captain Kahlor's legacy. In October 1904 another son was born to Margaret in Hampton: this sixth member of the family was given the name John. The ensuing period was one of domestic contentment for the Trebitsch household. Always something of an autodidact, Trebitsch occupied himself mainly with his books. Perhaps his demonstrated deficiencies in the classical tongues and in divinity stimulated his turn to the profane disciplines of politics and economics. During the next few years he read widely, if not deeply, in the classical texts of political economy and British liberal political

* There was no will. Probate records preserved in the Amtsgericht Hamburg state that, according to prevailing law, the estate was divided, one quarter going to the widow Kahlor and three quarters to the only surviving daughter, Mrs Trebitsch. (Gemeinschaftlicher Erbschein, 8 April 1904)

thought. When not busy with his books he travelled to London by train, 'on the look out', as his wife recalled, 'for a position which would enable him to come into contact with politicians'. Intimations of greatness, a desire to hobnob with the mighty, a taste for intrigue, a liking for public attention, a wish to boss other people around, fascination with the careers of Disraeli and of Napoleon — all these ruminations appear to have swilled around inside the ex-curate's head as he gazed out of his study window at suburban Hampton.

After about eighteen months of unemployment Trebitsch began seriously to look around for work. Perhaps Captain Kahlor's legacy had already dwindled under the impact of Trebitsch's massive book purchases. Perhaps he felt once again the urge to swing from a contemplative to an active stage in his life. Whatever the motive, he answered an advertisement for a post in a society engaged in temperance propaganda. The evils of drink, particularly its deleterious effects on the labouring classes, were at this time a focus of political controversy in Britain. Broadly speaking, the Unionist or Conservative Party was regarded as representative of the brewing interest (as well, of course, as that of the established church), while the Liberals, identified with nonconformity, particularly in the north and west of the country, were pledged to reform of the drink licensing laws in order to reduce drunkenness among workers — and incidentally, the profits of the brewers. The installation of a reformist Liberal government in December 1905 and the Liberals' sweeping election victory a month later heightened public discussion of the issue. In lighting on the drink question Trebitsch thus found a subject which neatly joined his former religious with his new political interests. His mission work had provided him with what might be regarded as excellent training for temperance agitation which was in this period conducted in a manner akin to that of proselytism for a revealed religion. Trebitsch was invited for an interview for the position — but he was not offered employment.[14]

Although he failed to get the job the episode marked a crucial turning-point in Trebitsch's life, for as a result of his application he made the acquaintance of one of the leading figures in the temperance society, Benjamin Seebohm Rowntree, a cocoa and confectionery manufacturer from York. Hearing that Trebitsch knew foreign languages, Rowntree offered him employment as private secretary and travelling social investigator in connection with research on land tenure systems in various European countries. Trebitsch informed his wife by telegram from York of his new position: 'Am permanently engaged as secretary to Mr Seebohm Rowntree to investigate different countries — Holland, Belgium, Germany, Denmark. Salary paid in advance. Leaving shortly.'[15] Returning to Hampton only to pack his bags, he told his wife he would be leaving almost immediately for Brussels. 'I had never seen him so happy before', she later recalled.

B. Seebohm Rowntree, who was to be Trebitsch's employer and patron from early 1906 until August 1909, and a central figure in his life until 1916, was a pioneer of empirical social research in Britain. His father, Joseph Rowntree, had started the family cocoa business in 1862. In 1881 he produced the world's first 'crystallised gum pastilles', and by 1887 four tons of gums and pastilles were being manufactured each week in the Rowntrees' model works at York. The firm's cocoa and chocolate products were consumed all over the world, and the twenty years after 1890 saw a fourfold expansion of the labour force, and large profits flowing into the Rowntree family's pockets. Seebohm Rowntree had started work in the cocoa factory at the age of eighteen and he retained his connection with the firm until his retirement. But his real interests lay elsewhere. A Quaker, a Liberal, a progressive employer, he was horrified by the squalor and deprivation which modern industrialism imposed on the working class. Somewhat in the spirit of his contemporaries Sidney and Beatrice Webb, he determined to contribute his mite to social improvement by the patient accumulation of social facts and statistics which were to serve as the essential foundation for reformist policies of the sort later pursued by the Liberal governments of Campbell-Bannerman and Asquith between 1905 and 1915.

Rowntree was a modest, endlessly hardworking, utterly unassuming, somewhat naive, and immensely generous man. His biographer, Lord Briggs, writes of him that he was 'quiet, sentimental, committed to a Quaker conception of trust'.[16] It would be utterly mistaken to regard his espousal of teetotalism as arising from a desire to protect the family's inland trade from competition by rival beverages. For Rowntree had inherited from his father a rooted belief in liberalism, political and economic, conceived almost as a natural outgrowth of Quakerism. In 1901 Rowntree published his first book, *Poverty, a Study of Town Life*, which, if it may not satisfy the rigorous statistical standards of modern professional sociologists, represented a major advance in techniques of social investigation and description in Britain. The Rowntrees were already influential in local Liberal politics in the north-east, but the publication of *Poverty* drew Seebohm Rowntree to the attention of progressive politicians at the national level, including the rising young radical David Lloyd George. Rowntree decided to follow up his research on the workers of York with a study of rural society and the problems of rural poverty and depopulation. These questions and the issue of land ownership and taxation were central concerns of the radical wing of the Liberal Party. Lloyd George, as President of the Board of Trade from 1905 to 1908, and even more as Chancellor of the Exchequer

3 Seebohm Rowntree

from 1908 to 1915, saw the land issue as crucial and Rowntree became one of his unofficial advisers on the subject. The study of land tenure systems was thus consciously envisaged as providing a basis for the new Liberal Government's policy on rural land.

Trebitsch's appointment as Rowntree's private secretary thus transformed him overnight not into a clerk in the cocoa works but into a social analyst charged with the formulation of what might well become public policy. The opportunity to travel and the introductions to important people furnished by his new employer delighted Trebitsch. Rowntree had opened for Trebitsch the door to a new world which thrilled and fascinated him. Instead of being imprisoned in his suburban domesticity Trebitsch could now indulge to the full his passion for thrusting himself forward to the attention of the famous and mighty. Moreover, as was indicated by Trebitsch's cable to his wife from York (with its reference to the prepayment of his salary — always an important point for Trebitsch), Rowntree was open-handed in his dealings with his employees. To Trebitsch he allowed not only a handsome salary but also almost unlimited expenses for travel and research with very little in the way of scrutiny of accounts. Rowntree subsequently affirmed:

> In connection with these investigations he [Trebitsch] . . . handled large amounts of money for me, virtually without control. Substantially it is the fact that he had opportunities for misappropriating moneys if he had wished to do so, without risk of being found out. I have no reason for supposing he misappropriated any of the considerable sums of money which I entrusted to him for the purposes of the investigations.[17]

Trebitsch's duties consisted of supervising a research team engaged in collecting and analysing statistics on rural social and economic conditions in Belgium and other European countries. For this purpose it would be necessary for Trebitsch to secure official publications and unpublished figures from the Belgian and other governments. Rowntree therefore arranged, through friends in the newly appointed Liberal government, for Trebitsch to be introduced to the Consular Department of the Foreign Office, which, it was hoped, would smooth the path for him in Brussels and other European capitals.

Thus began the relationship between Trebitsch and the Foreign Office that was to endure (to the endless exasperation of the Department and its officials) for more than three decades. Trebitsch arrived at the Foreign Office on 20 March 1906 with an introduction from Captain John Sinclair MP, the Secretary of State for Scotland in Campbell-Bannerman's Cabinet. Trebitsch explained his needs and was furnished with letters of introduction to the British Ambassador in Paris and the British ministers in Belgium and Switzerland. In addition the Department promised to send dispatches to these representatives informing them of the imminent arrival of Mr Rowntree's research assistant.[18]

Trebitsch set out immediately for Brussels and presented himself at the British Legation, arriving almost simultaneously with the dispatch sent on his behalf by the Foreign Office. On 23 March, the British Minister, Sir Arthur Hardinge, wrote to the Foreign Office: 'Mr Lincoln called on me yesterday with a separate introduction from you and I have already placed him in communication with various authorities, official and unofficial, who will assist him in the prosecution of his enquiries.'[19] In June, when Trebitsch visited Switzerland, he was accorded similar assistance there by the British Minister in Berne.

Trebitsch rapidly acquired a taste for this congenial mode of tourism, with all expenses paid and introductions into high official circles arranged on his behalf. He stayed at first-class hotels in the various cities he visited, enjoyed his favourite pastime of meeting Very Important Persons, and indulged his predilection for statistics (already evident in his reports on the Montreal mission) in his research for Rowntree. In July, when he projected a visit to Germany (allegedly on behalf of Joseph rather than Seebohm Rowntree), he addressed a letter to the Foreign Office requesting, more precisely demanding, further help. In its blend of the peremptory and the obsequious, the letter was characteristic of its author and merits quotation *in extenso*:

The Cocoa Works,
York.
27th July 1906.

The Consular Department,
The Foreign Office,
Downing Street,
London,

Sir,

As I am going to Germany now, to investigate certain questions connected with Temperance and Social Reform on behalf of Mr Joseph Rowntree, I will take the liberty of calling upon you to-morrow, Saturday, for letters of introduction to our Ambassadors or Ministers in Berlin, Munich, Dresden, Stuttgart, and in other places in the German Empire where we have accredited representatives. You will recollect, perhaps, that I was introduced to the Foreign Office last March by the Right Hon. Captain Sinclair,

MP and that you have been good enough to furnish me since with letters of introduction.

Hoping that you will be able to have the letters ready for me to-morrow, as I have to leave London to-morrow evening,

I am, Sir,
With my deep sense of gratitude,
Yours very sincerely,
I.T. Tribich Lincoln[20]

By this time, with Trebitsch demanding letters of introduction from the Foreign Office almost as if he were placing his weekly order for groceries, he was evidently developing into a tiresome nuisance to the Department and to diplomats abroad. Worse was in store. In September 1906 the Consular Department received what was described as a 'somewhat indignant letter' from the British Vice-Consul in Copenhagen, C.H. Funch, referring to a visit from Trebitsch:

> I took some trouble about him and lent him various books and also the only typewritten translation I had of: Act for procuring plots of land for labourers of April 22. 04. Mr Lincoln said he would have it retyped and return me my copy, but he never did so. He never returned the books and he never called on me or wrote to me at his departure, which he had said to a friend of mine that he would do.... If you should have Mr Lincoln's address I should like to get it so as to claim my books &c.[21]

The archives do not disclose whether Funch ever got his books back. Given what we already know of Trebitsch's elastic moral code, we may suspect that they were added to the creaking shelves of his private library. The incident was, in any event, a minor peccadillo compared with what was to follow.

In June 1907 a long letter from Trebitsch, addressed to Lord Edmond Fitzmaurice, arrived at the Foreign Office. It was typed on the private notepaper of Seebohm Rowntree and addressed to Fitzmaurice in his capacity as a junior Foreign Office minister. After dropping the names of Lord Carrington (President of the Board of Agriculture and Fisheries), Percy Alden (a radical Liberal MP), Captain Sinclair, and, of course, Seebohm Rowntree, Trebitsch explained that he was planning a further continental tour. He requested that Sir Arthur Hardinge be once again sent a dispatch asking him to give further help to Trebitsch, in particular by using his influence with the Minister of Finance in Brussels in order to gain access for Trebitsch to confidential documents in cadastral offices. No new letter of introduction would be required to the British Minister since

Trebitsch was already acquainted with him, but the very fact that Hardinge had been so helpful in the past rendered Trebitsch 'reluctant to approach him once more without a new support from the F.O. and this the more so as the matter is a difficult one'. Trebitsch then added:

> From Brussels I intend to proceed to Paris, with the same object in view, i.e. to establish the extent of the division of land in France — and I beg to solicit the same assistance for France. In this case also, no new letter of introduction will be necessary, for I am known at the Embassy. The letters of introduction given to me by the F.O. in March of last year proved very helpful in the case of Sir Arthur Hardinge, but I regret to say, not at the Embassy in Paris. I had the usual conventional assurances and promises of help, but very little real assistance.[22]

As before, Trebitsch's request was granted, a copy of his letter being sent to the British missions in Brussels and Paris 'for such action as they can properly take on Mr Lincoln's behalf'.[23] The animadversions on the past conduct of the Paris embassy were, however, discreetly omitted from the version of Trebitsch's letter dispatched by the Foreign Office.

Trebitsch's dissatisfaction with his reception at the Paris Embassy, already evident in the letter to Fitzmaurice, erupted into a furious row upon his return to France in the summer of 1907. In the British Ambassador in France, Sir Francis Bertie, he encountered, apparently for the first time in his dealings with British diplomats, a personality sufficiently akin to that of Trebitsch himself in his sense of his own importance to refuse to act as social secretary and factotum for a visiting foreign-born research student of obscure origins and insolent manners. Known in the Foreign Office as 'the Bull' ('an apt nickname', writes Lady Gladwyn, 'for somebody whose instinct was to toss and gore people at sight if they apeared likely to give him any trouble'), Bertie was a snob, an eccentric, a man of 'unparalleled coarseness', whose 'outstanding and undiplomatic characteristic was an extraordinarily blunt manner that sometimes amounted to downright rudeness'.[24] In Bertie Trebitsch seemed to have met his match: and yet, remarkably, it was not the distinguished plenipotentiary of the King-Emperor, but the young Hungarian research student who came off best. In this contest the matador rather than 'the Bull' dealt the decisive blow.

The first intimations of a storm across the Channel reached the Foreign Office in August 1907 in a private letter from Reginald Lister, Minister at the Paris Embassy, to William Tyrrell, Private Secretary to the Foreign Secretary, Sir Edward Grey. Lister explained that he had been asked a month or so earlier by Arthur

Ponsonby, the Prime Minister's Private Secretary, to extend help to Trebitsch in his researches. The embassy had done what it could, but had jibbed at a demand by Trebitsch that the French Foreign Ministry be asked to make him a present of official publications to the value of two thousand francs. When informed that this was out of the question, Trebitsch had written 'rather an impertinent letter' expressing dissatisfaction with his treatment at the hands of the embassy.

Trebitsch's 'impertinent letter' is still preserved in the archives of the British Embassy in Paris. Written from his luxurious quarters at the Hôtel de la Poste in Brussels, it was worded with an undiplomatic bluntness worthy of Bertie himself:

> Dear Sir,
>
> I am much obliged by the receipt of your letter & am sorry to see that you have so much trouble with the matter.
>
> I am greatly disappointed.
>
> It is quite true that it is unusual to ask for so many books, but the enquiry we are doing is unusual too. If the Embassy would but ask for the books, the french Govmnt. would gladly supply them. We have obtained twice as many books in Brussels.
>
> As to the price, I cannot agree with you that we are asking for 2000 frs worth of books. Their published value may be 2000 frs. but certainly not their actual value; in any case we have spent thousands of pounds on our french enquiry & we are not inclined to buy 2000 frs worth of books, which immediately after the publication of our volume on France will become useless to us.
>
> I thank you for your kind offer to consult documents at the library in Paris. A moments reflection will show you that this is impracticable. We must have the books constantly at our beck & call throughout the digesting of the french reports. Whilst I thank you sincerely for your efforts and exertions, I cannot let the matter rest as at present.
>
> We must obtain the books gratis & I am going to invoke the help of the highest quarters.
>
> I am, yours very truly,
> J.T. Tribich Lincoln

Presumably in order to forestall the threat implied in the final sentence of this letter, Lister wrote direct to Ponsonby, enclosing the offensive letter received from Trebitsch.[25] Bertie's no-nonsense attitude had evidently infected his junior staff and Trebitsch would thus appear to have suffered a definite rebuff.

The second round, however, demonstrated (what an entire generation of British diplomats were to discover again and again) that in the art of bouncing back after official snubs Trebitsch had no equal. The Prime Minister's Private Secretary, Ponsonby, had after all asked the Foreign Office for assistance to be given to Trebitsch. Faced with Lister's complaint Ponsonby resorted to the classic Whitehall method of settling awkward disputes — correspondence between private secretaries. He therefore sent a note, on 10 Downing Street writing-paper, to Sir Edward Grey's private secretary, Tyrrell, in which he explained that the Prime Minister 'wanted every help to be given' to Rowntree and his secretary. Granted the value of the books asked for from the French Government was high, 'but the Belgian Government supplied him with books to the amount of £150 because they realised that his book, when it appears, will be of very great service in Belgium.' Ponsonby added: 'I think the same applies to France.' As for Trebitsch, Ponsonby admitted that he did 'not appear to be a very tactful person, and I daresay the Embassy are rather annoyed with his supposing that these documents can be supplied as a matter of course'. But Ponsonby stressed that this was 'not quite a case of an ordinary individual applying out of mere curiosity or for his own convenience, but this great book which Rowntree is spending thousands of pounds upon will be a reference book of considerable value'.[26]

A flurry of Foreign Office minutes followed upon Ponsonby's note. There was some discussion of trying to get Rowntree to reduce the number of books required of the French Government. In the meantime, however, Trebitsch too had not been inactive. Percy Alden MP., who appear to have attempted to mediate between the Foreign Office and Trebitsch, wrote to Tyrell on 18 September: 'I have upbraided Lincoln & he promises to be wiser another time. Will you now give him a good letter of introduction from the Foreign Office to the French Govnt. asking them to do all they can on his behalf.... *So sorry* to trouble you again about this'.[27] The intervention of the member of Parliament, coming on top of the renewed interest in the matter shown by the Prime Minister's Private Secretary, left the Foreign Office little option. On 1 October an official dispatch was addressed to Bertie emphasizing the importance of Rowntree's research, and instructing the Ambassador to 'introduce Mr Lincoln to the proper French Authorities and ask them to be kind enough to grant him such facilities as they may be willing to afford him to aid him in carrying out his researches'.[28] The dispatch was given to Trebitsch for him to hand personally to the Ambassador. This virtual rebuke to the Paris Embassy represented a victory for Trebitsch in the absurd contest. Perhaps seeking to soften the blow, a private letter was sent at the same time to Lister, explaining that Sir

Edward Grey had provided the letter of introduction at the request of Percy Alden MP, and adding a hint that the embassy need not over-exert itself in favour of Trebitsch: 'There is no question of our bothering the F[rench] G[overnment] to present him with the publications he may want or to do anything unusual or contrary to custom. If he is given as cordial an introduction as possible to the necessary people he may be allowed to fight his own battles'.[29]

Trebitsch duly presented himself at the embassy and handed the British Government's instructions to Sir Francis Bertie. Appropriate representations were made to the French Government. The French Foreign Ministry accordingly arranged for Trebitsch to be given the publications he needed. In a letter of 3 December 1907, the French Foreign Minister, Pichon, informed Bertie that the Minister of Commerce, Doumergue, had supplied ten volumes, and that the Minister of Labour, Viviani, had sent thirteen.[30] Trebitsch was thus one of the few people to best Bertie in the art of the calculated snub. He administered a final twist, which evidently infuriated the embassy, by insisting that the books, so laboriously procured from the French authorities, should not be trusted to the vagaries of the ordinary mails, nor packed in Trebitsch's personal luggage, but rather should be dispatched by the Paris embassy to Rowntree's home in York. Apparently unable to contain himself, George Grahame, Second Secretary at the embassy, sent a private note to the Foreign Office complaining that 'Lincoln has shown a disagreeable spirit about the matter'.[31] On this untoward note the ridiculous affair ground to a halt.

What, it may be asked, was the point of this nonsensical contretemps? First, let us absolve Seebohm Rowntree of any responsibility for such an unnecessary and trivial controversy. Although Trebitsch wrote (admittedly with his employer's authority) on Rowntree's notepaper, it is inconceivable that the Quaker philanthropist would have countenanced stirring up such a fuss. And for what? After the thousands of pounds already spent on gathering research materials (and on maintaining the head of the research team in luxury hotels across Europe), is it imaginable that the cocoa millionaire would have grudged the paltry sum of two thousand francs (about eighty pounds) to pay for the urgently required French books? As for Trebitsch himself, by Rowntree's own admission he held virtually unlimited authority to spend money for exactly such purposes. Apart from the matter of the books he never evinced any notable propensity towards parsimoniousness in his disbursement of Rowntree's funds. Why then did Trebitsch make such a diabolical nuisance of himself to the officials of number ten Downing Street, the Foreign Office, the British embassies in five European capitals, as well as the personnel of at least three French government departments?

Here we approach a central feature of Trebitsch's personality — one which was to emerge repeatedly, although in strangely different forms, throughout his life. His was not merely a case of the man on the make who will do anything to secure admission to high society — although at one level that was part of the story. Nor did Trebitsch have anything to gain, directly or indirectly, by his pushful and arrogant behaviour, which was more calculated to alienate important people than to ingratiate him with the mighty. As for Trebitsch's later claim that his persistent nagging of British embassies and government departments constituted part of a long-term scheme to obtain British diplomatic secrets — that, as we shall see, may be dismissed as self-magnifying fiction.

To apprehend the springs of Trebitsch's odd, often contradictory, and sometimes self-defeating actions we must think of him as something other than a mere parvenu, busybody, or fantast. He was all of those things. But there was more. We have already observed in his early life his violent swings of mood, his minor irrationalities and apparent lack of a sense of proportion, his frequent inversion of conventional moral values, his increasingly solipsistic outlook, and the first stirrings of Manichee-like impulses bubbling in his head. As time passed, these tendencies were to develop into the dominant features of his personality. Eventually he was to convince himself that he was endowed with prophetic gifts, that he was a messiah of doom who could summon up dark forces which would crush all those who blocked his utterly self-oriented vision of the world. The full growth and expression of this psychosis still lay far ahead. We shall have occasion later to witness some of its more dramatic symptoms and to try to explore its aetiology. At this stage, as we begin to detect recurring patterns of strange behaviour, we may simply ask ourselves whether this is merely a case of a tiresome eccentric or that of a man whose mind was gradually succumbing to an ugly and gangrenous sickness.

In our excursus into Trebitsch's psychological condition and his quasi-diplomatic negotiations we have momentarily lost sight of Trebitsch's wife and family. So, it must be said, had Trebitsch, for from the moment of his appointment to the service of Seebohm Rowntree he saw less and less of his family, initiating a process which was to culminate ten years later in his virtual abandonment of them. In her recollections, Margaret Trebitsch writes charitably of her husband's conduct in this period. Trebitsch's new position necessitated another move for the family, from Hampton to York. But, writes Mrs Trebitsch, 'from that time onwards he was away most of the time somewhere on the continent'. Her account continues:

> Once I received a telegram to join him in Brussels at once. I took our youngest child with me. I was pleased to be with him again after so many weeks of separation. He showed me all the sights of Brussels, bought me beautiful clothes, and also a great deal to take home for all the youngsters. On the fifth day of my stay in Brussels he thought it would be better if I returned home as my mother would not like to be alone for so long. I was disappointed, as I had expected to be with him much longer.[32]

The wife's distress was increased by the suspicion (which, she tells us, later hardened into certainty) that Trebitsch was taking advantage of his long periods of absence from home to engage in an extra-marital liaison.

After nearly two years devoted in large measure to collecting information on the continent, Trebitsch returned to York, where he was now occupied in assisting Rowntree in the collation and analysis of the material for the forthcoming book. Thus settled in York, Trebitsch found an outlet for his surplus energies (as well as his love of public speaking) in part-time work as teacher in an Adult School in the city. During this period he also deepened his interest and involvement in politics, utilising the many openings afforded to him by the Rowntree connection. By August 1909 the bulk of the work on Rowntree's book was complete. Rowntree discharged Trebitsch with a remarkably generous unsecured loan of at least £10,000 (equivalent to at least £350,000 in 1988 purchasing power). The philanthropist later explained:

> I cannot recollect the total amount off-hand; it was over £10,000. I had no security for this money. I did this because I felt he had worked very hard for me for a number of years, and I was anxious to give him a start in business. I also lent him the money without security because I felt from my past experience I could trust to his honesty, without security.[33]

Land and Labour: Lessons from Belgium was published only in 1911. In a preface written in York in March 1910 Rowntree paid lavish tribute to his former assistant 'who for three years resided in Belgium, superintending the whole enquiry and also making certain investigations himself. Without his unsparing labour, tact, and skill many of the facts set forth in this volume could not have been collected.' The acknowledgement was addressed to 'Mr Lincoln MP'. How Trebitsch's but recently acquired surname had come to be dignified with this impressive handle we shall now discover.

CHAPTER 4

Mr Lincoln MP

The election of Ignatius Trebitsch Lincoln to the House of Commons in January 1910 as Liberal MP for Darlington stands out as one of the oddest aberrations in British political history. Other foreign-born citizens, other scoundrels, other penniless adventurers have irrupted into Parliament occasionally over the years. But the combination of handicaps under which Trebitsch laboured — youth, poverty, foreign birth and accent, as well as the defects of character which his previous career had already disclosed — was such that his election must be judged a massive personal achievement secured against immense odds.

The precise mechanism by which he managed, in April 1909, to obtain the nomination of the Darlington Liberal and Progressive Association is unfortunately shrouded from view, since the records of the association have been lost. But of the overriding importance of one connexion there can be no doubt: Trebitsch's nomination would have been unthinkable without the advantages derived from his period of employment by Seebohm Rowntree.

We have already observed with what little compunction Trebitsch had used Rowntree's name to winkle himself into the acquaintance of senior politicians and diplomats, how he had written on Rowntree's private notepaper as if it were his own, and how he had extracted thousands of pounds from the hapless philanthropist in support of vaguely defined business ventures. We should not think that Seebohm Rowntree presented Trebitsch with the seat by direct intervention. Darlington was no rotten borough and the constituency was not in the gift of the cocoa magnate. But the Rowntrees belonged to a handful of Quaker families whose influence in the commercial, intellectual and political life of the region was paramount. The most important newspaper in Darlington, the Liberal *Northern Echo*, formed but one strut in the great scaffolding of influence exerted by the Rowntree empire's diverse holdings.

In the course of Trebitsch's election campaign his links with the Rowntrees were fully exploited by his opponents. The chairman of the Darlington Liberal Association, James Cox, wrote twice to the *North Star* denying allegations that Trebitsch had been chosen as candidate thanks to the Rowntrees. Cox claimed that there had been no communication whatsoever between Seebohm Rowntree and the Darlington Liberals until after Trebitsch Lincoln's adoption as candidate, and he rejected imputations that the Rowntree enterprise 'or any individual thereof' was financing Trebitsch's election campaign. But as the *Star* (which supported Trebitsch's Conservative opponent) observed editorially, that was not really the point. 'Whether Mr Lincoln is being financed by the great cocoa entourage or not is altogether beside the question. All we inferred was that it has been through that gentleman's intimate personal and business connection with Messrs Rowntree that he has become known to Darlington in a political sense.'[1] This assessment may be broadly accepted: the *indirect* influence of Rowntree, the doors that were opened by the mere mention of his name, and the propagandist power of the *Northern Echo* must be regarded as the chief reasons for Trebitsch's nomination.

The importance of the *Echo* is evident from the fact that on 5 April 1909, a few hours *before* the local Liberal association's special meeting voted on Trebitsch's candidature, the Rowntree-owned newspaper published a lengthy profile of him, complete with flattering photograph, under the headline 'Darlington's Prospective Liberal Candidate.' The article presented a suitably cosmeticised pocket biography of the ex-missionary, pronouncing him 'a born politician' who had 'already made his mark as a public speaker'. No mention was made of his Jewish origin, but much stress was laid on his successful careers in journalism and the church, and a paragraph was devoted to his researches with Rowntree. With this encomium before their eyes it is hardly to be wondered at that the members of the Liberal Association, when they gathered that evening in the Mechanics' Hall, unanimously approved their executive's proposal that Trebitsch be adopted as Liberal candidate at the next election.

A bizarre (but not publicised) aspect of this astonishing decision was the fact that, at the time the Darlington Liberals proposed to dispatch Trebitsch as their representative to the imperial Parliament, the object of their enthusiasm had not yet been naturalised and was still a Hungarian citizen. Later Trebitsch artfully falsified the date of his naturalisation: for his first appearance in *Who's Who* (the 1911 edition, for which he submitted his entry after his election in 1910), he wrote 'naturalised 1908'. But this was a lie. His naturalisation certificate, a copy of which is preserved at the Home Office, is dated

5 May 1909, exactly one month *after* his formal adoption as a parliamentary candidate.

Trebitsch spent the next few months nursing the constituency, apparently in the confident expectation that he would be victorious at the next election. Trebitsch's optimism was admirable but not widely shared, for he faced a popular and formidable sitting Unionist, Herbert Pike Pease, who had succeeded his father as MP for Darlington in 1900.

The Peases were a further branch of that Quakerocracy whose wealth, public spirit, and zeal for good works permeated all aspects of life in Darlington. Indeed, we are told that 'it was impossible to avoid them even in death for they had, in 1877, donated a cemetery to the town'.[2] By the late nineteenth century the Pease interests had grown to envelop not only Darlington but several neighbouring constituencies for which members of the family sat at various times. The Pease holdings included ironstone mines in the Cleveland hills, iron and steel works, collieries and railway concerns, a family bank, and the locomotive works of the North-Eastern Railway, the largest employer of labour in Darlington. A crash in 1902 had weakened but not destroyed this tentacular economic power. Herbert Pike differed from most of his Pease cousins in being a Conservative rather than a Liberal; nor did he remain a Quaker, choosing to convert to the Church of England. But he maintained successfully the family political interest in Darlington, where he continued to enjoy the support of the Backhouse family, Quakers long prominent in the town. At the time of the Liberal landslide victory in the general election of 1906 Pease had shown his mettle by holding Darlington for the Tories with a majority of 288.

Yet even Pease had his Achilles' heel: in 1906 no Liberal had contested Darlington — a consequence of the Lib-Lab electoral compact by which it was agreed to leave the field open to a single anti-Conservative challenger in certain constituencies. Pease had as a result secured the votes of many middle-class Liberals who would not back a socialist. Now that a Liberal candidate was running in Darlington for the first time since the election of 1895, the middle-class Nonconformist vote might be expected to gravitate back to the Liberals in sufficient quantity to secure them the seat.[3]

Over the summer of 1909 Trebitsch conducted a number of outdoor political meetings, designed to introduce himself to the working-class electorate. On 8 September the Liberals organized a large public meeting in Darlington which induced the *Northern Echo* to hail Trebitsch's 'thorough grasp of the political questions of the day'. Not satisfied with what might be construed as faint praise, the editorialist dug deep into the quarry of political eulogy: 'There are, perhaps, few men in Parliament with so deep or so wide a knowledge as Mr Lincoln, and his most intimate friends have the strongest faith in his future as a statesman.'

The leading article continued with a surprising disclosure:

> The next month or two will be spent by him in pursuing a mission that shows how he has won the confidence of a Government which interests itself more deeply in the development of the nation than would appear even from its legislative efforts. Mr Lincoln, as is well known, is a native of Hungary, and one of the most fluent linguists in Europe. His ability to speak most European languages he proposes to put to excellent use, as we understand that in a few days he will be on his way to the Balkan States, armed with special letters of introduction and commendation from Sir Edward Grey, to pave the way for the expansion of British trade in that most promising field. He will visit practically all the Balkan states and Hungary to complete investigations as to the extent to which British capitalists and manufacturers, and through them the British workers, may benefit from the new spirit that is animating those states, all of which look to Britain as their friend.

The leader writer (evidently little versed in the subtleties of meiosis) pronounced: 'Although his opponents have, with scant courtesy, cast reflections upon his foreign origin, there is probably not another man in this country who is so well qualified to undertake the work' — which (according to the *Echo*) would undoubtedly do much for the industrial development of Great Britain.[4]

What motive lay at the back of this strangely-timed journey? When we might have expected that all Trebitsch's efforts would have been concentrated on the task of making himself known to the electors of Darlington, why did he rush off to south-east Europe? In spite of the *Echo*'s inflated panegyrics, the burgesses of this northern provincial town were unlikely to be swayed much in their political opinions by their candidate's jaunt to the Balkans. The reason must be sought elsewhere. We may safely dismiss Trebitsch's later efforts to dress his travels in a cloak of mystery, claiming that they had some devilish complicated espionage function. Equally imaginary (as we shall shortly see) was the suggestion that the journey was undertaken in the national interest at the behest of the British Government.

The truth seems to have been twofold. In the first place, Trebitsch undoubtedly wished to go home and boast to his friends and family in Budapest about his newly acquired political status. But beyond that there was, it seems certain, another (not unfamiliar) motive: money.

With his adoption as candidate for Darlington Trebitsch had very sensibly insisted on his family moving to live in the constituency, a prudent move if he were to have any hope of countering the inevitable accusations that he was an alien carpetbagger. His wife later recalled his saying: 'The people like to talk about their candidate as being one of themselves; one who lives amongst them and spends money in the town.'[5] A large house in Darlington, 'Park View', furnished and decorated by Maples, became the new Trebitsch-Lincoln habitat. In August 1909, with the work on land tenure complete, Trebitsch's employment as social investigator for Rowntree ceased. Although Trebitsch's patron appears to have continued to make generous subventions to his protégé, there could be no certainly that the flow of Rowntree bounty would continue for ever. Moreover, a man of Trebitsch's proud individuality naturally chafed at the bit of financial dependence (as we have seen already in the unhappy history of his relations with the Revd. McCarter). With the departure of the family from York, Trebitsch's income from teaching in the Adult School too was stopped. The trip to Europe was thus undertaken less in the national than in the personal economic interest (though Trebitsch doubtless persuaded himself that the two coincided): with the capital base so selflessly provided by Rowntree, Trebitsch had half-formed ideas of constructing an Anglo-Hungarian or Anglo-Balkan business empire under his personal direction. His political and business careers would thus happily complement one another.

Prior to his departure Trebitsch obtained letters of recommendation from the Foreign Office (as a prospective parliamentary candidate he no longer required the help of Rowntree in securing these). Dispatches were sent (as requested by Trebitsch) to the British embassies in Budapest, Belgrade, Sofia, Bucharest, Constantinople and Vienna, stating that Mr Tribich Lincoln was 'proceeding to the country in which you reside to study the commercial conditions with a view to the development of British trade'. The British envoys were accordingly instructed to furnish him with 'such assistance as you properly can for the furtherance of the objects of his visit'.[6]

Trebitsch's first stop was Budapest. He duly presented his credentials to the British Consul-General, Esmé Howard, to whom he explained that he was engaged in literary and commercial ventures which required that he be introduced to government ministers and other important people in the city. Howard accordingly introduced Trebitsch to the Hungarian Ministers of Commerce and Agriculture. In confidential conversation with Howard, Trebitsch disclosed that his object was to discover whether Hungary could offer a suitable field for the investment of British capital. Warming to his theme, Trebitsch explained to Howard that, together with other British investors, he was prepared to lay out as much as two million pounds — even more if the prospects were bright enough. He added, for

Howard's private information, that his backers included Sir Ernest Cassell (the wealthy Anglo-German banker and friend of King Edward VII) and the merchant banking firm of Samuel Montagu. Trebitsch supplemented these evidences of his grand connexions with the information that his friend Mr Rowntree was inclining towards the establishment of a cocoa factory in Hungary.[7]

Although Howard provided the introductions requested by Trebitsch and even accompanied him to meet one senior official, he reported to the Foreign Office that the Minister of Commerce had later expressed 'surprise . . . and even suspicion' concerning a proposal broached by Trebitsch for the establishment of an Anglo-Hungarian Bank. Howard himself, astonished by Trebitsch's arrogant mien and rapidly shifting business plans, wrote a private letter to a senior Foreign Office official:

> Who is your Mr Lincoln whom you have sent out to me? Il m'intrigue pas mal. A Hungarian born, with an English name tacked onto a Bohemian one, naturalized in England, educated in Canada, disfrocked parson (not by compulsion but by choice), Liberal candidate and prepared to make proposals for the investment of from 2 millions to 5 millions sterling of British Capital in Hungary — you will admit that he is a romantic character. And with all your F.O. taciturnity you simply tell me he is coming out to make investigations for the development of British commerce!
>
> Is it a blague that he has Cassell & Montagu & others behind him to the amount as he says of five millions? He has only been here a week: I have introduced him to everyone I could think of that would be likely to help him. . . . Please let me know a little more about him & if it is all quite serious.[8]

From Budapest Trebitsch moved on to Belgrade to re-enact the performance in his homeland. Once again the British embassy, in accordance with the instructions received from London, introduced Trebitsch to the Ministers of Commerce and Agriculture. Again Trebitsch confided his business plans to the British envoy: this time he claimed to be studying the possibility of opening an Anglo-Serbian Bank with a capital of £400,000. The British Minister in Belgrade subsequently reported to the Foreign Office that Trebitsch's scheme had been mentioned in a meeting of the Council of Ministers and that the Minister of Foreign Affairs had stated that the Serbian Government were prepared to accord Mr Lincoln all the facilities allowed by law. But the Foreign Minister also told his British colleague that the concession would not be granted until the company had actually been formed and the capital was forthcoming 'as they had recently had some unfavourable experiences in this respect'.[9]

These dispatches from Budapest and Belgrade ruffled sensitive official feathers in Whitehall. Inquiries were set in motion as to why Trebitsch had received letters of introduction, whether he really enjoyed the backing of powerful financiers, and what his political standing was. On the first point it was discovered that he had been given the introductions 'on the strength of the fact that he had had one before'. On the second, Mr Stuart Samuel, a partner in the firm of Samuel Montagu, declared that the merchant bankers had had nothing to do with him. And on the third, 'private inquiries at the Liberal Central Office' led the Foreign Office to the view that 'Mr Lincoln is not a person deserving much support'.[10]

Perhaps conscious that his Balkan peregrinations were not yielding tangible results, Trebitsch abandoned his intention of travelling to other countries in the region and returned to London. On his arrival he wrote to the Foreign Secretary, Sir Edward Grey, asking for an interview in order 'to report to you verbally the results of my journey and submit my plans'.[11] Grey proving to be otherwise engaged, he was interviewed by a senior official who was unimpressed by the man ('There is nothing British about him except his name and his naturalization.') and unconvinced by his commercial schemes.[12] The affair left a blot against Trebitsch in the collective memory of the department (where his antics in Paris over the books for Rowntree were still recalled). But for the time being the matter was consigned to the files.

Back in Darlington, Trebitsch discovered a suddenly changed political situation. When he had been adopted as candidate the previous April, there had seemed little likelihood of an election for some years: the House of Commons elected in January 1906 could constitutionally sit until 1913 without seeking another mandate. But the action of the House of Lords in rejecting Lloyd George's 'People's Budget' in 1909 provoked a first-rate political crisis which led Asquith's Liberal Government to call a general election in order to demonstrate the extent of their popular support against the recalcitrant peers. Trebitsch therefore found that instead of years, as had been expected, he had only a matter of weeks in which to make himself known in preparation for his contest in Darlington against the sitting local MP.

Trebitsch plunged into the campaign with energy, determination, and an arrogant bravado. At a Liberal meeting in the Drill Hall on 15 November 1909 he declared that the main question before the electorate was whether they were willing to submit to democracy becoming a farce. According to the report of the *North Star* he asked his audience whether they intended to vote for a man such as Pike Pease who fought against the people, 'or for such a splendid man as they had in him (Mr Lincoln)'. Aping Disraeli, he avowed: 'I am a

Jew. I am pround to belong to that race. I am a Jew with all the ability of a Jew. I have will power; I have lofty ideas, and I, I.T.T. Lincoln, though a Jew, will show the Tories of Darlington that I can fight.'

Such an opening was not to be missed by the local Conservative organ, which commented editorially:

> A little while ago, a small and by no means influential coterie of Socialistic Radicals introduced to Darlington as a prospective candidate a gentleman from Hungary. . . . He . . . is suffering from a bad attack of self-conceit, and . . . has found it necessary to direct the attention of such of the electors as take the trouble to attend his meetings to his opinion that he is a "splendid man". . . . We think some of that conceit will be taken out of him next January, if the general election takes place then. Meanwhile his peacock-like strutting adds to the gaiety of the borough.[13]

As we have already noticed, the *North Star* kept the issue of Trebitsch's Rowntree connexions in the public eye during the campaign; as a result, several of his meetings were disrupted by raucous catcalls and cries of 'cocoa!'

In spite of persistent Conservative attempts to draw attention to the Liberal candidate's links with Rowntree and his alien origin, Trebitsch campaigned doggedly on the issues of parliamentary reform and free trade. Drawing on his experience as a social investigator, Trebitsch overwhelmed his audiences with blue book statistics on the balance of trade and the comparative advantages of free trade and protectionism. His experience as missionary and as adult school teacher stood him in good stead as he confronted jeering opponents and sought to explicate the mysteries of international commerce with the aid of blackboard and chalk.

Characteristic of his campaigning style was a pamphlet, entitled *Powder and Shot*, issued about this time to the electors of Darlington. Arguing against the imposition of tariffs (advocated by his Conservative opponent), Trebitsch maintained that the wages of the working class and the general industrial position in free trade Britain were superior to those of protectionist Germany. As an illustration of the miserable condition of the German workers he pointed out that many were reduced to eating horse meat. In 1907, wrote the inveterate statistician, 135,239 horses had been slaughtered in Germany for human consumption. Even more horrible was the Teutonic commerce in dog flesh; the pamphlet gave a lengthy extract from an American consular report which stated:

> Complete figures in regard to the slaughter of dogs for food in the German Empire I have not been able to secure, but fragmentary

4 H. Pike Pease, Trebitsch's opponent in the Darlington election, 1910

> statistics indicate that the total number was about 7,000 — probably more rather than less. *In the City of Chemnitz alone, 698 dogs were slaughtered* in 1906, an increase of 88 over 1905. . . . *Neither is it unusual to find advertisements of dog meat, or for the purchase of dogs for slaughter.* Nor is it possible to read the German newspapers for any length of time without coming to the conclusion that a *great many dogs are killed and eaten that do not give up their lives under official inspection.*[14]

Trebitsch thus neatly deflected xenophobic prejudice from himself to German dog-eaters. The appeal was well calculated to cater to the

British concern for the well-being of certain classes of dumb animal, although the unkind critic might have observed that Trebitsch gave the appearance of running less in the Liberal interest than in that of the RSPCA.

In spite of the suspicions of Trebitsch which had already emerged at the Liberal Central Office, solid support was forthcoming from major political figures. Winston Churchill sent a message wishing Trebitsch 'success in the fine fight you are making for Free Trade, Land Reform, and Popular Government'.[15] David Lloyd George sent a letter of support — in after years to be preserved and displayed with pride by its recipient.[16] The Chancellor of the Exchequer did not visit Darlington to deliver one of his great speeches (as he had done on behalf of Pease's Labour opponent in the 1906 election), but other well-known Liberals joined Trebitsch on the hustings. Among these was Herbert Samuel, a recent Cabinet appointee, and MP for the nearby constituency of Cleveland. If Samuel's brother, Stuart, had mentioned to him anything of his exchange with the Foreign Office, Samuel did not allow this to affect his public endorsement of the Liberal candidate for Darlington. The minister congratulated the electors of the constituency who were 'fortunate in having so able and active a champion'.[17]

One former trumpeter of Lincoln's virtues remained curiously reticent during most of the campaign. The *Northern Echo*, while attacking Pike Pease vigorously, seldom so much as mentioned Trebitsch's name. Only on the eve of the poll did the Rowntree organ declare:

> Argument and closely-reasoned presentment of the people's cause have been the sole weapons of Mr Lincoln and his supporters. . . . The Liberal candidate has proved himself unassailable on the public platform. Of the attempts made to assail him on personal grounds we hope to have no reason to say anything.[18]

The ambiguity of the last sentence is disturbing. Perhaps the *Echo*'s leader-writer had belatedly learnt the art of litotes (of which he had been so conspicuously ignorant the previous April)? Or can it be that the discreet inquiries set in motion by the Foreign Office had alerted the Rowntrees to certain hitherto concealed aspects of their former employee's character? The latter seems the more probable explanation — particularly when we contrast the fierce Tory partisanship of the *North Star* in the Darlington campaign with the virtual effacement of the name of Lincoln (save in paid advertisements) in the *Echo*, previously such an egregious admirer of the man and his works.

Mrs Trebitsch later recalled the excitement of the final stages of the election campaign in December 1909 and January 1910: 'we had the unpleasant experience of being pelted by our opponents with banana

THE NORTHERN ECHO, SATURDAY, 15 JANUARY, 1910.

PROCLAMATION.

Be it known to you, O Men of the North, that the battle between the People and the Forces of Reaction starts at 8 o'clock this morning.

See to it that there are no laggards on the People's side.

Then Victory will be yours.

God Save the People!

PUT
IT
THERE

LINCOLN	X
PEASE	

THE BALLOT IS ABSOLUTELY SECRET

5 (*above*) 'Put it There'

6 (*right*) Trebitsch Lincoln, prospective candidate for Darlington, 1909

skins, stones wrapped in paper, and rotten eggs.' Then as now such excesses formed part of the festive merriment of British elections. More unusual were the gibes of 'damned foreigner' directed at the candidate's wife and the threat to stick a hatpin into her.[19]

The result of the election on 15 January 1910 was a sensation:

LINCOLN, J.T.T. (Liberal)	4,815
PEASE, H. PIKE (Unionist)	4,786
Liberal majority	29

The upset was notable not merely because of Trebitsch's exotic origins but also given the general political context. The January 1910 election constituted a setback for the Liberal Party: although they remained securely in power, they lost their overall majority in the House of Commons and were henceforward dependent on the votes in Parliament of Labour and Irish Nationalist members. Trebitsch therefore bucked the Conservative tide. Of course, the withdrawal of the Labour candidate was the crucial element. But it would be wrong to dismiss Mr Lincoln MP as an 'electoral freak'.* Without much assistance from the local Liberal press, Trebitsch, a stranger to Darlington, a novice on the hustings, a man who had himself never voted in a British election, a candidate whose most distinctive campaign plank had been the complaint that German workers ate the flesh of dogs, had, at the age of thirty, succeeded, where Disraeli (and countless others) had failed, in being elected to the House of Commons at the first attempt.

The victory was worthy of celebration. Not content with savouring his victory in his own constituency, Trebitsch embarked on a triumphal progress through neighbouring seats. At Stockton there was a fracas when a group of fish hawkers with their ponies and carts attempted to disrupt an open-air meeting while it was addressed by Trebitsch. At Thirsk he encountered boos, heckling, and a lusty rendering of the 'Glory Song'. One man shouted, 'We want no Jews here.' Trebitsch had great difficulty making himself heard, but he nevertheless carried on speaking doggedly. His speech, inaudible to most of the audience, was reported in the *Darlington and Stockton Times* of 22 January:

> "We have won at Darlington the greatest victory of this general election. The Tories had the strongest local man they could

* In an article in the *Manchester Guardian* of 15 December 1928, Arthur Ponsonby MP wrote of Trebitsch (he did not name him, but from the context it emerges definitely that he refers to him): 'On the whole... he was regarded as a man of no account or, at most, as an electoral freak.' In weighing this judgement the attentive reader will recall the intervention on behalf of Trebitsch in 1907 by the same Arthur Ponsonby (then Private Secretary to the Prime Minister).

possibly put against me. He represented Darlington for eleven years, and his father before him. He is a native of Darlington and notwithstanding all the association of the Peases with Darlington, Darlington people have shown that principles count with them more than names. They have brought out a poster in Darlington like they have here in Thirsk — 'The foreigner's got my job.' Well, he has got it. I am the foreigner, I have got Pike Pease's job."

Tories in the audience drowned most of the remainder of Trebitsch's remarks in derisive cheers and choruses of popular songs such as 'Antonio', 'Yorkshire Girl', and 'Kelly', but the orator rounded confidently on his opponents:

"You will make no impression upon me, shout as hard as you like," said Mr Lincoln. "My dear friends, there are 4,815 Darlingtonians standing behind me. You cannot upset that by any amount of shouting."

In her memoirs Mrs Lincoln relived the heady atmosphere of those days: 'Our delight was beyond words. Throughout the night we celebrated, and next day was again full of excitement. Telegrams arrived from all over the country and there were endless callers.'[20] Probably the most satisfying to Trebitsch of all these cables was one from the Foreign Secretary, Sir Edward Grey, who had virtually snubbed him only a few weeks earlier.[21]

Trebitsch's response to his election to Parliament was characteristic. Other newly-elected MPs might pore over Erskine May, struggling with the intricacies of parliamentary procedure, or ingratiate themselves at the whips' office. Learning that the new Parliament would not convene for several weeks, Trebitsch decided on another trip to Budapest. Naturally the Foreign Office was informed that the usual diplomatic courtesies would have to be extended to the peripatetic legislator by the British embassy in Budapest. When Esmé Howard heard the news that his self-invited guest was about to return, he wrote privately (with deplorable disrespect towards a popular tribune): 'I do not congratulate the people of Darlington on their choice of an MP but if Mr T. Tribich Lincoln comes back here I shall always treat him with the respect due to the Elect of the People and with the reserve necessary in dealing with a Liar.'[22]

On 28 January 1910, the *Pester Lloyd*, the distinguished German-language Budapest daily, published a lengthy account of Trebitsch's arrival in the city the previous day, his installation at the Hotel Hungaria, and his 'joyous reunion' with his widowed mother. Trebitsch accorded the paper an interview in which he enlarged on his life history and announced: 'I intend to stay here a week and deal with some business, since I want to serve my fatherland and promote Anglo-Hungarian economic relations.'

A day or two later Trebitsch visited the British Embassy and told Howard that he had 'practically arranged everything at this end for the establishment of an Anglo-Hungarian Bank in Budapest.' A week later he called again and showed Howard various papers concerning the proposed bank. In his dispatch to the Foreign Office reporting Trebitsch's visit, Howard added:

> Mr Lincoln further informed me very confidentially that he had run up against a most astonishing invention since he had been in Hungary of which he has purchased the option. This consists of a furnace by which all coal of whatever kind, even the worst forms of 'brown' coal, is utterly consumed giving off neither smoke nor gas. The arrangement is, he says, purely mechanical and of the simplest possible kind. He has already entered into communication with the First Lord of the Admiralty on the subject. He has himself seen the furnace at work, and declares the result to be little short of amazing.[23]

In a second dispatch on the same day Howard reported that Trebitsch had delivered a public lecture in Hungarian on February 7 on the subject of British politics. In the course of this speech before a large audience Trebitsch had apparently committed an undiplomatic gaffe by uttering unorthodox views on internal Hungarian politics. The Liberals of England (Trebitsch told his Hungarian audience) 'did not look with sympathy on Hungary's efforts towards independence' since these could only weaken the Dual Monarchy to the advantage of Germany and Russia. Trebitsch also gave vent to his view that 'the present agitation in Hungary for universal suffrage was inopportune' since it 'would only strengthen the Church and the Conservatives'.[24]

The reaction of Trebitsch's audience to these doctrines, strange in the mouth of a British Liberal, doubly so in one of Magyar origin, is not recorded. But the Foreign Office reacted with predictable irritation, fearing that if Hungarians thought that the MP's views represented official thinking in Britain they might be affronted. The file containing Howard's latest report was shown to the Foreign Secretary — who may now have begun to regret his cable of congratulations to Trebitsch after the election. On the front of the file was a caustic minute by Eyre Crowe:

> This gentleman is a Hungarian Jew recently naturalized here, who now hides his origin under the guise of an honoured name. It seems odd that a British constituency should elect to be represented by this variety of British subject in parliament . . . Mr Trebitsch Lincoln's tactless remarks about internal politics in Hungary and support to the Germans in and out of Hungary are likely to frustrate his efforts in that country.[25]

As we shall see, Crowe was later to outdo nearly all his Foreign Office colleagues in his loathing and contempt for Trebitsch. At this stage we may merely note that Crowe, the most implacable foe of Germany in Grey's Foreign Office (though Crowe himself had been born and educated in Germany, and married a German), was the first British official to suspect Trebitsch of over-friendliness to Germans.

The various business schemes initiated by Trebitsch in Budapest came to nothing. The Anglo-Hungarian Bank remained no more than a gleam in his eye. The plans for large-scale British investment in Hungary were, of course, castles in the air. The smokeless fuel scheme was communicated to the Board of Trade and the Admiralty but aroused no interest. Even the idea for a cocoa factory in Hungary proved to be a figment of Trebitsch's venturesome imagination: the beverage was in any case not widely consumed in that country.

With Parliament about to be opened in London, Trebitsch returned to England and installed himself at the National Liberal Club. Mrs Lincoln, whom Trebitsch now dubbed 'the first lady' of Darlington, remained precisely that: she did not join her husband in London and saw him only on his occasional weekend forays to his constituency.[26] When another son, named Edward Cuthbert Lincoln, was born on 6 April 1910 in Darlington, Trebitsch was away in London asking questions at the House of Commons.

By contrast with the spectacular series of events before and after his election, Trebitsch's brief term in the House of Commons was something of an anticlimax. In Darlington he had been the centre of attention and the focus of debate: in Westminster he was merely one of the most junior of hundreds of backbench members seeking to catch the eye of the Speaker and the press. A fellow Liberal MP., Arthur Ponsonby, later recalled:

> He attended debates fairly regularly, but when he spoke his strong foreign accent made me wonder how it was that any constituency could have returned him. In conversation he had an air of profound knowledge and compelling conviction, and he might be seen occasionally pacing the division lobby alone as if weighed down by an intent conception of great projects.[27]

Trebitsch's maiden speech was delivered on 23 February 1910 in the debate on the King's Speech. It was an unimpressive hotchpotch of tired campaign rhetoric on the theme of free trade. Trebitsch first bored the House with comparative figures of earnings in Britain and Germany and trade statistics of several countries, and then proceeded to try to entertain members with stale jokes and lengthy anecdotes which might have amused a friendly election audience but were hardly the stuff of memorable parliamentary oratory. The speech attracted little attention.[28] Trebitsch, however, was not easily put down. A week later he rose again, this time to intervene in a debate on the Temporary Borrowing Bill (necessitated by the House of Lords' refusal to pass the 1909 budget). After a few moments he was interrupted by the Speaker, who rebuked him for irrelevance. Trebitsch veered back to the subject of debate; he said little of any originality or substance; but he spoke with a vehemence (and an accent) that attracted notice. Moreover, whereas his maiden speech had been delivered at a time when many members would be eating their dinner, on this occasion he was more fortunate in his timing.[29]

Trebitsch won the reward that he most craved — publicity — although not quite in the form he might have expected. The *Punch* caricature, although crudely drawn and hardly flattering (particularly

PAKS VOBISCUM; OR, THE LINCOLN HANDICAP.
"We weel not zend ze Büdg-ett to ze Haus of Lörrdz to be zrown out on-ly a-gen!!"
(Mr. J. T. T. Lincoln—born at Paks in Hungary.)

7 Paks Vobiscum *or* the Lincoln Handicap (from *Punch*)

in the caption's implied reflection on his command of English), pleased Trebitsch enormously. In later years he would proudly cite the cartoon as evidence of his political importance and he reproduced it in print on more than one occasion. In a sense this was, for Trebitsch, the peak of his parliamentary career.

A few days before the *Punch* caricature appeared, Trebitsch was suddenly taken ill in Darlington and underwent an operation for appendicitis.[30] The illness put him out of action for a month. When he resumed his parliamentary duties he seemed to have lost for a while something of his earlier political gusto. During the whole remainder of his career in the House of Commons he delivered only one more speech. This latter, in the debate on Egyptian Administration on 13 June 1910, constituted his only memorable contribution to the proceedings of the House during his brief membership.

An earlier speaker from the Conservative benches had insisted on the importance of the British overseas 'fulfilling the functions of a superior race' and had declared that 'the black races must and can only be treated as subordinate to the race charged with the government of the country for the time being'.[31] Trebitsch rose to protest at these propositions:

> I submit that if the white man cannot rule races which we call inferior races save by resort to arms, then his prestige is already gone. I speak, I confess, as an Oriental myself. I have Oriental blood in my veins, and I cannot but laugh at the doctrine of hon. Members opposite that Orientals must receive treatment in some way different from that given to other peoples. May I be permitted to point out that one of the greatest men who ever lived, Jesus Christ, was an Oriental, and did He differentiate His treatment when dealing with Orientals?

After offering his proposals for improving Egyptian administration, Trebitsch concluded on a note of unctuous flattery: 'I admit that the situation is very complicated, and as a humble Member of the Liberal party I desire to compliment the Foreign Secretary and to express my admiration for the skill with which he has handled this question during the past two or three years.'[32]

Trebitsch's speech evoked the compliment of a lengthy retort from A.J. Balfour, the Leader of the Opposition. On the other hand, Grey, who wound up the debate for the Government, ignored the contribution of the Liberal member for Darlington. Trebitsch never spoke again in the House of Commons. Apart from his three speeches he had asked a total of seven parliamentary questions. These all dealt with foreign affairs and, while of little intrinsic interest, are revealing of the directions in which Trebitsch's thoughts were moving. Three of the questions concerned the tangled diplomacy of the Balkans following the annexation by Austria in 1908 of the provinces of Bosnia and Herzegovina. The first two of these were addressed to the Foreign Secretary, but Grey (as was common in the case of questions regarded as of lesser importance whether because of their nature or because of the standing of the member who asked them) delegated the job of replying to a junior minister.[33] Perhaps miffed at the implication that his questions were not worthy of the attention of the Secretary of State, Trebitsch addressed his third Balkan question to the Prime Minister — but the same junior minister was deputed to reply.[34]

If Balkan diplomacy was a natural object of interest for Trebitsch, given his history, the same could not be said of the field of concern disclosed by Trebitsch's remaining four questions. These all concerned the Orient: two related to the affairs of Persia (of these Sir Edward Grey deigned to reply to one); and two dealt with the sensitive diplomatic question of railway construction in China. The last of these (it was also Trebitsch's last question in Parliament) may be quoted in full:

> MR LINCOLN asked the Secretary of State for Foreign Affairs, whether, in view of the fact that the Japanese Government had opposed the construction of the Chinchow-Aigun Railway, which, apart from the junction, runs throughout on Chinese territory, he would say what action he proposes to take, in view of the Anglo-Japanese Treaty of 1905, one of the objects of which was the preservation of the common interests of all Powers in China by ensuring the independence and integrity of the Chinese Empire and the principle of equal opportunities for the commerce and industry of all nations in China?

The junior minister, Mr McKinnon Wood, replied loftily that the question was based on 'a misapprehension of the facts'.[35] How and why Trebitsch became interested at this time in the fascinating but esoteric rivalry between Britain and Japan in north China we do not know. We shall have occasion to return to this problem later. For the time being let us merely note that this theme, which was to dominate the final chapter of Trebitsch's life, was already germinating at this early stage in his career.

The Parliament elected in January 1910 was the second shortest-lived this century (the shortest was that of February 1974). The continuing impasse arising from the conflict between the Liberal Government and the Conservative-dominated House of Lords led the Prime Minister, Asquith , to call a second general election in the same year. In the normal course of events Trebitsch would have stood for re-election in Darlington in December 1910, but before the election took place it became clear that his parliamentary career was

8 I.T.T. Lincoln MP (front centre) with constituents, Darlington, 1910

over. The reason was not (apparently) any deficiency in his political performance. It was the old bugbear: money.

For the past year Trebitsch had been spending lavishly, recklessly, and with no thought for the morrow. He had forfeited his salaries from the Adult School at York and from Rowntree (although the flow of bounty from the cocoa magnate seems not yet to have dried up altogether). As an MP Trebitsch earned nothing, for the Liberal Government's plans for payment of members had not yet passed into law. In the course of his election campaign, Trebitsch, with typical effrontery, had applied for a loan of 'a few hundred pounds' to, of all people, Revd. Lypshytz, the east end missionary whose trust he had betrayed and whose wife's watch he had stolen.[36] The cleric's reply, if any, no longer exists. But the Darlington Record Office holds an IOU, signed by Trebitsch, in the sum of £100 made out to Mr James Blumer, a prominent local Liberal. This loan (never repaid) seems to have been used to help organize a successful but expensive political publicity stunt: in order to prove to the world the palpable superiority of English free trade principles over continental protectionism Trebitsch led a party of Darlington working men in the summer of 1910 on a tour of inspection of some of the less attractive industrial regions of Belgium. When they got back the workers all duly reported on the obvious inferiority of foreign countries cowering behind tariff walls — all, that is, save one awkward individualist who denied that Belgians ate horse-meat and complained that he would have preferred to attend the international exhibition rather than tour the slums with Trebitsch.[37]

Not content with the organization of this boondoggle, Trebitsch looked for other ways of throwing away money. He employed two private secretaries to assist in his political and business activities. In September 1910 he set up a company, the Anglo-Austrian Petroleum Syndicate, with a view to exploiting what appeared to be a potential boom in the oil industry.[38] (Of this more presently.) He invited relatives from Hungary to come to England and take up positions in his new enterprise. Among those who arrived were a nephew in his late teens and two of Trebitsch's younger brothers, the socialist Lajos (who had Magyarised his surname to Tarcai) and Simon (who went by the name 'Harry Trebitsch'). All looked to Trebitsch for support, not to mention the jobs he had promised. Disappointed, they moved on to the United States.[39] Mrs Trebitsch later remembered her husband's irrational response to her mild attempts to rein in his wild financial irresponsibility:

> I knew we were living beyond our means, but it was no use arguing the point. My husband's opinion was: "The more you spend, the more you are obliged to earn. It is no use trying to scrape and save small amounts; nobody got rich that way. Never be satisfied with what you are earning — try and earn more."[40]

By November 1910 Trebitsch's finances had deteriorated to a disastrous level. On 26 November Joseph Rowntree wrote to his son, Seebohm:

> I am very sorry to hear of the Lincoln smash, but one had got prepared for bad news. I hope you will take it as we took the dear woodcock dish at Marseilles some years ago when we concluded that as the dear bill had to be paid we wd not spoil our journey to Cannes by any regrets. There is really no reason why you shd lose 5 minutes sleep over the affair. My feeling is how thankful we shd be that the loss can be borne without any inconvenience. If you want any help with the Bank let me know. You wd have felt bad if Lincoln had turned out an honest man and had failed through want of help that might have been given. The experience gained may be of great help in your power of helping and giving advice to others in future years.[41]

Trebitsch was thus (as in the past) fortunate in the philosophic forbearance of his benefactors-turned-victims. But it was now plain even to the Rowntrees that Trebitsch could not be permitted to remain in parliament.

If we are to believe Trebitsch's own account, his retirement from the fray was voluntary and was greeted with dismay by the local Liberal association, which sought to persuade him to continue as candidate in the forthcoming election.[42] This was indeed the public stance of the association. But there are indications that the matter was not settled quite so amicably, that the ruined parliamentarian struggled desperately to keep his seat, and that considerable pressure had to be exerted behind the scenes in order to induce him to desist without creating a public scandal. (Quite apart from Trebitsch's finances, the Liberals probably had another good reason for wanting to be rid of him. In June 1910, the Austrian government, annoyed by some of Trebitsch's questions in Parliament instructed the Austrian Ambassador in London, Count Mensdorff, to inform Sir Edward Grey of some untoward details concerning Trebitsch's past. Among these were references to Trebitsch's juvenile career as a petty thief.[43]) Although Trebitsch's finances had been deteriorating for some time, he did not withdraw his candidacy until the last possible moment, so late that there was hardly time left before the election for the local Liberals to select a replacement. The Rowntree-controlled *Northern Echo* preserved a discreet silence throughout these embarrassing events. But its Conservative competitor, the *North Star*, scented blood. On 25 November it reported that a member of the Rowntree family had visited the town two days earlier and that local Liberals were engaged in anxious consultations. 'What is happening,' the *Star* continued, 'we do not, of course, pretend to know, but it would seem that steps are being taken by the wire-pullers to set Mr Lincoln aside.' On 30 November the same newspaper reported a statement by Trebitsch himself:

> Mr Lincoln said his retirement was a keen disappointment , but it was due to causes which he could not prevent. "We have tried our best to be in the battle. I have tried my best to so arrange matters that I would still have the privilege of working with you and fighting with you for the great and noble cause of Liberalism; and, ladies and gentlemen, I am not yet dead. I have not yet done with politics."

Trebitsch withdrew barely a week before polling day in Darlington. The Liberals rushed to select a new candidate who scrambled together a hasty campaign. Trebitsch himself appeared on the hustings in support of his successor and became embroiled in a new controversy with Pease. Predictably the Liberal lost, no less predictably blaming his defeat on the 'contumely and scandal' which had engulfed his predecessor.[44] Thus concluded, abruptly and sourly, Trebitsch's short but extraordinary career in British politics. As to his forecast that he would make a political come-back, this must have

9 Trebitsch Lincoln, *c.* 1915

seemed to most of his listeners a typical piece of unrealistic braggadocio.

Within twelve months the wheel of fortune had turned disastrously for Trebitsch. Just a year earlier he had returned in triumph to his mother and his homeland as a newly elected member of the British imperial legislature. Now he had lost his seat in parliament and was virtually bankrupt. He does not, however, appear to have been prosecuted to the point of a court declaration of bankruptcy. The reason may lie in the circumstances of his political displacement. It is not perhaps a far-fetched surmise that his creditors, among whom Seebohm Rowntree figured prominently, undertook to settle Trebitsch's financial affairs without untoward publicity in return for an assurance on his part of similar circumspection in the political sphere.

At a melancholy meeting at the Station Hotel in York in January 1911, Trebitsch confronted his assembled creditors, among them Seebohm Rowntree. Liabilities, it was immediately apparent, hopelessly exceeded Trebitsch's available assets. Rather than pursue the matter through the bankruptcy courts, the creditors agreed to a composition for the time being of five shillings in the pound; as to the remainder of his debts they consented to wait. 'We couldn't do anything else'. Rowntree later commented.[45] Few of those who attended the meeting can have expected to hear anything further of Trebitsch Lincoln.

CHAPTER 5

The Oil Bubble

In early 1911 Trebitsch, at the age of thirty-one, could look back on the wreckage of his political career; as for the future his prospects seemed bleak. He was saddled with debts of at least £1,700.[1] He had no job and no income. His family already numbered seven (Trebitsch, his wife, the widow Kahlor, little Ignatius, John, Edward, and Julius Tut), and his wife was pregnant again; the last of Trebitsch's children, Clifford, was born in May 1911. But Trebitsch was not downhearted. True to his philosophy that expenditure would somehow generate earnings, he took steps to increase his outgoings. There was nothing now left to hold him in Darlington, where his wife had in any case never been happy. 'Park View' was given up and the Trebitsch family moved back to the south of England. Their new home was a large house at Watford in Hertfordshire, just north of London, which Mrs Trebitsch later remembered as 'the place where I spent the happiest days of my life'. The house in Watford contained fourteen rooms and was furnished on a lavish scale. The family enjoyed the attentions of a staff that included a nurse, butler, cook, housemaid, charwoman and gardener. 'We lived', Mrs Trebitsch wistfully recalled, 'on the most extravagant lines'.[2]

Having failed in commerce in a small way, Trebitsch decided, consistent with his doctrine, to plunge into business at the deep end. The various Balkan banking schemes had never got off the ground, but Trebitsch clearly still felt that his linguistic skills and knowledge of the area gave him special advantages in the direction of British capital towards eastern Europe. His magpie-like attention had, as we have already noticed, been caught in 1910 by the apparently glittering opportunities of the oil fields of Austrian Galicia and Roumania. Long a magnet for speculative finance, these regions, at that time the closest major oil sources to the heartland of industrial Europe, seemed about to enter a massive boom development. Galician oil production had multiplied nearly sevenfold between 1899 and 1909 and English capital was already flowing towards Galicia, encouraged by special articles in *The Times* on 'The Virgin Oilfields of Galicia'.[3] With the British navy and other large energy consumers beginning to switch from coal to oil, resourceful entrepreneurs espied easy pickings.

Trebitsch now attempted to turn himself into a Galician Gulbenkian, investing tens of thousands of pounds of other men's money in options, pipelines, drilling rights and equipment. He formed a number of interlocking companies to pursue the *fata morgana* of east European oil. These included the Anglo-Austrian Petroleum Syndicate, incorporated in September 1910, and Lincoln and Company, established in March 1912.[4] These were both essentially private companies with little capital and little real existence save in legal documents. Very different were the two public companies launched by Trebitsch as the main vehicles of his enterprise, the Amalgamated Oil Pipe-Lines of Galicia, formed in May 1911, and the Oil and Drilling Trust of Roumania, established a year later. Although the records of these companies no longer exist, it is possible to trace their meteoric rise and fall with some precision from other sources, including official documents lodged at Companies House. The picture that emerges is not pretty, though it conforms strikingly to the knowledge we have already acquired of the less attractive aspects of Trebitsch's character.

Around him in his undertakings Trebitsch gathered an ill-assorted gallery of associates, some highly respectable, others of more questionable social standing. An established Edinburgh businessman, William Gardner Sinclair, agreed to serve as chairman of the Amalgamated Oil Pipe-Lines of Galicia. The company's board of directors included also a Norfolk banker, a member of Lloyd's, a Viennese oilman, and most decoratively, two princes, Hieronim Radziwill and August Lobkowitz. Among the staff of the company were Alfred Douglas Farmer, the company secretary (later Managing Director of the County Gentleman Publishing Company), a Belgian named Hotermans who had worked as Trebitsch's private secretary while he was an MP, and Trebitsch's young nephew Alexander Krausz, whom he had brought back from the USA to help organize the oil bonanza. Later, when Trebitsch's affairs began to go awry he fell in with other business collaborators, among them Charles Weingart, a German resident in London, and John Goldstein, a financier who traded as J. Grainger at 11 Duke Street, London.

How did Trebitsch, unemployed and virtually insolvent, pay for his vast domestic establishment, sink substantial capital into his oil companies, and even begin to transfer some assets to the trustee for his patient creditors? Part of the answer undoubtedly lies in Trebitsch's finesse as a confidence trickster. For a man who was insolvent, albeit not technically bankrupt, to launch public companies required a boldness bordering on the foolhardy. But Trebitsch possessed in overflowing measure the first requirement of the successful con-man, an absolute belief in himself. Moreover, he could introduce himself quite correctly as a former member of parliament. He could entertain at his magnificent house in Watford. He could travel to Berlin and Vienna and speak to bankers and oil magnates in their own language. He could invite associates to lunch at the National Liberal Club, where government ministers hob-nobbed with distinguished lawyers, newspaper editors, business-men and the occasional peer. He could show off his prized letter from Lloyd George, his caricature in *Punch*, and the dedication in Rowntree's book, and he could boast of his connexions in the Foreign Office and his meetings with senior politicians in many countries. But above all he could talk — volubly, self-importantly, flashily, at inordinate length, and yet plausibly. His experience as a missionary and as a politician in the rough-and-tumble of public debate provided an ideal grounding for his new vocation. He had learned how to win souls and how to win votes; now he drew on a battery of professional skills in order to accumulate more tangible assets.

The Amalgamated Oil Pipe-Lines of Galicia Ltd was launched with a public issue of shares in May 1911. The nominal capital of the company was announced in the company prospectus as £660,000, but the actual working capital of the enterprise was a good deal less. At the initial issue 440,000 shares were offered for sale at one pound each. Of these, the Vienna banking firm of Laupenmühlen and Co. underwrote the sale of 312,000. In order to promote the sale Trebitsch bought a big advertisement in *The Times*, outlining the benefits and large potential profits available to investors.

The result of the issue was disappointing. The records of Companies House give a complete list of the names and professions of purchasers of the shares as well as the number of shares taken up in each case. The investors represented a variegated cross-section of society, including butchers, grocers, solicitors, veterinary surgeons, printers, schoolmasters, musicians, wine merchants, 'spinsters', 'widows', 'married women', an actor, a draper, an artist, a constable, a number of clerks, a member of parliament, the managing director of the Savoy Hotel, a fellow of University College, Oxford, and one Aram d'Abro of the Hotel Majestic, Paris.[5] If Trebitsch had been running once again for election, such a broad range of support would have afforded him an impressive political base. But all these private investors took up only tiny lots of shares. A handful of bankers and stockbrokers bought somewhat larger lots. Even so the total number of shares sold at the initial issue was only 75,989. The underwriters were therefore obliged to buy up an unsold balance of 236,011 shares. As a result Laupenmühlen and Co., although they did not have a controlling interest, possessed by far the most powerful voice in the affairs of the company.

The prospectus for the share issue explained that the company had been formed 'to acquire a controlling interest in, and thus practically to amalgamate, six of the eight principal pipe-lines now operating as public oil-transport and oil storage companies in the well-known oil districts of Boryslaw and Tustanowice, in the province of Galicia, in Austria'. The document noted that since it was 'not intended that this Company should own, drill, or work Wells, the speculative element incident to these operations will be absent. The well-known character of the districts served by the pipe-lines ought to provide a steady, continuous business, and consequent profit.' In the section estimating future profits it was calculated that these would suffice to pay a ten per cent dividend while leaving ample provision for reserves, management expenses and even 'a substantial balance for further dividend'.[6] The issue was discussed a few weeks later in an article appearing on the front page of the financial section of *The Times* under the headline: 'British Capital and Galician Oil: Optimistic Finance'. This declared the objective of pipe-line amalgamation in Galicia 'healthy in itself' though it warned that 'the value of the undertakings [i.e. the pipelines to be amalgamated by the new company] has, according to the view of experts, been calculated at a comparatively high figure in the prospectus.' 'The prospect of profits,' the article added, 'is, however, necessarily contingent upon a cessation of the falling off in the production of oil.'[7]

Greater caution would, it turned out, have been justified. In 1910, when Trebitsch first began to manifest interest in Galician oil it had seemed as if production in the region, which had risen so dramatically in the previous few years, could only continue to increase. In fact, far from being on the threshold of a great boom, the Galician oil industry, it subsequently emerged, had already reached a peak from which, almost from the moment of Trebitsch's involvement, it began an inexorable decline. Production shrank from 2.077 million tons in 1909 to 1.761 million in 1910. This was attributed in part to temporary causes such as severe flooding in the oil producing areas. The following year, however, the decline continued, with only 1.455 million tons being produced, a drop of some eighteen per cent.[8] By late 1911, therefore, it began to dawn on oil experts that the trend towards reduced levels of production was permanent and was a result of the steady exhaustion of oil deposits in the region. The Boryslaw-Tustanowice district in which Trebitsch's company operated consisted of less than two square miles: scope for further exploration in the hope of new oil strikes was thus almost non-existent.

Not only was the market for the piping and storage of oil in Galicia thus suddenly and unexpectedly diminished, but the prospects of the new company were clouded by another difficulty. Trebitsch, it seems, had originally hoped to amalgamate all the major pipeline companies in the area, eight in number, piping altogether over 95 per cent of the district's oil traffic. Indeed, an announcement inserted in *The Times* (anonymously, but probably at the instigation of Trebitsch) prior to the public share issue had suggested that there already existed an understanding among all the eight pipeline companies that they would combine.[9] This was vigorously contested, however, by the managing director of the Karpath company, one of the largest of the eight concerns, piping more than a quarter of all the oil in the district. In a letter to *The Times* he denied that the Karpath company was a party to any such agreement; nor, he added, was it 'in any manner interested in the combination of the Pipe Lines'.[10]

No doubt Trebitsch hoped that the combination of six out of the eight pipelines in his 'Amalgamated' company would enable him to squeeze out the competition. The strategy seemed at first to be working. In September 1911 the 'Amalgamated' company's general meeting was informed that negotiations were afoot for the purchase of the other of the two independent lines, the Braganza.[11] This was the property of the Premier Oil and Pipe-Line Company, which eventually agreed to sell the Braganza line for £100,000, of which £40,000 was to be paid in cash and the remainder in shares. With seven out of the eight companies now joined in the 'Amalgamated' it appeared for a moment as if Trebitsch's dreams were about to be realized.

Instead, disaster struck. The slump in Galician oil production continued during 1912, further reducing demand for pipeline capacity and oil storage tank space. The competition from the Karpath company, rather than weakening, grew ever more determined. Meanwhile Trebitsch's control of the 'Amalgamated' company became shaky. In order to pay the £40,000 cash for the Braganza line he had been obliged to turn again to the Laupenmühlen banking firm, who (together with their associates) provided the money in return for shares in the company and additional seats for their nominees on the board of directors.[12] In May 1912, when payments fell due on earlier purchases by the 'Amalgamated' company, Laupenmühlen supplied a further £39,000 in return for more shares.[13]

By now the bankers were in effective control of the company. With no sign of an upturn in the prospects for Galician oil, and in the absence of any dividend or other return on their large investment, they decided to close the company down. The company's assets were therefore sold to the Premier Oil and Pipe-Line Company — the very company that had earlier disposed of the Braganza line! At an extraordinary general meeting of the 'Amalgamated' on 14 June 1912 the shareholders heard the chairman's justification for the sale:

> The shareholders might reasonably ask [he said] why a company started under such favourable auspices, and with apparently such good prospects, should so early in its career consent to be absorbed by another company, but from the outset it had been found that the successful management of their business presented much more difficulty than had been anticipated. In the first place, competition developed on more extended and strenuous lines than could have been expected.... Even after the acquisition of the [Braganza] Pipe-Line the opposition of the leading pipe-line outside the amalgamation [i.e. the Karpath] was very determined, and on top of this came the more serious trouble of the diminution of output of oil in the fields in which they were interested.[14]

Soon afterwards the 'Amalgamated' company was placed in liquidation.

Trebitsch's plans had thus backfired: his company emerged the victim rather than the victor of the take-over battle. With his company liquidated, how did Trebitsch emerge personally from this foray into commercial warefare? If one were to believe the garbled version of these events presented in Trebitsch's autobiography, it would seem that he sold out of the company before the end, and emerged with a profit of £18,000. His wife reports that he boasted to her that he had made £20,000 out of Galician oil.[15] While it is impossible to establish the precise truth, the reality appears to have been quite different. Documents filed at Companies House show that Trebitsch had not yet severed his relationship with the 'Amalgamated' at the time when it went into liquidation. He does appear to have disposed of most of his shares in the company, but only later. They were acquired by the bankers Laupenmühlen; since these latter had already lost heavily by their involvement in the 'Amalgamated', it is highly doubtful that they paid Trebitsch a further £18,000 for his shares. Indeed, although the documents are silent on the point, it is much more likely that they paid him nothing at all, but that they took the (by now almost worthless) shares in lieu of payment for some other liability incurred by Trebitsch.[16]

Trebitsch's claim to have made a big profit out of the Galician operation is further weakened by evidence presented in a court case in London in 1924[17]: this shows that in July 1912, that is immediately after the 'Amalgamated' collapse, Trebitsch took out a loan of £4,000 from the Eagle Insurance Company at a rate of six per cent.* He would hardly have incurred such a debt if he were really flush with large Galician oil profits. The most credible, although not the most charitable, interpretation of Trebitsch's boastings is that, in the course of the twelve months of operations by the 'Amalgamated', during which he was in day-to-day charge of the running of the company, he succeeded in syphoning off large sums of money for his personal needs. Not surprisingly the records of the company filed at Companies House include no statement of accounts.

Trebitsch's by now almost automatic reaction to financial shipwreck was to plunge into still deeper waters. In theory, his move from Galician to Roumanian oil in the spring of 1912 was not unintelligent. Whereas the downward slide of Galician oil production was continuing apace, Roumanian oil was holding its own and production was growing. Indeed total Roumanian production in 1911 exceeded Galician for the first time for several years. The switch from Galicia to Roumania therefore made some sense. Trebitsch's second great oil venture was even more fantastic in conception and even more grandiose in execution than the first, while following a similar path of rapid ascent and sudden and catastrophic fall.

Trebitsch laid the basis for his switch to Roumanian oil some time before the collapse of the 'Amalgamated'. His first move was the formation in March 1912, in partnership with his friend Charles Weingart, of a small private company, Lincoln and Co. Incorporated with a nominal capital of £5,000, Lincoln and Co., like its predecessor the Anglo-Austrian Petroleum Syndicate, was little more than a letterhead operation formed for such purposes as renting the suite of offices at Finsbury Court where Trebitsch maintained the headquarters of his operations.[18]

On 21 April 1912 Trebitsch obtained a concession to exploit an oil well at Mislişoara in the Buştenari district of Roumania.[19] Where he found the money to pay for this is not known: we may suspect that he diverted funds from the revenues of the 'Amalgamated', at that time on the verge of collapse. On 2 May he incorporated his new company, the Oil and Drilling Trust of Roumania. The board of directors this time included no princes, though Trebitsch

* Trebitsch paid back only £1,493.11s.2d, before defaulting. The loan had been guaranteed by William Sinclair and Charles Weingart. Weingart emigrated to his native Germany in 1913 and did not pay his share of the guaranteed balance. Sinclair was therefore obliged to pay the entire balance of £2,507.8s.10d to the Eagle Insurance Company. In 1924 Sinclair appealed to the Anglo-German Arbitral Tribunal, claiming half the sum, £1,253.14s.5d due from Weingart. The German Government contested the claim, but Sinclair was awarded the full amount plus interest at five per cent per annum plus £15 costs. Thus again did Trebitsch bite the hands that fed him.

managed to maintain an aristocratic flavour by the appointment of a Roumanian nobleman, Count Michel Callimachi. Trebitsch himself served on the board from the outset (in the case of the 'Amalgamated' he had remained discreetly in the background until after the public capital issue) as did his partner, Weingart. A measure of respectability in the eyes of potential English investors was lent to the enterprise by the appointment to the board of a retired admiral, Sir Compton Domville, GCB, GCVO. Farmer once again served as Company Secretary, and the staff included Trebitsch's nephew Alexander Krausz, as well as the Belgian former private secretary, Hotermans. (An announcement in the *Moniteur du pétrole roumain* described the latter as a 'very capable specialist engineer with vast experience acquired working in Galicia for the "Amalgamated Oil Pipe-Lines of Galicia Ltd."'[20]) The solicitor who acted for the company was Gilbert Samuel, brother of the financier Stuart Samuel and the cabinet minister Herbert Samuel: again one wonders why Stuart Samuel did not inform his brothers of what he had learnt concerning Trebitsch's character.

On 20 May 1912 an announcement appeared in *The Times* inviting subscriptions to a public share issue in the new company. As in the case of the 'Amalgamated' a year earlier, the prospectus for the new company affords an interesting example of 'optimistic finance'. Whereas the 'Amalgamated' had restricted its operations to the transportation and storage of oil, the new company's primary object was the extraction of the mineral from the ground. (The warnings in the previous year's prospectus against the 'speculative element' in oil drilling were conveniently forgotten.) Waxing eloquent in praise of the advantageous location and excellent quality of Roumanian oil, the new prospectus estimated profits in the first year at £20,000, and in the second at £65,000. It was explained that this projection was based on the expectation that the company would soon be operating no fewer than sixteen wells in Roumania, each producing an average of twenty tons of oil a day — yielding a grand total of 116,800 tons per annum. Indeed, the prospectus continued, such an estimate should be regarded as highly conservative, since it was 'well-known' that wells in the Buştenari district generally gave a much higher yield than twenty tons a day. (The wary reader might have noticed an echo of the reference in the previous year's prospectus to the 'well-known' character of the Galician oil districts — but presumably few investors engaged in such close textual analysis.) The share issue was underwritten on this occasion, not by bankers, but by Lincoln and Co. itself, which guaranteed the subscription of up to £25,000 of the £100,000 issue. Perhaps Trebitsch had grown wary of bankers — or perhaps bankers were now more careful in their reading of prospectuses.[21]

The results of Trebitsch's second share issue were even more disappointing than the first. As in the case of the 'Amalgamated', small investors took up tiny lots. Arthur and Richard Ladenburg, bankers, bought 478 and 1,912 shares respectively. The directors took about 2,000. But Lincoln and Co., in their capacity as underwriters, were obliged to buy 9,286 at one pound each. In other words, instead of raising £100,000 as was hoped, the issue raised barely £15,000. Since the new company paid Lincoln and Co. the sum of £6,000 for 'formation expenses' and £1,750 as an underwriting commission, it would seem that little was achieved by the entire operation save that Trebitsch sent a flurry of cheques from and to himself (in his different capacities) round his suite of offices in Finsbury Court. Just enough money remained, however, to purchase some drilling equipment and send initial remittances to Roumania in order that oil extraction operations could be started.[22]

Undaunted by the fruitless merry-go-round of the share issue, Trebitsch announced his own appointment as managing director of the new company and his imminent departure for Roumania to supervise the beginning of operations. Arriving in Bucharest, he set up temporary offices at the Hôtel du Boulevard, and set about engaging engineers and workmen, ordering machinery, and securing the necessary authorisations from government officials. He achieved rapid results on all three fronts. In August the *Moniteur du pétrole roumain* reported that sophisticated equipment, of the new 'rotary' type, had arrived at the port of Constanţa from the USA, and that highly qualified drill-workers had also reached Roumania.[23] Moreover, on 28 September the Roumanian Government, at a meeting of the council of ministers, accorded Trebitsch's company authority to operate in the country, a decision which was subsequently confirmed in a decree issued by King Carol.[24] With such a royal seal of approval the way now seemed clear for the success of the venture.

In the early stages of the enterprise Trebitsch frequently travelled between London and the Roumanian oilfields. But after a short time he decided to move his home and family to Bucharest. A large furnished house was rented at 5 Strada Cosma, not far from the royal palace, and the house in Watford was given up. Trebitsch's wife did not enjoy her new life in the third foreign country in which her husband had deposited her. Trebitsch often went away on long business trips without her; when he was at home there were arguments during which Trebitsch threw things at her.[25] Even worse, she discovered that her husband had taken a mistress.[26] She did not raise the matter with Trebitsch, but the realization that he had deceived her plunged her into gloom. Her husband's attempt to cheer her up by naming an oil-well after her was unavailing. 'Margareta' turned out in any case to be unproductive.

Although the installation of the new drilling equipment took much longer than expected and was attended by various technical difficulties, Trebitsch's mood remained buoyant. In November 1912 two of the main investors in his company, his friend Weingart and the banker Arthur Ladenburg visited Roumania and were conducted by Trebitsch on a tour of the oilfields. Ladenburg pronounced himself impressed with what he had seen and accepted a seat on the board of the company.[27] With the financial weight of his board thus strengthened, Trebitsch set off happily on a trip to the United States with a view to inspecting the latest oil industry machinery and visiting his chief suppliers. On his return he issued an announcement to the press claiming that he had signed a contract with Mr J.F. Lucey, head of the Southern Well Works Company of Chattanooga, Tennessee, producers of the 'Parker Rotary' drill. The contract gave Trebitsch exclusive rights to market the drill in Roumania. Trebitsch further let it be known that his company was about to embark on a major expansion programme for which purpose it was proposed to make a new capital issue of at least ten million francs (about £400,000).[28]

Trebitsch was now on top of the world. In order to celebrate his success, demonstrate his optimism, and show the world that he had now attained membership of the Roumanian oil elite, he issued invitations to fellow oilmen to visit his installations and inspect the 'Parker Rotary' machine. On 20 February 1913 Trebitsch welcomed directors and technical experts from other oil companies, who arrived in a special train from Bucharest. The excursion ended with a banquet for the guests with the catering entrusted to the chefs of the Hôtel du Boulevard in Bucharest. After dinner there were speeches and champagne toasts. The director of the government department of mines proposed the health of the host; Trebitsch drank to his guests; and tributes were paid to the commercial press whose representatives formed part of the festive throng. A few days later the *Moniteur du pétrole roumain* published a detailed report on the occasion.[29] For the next few weeks the *Moniteur* regularly carried full-page advertisements for 'Parker Rotary' drilling equipment, 'sole concessionaires for Roumania, The Oil and Drilling Trust of Roumania Ltd'.[30]

Such extravagance seemed to betoken astonishing success for Trebitsch's young company, still less than a year old. The reality, visible only in the fine print of official Roumanian oil production statistics, was darker. Apart from the oil-well at Buştenari, Trebitsch had purchased four other concessions giving him the right to drill for oil in neighbouring areas.[31] But not one of these ever produced a drop of oil for him. Even the Buştenari well yielded only a dribble. In February 1913, its best month under Trebitsch's ownership, it produced 224 tons. Total production for the period June 1912 to August 1913 was 2291 tons. Thus instead of sixteen wells producing an average of twenty tons a day, as forecast in the prospectus, Trebitsch had only one producing an average of five tons a day. And instead of 116,800 tons in the first year, as promised, the company even after fifteen months had produced barely two per cent of the projected figure.[32]

The revenues were therefore a tiny fraction of what had been anticipated. In the absence of satisfactory accounts we do not know what price Trebitsch obtained for the small amount of oil actually produced by his company. But at a generous estimate, given prevailing price levels, it cannot have been more than £4,000 for his entire production over fifteen months. Trebitsch did succeed in selling or leasing some of the 'Parker Rotary' equipment, of which he had bought huge quantities, most of which was lying idle. Perhaps this brought his total revenue to £5,000.

But at the same time Trebitsch had incurred, on behalf of the company, vast expenses. According to the only statement of accounts ever prepared by the company (of which more presently) no less than £108,127 was 'remitted to or spent on behalf of the Bucharest office to provide for drilling operations or other expenditure'.[33] 'Other expenditure' presumably included such items as the cost of the excursion and banquet by which Trebitsch sought to impress his fellow oilmen. Nor did even this large sum include such outgoings as the Managing Director's salary (an additional £1,875). With an income of (perhaps) £5,000 and an expenditure more than twenty times that sum, it is hardly to be wondered at that Trebitsch started looking round for additional 'capital' in the spring of 1913.

Trebitsch's plan for a further share issue of £400,000 or more never got off the ground. Perhaps he realized that 'optimistic finance' had its limits even with the credulous small investors who had taken up his previous offerings. The butchers, the actors, the widows, and the managing director of the Savoy Hotel must, after all, have noticed that the 'Amalgamated' had collapsed and that Trebitsch's present enterprise had not paid any dividend. Casting round for other sources of support, Trebitsch had the monumental effrontery to cable to his old employer, Seebohm Rowntree, inviting his assistance. The beneficent Quaker had apparently not yet fully absorbed his father's wise advice at the time of Trebitsch's first 'crash' in 1910; instead of ignoring his former secretary's plea, Rowntree sent an investigator to Roumania to look at Trebitsch's oil well 'with a view [as Rowntree later stated] to advancing him money'.[34] Presumably the report was negative, for there is no evidence that Rowntree sent any more money to Trebitsch (to whom, it will be recalled, he had already given more than £10,000).

In the absence of an oil strike, and with continuing heavy outgoings in wages and equipment costs, Trebitsch became increasingly desperate. The pattern of events in the last stage of the 'Amalgamated' was now replicated. The Ladenburg banking firm, whose interest in the company has already been noted, were invited to help. At first they provided only small infusions of cash in return for shares in the company. They thus gradually began to build up their shareholding.[35] But Trebitsch, presumably recalling his experience with Laupenmühlens a year earlier, did not wish to allow Ladenburgs to acquire a controlling interest in the company. This constraint forced him to look elsewhere for cash. His friend Weingart helped a little, but could not or would not provide enough. As a last resort Trebitsch turned to his acquaintance John Goldstein, the Duke Street financier. Goldstein later testified: 'I recollect having sent [Trebitsch] £500 or £600 every week by cable to Roumania for several weeks; that would be in 1913.' Goldstein was evidently a trusting man, for he added: 'I recollect having once cabled him £1,000 to Roumania. He has never given me any security or even receipt for this last £1,000.'[36] But even these substantial cash injections barely sufficed to keep the company going.

On 3 July 1913 disaster struck from a completely unexpected quarter. King Carol ordered the mobilisation of the Roumanian army. The participation of Roumania in the second Balkan war (in which she joined Turkey, Greece and Serbia in attacking Bulgaria) spelt doom for Trebitsch's tottering enterprise. The mobilisation dislocated Roumania's communications and rendered it almost impossible for Trebitsch to obtain further credit. Several of his directors had already resigned. Trebitsch now had no alternative: he turned once again to the bankers, this time Ladenburgs. They were not prepared to lend him money in the same trustful way as Goldstein; nor were they prepared to follow the example of the Laupenmühlens and advance credit in return for reams of worthless shares. But Arthur Ladenburg had been to Roumania, had seen Trebitsch's oil well and also the stockpiles of unused drilling machinery. He knew that the company had real assets. Ladenburgs therefore agreed to grant the company a mortgage of £25,000. The terms were far-reaching, not to say harsh. In the absence of repayment (apparently at any time laid down by Ladenburgs), the bankers would be entitled to foreclose on 'the company's undertaking and all its property whatsoever and wheresoever both present and future including its uncalled capital'.[37]

Even £25,000, however, was not enough to keep afloat a company whose expenditures exceeded its revenues by a factor of more than twenty. By the end of August 1913 nearly all the remaining directors had resigned. By 6 September Ladenburgs decided that they could go no further. On that date they applied successfully to the Chancery Division of the High Court in London for the appointment of a receiver to take charge of the affairs of the company.[38]

The receiver was a former colleague of Trebitsch on the Liberal benches in the House of Commons, John MacDonald Henderson MP. He found a shocking state of affairs awaiting him. He immediately called in a respected firm of auditors to examine the company's books. They studied the nearest that could be found to accounts; indeed, it could hardly be termed a balance sheet since it listed only liabilities. In addition to the vast remittances and expenditures in Roumania which have already been enumerated and the more than £25,000 owed to Ladenburgs, there was a further £38,796 due to 'creditors for machinery supplied', and another £1,337 owing to other creditors. This was quite apart from whatever might be due to the shareholders. According to the statement, the firm's total of outstanding obligations had reached £151,430. Against all this, it was true, might be set the company's assets in Roumania, but information as to the exact value of these was hard to come by. Meanwhile the company's bank account in London contained the meagre sum of £32.4s.6d. In the circumstances it is hardly surprising that the auditors reported that:

> owing to (a) the lack of vouchers and other information that should be available at the Company's offices, and (b) the failure of the Bucharest Office to make complete returns of their working and to account for the moneys remitted to, or spent for, them, we have not obtained all the information and explanations we have required. We are therefore unable to state that the above Balance Sheet is properly drawn up so as to exhibit a true and correct view of the state of the Company's affairs.[39]

Trebitsch, as ever defiant in adversity, returned from Roumania to attend a hastily called company meeting. The occasion was reported in *The Times* of 23 September 1913:

> DIFFICULTIES OF AN OIL COMPANY
>
> An extraordinary meeting of the Oil and Drilling Trust of Roumania was held yesterday to receive a report from the managing director on the position of affairs. Mr J.M. Henderson MP, the receiver, was appointed chairman.
>
> Mr T. Lincoln, the managing director, gave a lengthy account of a number of misunderstandings which had arisen between various persons, resulting in the company's being without working capital just when it was, it was stated, on the verge of success. Several speakers addressed the meeting subsequently and numerous charges and counter-charges were made.

> The chairman pointed out that the shareholders were more concerned with the question of saving their property than with personal differences. The great thing was to find fresh capital, and he believed that a scheme was afoot with that object. After further discussions, Mr Lincoln agreed to go out to Roumania as soon as possible in the interests of the company, and the meeting was adjourned for three weeks.

Any hope that Trebitsch might yet be able to salvage something from the wreck was vain. Even his closest collaborators now abandoned him. Charles Weingart went abroad suddenly and permanently; Lincoln and Co., now without any assets, stopped doing business.[40] Meanwhile, Mr J.F. Lucey, manufacturer of the 'Parker Rotary' drill, turned up unexpectedly in Roumania. In an interview with the *Moniteur du pétrole roumain*, he denied that he had ever granted Trebitsch's company exclusive marketing rights for his machinery in Roumania.[41] Trebitsch was in any case no longer in control of the company: although he was still nominally managing director, he could act only subject to the authority of the receiver. Trebitsch's temperament could brook no such subordination. At a board meeting on 23 December 1913 he resigned.[42] The affairs of the company were so tangled that it took his successors nearly a decade to try to sort them out. The shareholders, of course, lost everything, and the company was dissolved in 1922.[43]

Even after his resignation as managing director Trebitsch did not yet give up. Returning to Roumania, he tried to prevent either his former company or Ladenburg's bank from seizing the company's remaining assets. He seems to have succeeded in misappropriating some of the property of his own former company, a crime for which, as we shall see, he was later found guilty and sentenced to a term in gaol by a Roumanian court. He cannot have made much out of the disposal of his former property, for in early 1914 he was still in desperate financial circumstances. He decided to return to England, telling his wife, whom he left behind with the family in Bucharest, that he planned to promote a new company.[44] But, of course, there could be no question of this for a man of Trebitsch's tainted reputation.

The failures in rapid succession of each of Trebitsch's companies, and the spectacular nature of the most recent collapse, completely precluded any further adventures by Trebitsch on the London markets. Indeed he found himself hard up for the barest necessities of life. In February and April 1914 he was obliged to apply again to Goldstein, who advanced him small sums amounting to £45 as a 'friendly loan'.[45] By now there was almost nobody else left to whom Trebitsch could look for help. Apart from all his other debts, Trebitsch owed thousands to the patient Rowntree as well as £500 to one of his former private secretaries, William Robson.[46] By the summer of 1914 even Goldstein would no longer lend him money without security. He obtained a loan of £100 from another financier, Samuel Finklestone of Jermyn Street, against a promissory note falling due in October. But this sum was soon dissipated.

Trebitsch had often before operated at or beyond the frontier of legality. As an adolescent in Hungary he had been accused of three acts of thievery. There had been the incident of the theft of Mrs Lypshytz's watch. There had been question marks over his handling of the funds of his public companies. There had been his illegal disposal of the property of his former company in Roumania. Trebitsch's renewed lurch into criminal behaviour in July 1914 and afterwards should therefore occasion no surprise.

Early in that month he went to see Goldstein and asked for a loan of £1,000. Goldstein replied (according to his later testimony), 'No not to you alone; get me a good guarantor, certainly.' A few days later Trebitsch came back and told Goldstein that he had found a guarantor for the loan. He gave the name of the guarantor as Benjamin Seebohm Rowntree, and his address as the National Liberal Club. Goldstein, who by this time was evidently more wary than in his earlier dealings with Trebitsch, wrote to Rowntree at the National Liberal Club inquiring whether he would indeed guarantee the loan. He received a reply, to all appearances signed by Rowntree, confirming the guarantee. When Trebitsch called again later that day Goldstein advanced him £750.[47]

Trebitsch had, in fact, committed an ingenious fraud. The letter on National Liberal Club stationery, supposedly signed by Rowntree, had in reality been forged by his fellow-member, Trebitsch Lincoln. What had happened (it subsequently emerged in court) was that Trebitsch had walked into the club as usual, had gone to the table in the hall where letters for members were normally placed for collection, and had picked up Goldstein's letter of inquiry addressed to Rowntree. He had then written the purported reply guaranteeing the loan.[48] In its simplicity it was a near-perfect crime, moreover one which probably came easily to Trebitsch, who, we may recall, had already accustomed himself at an earlier period to writing on his employer's notepaper as if it were his own. Provided Trebitsch could pay back the £750 to Goldstein by the agreed date of 30 November there was no reason why the crime should ever be discovered. Trebitsch still possessed some documents which he thought might enable him to reclaim some of his oil concessions in Roumania. With this new, dangerously acquired capital the exponent of 'optimistic finance' clung tenaciously to his insensate dreams of commercial glory.

CHAPTER 6

Double Agent

The outbreak of the First World War on 1 August 1914 shattered any lingering hope Trebitsch might have retained of salvaging some remnants of his business. As the rival armies of the powers marshalled their forces throughout the continent, Trebitsch ordered his wife home from Roumania. Margaret Trebitsch packed the family silver and valuables in the central heating furnace of their house in Bucharest and set off for England with her two youngest sons. Her husband met her in Brussels, already under threat from the German army, and after a couple of days the reunited family hurriedly decamped to London. Poor Margaret Trebitsch, who had grown accustomed to the luxurious ambience of life in the shade of the royal palace in Bucharest, could not return to her much-loved home in Watford. Compelled to adjust suddenly and painfully to their reduced circumstances, the Trebitsches settled in a cheap boarding-house at 51 Torrington Square, W.C.[1]

Trebitsch now found himself in what were, even for him, desperate straits. He owed money to Robson and Finklestone; he had defrauded Goldstein; he could not even pay his rent — though, deploying his great gifts of persuasion in such matters, he somehow managed to induce the proprietor of the boarding-house to grant him credit. Once again insolvent, unemployed, and with a family to feed, boarding school fees to pay, not to mention his pressing creditors, Trebitsch faced another of the recurring crises of his career. This time, however, no guardian angel in the shape of a Burt or a Rowntree appeared to rescue him. He was alone.

Moreover, Trebitsch detected around him a subtle change in the atmosphere. The comfortable tolerance of Edwardian England was giving way, under the inexorable pressures of modern warfare, to a heightened xenophobia which paid little need to the niceties of naturalisation. As a former Hungarian citizen with a German-born wife, Trebitsch now found himself under suspicion on all sides.

He continued to frequent the National Liberal Club, though (as he later complained) he was 'several times insulted' there.[2] Like many other naturalised aliens at this time, Trebitsch was the victim of anti-foreign whispering: a former servant, Mrs M.L. Williman, previously employed as a nurse to the Lincoln children, denounced him to the Gloucestershire Constabulary. Fortunately for him, she could report nothing more damaging than the facts of his business and family connexions with Austria-Hungary — which were in any case in the public realm. The police took no action, although the information was stored in Special Branch files for later use.[3]

Momentarily Trebitsch seemed to have held his enemies at bay when, a fortnight after Britain entered the war, he secured employment under the War Office as a censor of Hungarian and Roumanian letters. Later, questions were asked in Parliament as to how he had obtained this position, and there were dark hints of improper influence by important persons.[4] We do not know who supplied the letters of reference which were furnished to the authorities on Trebitsch's behalf. Perhaps he wrote them himself. But there need be no undue mystery about the matter. For Trebitsch was indeed exceptionally well qualified for this lowly and harmless position in the military hierarchy. Had he not been acclaimed by the *Northern Echo* as 'one of the most fluent linguists in Europe'? His shoddy performance under examination in the dead languages was happily buried in the archives of Lambeth Palace — and anyway irrelevant to the successful performance of his War Office functions. If Trebitsch had only rested content with his censorship duties he might have lasted out the war in this comparatively safe billet.

Unfortunately the job was not suited to one of Trebitsch's restless and arrogant mien. For a former MP and company director to be reduced to the position of little more than a clerk in the Mount Pleasant Sorting Office at a minuscule salary was in itself an insufferable degradation. For one who had taken to writing other people's letters it might be thought that reading them would come as second nature. But this sedentary, boring occupation was gall to Trebitsch's soul. As a result he came to commit the ultimate crime of the postal censor: he started *writing on the letters*. His marginal annotations may have temporarily enlivened the dreariness of the passing hours at Mount Pleasant, but they secured him a reprimand from his superiors. This Trebitsch could not endure: he resigned, thus giving up, after only a few weeks, the only office of profit he ever held under the British crown.[5]

Trebitsch was now at his wits' end. His wife later recalled that he raved incessantly about money, dreaming that sheer will-power would, as in the past, somehow carry him through. The family's remaining jewellery was pawned, but this purchased only a few weeks' grace. Already the previous July, as we have seen, Trebitsch had taken the first fateful step into criminality. Now he took a second. The promissory note to Samuel Finklestone fell due in October and Trebitsch could not pay. Trebitsch offered Finklestone a bill of exchange for £200, dated 30 October, and payable three months afterwards, this at the discounted price of £150. The bill purported to be signed by Alfred Douglas Farmer, former company secretary of Trebitsch's ill-fated oil ventures, and was payable at the Commercial Bank of Scotland in Lombard Street. The bill reached Finklestone by post together with a letter apparently from Farmer authorising Trebitsch to negotiate the bill. Finklestone took steps to verify the signature; satisfied, he handed Trebitsch a cheque for a further £150.[6]

Ingenious though his defalcations undoubtedly were, Trebitsch's frauds suffered from the fatal flaw common to most such schemes: it would be merely a matter of time before the victim discovered his loss. In the effort to beat the clock Trebitsch found ever-greater difficulty in keeping up the pace necessary for success.

On 26 November Goldstein wrote to Trebitsch, reminding him that the promissory note, supposedly guaranteed by Rowntree in July, fell due for payment on 30 November. At the same time, Goldstein wrote a similar reminder letter to Rowntree. As usual, both the letter to Trebitsch and that to Rowntree were addressed to the National Liberal Club. On 30 November Goldstein received a letter from Trebitsch asking for an extension of the period for payment. On the same day a letter arrived for Goldstein, apparently written by Rowntree, offering to extend the guarantee for a further period. Rowntree's letter was written on National Liberal Club notepaper. Not questioning the authenticity of the Rowntree letter, Goldstein replied to (as he thought) Rowntree, agreeing to the altered date for payment.[7]

At this point Trebitsch seems to have lost his nerve. His renewed forgery had apparently won him further time to pay. But this merely lengthened Trebitsch's agony, for, with his elder sons returning to London from boarding school for the Christmas vacations, Trebitsch's expenses were once again mounting while his income was non-existent.[8] He decided on the risky expedient of confessing all and throwing himself on the Quaker philanthropist's (already much abused) good nature.

On 2 December Seebohm Rowntree walked into the National Liberal Club and found waiting for him the two letters from Goldstein as well as another from Trebitsch. Since Trebitsch had already replied to Goldstein in Rowntree's name we know that Goldstein's letters cannot have been left on the table merely through inadvertence. Trebitsch obviously hoped that by making a clean breast of the matter to his former employer he might induce Rowntree actually to honour the guarantee that had been forged in his name. In his letter to Rowntree Trebitsch wrote:

> Do not judge me. You have never been in such circumstances as I was repeatedly during the last twelve months. I was driven in desperation to do what I have done hoping to be able to meet it, which might have been the case but for the War . . . please for God's sake keep the matter as your secret. . . . Remember my wife (who of course knows nothing) and my five children.[9]

But even the long-suffering Rowntree had now had his fill. He wrote to Goldstein repudiating all knowledge of the transaction. The financier immediately replied, exonerating him of all responsibility. In a final gambler's throw Trebitsch went to call on Goldstein to plead for understanding. Goldstein later recounted: 'I told him I was very surprised he had done such a thing to me; and that I felt like locking him up there and then. He begged me to have mercy on him and said he would repay me my money. I told him to clear out. He said his wife was starving in Roumania or he would never have done such a thing.' Perhaps Goldstein was moved, for he waited nearly three weeks before reporting the matter to Scotland Yard on 23 December.[10]

Trebitsch was now under imminent threat of arrest for fraud. Coincidentally, in the same week as the events just described, Trebitsch (probably unknown to him at the time) was found guilty by a court in Roumania of misappropriating money and goods, the property of the Oil and Drilling Trust of Roumania. The Tribunal of Ilfou condemned him *in absentia* to seven months' imprisonment and payment of fifty thousand francs (roughly two thousand pounds) damages.[11] Even without knowledge of this conviction, Trebitsch seemed to have reached a dead end. If he was unlikely to have to experience the rigours of a Wallachian penal institution, the lesser discomforts of a British prison cell now stared him in the face.

At this point Trebitsch embarked on a series of moves which, while they failed in their immediate aim, were to win him international notoriety and to become encrusted in fanciful legend — much of it invented by Trebitsch himself. In this, the most fateful turn in his tortuous life, Trebitsch in effect launched himself into a new career. The former journalist, ex-missionary, unfrocked (if not actually defrocked) curate, failed politician, and bankrupt businessman sought to establish himself in the profession in which he was to become world-famous — that of international spy.

Trebitsch himself, as well as other writers, later claimed that his involvement in espionage long antedated the First World War.* Not a shred of convincing evidence has ever been adduced in support of such statements. Trebitsch's career in espionage almost certainly began no earlier than December 1914 and appears to have followed immediately from the fiasco of his dealings with Rowntree and Goldstein. If we sift out the truth from Trebitsch's later exercises in myth-making, it emerges that, a few days after his climactic interview with Goldstein, Trebitsch called on his former employers at the War Office and asked to be introduced to an intelligence officer. He was eventually granted an interview with Captain P.W. Kenny of MO5 (the Security Service later known as MI5), to whom he volunteered for work as a double agent. Trebitsch suggested that he be permitted to travel to the (neutral) Netherlands and enlist in the service of the German espionage network there. Once the Germans trusted him, Trebitsch argued, he would be able to feed them with snippets of information about British fleet movements. Eventually he hoped by this means to lure the entire German battle fleet out into positions in the North Sea which would be communicated by Trebitsch to the British. As a result the Royal Navy would be able to lie in wait for the Germans, ambush and destroy them. The consequent complete British mastery of the seas around Germany would bring about a swift British victory — to this satisfying dénouement the most important contribution would have been made by Trebitsch![12]

The scheme was a childish and ridiculous figment of Trebitsch's overwrought and self-dramatising imagination. Probably he anticipated that, in the aftermath of such a heroic feat of deceptive warfare, the small matter of his irregular finances would be somehow smoothed out by the authorities. Even if the plan did not produce total victory over the Central Powers, it might bring Trebitsch a personal triumph over his creditors. At the least it might afford him an escape route from Britain, where the police seemed likely to knock on the door of the Torrington Square boarding-house at any moment with the request that Mr Lincoln accompany them to the station to assist in certain enquiries.

* See Lincoln, *Revelations*, passim. Richard Deacon [pseud. = G.D. McCormick] in *A History of the British Secret Service* (London 1969) alleges (pp. 197–202) that Trebitsch 'entered the profession of espionage at a very early age and . . . religion was merely a rather curious cover for a long-term purpose. . . . There is no doubt at all that Lincoln acted as an adviser to Lloyd George on oil. . . . It is highly probable that Lincoln had been working for the German intelligence for many years, certainly in the period between 1911 and 1914.' These absurd statements (and other variations on these themes which have appeared in print over the years) belong to the realm of fiction. The reality of Trebitsch's life is fantastic enough without these embroiderings.

Predictably Trebitsch's proposal received short shrift at the War Office. According to Trebitsch (we do not have Kenny's account of the conversation), Kenny said to him at one point that the War Office might allow him to go to Rotterdam to find out how much cocoa was imported from Holland into Germany. If Kenny actually said this, it can safely be interpreted as (what passes in Whitehall for) a joke. It may be doubted whether information concerning the movements of quantities of cocoa was regarded as crucial to the British war effort. Trebitsch, however, detected no note of mockery in Kenny's voice. On the contrary, he wrote later that Kenny's remark 'at once showed me an opening'.[13] Trebitsch was, in effect, sent packing, and Kenny (like many other British officials before and after) must have thought he had heard the last of this preposterous schemer.

Although Kenny had rejected Trebitsch's application for employment and had to all appearances laughed off his naval project, Trebitsch decided that Kenny's response was sufficiently encouraging for him to set out for Rotterdam on his own account and start work on the scheme. Perhaps he intended to show the British intelligence authorities of what mettle he was made by returning as a fully-fledged (if freelance) double agent. Perhaps he planned all along to enlist genuinely in the service of the German Empire. Both interpretations are plausible — and both were subsequently (on separate occasions) offered by Trebitsch in justification of his conduct. The most likely explanation is also the simplest: Trebitsch did not know exactly what he was doing or where it would lead him, but with the police almost certain to arrest him at any time, the most urgent necessity was that he leave England immediately.

On 18 December Trebitsch arrived in Rotterdam travelling on a legally issued British passport. That he was allowed to leave the country should occasion no particular surprise: he was, after all, a former MP; Goldstein's information about his frauds was dispatched to the police only five days after Trebitsch's arrival in Holland, and even then does not appear to have occasioned much significant police activity. In Rotterdam Trebitsch obtained an interview with the German Consul-General, Gneist, to whom he offered his services as a double agent in the German interest. Gneist hardly appears to have taken Trebitsch any more seriously than Kenny. Trebitsch succeeded, however, in making enough of an impression on Gneist (who was actively involved in the German intelligence apparatus) for the consul to give him some harmless information to take back to England. It was not, after all, every day that a former British MP turned up to volunteer for the German espionage service. As a native of Hungary it would not have seemed improbable that he should wish to render some assistance to the ally of his homeland at this critical moment in its history. Trebitsch spoke fluent German (it was, perhaps, the language in which he felt most at home), and we have already observed several instances of his winning way with new acquaintances. Gneist risked little in giving Trebitsch the opportunity to prove himself by means of a trial run back to England.

Before leaving Holland Trebitsch prepared a lengthy memorandum for his German spymasters. Written in longhand on the notepaper of the 'Grand Café-Restaurant "Riche"' in Rotterdam ('Speciale Restaurant voor fijne Vischsoorten' — even on this undercover mission Trebitsch had not forsaken his taste for the good things in life), the document affords damning proof of Trebitsch's treason against his adopted country. But it also sheds a revealing light on the egotism and amateurishness of the freelance spy:

Rotterdam 30 Dec. 1914

1. It could happen that a number of times during a week or a number of times on the same day I may have to telegraph. In order not to arouse suspicion through the repeated dispatch of telegrams mentioning petrol etc. I should take several '*plain-language codes*'* with me and a corresponding number of names and addresses. I on my side will never cable under my own name but will use the following names — Robson, Hayward, Hyndman, Cox, Sinclair, Boxall. [At least four out of the six were names of former business associates of Trebitsch.]

2. The reports which I shall send in letters or newspapers will always be signed Lagauchetière. [This paragraph was crossed out, apparently by Trebitsch himself. It will be recalled that the mission house in Montreal in which Trebitsch had worked in 1902–3 had been situated at 374 Lagauchetière Street.]

3. From important places such as Harwich, Chatham, Dover, Portsmouth, Devonport, Edinburgh etc. I shall never cable ...

4. Thus we must encode all important harbours as well as military units, different kinds of warships, French harbours like Rouen, Havre, Calais, Boulogne, Marseilles etc. In this way I shall be in a position to send telegrams similar to the following: 'Three Dreadnoughts undergoing light repair in Devonport'; 'Two armed cruisers in dry dock in the Tyne'; 'Thirty thousand troops going the day after tomorrow from Southampton to Havre.'

* The letter, which is preserved in the archives of the German Foreign Ministry, was written in German. Words printed here in italics are in English in the original.

5. Since I shall have to act with extreme caution I shall leave London only for '*weekends*' . . .

6. Please never write to me. Should it be desirable to have a talk with me, please send the following telegram to me personally: *Lincoln, National Liberal Club, London. Your brother-in-law wires your mother-in-law seriously ill.** Eliassen. After receipt of this telegram I shall come to Rotterdam.

7. It goes without saying that my name must not be made known to your agents in England. I can act successfully only if nobody in England has even the slightest inkling of my activity . . .

8. I shall not be able to begin my activity at once after my return; firstly in order not to arouse any suspicion; secondly because I wish first to transfer my assets and my family to Switzerland.

9. Nevertheless I hope that even during that period I shall be able to get to know a number of things in the clubs from friends who are newspaper editors or in service with the Admiralty or the War Office etc.

10. Should something happen to me unexpectedly (for example, if I am arrested) I hope that the German authorities will make it possible for my family to travel from Switzerland to Hamburg to their relatives.

In what way should my wife (a German by birth) make herself known at the Imperial German Consulate in any Swiss city?

I also hope that in that case a reward corresponding to my services will be paid to my wife.

11. Should the sum which I take with me for expenses be spent I shall cable to one of the addresses which I have taken with me as follows: '*Book me saloon passage New York Dutch mailboat next week. Carr.*' And I ask that in that case a further sum be sent to me by cheque drawn on London with the following accompanying letter: '*I.T.T. Lincoln Esq., National Liberal Club, London S.W. Dear Sir, Mr H. Tillman of Bucarest* [This was another former business associate of Trebitsch.] *has requested us to forward you Frs. — which we are doing enclosed by draft on London in English equivalent. Kindly acknowledge receipt. Yours truly. (Signature).*'[14]

This incriminating document, with its all too predictable stress on the financial side of the arrangement, is unfortunately accompanied in the German archives by no minutes or other notations which

* Mrs Kahlor had returned to her home in Hamburg.

might give us some clue as to how the German secret service regarded their new employee.*

Trebitsch returned to London on 2 January 1915. He immediately went to see Kenny, to whom he offered to sell secret codes allegedly received from Gneist. In spite of the disinclination of the British authorities to pay Trebitsch a penny for the supposed codes (which did not fit any known German message), Kenny could no longer simply dismiss Trebitsch as a tiresome buffoon. He had, after all, established contact with German intelligence; given that fact, even a buffoon might be useful (or dangerous) in a minor way to the British war effort. Kenny accordingly referred Trebitsch to the Director of Naval Intelligence, Captain (later Admiral Sir) Reginald Hall.

'Blinker' Hall (as he was known in the navy by virtue of the facial twitch which initially disconcerted those who met him) had been appointed to the post only a few weeks earlier. An officer of indomitable personality, high intelligence, and considerable force of character, Hall was unlikely to be bamboozled by Trebitsch. He ordered inquiries to be made about the background and circumstances of his would-be agent and in the meantime he kept Trebitsch waiting to hear whether he would be paid for the material he had brought back from Rotterdam.[16]

As the days passed, Trebitsch's natural propensity to alarm propelled him into a state of high panic. By now surely Goldstein would have informed the police about Trebitsch's crooked dealings. Moreover, the extra time he had won from Finklestone (by means of the discounted bill on which he had forged Farmer's signature) would be up on January 30. About the middle of the month Trebitsch decided to try to force the hand of the authorities. He obtained an interview with the radical Liberal MP, Sir Henry Dalziel, proprietor of the popular Sunday paper *Reynolds's News*. To Dalziel Trebitsch spilled out the whole tale of his meetings with the British and German intelligence officers and complained of the delays he was

* A fragment of information, which came to light shortly before this book went to press, suggests an answer to this question. In June 1915 the Austrian Minister at the Hague sent a confidential dispatch concerning Trebitsch to the Austro-Hungarian Foreign Minister. The dispatch stated that according to information received from a secret informant who was in touch with the German Intelligence Service, Trebitsch 'did actually furnish the English Admiralty with false information on behalf of Germany'. Moreover the informant stated that 'thereby he had rendered very worthwhile services.' Surprisingly (given what we know of Trebitsch's desperate financial straits at this period) the informant alleged that he had asked for 'little or no' remuneration, leaving the impression (on his German interlocutors) that his primary aim was to 'rehabilitate himself in his land of birth'.[15]

10 (*left*) Trebitsch Lincoln *c.* 1915

11 (*below*) Captain 'Blinker' Hall (later Admiral Sir Reginald Hall, MP)

encountering at the War Office and the Admiralty. Dalziel undertook to report Trebitsch's complaint to his friend James Macpherson MP, who was working at the War Office. Shortly afterwards Dalziel encountered Macpherson in the House of Commons and mentioned his strange meeting with Trebitsch. Macpherson said that if Trebitsch's story was *not* true he was the greatest scoundrel Dalziel had ever come across. But Dalziel must have been at least partly persuaded of the authenticity of Trebitsch's complaint for he urged Macpherson at least to listen to what the would-be spy had to say.[17]

As the ominous deadline of 30 January approached, Trebitsch made ever more frantic attempts to escape from the vice closing in around him. Macpherson did not grant him an interview but Trebitsch sought desperately to attract the attention of important people who might exert the necessary influence on the intelligence authorities. Hitherto doors of high dignitaries in several countries had opened to him as if by magic; but at this critical juncture in his life they all seemed barred against him. A letter to his former parliamentary colleague Winston Churchill, the First Lord of the Admiralty, evoked a curt response from Churchill's private secretary to the effect that his case was in the hands of the Director of Naval Intelligence.[18] Trebitsch phoned Dalziel pressing him to induce a greater sense of urgency in the government departments. He told Dalziel that the time given him by the Germans to send a message back to Rotterdam was running out. His time was, of course, almost gone — but with his creditors rather than the Germans. In his desperation he even hinted at this by asking Dalziel to advance him money, pending a decision by the authorities. Dalziel's response was a predictable negative. With next to no hope left of raising enough from the government to pay Finklestone in time, Trebitsch tried a new tack. He approached the editors of several London newspapers, offering to sell them his story as well as copies of his correspondence with the British intelligence departments. All his overtures were rejected — as was inevitable since the publication of such documents, however harmless their contents, would have constituted a criminal offence.[19]

Trebitsch's antics were now becoming a troublesome and potentially embarrassing nuisance to the authorities. On 28 January he was summoned by telegram to the Admiralty and told to take along his passport. Margaret Trebitsch later recollected that he seemed uneasy before he went there, although, with his characteristically self-deluding optimism, he speculated that perhaps he might be sent away on a mission.[20]

The ensuing interview with Captain Hall marked a turning-point in Trebitsch's life — one on which he was to ruminate for years afterwards with thoughts of revenge. Hall was one of the few among Trebitsch's interlocutors who seems to have succeeded in dominating his generally irrepressible personality. The prematurely bald, perpetually blinking, no-nonsense naval officer informed Trebitsch that his services were not required by the British Government in any capacity and that it was not proposed to pay him anything for the supposed codes he had obtained in Rotterdam. To Trebitsch's alarm Hall added some remarks indicating that he was well aware of the fraud perpetrated by Trebitsch on Goldstein and Rowntree.[21]

The interview was a terrible shock to Trebitsch. His dreams of being dispatched abroad on an official mission gave way to fear of imminent arrest for fraud. Caught rat-like in a trap of his own construction, Trebitsch made one last attempt to twist free. He wrote a final plea to Dalziel:

51 Torrington-square, W.C.
January 29, 1915

Dear Sir Henry Dalziel,

I have been called by telegram to the Admiralty. I saw the Director of the Intelligence Division. They WON'T give me anything, because they found out a certain thing in my recent past which, although it has nothing to do with my work, or with their service, or with the value of my work, influences them or rather prejudices them, against me.

This is cruel, mean, unjust, un-British! They are trying to take an unfair advantage of me which is devilish.

Please, for the sake of righteousness, do not allow this!!

If they do not remunerate me, at any rate to some extent, I shall be exposed, with my wife and children, to great hardship and misery.

Is it right to use my information and then, after four weeks, to turn me down?

They ought to be ashamed of themselves. I pray and trust that you will not permit this to take place.

Excuse me for having troubled you.

Yours truly,
I.T.T. Lincoln[22]

What exactly Trebitsch for a moment hoped Dalziel might be able or ready to do for him is unclear — and was probably so to Trebitsch himself. In any case, he did not wait to find out. He told his wife that he would have to leave the country immediately, and he set about making plans for his escape. His wife remembered the state of utter exhaustion and depression into which he plunged during his last few hours in London.[23] Just before he left he somehow managed to persuade his former secretary, William Robson, to buy 'certain papers, connected with an Oil Company' (as they were later described in a police report) for about seventy pounds.[24] The greater part of this sum seems to have been applied to Trebitsch's travel and other personal expenses, for he left his wife with only two pounds and an unpaid bill of seventy-five pounds for back rent. He told his wife he was going to America, but he did not give her any explanation for his sudden departure, saying only that he would tell her everything when they met in the United States. At five o'clock on the morning of 30 January 1915, Trebitsch got up, said goodbye to his wife and sons, and crept out of the boarding-house.

For most of the rest of his life Trebitsch was a man on the run. He behaved like a hunted fugitive even when the police of several countries had stopped looking for him. Indeed he seemed almost to invite their attentions, relishing the role of international outlaw. The restless wanderlust which we have already noticed as a prime characteristic of the respectable phase of his life was now heightened as he moved into the shadowy realm of illegality. Moreover, although he was to be re-united with his wife and sons for brief periods, his abandonment of his family in their mean lodgings in Torrington Square essentially marked the end of his married life. Trebitsch was a wanted man, but in a sense he was also now, for the first time, a free man. He had no responsibilities to employers, parishioners, constituents, shareholders or creditors. Unconstrained by legality, whether canonical, commercial or criminal, and with little concern for the fate of his still devoted and faithful wife, Trebitsch could now allow his natural selfishness to flower into a bloated and grotesque bloom.

CHAPTER 7

Spy At Large

Two days before Trebitsch left home Captain Hall had arranged for information to be circulated to all ports that, as criminal charges were pending against him, he should not be allowed to leave the country. But the actions of the police and port authorities seem to have been sluggish. Trebitsch later boasted that he had succeeded in giving Hall the impression at their final interview that he might head back to Rotterdam. As the nearest neutral haven, where he was, moreover, known to have a German contact, the Netherlands seemed a likely destination. On this point Hall seems to have been taken in, for, after an inexplicable and inexcusable delay of more than a fortnight, a telegram was dispatched on 16 February 1915 to the British Consul-General in Rotterdam:

> Urgent. Telegram from Admiralty. Ignatius Trebitsch Lincoln. A warrant has been issued in this country for the arrest of the undermentioned [*sic*] person for the undermentioned offence. Apply for provisional arrest with a view to extradition. Necessary documents will be sent as soon as possible through regular channels. Please acknowledge receipt of this by cable, and also telegraph when accused has been arrested. Forgery. Accused is travelling by the undermentioned steamship, which is expected to arrive at the undermentioned port at or about the date mentioned below. *Rotterdam.* Rotterdam tomorrow at the latest. Age 36, looks older, height five feet nine inches, stout, hair black, bald on top of head, eyes black, ears large, fresh complexion, wears eyeglasses, Jewish appearance, very excitable.[1]

Once the telegram had been deciphered and the various undermentionings explicated, the Consul-General took prompt action. But two days later he cabled back to London: 'Careful examination of passengers and crew was made in the presence of one of my Vice-

Consuls who saw Lincoln when he was last in Rotterdam but no trace of him was found.'[2]

By this time Trebitsch was, in fact, already safely installed in New York. He had travelled there under his own name as a passenger on the ocean liner *Philadelphia.* In the course of the voyage he struck up an acquaintance with a German woman, Annie Jundt, who was travelling with her three children and her sister. The Jundts had lived in England for many years but the anti-German mood of the early months of the war had induced them to emigrate to the USA. Annie's husband, Charles, had gone ahead of the rest of the family and found work in New York. They were now sailing to join him. Annie Jundt, aged thirty-five, was a little below Trebitsch in height; she had dark brown hair and a very white, almost anaemic complexion. Trebitsch later stated that he had had sexual relations aboard ship both with Annie Jundt and with her twenty-six-year-old sister Olive. In the case at least of Annie, there seems little doubt that the claim was true. Interviewed by the police, some months afterwards, she admitted that she had 'become intimate' with Trebitsch; later she denied it — but the denial seems to have been intended primarily for her husband's consumption. As we shall see, Mrs Jundt's behaviour during the few months of her relationship with Trebitsch lends colour to his claim that it was more than merely platonic.[3]

On arrival at the port of New York on 9 February, Trebitsch bade farewell to the Jundts, who were soon reunited with Charles Jundt. Before he could enter the United States, Trebitsch had to make a formal declaration to the immigration authorities. He gave his address as 'Wayside, Watford' — the home he had, of course, given up more than two years earlier. He announced his profession as 'merchant', declared according to the usual formula that he was not a polygamist or an anarchist, claimed that he intended to return to England within five weeks, and stated that he would be staying at the Knickerbocker Hotel in New York City.[4]

Trebitsch had stayed at the Knickerbocker on his previous visit to New York in January 1913, but with hardly any money in his pocket he was in no position to re-establish residence at this expensive hostelry. Trebitsch's younger brother József, who now called himself Joseph Schlesinger, was living in New York at this time. But he had little small change left over from his wages as an elevator mechanic to support Trebitsch's lavish life-style. Another brother, Harry, was also in New York working as a waiter; when Trebitsch met him shortly after his arrival they had a row. Trebitsch accused Harry of stealing money from him at the time of their last meeting in London (when Harry had briefly worked for one of Trebitsch's oil enterprises). The next day Trebitsch wrote Harry a fierce letter accusing him of lack of 'moral backbone' and demanding ten dollars immediately and five dollars a week thereafter until the whole amount stolen had been repaid. Harry apparently took fright, for he disappeared: soon afterwards he volunteered for the US Army and was sent to Schofield Barracks in Honolulu.*[5]

Trebitsch had better luck with a third brother, the socialist Lajos (now called 'Louis'), who, providentially for Trebitsch, also resided in New York at this time. Although practically penniless himself, he managed to scrape up some money for Trebitsch. Over the next few months he lent Trebitsch a total of $130, most of it borrowed money. Thus fortified, Trebitsch began to seek a more substantial fortune, although it seems that he did not consider the drastic expedient of trying to get a job.

Three or four weeks after his arrival in New York Trebitsch called at the barber's shop where Charles Jundt was employed, and asked for a shave. Jundt later told the police: 'While there [he] made known to me that his name was Lincoln and that he had come to this country on the same ship with my wife. I having heard my wife and sister-in-law speak of this man's kindness to them while on board the ship, invited him to call at my house, which he did about three weeks later.'[6] Unknown to Charles Jundt his wife advanced some money to Trebitsch, the first of a long series of loans.[7] Trebitsch eventually found lodgings at the home of a Mrs Schetter at 624 West 135th Street in Manhattan. The landlady's married daughter, Anna Fleisch, became the recipient of Trebitsch's attentions (even as he continued his occasional visits to Mrs Jundt) and she soon became Trebitsch's lover.[8]

* Before leaving New York Harry wrote to the British Ambassador in Washington offering to provide information about Trebitsch's whereabouts in return for money. The offer was declined. Harry soon began to regret his precipitate action in volunteering for the army, particularly as the USA began to move closer to war with his native country. His readiness to betray his brother ultimately backfired on him disastrously. Some time later, when the US authorities began to take an interest in Trebitsch's activities, the order was given that Harry should be watched. No treasonable activity was observed, but sadly for Harry he was detected in other illegal actions. On 16 August 1918 he was found guilty by a court martial on five charges of 'sodomy' with a fellow soldier. According to the brutal code of the time he was sentenced to five years' imprisonment with hard labour. The sentence was later reduced to two years, but much of this was served under the harsh regime of the US Disciplinary Barracks at Alcatraz, California. Thus again did Trebitsch (albeit in this case unwittingly) wreck the lives of those he touched. Poor Harry never really recovered from his ordeal. In 1933 he showed up suddenly at the British Consulate-General in New York, said he was writing a book about his notorious brother, and asked for official British cooperation. The Consul pronounced Harry 'a rather unprepossessing individual', though he did forward the request to London. The application was rejected.

At the time of his arrival in the USA Trebitsch appears to have hoped that German government representatives in America might provide him with financial support in recognition of his services to the German cause. He contacted the German Embassy in Washington and seems to have offered information concerning British intelligence.[9] The German military attaché in Washington, Captain Franz von Papen (later to serve as penultimate Chancellor of pre-Hitler Germany), and the naval attaché, Captain Boy-Ed, were both engaged in the course of 1915 in a string of espionage and sabotage conspiracies of a botched and amateurish character almost worthy of Trebitsch himself. At the end of the year, indeed, they were to be expelled from the United States on this account. Whether Trebitsch actually met von Papen is not known. German cables, intercepted by British intelligence, indicate that Trebitsch got little out of the German diplomats in the USA. On 10 February 1915 (one day after Trebitsch's arrival at New York) a cable from the German Embassy in Washington to Berlin gave particulars concerning Trebitsch and asked for instructions. No immediate answer seems to have been sent, for a reminder was dispatched to Berlin on 23 February. Finally, on 4 March, the reply came, warning the embassy to 'have nothing to do with' Trebitsch.[10]

It was not until May that Trebitsch managed to earn a temporary respite from his financial difficulties by selling two sensational articles about his supposed career in espionage to the New York *World*. These pieces, which appeared on successive Sundays in the newspaper's magazine section under screaming headlines, presented Trebitsch as one of the world's great master-spies. After opening with a romanticised and suitably expurgated account of his life up to the time of his election to Parliament, Trebitsch launched into an extraordinary mélange of self-justification, self-aggrandisement, and spurious heroics. His inconclusive and utterly unimportant contacts with British and German intelligence organs were enlarged and exaggerated into a tangled web of intrigue and deception, carried out in the German interest in order to avenge the ill-treatment of Germans and Austro-Hungarians in England — as manifested in the insults received personally by Trebitsch in the National Liberal Club. Trebitsch declared brazenly: 'I knew that what I was going to do was technically high treason, but my blood was boiling in me at all the calculated barbarities inflicted by a haughty, perfidious race upon innocent people.'[11] Accompanying the text were reproductions of some of Trebitsch's most prized mementoes: his certificate of appointment as an Anglican deacon in Canada in 1902, his letter of support from Lloyd George at the time of his election campaign in January 1910, the 'Lincoln Handicap' caricature from *Punch* of

The World Magazine, May 23, 1915

Revelations of I. T. T. Lincoln, Former Member of Parliament, Who Became a German Spy

AMAZING CONFESSION OF A NATURALIZED SUBJECT OF ENGLAND, WHO, FOR REVENGE, SOUGHT TO BETRAY HIS ADOPTED COUNTRY TO HER ENEMIES.

How He Obtained Important Secrets Regarding Germany's War Plans and Attempted to Use Them to Gain the Confidence of the British War Office—When Suspected He Fled From England and Sought Refuge in New York.

In the following narrative, the details of which are fully authenticated by letters and documents which the editors of this magazine have in their possession, some of which are here reproduced, Mr. Ignatius Timotheus Tribich-Lincoln tells his own story in his own words. He arrived here some weeks ago, having made his escape under circumstances of considerable difficulty from England. Lincoln has had an amazing career. A native of Hungary and a converted Jew, he has been successively a Presbyterian then an Anglican minister in Montreal, Canada, a curate in England, secretary to H. S. Rowntree, the cocoa magnate, and in 1910 a member of the House of Commons.

Mr. Lincoln is married and has four sons. His eldest son, an adopted child, is now serving in the British army. This young man is actually at the front in France.

By I. T. T. Lincoln.

Copyright, 1915, by The Press Publishing Co. (The New York World).

THE following paragraph appeared in The World on the 29th of April:

CODE OF SPY USED TO SPY ON GERMANS.

British Correspond With Kaiser's Workers Under Name of Kuepferle, a Prisoner.

(Correspondence of The World.)

LONDON, April 19.—Anton Kuepferle, the American citizen of German birth, who hails from Brooklyn, and is held for trial on a charge of supplying Germany with information concerning the movements of British troops and ships, is said to have been the means of affording British detectives much inside information concerning the workings of the German spy system, with headquarters in Holland.

Kuepferle's arrest was kept a secret for nearly two months. Meantime it is reported that Scotland Yard men were using the prisoner's name as a means of communicating with German officials in Holland. In Kuepferle's baggage sheets of paper for use with invisible ink were found. Imitating Kuepferle's handwriting, the detectives are said to have written letters to German spy chiefs, between the lines of which they traced in invisible ink all sorts of questions asking further instructions. A rapid fire correspondence is reported to have continued until Kuepferle had actually been in jail for many weeks.

A PLAIN recital of facts. A colorless, I might almost say uninteresting, or at any rate stale, piece of news.

The only interesting, dramatic turn in the report is provided by the statement that Scotland Yard actually did correspond with German officials in Holland in the name of Kuepferle—unknown to the German Secret Service. This is indeed interesting. The climax, however, is to be found in the facts that the German Secret Service knew that Kuepferle's alleged reports came from Scotland Yard and the requested instructions they ostensibly sent to Kuepferle were indeed meant to mislead the British officials.

The English thought they were fooling the Germans, while as a matter of fact they were being fooled. I happened to be one of the *dramatis personae* in this intrigue and counter-intrigue, in the plotting and counter-plotting, in the deep laid scheming of one brain against the other.

It is a story full of human and dramatic interest, the details of which are known only to me outside of some officials of the British and German Secret Services. I have hitherto refrained from publishing it, but now that no harm can result for those whom I intended serving and now that Kuepferle's arrest is officially made known, there can be no possible objection to setting down the story.

To make myself perfectly clear, I shall begin at the beginning and tell exactly who I am, so as to make plain my course and the reasons that actuated me.

I am a native of Hungary, of Jewish extraction. In 1900 I became a convert to Christianity and entered upon a study of theology in Germany, moving in 1901 to Canada and continuing and completing my theological studies in the Presbyterian College of Montreal.

In 1902 I was appointed Jewish Missionary in Montreal by the Presbyterian Church. But I am of an

My intention was to return to Canada, but instead I went to England (September, 1903) and became curate of a parish in the Archdiocese of Canterbury.

I, however, soon found that there was a world of difference between being an Anglican Missionary in the free and easy clerical atmosphere of the Dominion and being a curate in the Established Church in England. For fourteen months I continued to administer to the spiritual needs of a country parish—but at last I could not do so longer. I left my parish with the determination never again to take up clerical work. Accordingly I wrote a frank letter to the Archbishop of Canterbury, who released me from my duties.

I left the church and with it clerical work with the fixed determination to enter British politics. My vicar to whom I told of this and of my intention of becoming an M. P., replied "You are mad. You can never become an M. P. in England. There is too much against you."

At this time I was not yet naturalized in England.

Paks Vobiscum; or, The Lincoln Handicap—"We weel not zend Budg-eit to ze Haus of Lorrdz to be zrown out on-ly again!!" (Mr. I. T. T. Lincoln—born at Paks in Hungary.)

From Punch, March 9, 1910.

I quietly replied to my vicar: "Mark my words, within six years I shall be an M. P." As a matter of fact, five years and eight months from this date I was a British Legislator, having been naturalized a few months previously.

After leaving the church I became the private

family influence I tried to make up by brain power. When the poll was declared on the election night I was elected by the small majority of 29. It was a difficult task, yet I accomplished it.

I received congratulations from many of the most prominent men in England, including Sir Edward Grey.

I was not long in the House before I made my maiden speech, which drew forth praise from Mr. Lloyd George and conferred upon me the rare and much coveted distinction of having my caricature on the political page of Punch.

I was elected to Parliament in January, 1910. It may be recalled that that year was a time of acute political strife in England, the conflict between the House of Lords and the House of Commons having been brought to a head by the defeat in the Lower House of Lloyd George's famous budget. The Government dissolved Parliament and appealed to the electorate in December, 1910. To fight an election means heavy personal expenditure, and not being in the position to finance two elections in the same year, I did not allow my name to be put forward as a candidate for re-election.

After that and until the outbreak of the war, I devoted myself to my business interests in Roumania and Galicia, intending to return to the House of Commons at some later time.

But the war upset all my intentions and plans and forced me into an attitude of hostility to the policy of England which eventually led me into the dangerous but highly fascinating sphere of Secret Service work.

The outbreak of the conflict did not surprise me. For years I foresaw its coming.

According to my reading of contemporary history, two fundamental causes, in addition to others, have brought about the present war:

(1) Great Britain's jealousy of German industrial and commercial expansion.

(2) Great Britain's unheard of and preposterous pretensions to rule all the seas, and rule them alone.

The first is so patent to all observers that I need not adduce any facts or indications in support of it.

As to the second, I should like to point out that the great increase in the German navy was really begun after the Boer War, during which the German mail steamer Bundesrath's holding up and search for alleged contraband inflamed German opinion.

On May 6, 1909, in a speech I delivered in my constituency as Parliamentary candidate (I had to be careful what I said) I made the following remarks:

"Taking the present condition of things, we cannot abolish the navy. We must have a strong navy, and if Germany is going to build thirty-three dreadnoughts, it would be folly on the part of Great Britain to be unprepared. But why are the Germans building thirty-three dreadnoughts? Because Great Britain made

12 The first of Trebitsch's sensational articles in the New York *World* magazine section, 23 May 1915

March 1910, and a couple of trivial notes from Captain Kenny of the War Office arranging times and places of meetings with Trebitsch.

Trebitsch was later to deny the authenticity of these articles, claiming that they had been altered beyond recognition by the editorial staff of the newspaper. But (as we shall see) Trebitsch was to deny responsibility for the greater part of his substantial literary output over the next two decades. The *World* may have added some finishing touches to Trebitsch's already hyperbolic and overblown prose style, but there can be little doubt that these effusions, while in content highly coloured perversions of the truth, were authentic products of Trebitsch's self-absorbed and feverish imagination.

The publication of these articles may have temporarily alleviated Trebitsch's financial difficulties, but in the longer term they landed him in terrible trouble. So long as he was merely a fugitive on a squalid fraud charge he could safely be ignored by British security authorities once he had made his initial getaway. The supposed exposé in the *World* transformed the position from the point of view of the British Government. Trebitsch's two articles were tremendous propaganda coups for Germany: for a former British MP to announce publicly that he had worked as a spy in the German interest represented a humiliating snub to Britain in the battle for American public opinion at a critical stage in Anglo-American relations. That Trebitsch should be able to publish these articles in the American press (whence their gist was transmitted to the British newspaper-reading public*) was hardly to be borne by the British security services. Accordingly, Captain Hall and his colleagues instituted steps to secure the arrest and extradition of Trebitsch to face trial in England on charges of fraud.[12] Since the United States authorities appeared only mildly interested in devoting resources to the capture of Trebitsch (who had not, after all, committed any known crime against American law), the private detective agency of Pinkerton's was engaged by the British Government to locate the fugitive.[13]

Trebitsch was arrested in Brooklyn 'at the instigation of the British Consul in Manhattan' on the evening of 4 August 1915. Arraigned the next day before Judge Van Vechten Veeder in the Federal Court in Brooklyn, he was charged with being a fugitive from justice in England. Trebitsch defiantly admitted that he had been a German spy, but the charges laid against him referred exclusively to fraud: these Trebitsch indignantly denied, declaring that they were merely a subterfuge of the British Government to secure his return to England. He was remanded without bail for a fortnight

* Publication in the British press was delayed for two weeks — almost certainly by British censorship.

pending the arrival from England of the documents which would be necessary in order to prove that a prima facie case against him existed, whereupon extradition might be granted. In the meantime he was detained in the Raymond Street Jail in Brooklyn.[14]

In the course of further hearings in the next few weeks Trebitsch stuck to his to his claim of innocence of fraud — and with equal insistence to his admission of guilt of espionage. This line of defence, however, impressed neither the British authorities nor the American court. 'A poor sort of defence this', one Foreign Office official minuted. 'Lincoln will have to think of something better if he wants to get off.'[15] Judge Veeder was hardly less scathing in his comments from the bench:

> A state of war does not affect the situation in the slightest degree. Great Britain is not under martial law. Her courts are open and it must be allowed that justice will be done. The defendant is wanted for forgery and can be tried for that offense only. He cannot be tried for any political offense that occurred prior to the alleged commission of the crime for which extradition is asked.[16]

Attempts by Trebitsch's lawyers to secure delays on various legal pretexts were roundly condemned by the judge, who said 'it was common in extradition cases to bring to bear all the fictitious niceties of a criminal trial at common law'.[17] On 10 September, Judge Veeder ordered Trebitsch's extradition to England.[18]

The decision seemed clearcut and his deportation to England imminent. But (not for the first time) Trebitsch managed, over the next few months, to lead the officials of two governments a merry dance, as by one contrivance after another he succeeded in avoiding transfer to British custody. In the light of the Brooklyn court's decision, Chief Inspector Ward of Scotland Yard was sent out to New York, accompanied by a police sergeant, to convey the fugitive back to Britain. But when the two officers arrived in New York they found that, although the Secretary of State had actually issued a warrant for Trebitsch's extradition, he could not be handed over until the judge had disposed of a writ of habeas corpus which had been entered on the prisoner's behalf. Counsel for the British Consulate encountered repeated frustrating delays in securing dismissal of the writ. The British officials involved in the case, puzzled at the judge's sudden attention to the 'niceties' he had hitherto disparaged, began to suspect his motives. In his report to his superiors, Inspector Ward gave vent to both his frustration and his suspicion:

> I determined to see the Judge myself, and, if possible, ascertain if he was purposely holding the matter over, accordingly, on the 1st November I attended the Court and with the aid of the Marshal

> succeeded in getting an introduction to him as he was leaving the Bench. He appeared very pleased to see me and asked many questions about places in England which he had apparently visited some years ago. I discreetly approached the question of Lincoln, and he said he could not see why we were so anxious to get away with the prisoner having regard to the fact that he was now in custody, and furthermore, that in view of the extreme danger now existing in London from Zeppelins he considered we were all much safer in America than we should be in England. I attempted to dispel this idea from his mind* but he said he had received reliable information that London was practically devastated during the recent raid. His conversation then turned to the War and the trend of it clearly demonstrated his pro-German views and I came to the conclusion that he was deliberately delaying the decision of the Writ to give the prisoner every opportunity for a further appeal.[19]

In a condition of much disgust at the opportunities for delay in the American system of justice, Ward determined to return to England. Before leaving he asked for permission to interview Trebitsch, hoping that he might persuade him to return to England voluntarily. According to Ward's later report, Trebitsch replied: 'Oh no. I shall never go to England, that is unless the British Government withdraw the charge against me. Then I will go willingly.' He suggested that Ward might persuade the British Consul in New York to arrange for the withdrawal of the charge. Ward refused this impossible request and returned to England with empty handcuffs.[20]

The injury was in this instance preceded by insult: before Ward arrived back in London a telegram from Trebitsch reached the Foreign Office: 'Scotland Yard detectives after month fruitless waiting returned today without me. Cannot British Govt find other uses for public funds than vindictive persecution of me?'[21] The telegram was addressed to Sir Edward Grey (whose own congratulatory cable sent to Trebitsch at the time of the Darlington election had been one of the prize exhibits published by the former MP in the *World*). Whether because of the press of business or out of a delicate solicitude for the Foreign Secretary's peace of mind, the officials concerned with the case did not send Trebitsch's cable up for the minister's personal inspection. A copy was forwarded to the Home Office with the accompanying comment: 'No doubt this person has the interests of the British tax-payer very much at heart. It is a most impertinent message, and it is to be hoped that the sender

* By a tragic irony, Ward was himself later killed by a bomb dropped from a Zeppelin.

may soon be inside an English gaol where he will not have the facilities which he now enjoys for wasting his money,'[22]

The conditions of Trebitsch's detention in Raymond Street jail were indeed unusually liberal. In a letter to his wife in England, written from prison, Trebitsch sounded a surprising note of confidence and satisfaction:

> The warden and all the keepers treat me very well, and I have many privileges denied to all other prisoners. Some of the keepers spend hours every day in front of my cell talking to me. Some Germans also occasionally visit me and provide me with cigars and cigarettes which is a great comfort. It is through the kindness of a German totally strange to me that I could engage two lawyers to represent me before the courts. Last week I got some [money?] too.[23]

The unnamed Germans who provided such consolation for Trebitsch in his predicament included Annie Jundt and Anna Fleisch. Both paid him visits and lent him money — in the case of Mrs Jundt amounting to a total of more than three hundred dollars (all without the knowledge of her husband).[24]

Meanwhile Trebitsch took advantage of his enforced free time to write a book about his supposed exploits as an international spy. Prior to his arrest he had secured a contract with the New York publishing house of McBride & Co., and he now completed the text with a view to early publication. He appears to have hoped that he might use the imminent appearance of the book as a lever to induce the British Government to withdraw its extradition request.

The wheels of the American legal system continued, however, to grind slowly but inexorably forward. On 20 November Judge Thomas Chatfield, sitting in the US District Court in Brooklyn, dismissed Trebitsch's writ of habeas corpus.[25] His attorneys announced immediately their intention to appeal to the US Circuit Court of Appeals, and if necessary to the Supreme Court. But for Trebitsch the writing was on the wall.

Yet, ever resourceful when cornered, Trebitsch tried a new tack. He addressed a letter to the head of the Bureau of Investigation (predecessor of the FBI) in Washington in which he offered to provide the American government 'quite important trails' on German under-cover activities in the USA.[26] The activities of Papen, Boy-Ed and other German representatives in the USA had aroused considerable public and official concern at this time; the Bureau consequently considered Trebitsch's offer very seriously. A few days later Trebitsch wrote a further letter in which he proposed, as 'striking proof of my ability to materially assist the US Government', to decipher coded German cables which (it had been reported in the press) had recently been intercepted by the US authorities.[27]

On 7 December, Agent William R. Benham of the Bureau of Investigation visited Trebitsch in Raymond Street jail. On the instructions of the Chief of the Bureau, Benham told Trebitsch 'that it was not proper under the circumstances for this Government to interfere in the extradition proceedings instituted against him.' Benham added 'that the most that could be done would be to endeavor to secure some favorable consideration for him from the British authorities if he will furnish the information he states he has'. After a long wrangle with Benham, Trebitsch wrote out a lengthy memorandum, in which he provided next to no solid information, but offered to furnish the US Government with letters he had received from the German Embassy in Washington; he craftily baited a hook for the Bureau by suggesting that he was 'willing to start work at once' on decoding the German cables 'even whilst the US Government will sound the British Government with a view of my being liberated'. He insisted only that he be granted 'sufficient facilities' to conduct this work, and asserted: 'I do not want to escape. I want to regain my liberty by proper steps.'[28]

The Bureau committed the great blunder of nibbling at Trebitsch's bait. The next day Agent Benham was sent to call on Captain Guy Gaunt, the British Naval Attaché in Washington. Benham went over with him the data which Trebitsch claimed he could furnish and asked 'whether or not the British authorities would be willing to give any consideration to Lincoln if he actually furnishes the material which he states he has'. Gaunt, an astute man whose job included counter-intelligence functions, appeared to Benham 'to possess quite an accurate knowledge of Lincoln's history'. Gaunt replied that he had little or no confidence in Trebitsch's ability to provide any useful information, but he promised to send a long cable to London for an authoritative response.[29] The reply from the Admiralty a few days later was predictable: Gaunt was instructed tersely that Trebitsch's 'offer should be promptly and firmly declined'.[30]

If the Bureau's initial reaction to Trebitsch's 'offer' had been over-credulous, its subsequent handling of the prisoner may only be described as grossly incompetent. The British rejection of Trebitsch's proposal was not relayed to him by the Bureau of Investigation. He was instead encouraged to believe that he might earn his freedom by successfully performing the decipherment of some German cables. On 14 December Agent Benham again visited Trebitsch and turned over to him three coded German cables. After a cursory examination Trebitsch pronounced these to be written in a 'combination code' (a code within a code), and confidently declared that he expected to be able to decipher them 'within the next day or two'.[31]

Under the extraordinarily mild regime of the Brooklyn house of correction, Trebitsch was afforded full facilities for his work on behalf of the Bureau of Investigation. Each day he was permitted to leave the prison for several hours at a time, accompanied by a federal marshal, in order to work in the Brooklyn Federal Building, where an office was laid at his disposal. Whether with official cognizance or not, Trebitsch found it possible to retain large sums of money while in confinement (loans from his women friends and from other sympathisers); he deployed these remittances to good effect in suborning his guards. Convivial as ever, he began organizing small social outings for himself and selected friends. In later testimony to the Bureau of Investigation Anna Fleisch confirmed that while Trebitsch was in prison she had been out to dinner with him and other guests on at least three occasions. Among those present at all of these gatherings was Deputy Marshal George Proctor, who had been placed in charge of the prisoner. Trebitsch seems to have picked up the bill for food and drink consumed at these parties. Judge Veeder himself was astonished one day, while dining at the Clarendon Hotel in Brooklyn, to see Trebitsch there 'with a party including women . . . having a very gay time'. The judge lodged a complaint with the federal marshal's office protesting at the unusual privileges apparently accorded the prisoner. But the lunches and dinners continued, and on one occasion Trebitsch was even permitted to visit a friend at home.[32]

Meanwhile Trebitsch made slow progress in his attempts to decipher the German codes. On 16 December he notified Agent Benham by telephone (his conditions of confinement evidently included free access to the Bell Company's system) 'that he believed he had discovered the key to the code' and that 'he hoped to be able to finish the decoding of the cablegrams during the day'. Agent Benham's report on this alleged breakthrough contains an unsigned notation: 'Caution about possible escape.'[33] But no such precaution was taken, nor were the remarkable terms of Trebitsch's imprisonment amended. During the next few days Trebitsch continued to make optimistic telephone calls to Agent Benham. On 18 December he announced to Benham that he had 'entirely mastered the key to the code of the cablegram . . . and that only mechanical work remained'.[34] Two days later he claimed he had made further 'excellent progress' and hoped the work would be completed that very day.[35] At 11.00 am the next morning he telephoned Benham yet again to say 'that he needed the services of an Expert Accountant for an hour or two in order to complete the work of decoding'.

Brooklyn Federal Building. The accountant (Benham reported) 'proceeded to assist him in the matter, but before long it was dis-
Brooklyn Federal Building. The accountant (Benham reported) 'proceeded to assist him in the matter, but before long it was discovered that Lincoln's various combinations of the alphabet were incorrect'.[36]

Undaunted, Trebitsch, later that day, prepared a further lengthy memorandum for the Bureau, setting out his initial findings and urging that his research staff be augmented by the addition of a 'code mathematician', with whose assistance, he asserted, he 'would be able to settle the whole thing very quickly'.[37] Although the Bureau's senior officials were by now gradually beginning to realize that the prisoner was leading them a merry dance, Trebitsch was permitted to remain at work aided by the Bureau's accountant. He sent Benham several letters, two of them written on the official note-paper of the United States Marshal, announcing further advances in the science of cryptanalysis. His last such communication, dated 15 January, boasted that he was 'within an ace of final solution'.[38]

On 21 January 1916, Trebitsch's book, entitled *Revelations of an International Spy*, was published in New York. An expansion, and to a large extent a re-hash, of the *World* articles, it was revealing of little save monumental self-glorification and obsessional perversion of the truth by its author. Trebitsch now alleged that his career in espionage had begun years before the war, while he was still employed by Seebohm Rowntree. His tiresome nagging of British diplomatic posts in several European countries was presented as part of a diabolical espionage scheme, though the exact purpose of his activities remained shrouded in mystery. Trebitsch wreaked a belated revenge on those officials and diplomats who had thwarted or (in his eyes) insulted him. Sir Francis Bertie and other officials of the British Embassy in Paris, whose unhelpfulness over the matter of the books evidently still rankled, came in for particularly venomous treatment. Towards his former employer and benefactor, Rowntree, to whom he owed so much, Trebitsch adopted a peculiarly unattractive tone of schoolboy-like jeering, as he recounted how he had wasted Rowntree's time and money in pretending to engage in social research while really (so Trebitsch now averred) spinning webs of intrigue in the chancelleries of Europe. It was a shabby return for the years of forbearance and generosity on the part of the Quaker industrialist, showing to what depths Trebitsch's inverted moral sense had sunk. For the rest, the book was a surprisingly dull farrago of invention and misrepresentation, larded with long passages on the supposed techniques of international espionage — secret codes, invisible ink, and the like. The book's first edition of about 4,500 copies sold out within three months. It was not reprinted*, and in February 1917 the plates were sold to a junk dealer as scrap.[39]

Six days before the book was published Trebitsch escaped from custody. The ease with which he slipped away was almost laughable, and the official negligence thereby disclosed scandalous in the extreme. On the day of his escape Trebitsch had been working as usual in the marshal's office in the Federal Building in Brooklyn. At the time of his disappearance he had been in the custody of a young, recently-appointed US Deputy Marshal, Francis J. Johnson. After he had finished work in the Federal Building, Trebitsch left, in the company of Johnson, to return to the Raymond Street Jail. The two men were later reported to have been seen in Fulton Street in Brooklyn, Trebitsch walking a few paces in front of his custodian smoking a cigar. At the corner of Fulton Street and Pierrepoint Street, they stopped for a meal at 'Joe's' restaurant. Trebitsch asked for permission to go to the lavatory: Johnson waited but the prisoner never returned. The inexperienced deputy's feelings may readily be imagined. His disgrace was further compounded by his failure to report the escape for nearly two days, thus allowing Trebitsch precious time to secure his getaway.

The embarrassment of the United States Government was painfully acute, and there ensued a great deal of buck-passing. The acting Attorney General condemned the 'amazing negligence' of Deputy Johnson, and the Justice Department demanded detailed explanations. Judge Chatfield issued a statement denouncing the prison and police authorities: 'The deputy', he declared, 'had no right to take his prisoner into a restaurant. The Government makes provision for feeding the prisoners elsewhere.' US Marshal James Power, from whose office Trebitsch had departed with Johnson, repudiated the judge's strictures, arguing that the escape was 'the result of perfectly inexcusable carelessness and absolutely nothing more serious'. And in a long exculpatory letter to the Attorney General, Marshal Power pointed out that the special privileges accorded to Trebitsch had been granted at the explicit request of the secret agents operating under the Justice Department who had declared that 'the work he (Lincoln) was doing was very important'. As for the Bureau of Investigation, one of its agents was quoted as saying: 'We simply must get that man.'[40]

The consternation of the Americans was matched only by the vexed irritation of the British. Counsel for the British Consulate-General in New York called the escape 'the greatest piece of carelessness on the part of officers sworn to uphold the law that I have

* A Spanish translation was published by the German Information Service in Mexico in 1918.

ever heard of'. In the Foreign Office the news was received with indignation — 'most annoying', wrote one official.[41] The Home Office (where Trebitsch's former platform partner Herbert Samuel had just assumed office as minister) decided to ban Trebitsch's book. The customs authorities were instructed to prohibit its importation to Britain — although the order seems later to have been withdrawn upon declarations by the War Office and the Admiralty that the book was considered harmless.[42] Perhaps concerned lest his earlier commendation of Trebitsch be dredged up by some enterprising reporter, Samuel pressed the Foreign Office to seek urgent measures to secure the recapture of the fugitive.[43]

The Bureau of Investigation, conscious of the public attention aroused by the case, initiated a wide-ranging man-hunt for Trebitsch. Special agents from outside the state were drafted into New York. His brothers, Joseph Schlesinger, Louis Tarcai, and Harry Trebitsch were tracked down respectively in New York, Philadelphia and Honolulu. Mail addressed to Schlesinger and Tarcai was intercepted, and Schlesinger's telephone was tapped. (The Bureau agent who was listening reported that most conversations on the line appeared to be in Hungarian — with which tongue he was not familiar.) Various women friends of Trebitsch were questioned, among them Annie Jundt and Anna Fleisch. May Dougherty, a manicurist at the Equitable Insurance Building, who had been a guest of Trebitsch for lunch at the Clarendon Hotel in Brooklyn, was followed walking her dog down Central Park West. All Trebitsch's known contacts, including his publishers, were interrogated. Reported sightings as far afield as Baltimore, Albany and Chicago were investigated fruitlessly. Reports by agents engaged in the search filled hundreds of pages without providing a single relaible clue.[44]

Meanwhile the object of all this activity had effected a safe getaway. Soon after leaving Deputy Johnson, Trebitsch turned up at the Jundts' home on West 125th Street in Manhattan. Charles Jundt (a barber by profession) shaved off Trebitsch's moustache, and Annie Jundt burned his light brown derby hat, substituting for it a less conspicuous cap. From the Jundts Trebitsch proceeded, by prior arrangement, to the Silver Lake Park Hotel belonging to German friends of the Jundts in White Plains.[45] By the time Deputy Johnson reported his escape Trebitsch was thus securely in hiding outside New York City.

On the fourth day of his freedom Trebitsch performed a characteristic act of bravado. He walked into the office of the *New York American* newspaper and gave an impromptu press conference to the astonished editorial staff. He explained, in terms reminiscent of his Darlington election campaign, that the reason his enemies feared him so was that he was 'one of the brainiest of men'. He threatened to raise the standard of revolt against British rule in Central Asia, asserting preposterously (and, as we shall see, prophetically) that the British authorities knew he 'was disguised as a Buddhist monk in Central Asia for the purpose of spying there, and that he was going back to Asia to "get even with England" by fomenting trouble there'.[46]

Trebitsch thereupon slipped away again, without the alarm having been raised by the newspaper's employees. During the next few weeks he dispatched a series of boastful letters to the press, partly, it seems, with the object of promoting his book, but chiefly with the aim of feeding his obsessional craving for publicity. Becoming dissatisfied with his accommodation at White Plains, Trebitsch arranged to move to an isolated farm at Red Bank, New Jersey, where he stayed with a German who specialised in removing the carcasses of dead livestock. Trebitsch was expected to work for his keep, but he found the job of animal undertaker uncongenial and soon quarrelled with his host. Once again he moved on to stay with another group of pro-Germans. Finally, he returned to Manhattan and rented a room under an assumed name from a Hungarian furrier on West 30th Street. His behaviour while on the run did not endear him to his various protectors, and in the end he was betrayed by one of his German acquaintances who made a secret arrangement with the Bureau of Investigation to set a trap for him.[47]

Trebitsch was recaptured, after thirty-five days of freedom, on 20 February 1916. At the time of his arrest he was walking down Broadway where he had arranged to meet a German friend — in fact, his betrayer. Waiting Bureau agents grabbed him and took him back to Raymond Street Jail. Reporting on the arrest to the Chief of the Bureau in Washington, a Bureau agent commented that he had 'never seen a happier lot of federal officials' than at the time of Trebitsch's arrest. One of them seemed ready to 'explode from glee and sheer exultation'.[48] The recaptured prisoner was found to be carrying $58.20, two pawn tickets on a shop on Amsterdam Avenue where he had pledged suits of clothes for $5, and (presumably his most precious possessions) 'a pocket-full of clippings about himself'. After his arrest he talked non-stop, congratulating the police on catching 'the cleverest man in America', raving against the American Government for its readiness to deport him, and shouting: 'I'm a British subject, but I hate England. These charges of forgery have merely been trumped up in order that I may be shot as a spy.'[49]

To the intense annoyance of British officials, who suspected that Trebitsch's escape had been effected with official German help and that he continued to be in receipt of German aid, extradition proceedings remained bogged down in legal technicalities. Trebitsch appealed to the US Supreme Court, which did not issue a ruling until early May. In the interim Trebitsch very nearly succeeded in escaping again, this time by means of an elaborately conceived scheme in which he sought to enlist the aid of local gangsters. The plot was discovered and two gaolkeepers joined the unfortunate Deputy Marshal Johnson among those rendered unemployed through contact with Trebitsch. Finally, on 8 May, the Supreme Court issued a mandate requiring the return of Trebitsch to England to answer a charge of forgery.[50] On 26 May the indefatigable Chief Inspector Ward, who had crossed the Atlantic again in pursuit of his prey, took charge of the prisoner, who was driven at top speed across New York to the liner *Cameronia*.[51]

Trebitsch no doubt hoped that he would be able to exploit the opportunities for delay in the English judicial machine to as good an effect as he had in the American. In this he was disappointed. His case proceeded with almost ruthless speed. Trebitsch landed at Liverpool on 5 June. The next day he appeared at a preliminary hearing at Bow Street Police Court. He was charged with forgery, and Rowntree, Goldstein and Finklestone all appeared to give evidence against him. Trebitsch was remanded in custody.[52] At a further hearing a week later an application by Trebitsch for legal aid was denied.[53] On 19 June Trebitsch appeared at a third hearing and was allowed to cross-examine Rowntree, Farmer and Goldstein. Chief Inspector Ward said that, at the request of the prisoner, he had asked Winston Churchill, Captain Hall, Captain Kenny, Sir Henry Dalziel and others to attend as witnesses for the defence, but that all had refused. Trebitsch then addressed the court in a two-hour tirade in the course of which he broke into tears on several occasions. He recounted the story of his life and (reversing the line of defence he had used in the USA) admitted the forgery charges but declared that it was a 'devilish lie' to accuse him of treason.[54]

When Trebitsch's case came up for trial at the Central Criminal Court on 4 July, he pleaded 'Not Guilty' to an indictment charging him with forging and uttering a guarantee purporting to be signed by Rowntree for £750, and with forging and uttering a bill of exchange for £200 purporting to be accepted by Farmer. Trebitsch, not having been granted legal aid, was obliged to defend himself. In a speech lasting two-and-a-half hours he rambled again through the labyrinth of his espionage activities, attempting to prove that he had worked exclusively in the British interest. But as the judge observed, all this was irrelevant to the charges he was called upon to answer.

The jury returned a verdict of guilty without even retiring.

Mr Justice Scrutton accordingly sentenced Trebitsch to three years' penal servitude.[55] He was taken from the court and eventually removed to Parkhurst Prison on the Isle of Wight.

Trebitsch thus paid a heavy price for his crimes. In a sense there was some truth in his claim that the British Government would not have proceeded with the extradition request against him had it not been for his espionage activities. But of course, the essence of the matter was not the activities themselves, which were a minor nuisance rather than a significant threat, but the burst of anti-British publicity arising from them; for it was this that had moved Hall and his colleagues to take measures to secure Trebitsch's return to England. Trebitsch's sentence was not lenient — but he had the misfortune to be tried at a time of mounting public hostility to aliens in general, and against spies and enemy agents in particular. A fellow prisoner in June 1916 (whom he later claimed to have met in gaol) was the British knight, German agent, and Irish nationalist, Sir Roger Casement, executed for treason shortly afterwards. Perhaps, in the circumstances, Trebitsch was lucky not to suffer a similar fate.

The British Government too paid a high price: $3,575.81 had to be found to cover just the American legal fees for the case. A further bill for $119.78 was presented for Trebitsch's (laxly guarded and luxuriously provided) maintenance in the Raymond Street Jail in Brooklyn.[56] And of course all the costs of Chief Inspector Ward's passages across the Atlantic, the passages of a police sergeant and of Trebitsch himself, the entire costs of the British legal proceedings, as well as the custodial expense of Trebitsch's three years in Parkhurst Prison — not to mention the severe waste of official time on the case over the previous eighteen months — all this fell on the British tax-payer.

But the heaviest price for Trebitsch's ludicrous and egotistical behaviour was borne by his long-suffering wife and family. After her abandonment by her husband in January 1915, Margaret Trebitsch had sunk into utter destitution, dependent for her survival on the charity of the Salvation Army. Her elder sons had to be withdrawn from boarding school. Julius volunteered for the British army and served as a bombardier with the artillery at the Dardanelles. Ignatius junior too was later to join the army, and for him a peculiarly horrible destiny lay in store — one for which his father's criminality was held by some to be partly responsible.

Throughout her ordeal Margaret Trebitsch stood loyally by her husband. She corresponded faithfully with him while he was in gaol. She told the press: 'My husband may have done wrong, but I say with all my heart that I do not regret one minute of my married life. No woman ever had a better husband and no family had a

13 Margaret Trebitsch Lincoln

kinder father.... He was the cleverest man I ever knew.'[57] During his detention in Brixton Prison before his trial she visited him and brought him food. In court she wept. And after his release from prison more than three years later she was ready to return to him as soon as he gave the word. Of all the victims of Trebitsch's long career of confidence trickery his wife was surely the most injured, and yet throughout the most steadfast in her faith in him.

CHAPTER 8

Fairy Tales

Some men react to prolonged incarceration by resorting to literary creativity as an outlet for their frustrations, grievances and yearning to be free. Granted, Trebitsch was no John Bunyan or Silvio Pellico, but he possessed a facile pen and vivid imagination and was not altogether devoid of literary flair. Parkhurst, however, offered an environment less conducive to writing than Raymond Street Jail in Brooklyn, where Trebitsch had produced his *Revelations*.

In September 1916 Trebitsch wrote the first of a long series of petitions complaining of his treatment in prison, demanding reconsideration of his case, and inveighing against the Director of Naval Intelligence, Captain Hall, whom he held accountable for his plight. But he evidently felt cramped by the standard petition form, which permitted a statement of no more than two pages in length. His demand for facilities to produce a communication to the Prime Minister covering 'upwards of 100 pages or more' was rejected with an official comment, 'Apparently he thinks writing fairy tales would be an easier and more agreeable occupation than ordinary prison labour.'[1] The flow of petitions continued unabated, irritating the authorities to such an extent that in August 1917 the governor of Parkhurst informed him that the privilege of petitioning would be withdrawn for a period of twelve months. Thus baulked of his one remaining outlet, Trebitsch suffered something close to a general mental and physical breakdown. In early 1918 he was removed to the prison hospital, where he remained for most of the rest of his imprisonment, enjoying reasonably mild treatment.

Trebitsch's personality, of course, was not one that could adapt easily to the boredom, routine and discipline of prison life. More than for most men, liberty of movement was for him a desperate need, for which he had an almost narcotic-like craving. No less acute must have been the sexual frustration of this unregenerate philanderer. Possibilities of escape were almost nil: his British (unlike his American) gaolers did not take him on excursions to nearby restaurants; and even if he had broken out of Parkhurst, there could have been little hope of leaving the island without being detected.

Trebitsch could not respond to this predicament with philosophic indifference. Patience, equanimity and stoicism in the face of adversity had never been his forte. Instead he brooded with the mixture of self-pity, romanticism, and alternating rages and depressions that henceforth formed the fixed patterns of his emotional behaviour.

Trebitsch's writings in prison as well as his later comments suggest that one thought above all others dominated his mind throughout his imprisonment — the idea of revenge.[2] Like Edmond Dantès in his dungeon in the Château d'If, Trebitsch passed his time during his confinement by drawing up a vast and exotic scheme for retribution against his torturers. These latter he identified as Captain Hall in particular, and the British Empire in general. Like the Count of Monte Cristo, Trebitsch dreamed of reclaiming a fabulous fortune, but he aimed to surpass even Dumas's hero by somehow attaining leadership of immense revolutionary forces that would destroy the British Empire. This conceit, in various forms, obsessed Trebitsch for the rest of his life. It was a mad, vindictive, and utterly unrealistic ambition. And yet his dream came closer to realization than anyone save a madman could have predicted.

Trebitsch became due for release from prison at the end of his three-year sentence in the summer of 1919. The question of what to do with him exercised the British authorities, who were determined that he should be given no opportunity to make a further nuisance of himself in the United Kingdom. Accordingly, in December 1918, the Home Secretary (acting on the advice of Colonel Vernon Kell, head of MI5) resorted to a rarely-used procedure and revoked Trebitsch's certificate of naturalisation on the ground that he had 'shown himself by act to be disloyal to His Majesty'.[3] The government further decided to deport him from the country as soon as his prison term was over.

Trebitsch was first transferred from Parkhurst to Pentonville Prison in London, and then, on 2 July 1919, was discharged. He was not, however, set free. Two officers from Scotland Yard met him at the prison and escorted him by train to the port of Harwich. *The Times* the next day announced that he would sail from there 'in accordance with the expulsion order made against him by the Home Secretary'. But Trebitsch was not deported that day. At the last moment a message was received cancelling the order. On orders from Sir Basil Thomson, Director of Intelligence at Scotland Yard, Trebitsch was returned to London and lodged in Brixton Prison. This unexpected reversal provoked questions in Parliament to which the Home Secretary responded with the vague explanation:

> The deportation of this man was suspended on receipt of information which made it appear undesirable to allow him in present circumstances to return to his own country. He remains in internment and his repatriation will be carried out later.[4]

Behind this unrevealing statement lay a complex of political circumstances of great importance for an understanding of the next phase of Trebitsch's career. The three years of his confinement had, of course, seen dramatic changes in international politics. The United States, in April 1917, had abandoned neutrality and joined Britain, France, and Italy in the war against the central powers. In November 1917 the Bolsheviks had seized power in Russia. In November 1918 Germany had consented to an armistice which effectively marked her defeat. Her allies, Austria-Hungary and the Ottoman Empire, had already collapsed. With defeat came revolution, sweeping away the power structures of the old empires. In Germany a republic was declared, and the Kaiser and his family fled to Holland. Throughout central Europe the example of the Bolsheviks inspired imitative revolts. Among these was the short-lived Hungarian soviet republic, established by Béla Kun in March 1919. At the time of Trebitsch's discharge and turn-about at Harwich, the Kun government was still in power, much to the annoyance of the British and French authorities, who feared the contagious influence of Bolshevism on the working classes throughout Europe.

Trebitsch himself had no previous known connection with the extreme left. Nevertheless Sir Basil Thomson wrote:

> Having information of the disturbed state of Buda Pesth during the last few days, I thought it very undesirable to repatriate a man like Trebitsch Lincoln, who would at once throw himself into the Bolshevik camp and feed the Communist Government with lies about the intentions of the Entente. Lincoln is probably of superior ability to any member of the Communist Government and he might easily become a sort of Lenin of Central Europe.[5]

Beyond this direct fear — in itself a tribute to Trebitsch's capacity for troublemaking — may have been a further indirect apprehension on the part of British intelligence authorities, arising from the socialist connections of Trebitsch's younger brother, Lajos Tarcai.*

* Before his emigration from Hungary in 1910, Tarcai had been a leading member of the Hungarian Social Democrat Party, serving on the party executive. He adhered to a short-lived opposition group within the party, known as the 'Karl Marx Society'. After his arrival in the USA, Tarcai edited the Hungarian-language socialist weekly, *Elöre* (Forward); later he founded another newspaper in Cleveland, *Az Ujság* (The News), as well as contributing to a variety of left-wing periodicals. He is mentioned in a letter dated 4 April 1918 written by the Hungarian Group of the Russian Communist Party (Bolshevik) to the party's central committee. This

In any event, Trebitsch was obliged to spend another six weeks in custody. On 2 August 1919 the Béla Kun régime fell after 133 days in power, ousted by right-wing Roumanian forces who occupied Budapest. Nine days later Trebitsch was deported from Harwich on the *Lutterworth*, bound for Rotterdam.

The British Government's apparent expectation was that Trebitsch would return to his country of origin, Hungary. But the police escorted him no further than the cross-channel steamer, leaving him to make his own way home once he landed on the continent. Trebitsch's mother was still alive, and many of his large clan of relatives still lived in Budapest. He did not, however, return immediately to the bosom of his family. By now he had probably heard of the judgement issued against him by the Roumanian court in 1914. The receiver of his former company, the Oil and Drilling Trust of Roumania, was still pursuing the matter of the firm's missing assets on behalf of the creditors.[7] With Roumanian forces in occupation of Budapest it would have been foolhardy for Trebitsch to risk arrest and a further spell of imprisonment by returning there. Trebitsch went instead to the one other country where he might expect to receive a warm welcome after three years in prison in Britain as a self-confessed spy.

Germany in the summer of 1919 was in a condition of political, social, and economic turmoil. Polarisation between left and right had been accentuated by the brutal fighting of the previous winter, when a revolt in Berlin by the extreme left 'Spartacists' had been suppressed with murderous zeal. In the spring a short-lived soviet republic in Bavaria was overthrown amid further bloodshed. In both cases the government of the republic had been compelled to rely on the support not only of the army but also of the so-called 'Free Corps',

letter, which discussed the group's revolutionary plans, stated: 'III . . . 3. Liaison with America. Comrade Tarczai [*sic*], who had left the Hungarian Social Democrat Party some time ago and emigrated [to America] and now lives there, is working in the same direction. This is of great importance because approximately two million Hungarian proletarians live in America.' There is no evidence that Tarcai was, in fact, contacted at this time by Moscow. But British Foreign Office files concerning Trebitsch, dating from before the First World War, included occasional references to his brother and to the latter's socialist activities. All files concerning Trebitsch were probably checked as a matter of course prior to his release. It may well be, therefore, that the possibility of some link between Tarcai and the Kun régime contributed to the British Government's decision to prolong Trebitsch's imprisonment.[6] (FBI files on Tarcai, released to the author under the US Freedom of Information Act, show that Tarcai was dogged by sporadic FBI surveillance, on account of his socialist connexions, until as late as the 1960s. He died in Cleveland in 1971.)

semi-anarchic gangs of free-booters, mainly exservicemen, fiercely hostile to the left, and a law unto themselves.

In this ugly political climate the news arrived on 28 June of the signature by German representatives at Versailles of the treaty of peace, with its draconian provisions for the cession of territory, limitation of armaments, occupation of the Rhineland, and payment by Germany of vast reparations to the victorious powers. The addition of the so-called 'war guilt' clause, attributing all blame for the outbreak of the war to Germany and her allies, deepened the psychological blow. Resentment of these humiliations gave a powerul weapon to enemies of the infant republic. The severe social dislocations caused by the end of the war, most notably the demobilisation of millions of soldiers, added to the unrest. The notion that the German army had not really been defeated by its enemies on the field, but had been subjected to a 'stab in the back' by internal enemies, notably socialists and Jews, found a ready audience. In this atmosphere of mutual recrimination, suspicion, and hatred, the old verities seemed to many Germans to have lost all meaning or relevance; left and right alike groped for new political bearings; traditional standards of respectability and public conduct were swept away in the poisonous swirl; the rats began to crawl out of the gutter.

As Trebitsch stalked the pavements of Berlin, once again unemployed, friendless, and starving, he found that his private mood of impotent vindictiveness tallied exactly with the general atmosphere. Once before, he had been driven abroad by the British authorities, and had roamed the streets of a great city searching for some means of sustenance. The solution in 1915 had been the sensational anti-British articles in the New York *World*. For all its appearance of discontinuity and aberration, Trebitsch's life often repeated itself with an almost scientific predictability. So it was that he now resorted once more to the pen, both as an instrument of revenge and as a way of earning a living.

Two weeks after his arrival in Berlin Trebitsch published two violently anti-British articles in the *Deutsche Zeitung*, in return for which he was paid an honorarium of two hundred marks. If he had hoped that the piece would catapult him into the public eye, as had his 'revelations' four years earlier, he was disappointed. *The Times* of 1 September briefly noted 'Trebitsch Lincoln's sneer', but otherwise the world refused to take notice. From the point of view of publicity Trebitsch's forum was ill-chosen. For the *Deutsche Zeitung* was an extreme-right-wing rag, with a circulation of only 21,000, and operated on the borders of legality; indeed, only the previous week it had been issued an (unenforced) order to close.[8] Trebitsch could probably find no more legitimate paper willing to buy his envenomed outpourings. But what he lost by way of an audience he gained in other ways, for it was by means of this hate-filled effusion in a minor nationalist organ that Trebitsch first inserted his foot in the door of his new home — the world of right-wing German politics.

Reinhold Wulle, editor of the *Deutsche Zeitung*, was Trebitsch's first acquaintance in this new arena, and became his first patron. It may seem odd that Wulle, a violent nationalist, proponent of right-wing terrorism, and advocate of a *völkisch* dictatorship,[9] should have taken up with Trebitsch, a former Liberal MP, foreigner, and (at any rate by birth) a Jew. But Trebitsch could present formidable credentials which more than compensated for his dubious origins. Had he not, after all, served the German cause during the war as a spy? Had he not suffered the rigours of American and British penal institutions as a consequence? If challenged, Trebitsch could pull out his yellowing wad of press cuttings (which we may be sure he had preserved intact throughout his recent ordeals) and point with pride to his earlier triumphs in the art of anti-British propaganda. Burning as he was with an unquenchable hatred of the British empire and all its works, Trebitsch was to be outdone by no-one in his insistence that the result of the war could and would be reversed. Moreover, Trebitsch spoke and wrote almost perfect German. And his rambunctious, agitated, expletive style fitted the mood of the moment. In short, Wulle discovered in Trebitsch the perfect journalistic collaborator.

The degree of respect in which Wulle held his new associate is indicated by a letter that he dispatched to Trebitsch together with his honorarium. Evidently he had been much impressed by Trebitsch's boasts concerning his friends in American journalism, for he inquired whether Trebitsch might perhaps be able, through these contacts, to recommend a correspondent in America who could report to the *Deutsche Zeitung* from a German nationalist point of view.[10] Trebitsch replied with the news that he was planning a visit to Rotterdam the following week during which he would 'have talks with the representative of about 320 syndicated American papers'. He was certain that as a result of these talks he would succeed in recommending a suitable man to Wulle. Trebitsch added, somewhat mysteriously: 'I would be very glad to have a talk with you before my departure for Rotterdam. I should like to tell you about the aim and purpose of my journey there which is connected with the other question.'[11] The nature of this 'other question' and the motive for Trebitsch's hasty trip to Rotterdam, whence he had arrived barely a month earlier, were soon revealed.

Trebitsch travelled to Holland to visit the ex-Kaiser. The deposed monarch had been living in exile there since November 1918. The

Dutch, who had prudently remained neutral throughout the war, had not exactly welcomed the unexpected arrival of their royal guest. But they gave him asylum and bravely rebuffed pressure by the British and the French to yield him up to stand trial as a war criminal.[12] Since his arrival Wilhelm had been accommodated in a moated castle at Amerongen, the property of a Dutch nobleman, Count Bentinck. However, in late 1919, the ex-Kaiser's position in Holland was rendered extremely delicate because of the effects on Dutch opinion of the publication of German documents, apparently of an incriminating character, concerning his role in the crisis of July 1914. The Dutch wavered and wondered whether to hand him over to the Entente powers; some German nationalists plotted his return home; and the less enlightened sections of the British press clamoured for him to be hanged. Meanwhile the object of these conflicting aspirations pottered around on the Amerongen estate, walking, shooting, and cutting down trees, all the time preserving a wise, if uncharacteristic, silence.[13] An interview with this man at this time would be a scoop of international proportions, and it was in pursuit of this journalistic dream that Trebitsch set out for Amerongen. No doubt he felt confident that if he attained his objective he would at the same time be able to offer Wilhelm valuable political advice.

The trip to Amerongen had about it an air of absurdity reminiscent of William McGonagall's abortive visit to Queen Victoria at Balmoral. Like the Scottish poetaster, Trebitsch failed to meet the monarch; but unlike him he was received by members of the royal entourage. He did not secure an interview with the former emperor, but on the other hand he obtained a reward no less dear to his heart: Trebitsch was himself interviewed, and his words were given much prominence in the world press. The London *Daily Graphic* dramatised its report with five headlines: 'Spy "Envoy" to Ex-Kaiser: Lincoln's Special Mission for Pronouncement from the Fallen War Lord: Wilhelm Remains Silent: Lincoln's Secret: Ex-MP Fails in His Promise to Startle the World'.[14] The *New York Times* devoted an entire column to a dispatch on the incident, quoting Trebitsch's statement that he had had no more than 'a few pleasant chats of a purely personal and private nature'. Trebitsch further declared that he would devote his life to working against England, and he added, 'I am already beginning.'[15]

Trebitsch's journey to Amerongen had a further beneficial side-effect in extending his circle of friends. He was accompanied on the trip by an American journalist, Alfred G. Anderson, an employee of the Hearst newspaper chain — presumably the 'representative of about 320 syndicated American papers' about whom he had written to Wulle. Soon afterwards Anderson was recalled to America, whereupon Trebitsch took the opportunity to engage the services of the newspaperman's former secretary, a certain Mrs Lenkeit.[16] The relationship seems to have blossomed into close intimacy, thus fulfilling a dual purpose for the sex-starved ex-convict. Anderson's replacement as Hearst correspondent in Germany, Karl von Wiegand, was also to serve a useful function for Trebitsch. A German-American who sympathised strongly with the nationalist right in Germany, Wiegand collaborated with Trebitsch during the following months in placing articles on German affairs in the American press.

But Trebitsch's most important new friend, and one who became his closest confidant for the next year, was of an altogether different stamp. Colonel Max Bauer was admired as one of the most remarkable men in Germany. A strategic thinker of force and originality, Bauer had served on the General Staff during the war as a senior adviser to General Ludendorff. After the armistice he published a trenchant booklet analysing the causes of the German defeat — this he attributed primarily to the bungling of weak-kneed politicians and their interference in the proper sphere of the High Command. If only the soldiers had been allowed to get on with the job unhindered by civilian busybodies, Germany, he believed, might have been saved. A military dictatorship under his hero, Ludendorff, would (so Bauer maintained) have resisted the attempts of Germany's internal enemies to weaken her while she was under external attack.[17] It was an ahistorical, self-serving apologia for the German army, and particularly for Bauer's commanding officer — but written with a power and lucidity which enhanced Bauer's reputation and led some rightists to look on him as a 'coming man'.

Bauer's personality presented striking contrasts and strange contradictions. He had a sharp and agile intellect; but he was prone to superstition. He despised women and condemned their sex in morbid terms; yet he could inspire adoration in the few females he admitted to his severely masculine life.[18] He was an extreme right-winger; but he dallied with the far left, and in the second half of 1919 held several friendly discussions with the Bolshevik agent in Berlin, Karl Radek. (Radek said that he moved like a cat and made a most unwarriorlike impression.[19]) To Radek he proposed a coalition of the German army, the German working class, and Russia, against the common enemy, the Entente powers. Yet this German nationalist, who so hated Britain and France, paid a call in July 1919 on the head of the British military mission in Berlin, General Malcolm, to discuss possible British support for his plans for a right-wing revolution in Germany.[20] Bauer was a rabid anti-semite (he stressed his hostility to Jews in a cordial correspondence with Adolf Hitler in April 1923);[21] but he nevertheless formed a close political and per-

14 Colonel Max Bauer

sonal union with a man who made no secret of his Jewish descent. The explanation probably lies in the similarity of their characters: they shared a zest for adventure, a love of intrigue, a complete lack of scruple, an irrepressible wanderlust, ruthlessness, self-regard, and utter contempt for conventional moral values. In a sense, Bauer and Trebitsch were made for each other.

In Trebitsch's first letter to Bauer, on 1 October 1919, he enclosed an introduction from Wulle, and requested an interview with the colonel. Trebitsch must have realized the importance of the coming encounter, for he emphasized: 'I would ask you to be kind enough to take account of the need for this meeting to last a number of hours.'[22] They met for the first time a few days later. We have no record of the occasion, but all the evidence suggests that Trebitsch made an immediate and profound personal impression on Bauer. The beginning of this relationship, indeed, calls to mind Trebitsch's first meetings with the Revd. Burt and with Seebohm Rowntree. Like these earlier patrons, Bauer was enormously taken by Trebitsch's intelligence, his gift for rapid absorption of data and for lucid exposition, his forthright and (apparently) open personality. Like the Anglican parson and the Quaker industrialist, Bauer took Trebitsch under his wing, nurtured him, defended him against attacks, introduced him to a wide circle of acquaintances, and (again like his predecessors) clung to a credulous faith in his protégé long after any rational man would have concluded that Trebitsch was a scoundrel. That Bauer (unlike the unwordly Burt and the saintly Rowntree) was himself a scoundrel may help explain the initial attraction, but in a way it renders even more mysterious Trebitsch's enduring hold over a friend whom he betrayed and humiliated.

From October 1919 onwards Trebitsch became Bauer's closest political collaborator. Trebitsch organized his publicity in the American press and fed him political memoranda. Bauer introduced his new acquaintance to Ludendorff as well as to other nationalists who were loosely grouped in an organization called the Nationale Vereinigung. This society bound together various disparate rightist elements, among them military officers such as General von Lüttwitz and Captain Pabst, far-right public officials such as Dr Wolfgang Kapp, industrialists such as Hugo Stinnes, and an assorted crew of journalists, lawyers, and other disgruntled patriots.[23] The group spanned the respectable old right of imperial Germany and the new right of the streets. Bauer himself bridged this divide in his own person, and it was perhaps symbolic of this union that the first introduction that he arranged for Trebitsch was with a most exalted personage.

Trebitsch, as we already know, was a man who did not give up easily. He had apparently set his heart on meeting a Hohenzollern, for, just a few days after his rebuff at Amerongen, he wrote to Bauer announcing that he planned another visit to Holland and adding:

> I wonder whether it might not be possible during my stay in Holland for me to visit the Crown Prince. Of course, it is not a

question of an interview; on the contrary, my visit, if possible, should be kept strictly secret. The purpose I have in mind would be that I should have a personal talk with the Crown Prince about general, but nevertheless important political questions and thus be able to give a personal impression of him in my articles.[24]

Bauer had served with the German Crown Prince Wilhelm during the war and admired him greatly.[25] He readily complied with Trebitsch's request for an introduction, though he warned: 'I do not, of course, know whether His Imperial Highness will receive you.'[26]

The heir to the defunct imperial throne had shared his father's exile since the previous November, but he was not allowed to partake of the amenities of the castle and estate at Amerongen. Instead he was consigned to an empty parsonage on the small island of Wieringen in the Zuider Zee. The house had no water or electricity and the crown prince lived there alone except for two servants and two aides, Freiherr von Hünefeld and Major von Kummer.[27] The prince inherited many of his father's defects without possessing the Kaiser's occasional brilliance and erratic energy. During the war he had acquired a sordid reputation as a womaniser and orgiast, and as a result he was not popular either in the army or the country. On Wieringen he moped ineffectually, lamented the absence of a bathroom, and went for long walks by the sea. But whereas the elder Wilhelm maintained a sensible silence, the younger made the mistake of issuing pronouncements which seemed to indicate ambitions to return to Germany in some political capacity, perhaps even in place of his father on the throne.[28] Into the dreary monotony of the crown prince's life at Wieringen there now burst Trebitsch.

Trebitsch's claim that he was received by the crown prince has been accepted by some historians. But it is totally without foundation, as can be seen from the following account of Trebitsch's visit, written a few days later by Freiherr von Hünefeld:

On the 14th of this month a telephone call was received at the Pastorie from the Hague from a man speaking German with a foreign accent who asked for the Adjutant to His Imperial Highness to come to the phone. Major von Kummer, who thereupon came to the phone, learnt that the caller did not want to give his name because he feared that the conversation could be overheard, that he carried a letter of introduction from Colonel Bauer in Berlin and requested an interview about a very important matter. Major von Kummer had the letter read out to him and arranged the visit of the unknown gentleman for the following morning in Wieringen. On the morning of the 15th the gentleman appeared, and introduced himself as the political writer and industrialist

Trebitsch Lincoln. He was received by Major von Kummer in my presence. Lincoln produced the letter from Colonel Bauer . . . and he said: 'By birth I am a Hungarian. About twenty years ago I migrated to England and there became a British citizen. Some years before the war I was elected to the House of Commons. In Parliament I always worked for Anglo-German understanding and even after the outbreak of the war I did not give up my work for the German cause. The result of my activity, of course, was that I became inconvenient to the British authorities. In order to protect myself against persecution I fled to America and there made propaganda in word and in writing for Germany. After America's entry into the war, England succeeded in having me extradited. I was then imprisoned in England until mid-August of this year. Then I was deprived of British citizenship and deported. I went to Germany, the home-country of my wife. In Germany I soon recognized that it would be completely impossible to rebuild Germany with the republican régime. I contacted George [*sic*] Wulle, the manager of the *Deutsche Zeitung*, for whose organ I wrote two articles. Through Wulle I got to know Colonel Bauer, about whose military work I need say no more as it is certainly known to you.'

Having thus passed lightly over some of the less creditable episodes in his past, Trebitsch moved on to an exposition of his political views. Perhaps seeking a private revenge for his summary dismissal from Amerongen, Trebitsch now sought to turn the crown prince's entourage towards the thought that the ex-Kaiser might be displaced as claimant to the German throne:

'Now it is my view [so the rendering of Trebitsch's lengthy monologue continued] that such matters cannot be conducted by force and that a civil war would be damaging rather than useful. It seemed to me that a *conditio sine qua non* for achieving our aim would be propaganda and the agreement of one of the now victorious great powers. This aim, however, until now has lacked a person around whom adherents would rally. The Emperor was ruled out both on account of his previous history and because of the inexpugnable revulsion against him by America, whose support I had hoped to win. About the Crown Prince I held the same views as were held by most people both here and abroad until recently. Colonel Bauer taught me to see that I had been wrong and I soon recognized that no-one other than the Crown Prince was possible.'

The two adjutants listened in some amazement to Trebitsch's speech. It seems that they did not find an opportunity to say much themselves, such was the volubility of their self-invited guest. As to a meeting with the crown prince, Hünefeld's account is quite explicit: 'In order not to compromise himself His Imperial Highness refused to see Lincoln.'[29] But they evidently had some difficulty shaking Trebitsch off, for on the next day Hünefeld met Trebitsch again, this time at Schagen, a small hamlet on the mainland near Wieringen. At this second meeting Trebitsch enlarged on his earlier proposals. He suggested that suitable propaganda in the USA might induce the American administration to acquiesce in a Hohenzollern restoration. As for the ex-Kaiser, he offered to employ his journalistic skills in planting news reports to the effect that the former monarch had gone mad — thus opening the way for his son to claim the throne.

Following his meetings with the crown prince's aides, Trebitsch prepared a long memorandum which he dispatched to Wieringen. This document combined, to a breathtaking degree, loyal support for the crown prince with brutally candid criticism of the young pretender's recent public statements. The document contained the surprising disclosure that Trebitsch had been received at the American Legation in the Hague, where he was 'carrying on important negotiations about the reestablishment of the Hohenzollern monarchy'. He cautioned that these discussions must be kept 'absolutely secret', adding that he had been officially informed that, while the United States government could not openly support the monarchists, it would not stand in the way of the peaceful restoration of a constitutional monarchy. (Trebitsch did indeed call at the Legation, where he asked for a United States visa, to be provided in return for information about German monarchist plots — the first of many similar fruitless applications by Trebitsch over the next eighteen months.[30])

Trebitsch forewarned the crown prince's adjutants that he planned within the next few days to 'publish or cause to be published the mental state of His Majesty.' He asked that his recommendations be conveyed to the crown prince, mentioning that he had much more to say but that he would 'wait with that until I have the longed-for opportunity to be presented to him personally'. And Trebitsch concluded with a rhetorical flourish:

> We have no time to lose, for it is the aim of my plans to establish the monarchy in Germany *immediately after the elections.** I beg you not to argue that the time is not yet ripe. The time is always ripe when a strong-willed man wills it so. Caesar wanted to abolish the republic and civil wars, to bring order into the world and to

* The first elections under the Weimar constitution were to take place in 1920.

> make himself master of the world. And he achieved this in spite of all obstacles and difficulties. Jesus wanted to sweep away the garbage of old Jewish superstition and realize his ideas, and he achieved this in spite of all hindrances.[31]

Trebitsch thus switched within a few paragraphs from a severe critique of the crown prince's indiscretions to a (to unprejudiced eyes, hilarious) comparison of the debauched Wilhelm with the Saviour of mankind. Or was Trebitsch perhaps thinking in these sublime terms not of the miserable royal exile but of — himself? Patently absurd though it may appear, this is a question which will recur later.

Trebitsch's unsolicited advice and bold projects were received with outward courtesy but private distaste. Hünefeld told him that he did not believe the Kaiser was mad 'in the medical sense', and he made Trebitsch promise not to quote either Kummer or himself on that subject.[32] Kummer sent Bauer a report on Trebitsch's visit in which he asked the colonel to persuade his friend to 'break off his communications with Wieringen'. The adjutant apparently felt that Trebitsch, while briefly enlivening the dull round of life on the remote island, was not to be taken very seriously: 'Mr T.-L.', he wrote to Bauer, 'may have good ideas and the best will, but he gives the impression of a nervous, not to say hysterical person. He is extraordinarily pushy and may thus easily compromise one. But still I treated him in a very friendly way for reasons of both conviction and utility.'[33]

Innocent of the unfavourable impression he had left at Wieringen, Trebitsch returned to the Hague, and thence to Germany, in high good humour. His self-satisfaction was apparently enhanced by other transactions which he had conducted during his brief stay in the Dutch capital. He had made the acquaintance there of the wife of the Dutch consul in Cologne, Frau Nieuwkamp-Sohst, a person of some standing in society who was much involved in charitable work on behalf of German and Austrian prisoners-of-war. Somehow Trebitsch induced the lady to make him a loan of the substantial sum of two thousand Dutch florins — which he promised to repay within four days. The money was never paid back. After six months Frau Nieuwkamp placed the matter in the hands of a lawyer, and (as will be seen) the case was pursued through the courts for more than a decade, but to no avail.

Frau Nieuwkamp may have had a secondary motive for her relentless legal pursuit of the debtor; for Trebitsch may have dispossessed the consul's wife of more than mere money. As a visitor to her house in the Hague, Trebitsch met another woman, a certain Fräulein Else von Nägelein, a Berliner who was also engaged in

15 Trebitsch Lincoln, photographed in Berlin in 1919

work for the POWs. Trebitsch claims to have performed a minor service for her, using his connexions at the American Legation. Whatever the truth of that, the two struck up a friendship which was resumed later in Berlin. Jealousy may well have been the inspiration for Frau Nieuwkamp's long campaign for the repayment of her loan.[34]

Back in Berlin, Trebitsch prepared a plan of action which he submitted to Bauer. The scheme called for the elimination of the ex-Kaiser as a candidate for the throne by means of the release of a news report that he was mentally ill. Using Trebitsch's contacts with American newspapermen, a series of articles would be published in the foreign press, with the design of drawing public opinion towards the idea of a constitutional monarchy in Germany under the crown prince.[35] Parts of this programme were actually implemented. Shortly afterwards rumours began to spread that the ex-Kaiser was 'distressingly garrulous, to the point of showing a loss of mental faculties'.[36] Whether these reports originated with Trebitsch or in the actual behaviour of the former Emperor is unknown. In any case the British Ambassador at the Hague refused to believe them, and all that happened was that the already tense relations between the two Wilhelms degenerated further. Meanwhile Trebitsch succeeded, through the good offices of his friend Wiegand, in placing some pro-monarchist articles in American newspapers.[37]

Bauer's confidence in Trebitsch was unshaken by the disparaging opinions emanating from Wieringen. He continued to proffer Trebitsch full support in his schemes, and he even seems to have derived some of his own political plans from his enthusiastic associate. At any rate, the views of the two men dovetailed perfectly at this period.

The blind trust which Bauer reposed in Trebitsch only a few weeks after their first meeting is illustrated with dramatic clarity by his response to a vitriolic public attack on Trebitsch by a fellow right-winger, Count Ernst Reventlow. In many ways Reventlow resembled Bauer himself: he too dabbled in Russian politics, intriguing with both Radek and right-wing Russian émigrés; a violent anti-semite, he inveighed against the 'indefatigable propaganda of Jewry within German liberalism and German social democracy'.[38] Like Bauer, Reventlow was an admirer of Ludendorff; their political outlook was almost identical. An attack on Trebitsch by this man was therefore highly dangerous, for it might impair the high regard in which Bauer held his friend.

The first onslaught came in a newspaper article published by Reventlow in the *Deutsche Tageszeitung* on 7 October 1919, just as Trebitsch was leaving Berlin for Holland. The article denounced

Trebitsch's 'fairy tales', denied that he represented anybody in the monarchist movement, suggested that his visit to Amerongen might well have been a republican provocation designed to discredit the monarchists, and warned right-wingers against any intercourse with him.

The attack could hardly have been timed more threateningly for Trebitsch, coming, as it did, so soon after the establishment of his alliance with Bauer, and on the day of his departure for Wieringen. As soon as he read the article he wrote in some panic to Bauer and Wulle, asking for their help and advice. Both sent him reassuring replies,[39] and Trebitsch let the matter drop until he returned to Berlin. But the insult rankled and Trebitsch resolved to obtain satisfaction. He persuaded Bauer to write to Reventlow on 15 November. Bauer declared emphatically that he had known Trebitsch 'for some time' [in fact, the acquaintance was at most six weeks old] and that he could 'only say that he has worked successfully and reliably in the direction that we desire'.[40] Reventlow's reply was hardly conciliatory: he insisted that the visit to Amerongen had greatly harmed the monarchist cause, and he added for full measure that any propaganda organized by Trebitsch in the United States would be worthless.[41] Furious at this further depreciation of his value to the monarchist movement, Trebitsch initiated legal action against Reventlow — but the case was dropped when Trebitsch's lawyers prudently asked for payment for work done before they would proceed further.[42]

Bauer's staunch defence of Trebitsch in the Reventlow affair cemented their friendship. The political collaboration of the two men now became even more intimate. When Trebitsch conceived a plan for the foundation of a new right-wing newspaper (a potential platform for himself against the likes of Reventlow), Bauer arranged for an officer of the Nationale Vereinigung to request that Trebitsch be received by the former Vice-Chancellor and right-wing politician, Karl Helfferich.[43] A dubious response from Helfferich, who suggested that 'for the moment I would leave out Mr Lincoln', evoked another letter by Bauer proclaiming his faith in Trebitsch.[44]

By the end of the year Trebitsch could look back on a remarkable turn-around in his fortunes. In August he had landed at Rotterdam as a penniless refugee. By December he had gained an entrée to the most exclusive circles of the right-wing German political establishment; his political advice was heard with respect by Ludendorff and Bauer; his articles were printed in the conservative press. True, he had acquired enemies in Frau Nieuwkamp and Count Reventlow, and detractors in Major von Kummer and Helfferich; but his bonds of friendship with Bauer had overcome all such hostile critics. In his moments of relaxation Trebitsch could enjoy the society of other friends such as Mrs Lenkeit and Fräulein von Nägelein. As for his financial position, if not secure, it was at least sufficient for the time being to enable him to live in the style to which he had once again grown accustomed.

The loan from Frau Nieuwkamp did not, however, keep him going very long, and — probably for this reason — Trebitsch began at about this time to consider the possibility of re-establishing his Roumanian oil business.[45] His young nephew Alexander Krausz, who had worked with him in the Oil and Drilling Trust of Roumania before the war, arrived in Berlin from Budapest in November 1919.[46] He brought family news and information about the political atmosphere in Budapest, which had recently been evacuated by the Roumanian occupying army. A Hungarian government of the extreme right, under the leadership of Admiral Miklós Horthy, took power and launched a bloody 'white terror' against the remnants of the Béla Kun regime, as well as leftists in general, Jews, and others with whom the 'whites' felt they had scores to settle. Trebitsch, however, seems to have had no fears now that the Roumanians had decamped, and he decided to return to Budapest for the new year. During his visit he was reunited with his aged mother and his extended family.[47] He made no progress in resurrecting his business interests, but he succeeded during his visit in obtaining one important possession: a Hungarian passport issued to him in the name of 'Ignácz Trebitsch' on 30 December 1919. Now that he had been deprived of his British nationality this was a specially precious document, even though its validity extended for only three months.[48]

Reinvigorated by his holiday in Budapest, Trebitsch returned to Berlin on 6 January, ready to plunge once again into the thick of right-wing political activity and intrigue. But within a few weeks he had become deeply disillusioned with all of his associates, apart from Bauer, and with the crown prince. On 29 January 1920 he wrote a long letter to Bauer announcing that he planned to withdraw from any further political activity. He declared that matters were not being handled correctly. He did not criticize Bauer personally, but those around him. Of course, Trebitsch wrote with a certain effrontery, he did not aspire to be leader of the movement himself. But he criticised those who urged delay. Now was the time for action. He condemned the crown prince's adjutants for not calling on Bauer during a recent visit to Berlin. And he denounced the crown prince himself for interfering in the work of those who were active on his behalf. Trebitsch insisted that, if the prince must make statements to the press, these should be submitted in advance for approval by a central press bureau (presumably Trebitsch had it in mind that he would preside over this office). He particularly objected to a recent conciliatory statement by the prince concerning England. There could be no question now, Trebitsch wrote, of any further efforts at propaganda in favour of the prince in the American press. If Wilhelm behaved in such an arbitrary way now, what was to be expected of him as a monarch? What would a constitutional monarchy under him mean? Were the Hohenzollerns as politically inept as the Bourbons? If so, it was a miserable shame! In any case, Trebitsch concluded, unless Bauer could organize the movement in a uniform way, there was no point in Trebitsch's continued participation.[49] It is an indication of Bauer's political innocence that he forwarded this astonishing document to the crown prince, with an accompanying letter following the same line as Trebitsch, albeit in rather gentler terms.[50]

Meanwhile Trebitsch, having vented himself of this tirade, left once again for Budapest, this time in the company of Mrs Lenkeit. This second visit to Hungary was very different in character from the first, which had been a purely family affair without any political overtones. On this occasion, Trebitsch arrived in Budapest bearing a letter of recommendation from a senior official of the German Foreign Office, von Kaufmann, addressed to the head of the German diplomatic mission in Budapest, Count Egon von Fürstenberg. The letter introduced Trebitsch as a journalist 'who intends to come for some time to Hungary in order to study the political situation there, and who asks to be received by you, dear Count'.[51] The letter had presumably been obtained through one of Trebitsch's political connections in Berlin.

Here we may, in passing, note again the repetition of a pattern; those endless (and pointless) letters of introduction which Trebitsch had obtained from the British Foreign Office in earlier days. Fürstenberg was now cast in the role once performed by the British Consul-General in Budapest, Esmé Howard — that of enforced host and factotum for a self-invited guest. Fürstenberg's opinion of Trebitsch eventually descended to almost as low a point as had Howard's,[52] but for the time being he was obliged willy-nilly to conform to the customary usages of diplomatic protocol and comply with the request from Berlin.

Once again Trebitsch forced a foreign diplomat to lay out a red carpet for him in his own native country. Thanks to introductions from Fürstenberg, Trebitsch obtained access to senior officials of the newly-installed right-wing régime in Budapest. When Trebitsch quarrelled with the staff in his hotel he appealed for intervention by the Hungarian Foreign Ministry; whereupon the head of the ministry's press department, Tibor von Eckhardt (a man who was later to play an important part in Hungarian political life and in Trebitsch's conspiratorial activities), wrote to him:

> Please forgive the difficulties which have resulted from the self-willed conduct of the hotel personnel in the matter of your accommodation. As I learn today from a report of the man responsible for lodging in the capital, both rooms were reserved when I told you so, but the hotel kept them for only one day; although forbidden to do so they gave them to somebody else the next day. In order to avoid similar excuses there are now two rooms reserved from tomorrow, the 20th, at the Hotel Astoria for you, Mr Editor, and for Miss [*sic*] Margaret Lenkeit, and I ask you to make use of them.

The letter inevitably provokes unkind questions in the mind of the reader. Of what periodical did Trebitsch claim to be editor? Why was Trebitsch's secretary concealing the fact of her marriage? Did they in fact make use of both of the rooms? Enclosed with the letter was an invitation from the Hungarian Prime Minister for 'Monsieur Lincoln Trebics' (accompanied by 'Miss' Lenkeit) to attend a soirée at the Prime Minister's home on the occasion of the opening of the session of the National Assembly. At Eckhardt's behest a cavalry officer was sent to call by car for Trebitsch and his companion to take them to the premier's residence.[53] The contacts which Trebitsch thus forged at the very highest levels of the new Hungarian establishment were to be of great utility to him a few months later. But in early March he abandoned the luxury of the Hotel Astoria and the pleasures of Budapest high society, and hurried back to Berlin. He arrived just in time to join a revolutionary government and thereby to earn a minor niche in modern European history.

CHAPTER 9

The Kapp Putsch

The five-day German revolution of March 1920, in which Trebitsch played a prominent part, was from the beginning a botched affair. At the time this short-lived attempt to overthrow the Weimar constitution and the Versailles treaty seemed like a historical aberration, a rearguard effort by the army and a few half-baked reactionaries to restore the old order and reverse the consequences for Germany of defeat in the war. The determined resistance of the German working class, whose general strike was held to have foiled the coup, appeared to contemporaries an indication that a seizure of power by the extreme right was henceforth ruled out. But in a longer perspective the Kapp putsch seems less an anachronism than a portent. Hitler's 'beerhall putsch' in Munich followed in November 1923; and in January 1933 Hitler ascended to power by constitutional (or quasi-constitutional) means. There was nothing pre-determined or fore-ordained about this progression. Hitler himself saw the 1920 rebellion as an object lesson in how *not* to organize a right-wing revolution. The Kapp putsch began as comic opera and ended as melodrama; but it may also be seen as a dress rehearsal for a tragedy.

The insurrection was essentially the work of disaffected units of the German army, but the prior planning was carried out by a mixed group of army officers and civilians, among whom Generals Ludendorff and Lüttwitz, Colonel Bauer, Major Pabst, Dr Wolfgang Kapp, and Trebitsch were central figures. Kapp, a conservative ex-bureaucrat, emerged as head (or rather figurehead) of the putschists.

Rumours of an impending monarchist revolt were rife throughout late 1919 and early 1920. British intelligence, which learnt of the coup preparations directly from Bauer's efforts to engage their sympathy, warned the German Government of what was afoot.[1] The rapid fall in the value of the mark and growing resentment of the terms of the Versailles treaty intensified unrest during this period. The governing coalition (composed of social democrats and centrists) and the president of the republic, Friedrich Ebert, were assailed as much from the far left as from the right: the government and the republican régime lacked authority, and in the eyes of many lacked legitimacy too. Talk of resistance was aroused in the army by the insistence of the victorious powers on the demobilisation and virtual disarmament of the German armed forces. This slow-burning fuse eventually ignited the revolt.

As we have seen, as late as 29 January 1920, in spite of the rumblings of discontent and rumours of revolution, Trebitsch had despaired of any effective action by the conspirators. But during his five-week absence in Budapest a series of dramatic events induced a coalescence of the forces which ultimately produced the putsch. On 3 February 1920 the Allied powers presented Germany with a note containing a list of nearly nine hundred alleged war criminals (among them the crown prince, Hindenburg, Ludendorff, and other royal, military and political personages) whose surrender for trial was demanded. The reaction among the German population was one of bitter indignation, and the government was further humiliated and weakened. On 9 February the crown prince sent a telegram to the Allied governments offering to substitute himself for the other persons on the list.[2] The Kaiser was furious at this, and the episode was seen on all sides as yet another example of what a British intelligence report called the prince's 'inborn political tactlessness'.[3] Even Bauer now no longer insisted on the crown prince's claim to the throne as a major objective of a revolution, and during the next few weeks the conspirators presented the curious spectacle of preparing a monarchist coup without, however, putting forward any royal candidate.[4]

What precipitated the revolt was a profound movement of protest within the German army. On 9 February, at a meeting of staff officers and departmental chiefs attended by General von Seeckt, there was talk of resistance.[5] The next day General Malcolm, chief of the British military mission in Berlin, heard that a coup was imminent. He immediately informed the British Government, and on the basis of this and another report, the British chargé d'affaires in Berlin, Lord Kilmarnock, again warned the German Government that trouble was brewing.[6] Alarmed by this information, which tallied with news received from several other sources, the German Government decided to assert its authority. In order to demonstrate its strength and at the same time diminish the potential threat from the military, the government issued an order on 29 February for the disbandment of two marine brigades stationed near Berlin.[7] On the following day General Lüttwitz appeared at a parade of one of these units, headed by Captain Hermann Ehrhardt, at their camp at Döberitz, twenty-five kilometres from the centre of Berlin. A

Lutheran chaplain delivered a sermon which culminated in a demand for the restoration of the German monarchy. Lüttwitz addressed the troops declaring that he would not tolerate the demobilisation of the brigade.[8] After this open defiance of the government by Lüttwitz the conflict swiftly came to a head.

On 3 March Trebitsch left Budapest, arriving back in Berlin three days later. His 'withdrawal' of five weeks before was forgotten. Spurred on by the political developments during the intervening period, he returned to Bauer's side, and with him plunged into a week of intense conspiratorial activity. Ludendorff's first wife, in her memoirs, recalled Trebitsch's presence at the meetings of the inner circle of plotters (among them Lüttwitz, Bauer, Pabst, and Kapp) in Ludendorff's flat overlooking the Tiergarten.[9] On 8 March Bauer paid another call on General Malcolm, to whom he spoke (as Malcolm later reported) 'vaguely of the danger of Bolshevism and the need for stronger Government in Germany'. According to Malcolm, Bauer 'did no more than hint at a "putsch"', but the British general took the opportunity to warn him 'that England would not stand anything of the kind and that any unconstitutional action ... would be sheer madness'.[10]

On 9 March Trebitsch was reported by an eye-witness to be 'very elated and joyful'. He said that he would be 'a very rich man in a day or so', that a revolution was about to take place, and that the leaders of the coup 'were only waiting for him'.[11] The next day the German Government sought to crush the incipient army revolt by ordering the transfer of the Ehrhardt brigade from the authority of General Lüttwitz to that of Admiral von Trotha.[12] But the loyalty of the admiral too was doubtful, and that evening Lüttwitz stormed in to see President Ebert, to whom he presented an ultimatum. Ebert rejected Lüttwitz's demands for the immediate dissolution of the constituent assembly, the holding of new elections, the appointment of non-political 'experts' to government ministries, his own installation as commander-in-chief of the entire armed forces, and the withdrawal of the demobilisation orders.[13]

Lüttwitz had taken this sudden, apparently impulsive move without previously consulting or even informing Kapp, the nominal leader of the conspirators.[14] Lüttwitz's action forced the hands both of the government and of his fellow-plotters: each side realized it must now act or risk arrest by the other. Meanwhile news of an imminent revolt leaked out to the press. The government announced that Lüttwitz had been relieved of his army command on ground of insubordination, and orders were issued for the arrest of Kapp, Bauer, and two other conspirators (but not Ludendorff, Ehrhardt, Pabst, or Trebitsch). Faced with the apparently firm resolve of the government, some of the conspirators hesitated. Kapp vacillated and went into hiding.[15] Trebitsch was beside himself with fury at the faintheartedness of his collaborators and was heard to remark, 'the whole thing has crashed — these silly, thick-headed Germans!'[16]

But on the next day, 12 March, Trebitsch attended a crucial meeting of the leading conspirators: those present included Kapp, Lüttwitz, Bauer, Ehrhardt, and two or three others. Ludendorff and Pabst did not turn up, but Pabst sent along a representative who spoke against a coup, declaring that 'nothing has really been prepared'. Ehrhardt replied with some heat that it was now too late to withdraw: 'the putsch must take place'.[17] Bauer made a speech advocating tough measures and the declaration of a military dictatorship.[18] Trebitsch's contribution to the discussion (it strains the imagination to think of him as remaining silent at such a moment) has unfortunately not been recorded. At any rate, we may be confident that he was among those who favoured an immediate seizure of power. The plotters decided that the Ehrhardt brigade would march on Berlin the next morning.

Early that evening Trebitsch was once again in high spirits. According to a reliable report 'he became more cheerful and said that things were righting themselves in favour of the revolutionaries, and that if all went well they would be the masters in the morning, but that he would know definitely by 10 p.m. that night'. The news was evidently encouraging, for at ten o'clock the same evening Trebitsch appeared in the hall of the Adlon Hotel smoking a large cigar. He laughed and said: 'Tomorrow morning at six a.m. I shall march in with the troops from Döberitz to the Brandenburg Gate'. He talked of sending a note to his friend Wiegand (the Hearst newspaper chain representative), who was staying in the hotel, telling him to be up in time in the morning.[19]

That same evening of 12 March, the government, on hearing that rebel troops were about to march on Berlin, momentarily lost its nerve. The Defence Minister, General Noske, who had drowned several leftist uprisings in blood, shouted, 'Everyone has deserted me; nothing remains but suicide!'[20] But the minister did not take his own life. Instead, together with the President and most of the cabinet, he withdrew from Berlin to Dresden. The German capital was now defenceless against the putschists, and the government's flight left a vacuum at the centre of the administration of the state.

The rebel capture of power the next morning was bloodless and almost effortless. Ehrhardt's troops marched in from Döberitz: at the Brandenburg Gate they were met by Kapp clad in a morning-coat, top hat and spats.[21] Ludendorff, Lüttwitz and the other conspirators also arrived. The rebel forces occupied all the main points of the city without encountering any opposition. Kapp moved into the vacant Chancellery building and issued a proclamation declaring himself Chancellor and dissolving the constituent assembly.

The new government promised to liberate Germany 'from the misery, corruption and crime' allegedly fostered by its predecessor.[22] General Lüttwitz was appointed minister of defence, and Kapp set about trying to fill the other cabinet posts. But he encountered some difficulty in this, partly because few persons of any weight could be found who were willing to serve under a man widely regarded as a nonentity, and partly because of his own irresolution and unbusinesslike methods. Indeed the atmosphere in the Chancellery throughout the coup was one of utter confusion. Bauer himself termed it an 'unbeschreiblichen Wirrwarr' (indescribable muddle).[23] Although he remained somewhat in the background in the early stages of the coup, he went to the Chancellery building and took a hand in trying to organize the administration. But he had little success since the nominal Chancellor seemed to lack the first elements of governmental capacity, the Allied powers refused to grant the new government recognition, and many civil servants stayed away from their offices.

Amidst this chaos, however, at least one man happily accepted appointment to an official post in the new régime, and appeared to know exactly what he was doing and what he wanted. Early on that Saturday morning Trebitsch put his head round the door of his friend Wiegand's room in the Hotel Adlon and handed him a copy of Kapp's proclamation.[24] At 8.30 am Trebitsch drove in a motor car to the Hotel Excelsior with an escort of two soldiers. Entering the breakfast room with his guard of honour, he announced to the startled guests: 'Power is in our hands.'[25]

Later that morning Trebitsch appeared at the main telegraph office in Berlin, where he met a former naval officer, Captain-Lieutenant Lensch, a radio specialist who had been ordered by Ehrhardt to ensure the orderly continuation of the wireless telegraph service in some unspecified form of association with Trebitsch. In legal testimony three months later, Lensch recalled the sequel:

> From the Telegraph Office Trebitsch and I returned to the Reich Chancellery. Trebitsch rushed upstairs whereas I remained in the ante-chamber. Some time later he returned and said that the two of us were to look after all press matters in the Foreign Ministry; he was to deal with foreign press matters, and I with the others. I was to go to Kapp. When I got there, there was a big meeting and Kapp spoke only a few words to me. From the outset I represented to him that I was not the right man for that position and I said that I was an official of the wireless office. His answer was

something like this: 'That's nothing to do with it. This is what's going on here. I order you to issue all instructions in the press department that you find necessary.' I assumed that as a civil servant it was my duty simply to obey the order of a government that was now in existence *de facto*, and I thereupon went with Trebitsch to the Prince Frederick-Leopold Palace at the Wilhelmplatz, where the press department of the Foreign Ministry was located.[26]

At the press office there was total confusion. On the way there Lensch had met another of the conspirators, a shady lawyer and convicted embezzler named Bredereck. Lensch told him (according to Bredereck's later testimony): 'Kapp said to me that I should provisionally take over the press work. But I don't understand anything of that. You come with me!' Soon after Bredereck reached the press office a telephone call came from one of the right-wing newspapers, the *Kreuzzeitung*, complaining that the paper's office had been occupied by the security police. The *Kreuzzeitung* was a strong supporter of the coup and the supposed press chiefs were amazed to learn of the police move. Lensch told Bredereck to go to the Chancellery and ask what was the point of having a press office if the press was forbidden to appear. After being sent from one person to another, Bredereck found a man who claimed to exercise police authority. He said he had forbidden all newspapers to appear lest the public become disquieted. Bredereck protested that the disquiet would be greater if the press did not appear. But the official would not listen. 'He treated me in a military fashion, more or less like a raw recruit,' Bredereck recalled. 'He said curtly, "Turn left! That's it! The press won't appear! I have made arrangements to have all newspaper buildings occupied!"'[27] In fact, the entire Berlin press remained closed for the duration of the putsch.

With the local press thus arbitrarily and totally locked out by the government, the sole remaining function of the government press office was to deal with the foreign press. One member of the office remembers their surprise when they heard that Trebitsch was to be their new chief: 'We were all taken aback when we heard his name.'[28] Another official provides a vivid picture of Trebitsch's high-handed ways with his new staff:

[There] was a door between the room of the press chief, which was occupied by Captain-Lieutenant Lensch, and my room. I had given orders . . . to have it locked, so that none of the gentlemen next door could make his way into my room. Shortly afterwards one of these gentlemen asked me who had had the door locked. I said that I had done so. When, after a while, I left my room, I found on my return that the door had been forced open. I went

> into the next room and asked who had opened the door or had had it opened. I said I must protest most strongly. Thereupon, to start off with, Captain-Lieutenant Lensch demanded that I speak in a more moderate tone of voice. I replied that I could not find another tone towards people who opened other people's doors. At that point there emerged from out of the crowd of people standing there a rather large gentleman [Trebitsch] who said it was he who had opened the door. What was more, he said, *quite a lot of other things would be happening to me*. When I asked him by what right he addressed me in this manner, he said that he had been entrusted by Colonel Bauer with responsibility for foreign propaganda. I said to him that as far as I knew he was a foreigner himself, and that I was astonished that German official functions had been assigned to an alien. His answer was that until now foreign propaganda had been conducted on false principles and he was going to demonstrate how it was to be done properly.[29]

The consternation inside the press office at Trebitsch's appointment and at his arrogant bullying was, however, as nothing compared with the international uproar when the news was broadcast that the former British MP and convicted forger had now been appointed to an official position in the German Government. Trebitsch's new eminence gave him absolute authority to censor all outgoing press telegrams dispatched by foreign correspondents in Berlin. This was a power on a very different level from his earlier menial duties as postal censor at Mount Pleasant sorting office in 1914. He performed his new functions with a ruthless zest, exercising his blue pencil almost indiscriminately, and taking a malicious delight in the fact that he had now turned tables on the British press which had printed most unkind reports about him at the time of his trial in 1916.

Trebitsch began his censorship activities by simply tearing up the cables of British correspondents and throwing them into the wastepaper basket.[30] The representative of the *Daily Telegraph* reported on the evening of the first day of the coup:

> Whatever qualities the new German Government may lack, tact is not among them. It has had the supreme delicacy to appoint as the official who has to deal for it with the British and American newspaper correspondents, and to censor their telegrams — none other than Trebitsch Lincoln, ex-Liberal MP for Darlington. This gentleman refuses to pass anything that does not correspond with his idea of truth, and that his idea does not correspond with mine will be clear from the fact that he suppressed in its entirety the first telegram I handed to him. Mr Lincoln's theory, in fact, is that the truth about the latest coup d'état in Germany begins and ends with

> what he has to say about it. That is why I am choosing another vehicle than the telegraph to convey some information to your readers.[31]

Other foreign correspondents encountered similar obstructionism from Trebitsch and also resorted to unorthodox channels in order to dispatch their reports. *The Times* correspondent in Berlin, H.G. Daniels, wrote on 13 March:

> Owing to the great difficulty in forwarding messages by telegraph, I am sending this by mail. The first obstacle is the censorship of British messages, which has been placed under I.T. Trebitsch Lincoln, and he is exercising his power in a most arbitrary manner. He insists on arguing with correspondents sentence by sentence in regard to their matter, and under the cloak of censorship seeks to influence them by expounding what the present *régime* wants said. His method is to refuse to pass whole messages, telling correspondents to rewrite them.[32]

The *Daily Chronicle* correspondent declared indignantly:

> After a fairly thorough experience of censorships all over Europe, I can only say that it is the most intolerant that I have ever come into contact with. It is a political censorship in its worst form. The merest expression of opinion, and that by correspondents who know what they are talking about, the slightest deduction, the most ordinary speculation, in short, the slightest liberty, are to it anathema maranatha.[33]

So incensed were the British press reporters in Berlin that, on the afternoon of the first day of the coup, they formed a deputation, headed (by a process of natural selection) by the correspondent of *The Times*; they called on the British chargé d'affaires, Lord Kilmarnock, and demanded that Trebitsch be 'outed' from the censorship. In a letter to his London office, the *Times* man commented: 'I never saw the Press really moved as they were when Trebitsch appeared.'[34] Kilmarnock, of course, could exercise no authority over the dispositions of the Kapp government, the less so since the Allied diplomatic representatives in Berlin had decided that morning 'to hold no communication with [the] so-called new Government'.[35] But he agreed to report the journalists' protest to the Foreign Office in London.[36]

Already by the evening of the first day of the revolution it was becoming evident that the new régime faced strong opposition not only abroad but also among the German population. The response of army units outside Berlin had been mixed, some supporting the coup, some remaining loyal to the Ebert government in Dresden, and others again biding their time in order to see how things fell out. In Berlin the police and the security police ('Sipo') initially supported Kapp. The change in government in Berlin was immediately followed by the removal of the socialist provincial premier of Bavaria, Johannes Hoffmann, and his replacement by a conservative, Dr Gustav von Kahr. But many other regions of Germany refused to acknowledge the authority of the Kapp government, and in places fighting broke out between army units and anti-militarist leftists. A general strike was called by the left: within a short time, and in spite of the absence of newspapers, word of the strike call spread, and the work stoppage in Berlin became almost universal. Even the telegraph clerks at the Berlin Post Office refused to heed Trebitsch's authority, and by the third day of the coup they had taken matters into their own hands, transmitting only those messages they liked, and declaiming (in a message of their own to the General Post Office in London): 'Let us hope that the power of a clique of soldiers and officers soon will come to its end. We are a democratic people now and know well that we are in bad hands when we help the new Government. Let us hope that these mad dogs and criminals will go to the devil.'[37]

Trebitsch refused to allow news of the working-class opposition to the government to be dispatched abroad. When, late on the evening of 13 March, the correspondent of the (Liberal) *Daily News* said to him, 'Are you afraid of the truth about the movement reaching the British public?', Trebitsch replied: 'It all depends on the conception one has of the truth. Correspondents of British Liberal newspapers always labour under the delusion that any movement which does not originate from the Extreme Left in Germany must necessarily be reactionary. This Government is neither reactionary nor monarchist; and I object to the British Government being told that it is.'[38] Trebitsch's statement may be seen as more than mere public relations camouflage, for in fact, the new government, and in particular Bauer, understood that their only hope of success lay in some accommodation with the extreme left. Bauer even favoured including left-socialists and communists in Kapp's cabinet.[39] Communist leaders were seen entering the Reich Chancellery building several times during the coup.[40] And indeed the Kappists continued their contacts with various elements of the left up to the very end of the putsch, but without persuading them to cooperate with the government or end the general strike.[41]

At 8.15 p.m. on 13 March Trebitsch told the *Daily Telegraph* correspondent that the Kapp Government was master of the situation nearly everywhere in Germany. But by the following morning, the second day of the revolt, he was obliged to admit that opposition was greater than he had anticipated. That morning, 14 March, the general strike took effect in earnest, and its effects were brought home to Trebitsch in a direct manner.

The scene was the breakfast room of one of the leading Berlin hotels (either the Hotel Adlon or the Hotel Excelsior, where Trebitsch had created such a stir on the previous morning). The episode was recorded with undisguised glee by the *Daily Telegraph's* man on the spot:

> At breakfast I had an experience which I thoroughly enjoyed, after what I went through at the Press Bureau of the Foreign Office yesterday. Bacon and eggs were served to me at one end of the hotel restaurant, while cold meat was refused to Herr Trebitsch at the other. The only other guests in the restaurant at the moment were two Americans, altogether ignorant of German, who had just arrived from Paris, and were prodigiously puzzled as to what was going on here. The reason for the differentiation between Herr Trebitsch and myself was this. The works council of the hotel had decided, as long as the staff was in the hotel, to go on serving members of the Entente Missions, and, for some reason or other, chose to give the foreign correspondents the benefits of this privilege also. As Herr Trebitsch, who had vainly argued the question of his cold meat, which was admitted to be in the larder, came over to my table to invite me to the [press] conference with the Chancellor, he was able to satisfy himself that I was having a really excellent breakfast.[42]

Later that morning Trebitsch, 'in his capacity of Director of Foreign Press Affairs', presided over the only press conference given by Kapp during the five days of his Chancellorship.[43] The occasion was not a success. Kapp delivered a prepared statement 'in metallic tones'.[44] His declaration that the full list of his ministers would be published 'in a few days' hardly enhanced the authority of his gimcrack administration.[45] The *New York Times* correspondent called the Chancellor a 'reactionary Hotspur' in his report the next day.[46] Kapp's ineffectual leadership and his lack of grip on events led to a rapid loss of morale by the putschists.

Nothing illustrates the ineptitude of the Kapp government better than another episode on the morning of Sunday, 14 March. The president of the Reichsbank, in testimony given after the collapse of the coup, recalled:

> An officer arrived who presented me with a written request, signed 'Kapp, Reichskanzler', demanding that half a million marks be put immediately at his disposal, and informing me that the money had to go that same afternoon at two o'clock to Munich. I rejected this request and declared that orders for payment drawn

on accounts belonging to the Reich could be made only through regular cheques, that is to say that the cheque had to be made out by persons who had the legitimate right to dispose of these accounts. It was impossible for the Reichsbank to honour orders for payment by 'Reichskanzler Kapp'. Besides, it was Sunday today and the Reichsbank was closed.

Successive attempts over the next few days to persuade the state bank to disgorge the funds urgently required by the Kapp régime met with similar ill success. Exasperated by this refusal, the government ordered Ehrhardt to go to the bank and obtain money by force if necessary: whereupon he replied that a German officer could not appear in the guise of a safe-cracker. The money was never released.[47] This strangely scrupulous revolutionary régime, which shrank from employing force in order to be able to pay its own bills (including most importantly the wages of its troops), quickly lost all semblance of control over the machinery of government.

Against this background of general disintegration Trebitsch's slender authority in his own more limited sphere was ebbing away. In the press office, as we have seen, his actions were challenged by at least one of his subordinates. In the telegraph office the clerks had taken power into their own hands. And after their experience of the first day or two, many of the foreign correspondents stopped submitting their dispatches to Trebitsch for censorship and resorted to a variety of expedients for evading his control. Trebitsch moved his main base of operations from the press office to the Chancellery building itself and there were even rumours that he had been dismissed from his post.[48]

In the increasingly desperate situation Trebitsch resorted to outright lies in an effort to shore up the position. He told the foreign correspondents that he had spoken to General Malcolm, who had assured him that the British Government favoured the new régime. The lie was promptly nailed by the *Daily Telegraph* correspondent, who plainly felt that he had gained the upper hand ever since the incident in the hotel breakfast room. He promptly jumped up and said that the British chargé d'affaires had strenuously denied any such allegation of British support for the coup. Both Kilmarnock and Malcolm were much exercised over this accusation, the latter perhaps fearing lest a false construction might be put on his parleys with Bauer in the period before the coup. Since no Berlin papers were allowed to appear, it was difficult for them to issue a denial effectively. But Kilmarnock took the unorthodox step of calling in the editor of the *Vossische Zeitung* and arranging for a denial to be placarded in the windows of the fifty or so agencies of the paper.[49] Indeed, Kilmarnock was so incensed that he complained to the former German Foreign Minister, Count Brockdorff-Rantzau, who went straight to the Chancellery building, asked to see Kapp, and when told that the Chancellor was busy, barged into a Cabinet meeting without knocking and told Kapp that Kilmarnock had termed the report nothing less than 'un sacré mensonge'. But rumours of British involvement persisted for several weeks in spite of further denials by Kilmarnock, by Malcolm, and even by the Prime Minister, Lloyd George, in a statement in the House of Commons.[50]

By Monday, 15 March Trebitsch had begun to share the general exasperation with Kapp's ineffectual leadership. He began to talk of the replacement of the civilian government by a military dictatorship.[51] The next day he tried to rally support for the government by spreading another rumour. He called a press conference and announced that grave events were impending. A communist counterputsch was expected that very evening. The communists, he asserted, had even set up an alternative government, whose seat was somewhere in the north of the city. Now therefore was the time for all national forces to unite against the Bolshevist threat.[52] In an interview the next day with *The Times*, Bauer repeated these statements with further embroidery.[53] That Bauer, who had only a day or two earlier been deep in confabulation with communist and other leftist leaders, should now invoke the Bolshevik bogey was a sign of how close the government was to complete collapse.

By the morning of 17 March it was clear to all concerned, including the 'Chancellor' himself, that Kapp would have to go. At first, Kapp thought he might save something from the ruins by negotiations with the legitimate government in Dresden; but such hopes soon proved illusory. Trebitsch was by now admitting to foreign correspondents that the situation was 'wobbly'.[54] On the morning of 17 March news came that not only all the established political parties (including those of the right) but also the Berlin security police were turning decisively against the régime.

At this critical juncture Trebitsch went, possibly at Bauer's request, to see the one man who, they believed, might yet save the situation. General Ludendorff had not taken office in the Kapp government, but he had participated in the conspiracy leading to its formation, he had been present at the Brandenburg Gate on the morning of the first day of the coup, and he had been consulted frequently by the putschists during the course of the insurrection. Trebitsch succeeded in finding the general and read the following statement to him:

> As a collaborator in the preparation of the coup, I feel that I have the right to put the following to you. A fateful lack of resolve

> produced immense calamities during the war. We who have made these revolutionary preparations will be called frivolous criminals by history. If we do not act today, it will be too late tomorrow. And we alone will be held responsible for the disasters that will befall the whole country. Your Excellency knew about the preparations and your Excellency must not now abandon us. What shall the brave troops say who faithfully followed their leaders and were willing to give their blood to establish a new era if we now leave them in the lurch?

Authorship of this appeal has been attributed to Trebitsch;[55] but it is more probable that the author was Bauer and that Trebitsch acted here as his agent.* Ludendorff's response is unknown. But presumably even he now realized that the rebellion had been a gigantic and irretrievable flop.

On the afternoon of Wednesday, 17 March, Kapp resigned. General Lüttwitz briefly toyed with the idea of establishing himself as a military dictator, but he was soon disabused of the notion.[57] Fearing retribution, Kapp wisely fled to Sweden. (Less wisely, he later returned to stand trial in Germany: he died in a German prison.) Lüttwitz returned to his suburban villa, whence he made his escape a few days later to Hungary. Confused fighting continued for some days between armed workers and frightened soldiers in Berlin and elsewhere, but the authority of the Ebert regime was soon restored throughout the country. In Bavaria, however, the conservative provincial government of Kahr remained in power, and Munich henceforth became a refuge and rallying-point for opponents of the Weimar republic.

Freed of the attentions of their former censor, the foreign correspondents could now turn their pens like hatchets against their former tormentor. The most vicious blows, perhaps not surprisingly, were wielded by the *Daily Telegraph* correspondent, who wreaked his revenge on Trebitsch in grand style:

> The personnel of the Kapp Government was an extraordinary mixture of idealism, roguery, and dull animalism.... Of the

* The document was captured by the German police at Trebbin on 3 May 1920 (see below p. 164); it was read into the evidence of subsequent court proceedings at which Ludendorff acknowledged that Trebitsch had read it out to him. But Ludendorff refused to make any further comment. The document is not signed. If Trebitsch had written it as a letter he would surely have added his signature. If he had gone to talk to the general on his own account it seems unlikely that he would have written out the statement in advance: he was rarely, after all, at a loss for words. The most likely explanation is that he went as Bauer's emissary. In this regard the reference to the war is suggestive. Unfortunately, Ludendorff's papers, which might shed some light on this minor mystery, remain in private hands and are not accessible to historians.[56]

> villains of the piece undoubtedly the finest example was Trebitsch Lincoln. There is something almost Olympian about this man's scoundrelism. He has been handicapped by Nature with a face in every feature of which deceit, dishonesty, and brutality are written for all who run to read, and yet he has been a clergyman in the Church of England, a Liberal member of the British Parliament, and adviser on foreign politics of the German usurper who put himself forward as the champion of purity and truth. More than that, as an Hungarian Jew he got into the confidence of a clique consisting exclusively of anti-Semites of the most virulent type. Nothing could be more typical of the political childishness of the Kapp gang than the fact that they chose this man to be their link of communication with the British Press. . . . Every day we were told that Trebitsch Lincoln had gone or was going, but he kept on popping up like a Jack-in-the-box almost till the end. After he had disappeared from the Press Bureau he was seen by someone installed in a stately suite of apartments in the Chancellor's Palace. What Trebitsch was really doing in that galley, and how he got into it, are still mysteries. . . . I have heard it variously suggested that he was in the movement as a Bolshevik, as a British, and as a French spy. Possibly he was all these. . . . The world will watch with interest to see at what point this really remarkable rogue will crop up next.[58]

A strange coda to the Symphonie Fantastique of the Kapp Putsch was played out in its final moments. Trebitsch was among the last of the conspirators to leave the Reich Chancellery building. Either there or at the Hotel Adlon on the last day of the coup Trebitsch encountered two young men who had flown up from Munich in a hurry to join in the movement against the Weimar republic: one was a poet and journalist, Dietrich Eckart, the other was his close friend, Adolf Hitler. Unfortunately our sources for this meeting are scanty — and in one case fraudulent.* But although we have no eye-witness account, there exists a description of the incident which may be taken as genuine. This is to be found in the memoirs of Hitler's press chief, Otto Dietrich, published posthumously in 1957:

* A supposed report by Hitler on his Berlin visit, dated 29 March 1920, is printed in Eberhard Jäckel and Axel Kuhn, eds., *Hitler: Sämtliche Aufzeichnungen 1905–1924* (Stuttgart 1980), document 89, p. 117. I am informed by Professor Jäckel that he now considers this document to be a forgery performed by Konrad Kujau, perpetrator of the notorious 'Hitler Diaries' hoax. Several standard books on Hitler repeat the story of his meeting with Trebitsch, sometimes with circumstantial detail, but none provides a satisfactory eye-witness source.[59]

> Eckart had distinguished himself as editor of the magazine *Auf Gut Deutsch*. . . . With Eckart Hitler piled into an open sporting plane and flew off to Berlin in order to be on hand for the Kapp Putsch. (This was Hitler's first flight.) Kapp had set up his headquarters in the lobby of the Hotel Adlon in Berlin. While waiting there Eckart and Hitler saw Kapp's newly-appointed press chief, Trebitsch-Lincoln, going up the stairs to Kapp's rooms. Trebitsch-Lincoln was reputed to be Jewish. Eckart promptly gripped Hitler's arm and drew him towards the door, saying, "Come on Adolf, we have no further business here." Whereupon they left Berlin. Hitler often described this incident in conversation.[60]

Oddly enough, Trebitsch, who was seldom backward in retailing stories of his meetings with the high and mighty, never seems to have mentioned this occasion. Possibly the corporal from Munich seemed so insignificant that he forgot all about it. Or perhaps (and this is suggested by Dietrich's version) the two visitors did not actually talk to Trebitsch but merely saw him on the stairs.

There seems little reason to doubt Dietrich's veracity in this matter. He can hardly be accused of profiteering or sensationalism in a book which he deliberately withheld from publication until after his death. Nor was the entire story a post-war invention, for in an earlier book, published in Germany in 1934, Dietrich had already hinted at the encounter, though without filling in all the details: to allege the slightest contact between Hitler and Trebitsch (by Nazi standards, a Jew) in 1934 would have been, to say the least, a risky venture — unless, that is, Dietrich knew that the Führer himself was the source.[61] That Eckart and Hitler flew to Berlin after the outbreak of the putsch is in any case well-documented fact.[62] As for the sequel it seems, *prima facie*, believable, We have already observed Trebitsch's penchant for making himself conspicuous in the Hotel Adlon. What could be more natural than for the Bavarian journalist with a soldier in tow, on turning up at the government's headquarters, to be directed to the head of the foreign press office (the inland press bureau seems by this time to have been in a state of complete collapse)? Of all Hitler's early associates Eckart was perhaps the most rabid in his antisemitism: his reported reaction is entirely in character. Both the nature of the source, albeit secondary, and the story itself therefore merit credence.

In one sense, of course, this brief encounter can be classified as little more than a piquant cameo. But seen in the context of Trebitsch's later relations with Nazi Germany, as well as of his activities in the immediate aftermath of the Kapp putsch, it assumes in Trebitsch's biography a larger emblematic significance.

CHAPTER 10

The White International

Unlike other members of the deposed Kapp régime, Trebitsch did not flee Berlin immediately after the collapse of the coup. When the Ebert régime resumed the reins of power a day or two later he deemed it prudent to go into hiding. For a few days he lived under a false name at the Hotel Moltke; later he moved to other addresses.[1] When news reached him that the government was preparing an indictment against him, Trebitsch began to make plans for his escape. He still held the Hungarian passport, valid for three months, which had been issued to him in Budapest on 30 December. On 22 March he went to the Hungarian Legation in Berlin, where he obtained an interview with a senior diplomat. Trebitsch explained that he had participated in the Kapp putsch and he inquired what the attitude would be of the Hungarian Government in the event of his seeking refuge in Hungary. He was told that the matter would have to be handled very discreetly 'on account of the Entente'.[2]

Two days later Trebitsch was issued with an identity document in the name of 'Wilhelm Ludwig' by the Reich Central Office for Military and Civilian Prisoners-of-War.[3] This was the first of what was to develop into a large and cosmopolitan collection of passports and other official documents, some forged, others genuine, which Trebitsch was to amass over the following months. He owed this first item to his friendship, begun in Holland the previous autumn, with Elsa von Nägelein, who, it will be recalled, was engaged in work on behalf of prisoners-of-war. A Berlin police report a few weeks later stated that Trebitsch had been seen around town with Fräulein von Nägelein and described the subterfuge by which the identity document had been obtained. The writer of the report commented that Trebitsch was obviously 'on very good terms with Fräulein von Nägelein' and that he appeared to 'trust her to a very high degree'.[4]

As during his previous period on the run (in New York in 1916),

Trebitsch could not resist cocking a snook at the authorities by making the occasional public appearance. On Saturday, 27 March, the *New York Times* correspondent in Berlin reported:

> Trebitsch Lincoln is a bolder man than General Ludendorff. While ... Ludendorff fled in such a hurry he left his servant to suppose he had merely gone for his morning walk, Lincoln remains in Berlin. He is still here, making no particular efforts to hide himself. He proposes to leave the capital on Monday evening. He goes about the streets and even strolled down Wilhelmstrasse a few times looking, most likely, amusedly, at the window of the Foreign Office, where, as he must know, an indictment has been drawn up against him. But he laughs at it, for he has learned that the authorities, evidently ignorant of the canceling of his British citizenship prior to his expulsion from England, hesitated to take action against him, because he was a British subject. He openly admitted to me the day before his disappearance from the Foreign Office that he had been helping for six months to bring about the Kapp coup. Now he brags he has remained in Berlin to wind up the business of the plotters and insure their escape ... He boasts that the failure of the coup is not so complete as most people think and that the good seed has been sown. "We shall come again," he boasts, and he takes pride in the way in which the Extreme Left Independent Socialists have been roused against the other parties. He still places his faith in the union of Conservative and Communist, of reactionaries and Reds.[5]

This reference to collaboration with the extreme left (a theme we have already noticed during the Kapp putsch) may have been more than optimistic political rhetoric. According to one account, Trebitsch and Bauer (as well as a third Kappist fugitive) obtained false identification papers around this time from the quasi-official Soviet representative in Berlin, Victor Kopp. The source for this story is a series of statements presented to British and American intelligence agents in central Europe in 1920 and 1921 by Trebitsch's nephew Alexander Krausz who had been with him in Berlin at the time of the Kapp putsch.[6] Krausz had fallen out with Trebitsch over a financial dispute, and sought revenge by spilling out all he knew of Trebitsch's activities.

The allegation of Soviet assistance is buttressed by a certain amount of circumstantial evidence. Kopp had been involved in the contacts before the coup between the Kappists and Radek.[7] The main purpose of his mission in Germany was to negotiate an agreement on the repatriation of prisoners-of-war between Russia and Germany: Kopp may on this account have wished to ingratiate himself with German army circles by aiding the fugitive militarists. Further verisimilitude is given to the story by an extraordinary article by Radek, published in *Izvestia* on 16 March 1920: this argued that the emergence of a reactionary, anti-Entente government in Germany might serve Soviet interests; it could, Radek suggested, help prevent a unified capitalist, anti-Soviet front; and it might also lead France's vassal, Poland, to turn in a defensive posture against a revanchist Germany, rather than fighting gainst Russia.[8] On the other hand, Bauer's private papers contain no confirmation of Kopp's aid; nor is the report corroborated by any other source. The matter is of more than passing significance in view of the later immixture of both Trebitsch and Bauer in Russian political affairs. But in the current state of evidence the wisest verdict is probably one of not proven.

With or without Kopp's help, Trebitsch left Berlin towards the end of March and went to Munich. Many other former Kappists, among them Ludendorff and Bauer, were gathering in Bavaria, where the right-wing Kahr government afforded them unofficial sanctuary. The Munich police, at this time headed by Ernst Pöhner, not only turned a blind eye to the presence of these wanted men, but actually gave them help in the form of false identity documents.[9] (Pöhner 'was the only higher State official who even then had the courage to be first a German and then an official' — Hitler's tribute to him in *Mein Kampf*.)[10] On 29 March the Munich police department issued Trebitsch with a personal identity document in the name of 'Heinrich Lamprecht'.[11] Two days later Trebitsch appeared at the Hungarian consulate in Munich and was given a new Hungarian passport, valid for one month, to replace the one that had just expired. This was issued to him under the name 'Vilmos [Wilhelm] Ludwig'. His profession was given as journalist and his domicile as Munich. Trebitsch now seems to have been taking some trouble to disguise his appearance, since, according to the personal particulars entered on this document, his most distinctive feature, the once luxuriant moustache, had again been shaved off.[12]

Bauer was staying with friends in a villa at Partenkirchen, about fifty miles south of Munich, near the Austrian frontier. He too had adopted an assumed name, 'Dr Becker', and occupied his time in writing a pamphlet about the Kapp putsch.[13] In it he attempted, in a curiously tortured fashion, to furnish a vindication of the revolt's aims.[14] But it ranks as one of Bauer's less impressive literary efforts. Possibly his heart was not really in it, for in his private correspondence at the same time, far from presenting an apologia for the Kappists, he was unsparing in his denunciation of their 'inconceivable imbecility' and 'cowardly capitulation'.[15] Relations between Bauer and Trebitsch remained, however, unimpaired by the political transformation of the previous weeks. When Bauer finished the manuscript in early April he entrusted it to his friend to take to Berlin — possibly with a view to finding a publisher.

Trebitsch thus returned to the capital in the second week of April. According to a Berlin police report he was seen on 12 April in the lobby of the Hotel Fürstenhof in the company of his friend Fräulein von Nägelein. On the same day (the report continued) he met the correspondent of the *Chicago Tribune*, Barker Brown, in the hotel's coffee-shop and offered him notes by Bauer concerning his contacts with the British prior to the putsch. Trebitsch demanded $2,500 for these papers, but both Barker Brown and another journalist to whom they were offered said no.[16] Trebitsch also met a string of other journalists in Berlin. On 15 April General Malcolm noted in his diary:

> Mrs Hardinge [the correspondent of the *Daily News*] came in this morning. I knew that she had had a long interview with Trebitsch Lincoln so asked her about it. She says he is almost openly organizing a new putsch with the idea of making Bauer, of whom he has a marvellous opinion, President (or Chancellor) — says putting up Kapp was the greatest mistake. He assured her that his party had the support of Winston Churchill, received through Cologne . . . Except in so far as Winston Churchill is concerned there is just the shadow of truth in it, and this, no doubt is the foundation of all the stories of British support.[17]

The Berlin press had in the meantime picked up some rumours of Trebitsch's indiscretions, and some papers (among them that of his old enemy Count Reventlow) attacked him as an English agent — further infuriating Lord Kilmarnock.[18]

Largely because of Trebitsch's own behaviour, things were now becoming uncomfortable for him in Berlin. After some delay, a warrant had at last been issued for his arrest, and the police were on his heels.[19] If the purpose of Trebitsch's visit to Berlin was to hawk Bauer's manuscript he does not seem to have accomplished it very efficiently. Neither the pamphlet nor the notes by Bauer were sold. In fact, Trebitsch did not even look after the manuscript properly, since he lent it to Fräulein von Nägelein, and she subsequently left it behind at a restaurant.[20] The pamphlet was later published not in Berlin but in the more favourable political climate of Munich. Having failed to sell Bauer's papers, and with the police now uncomfortably close, Trebitsch decided to leave Berlin. In a hastily written note to his friend Wiegand on 15 April he announced: 'I have to leave Berlin on very urgent business, but shall be back within a few days when I will communicate with you.'[21]

Trebitsch returned to Bavaria, eventually reaching the house at Stefanskirchen near Rosenheim where Ludendorff was staying as the guest of a friendly nobleman. Bauer was there and other former Kappists came and went. At this meeting and others during April and early May the groundwork was laid for a new conspiracy. Ludendorff, Bauer and Trebitsch were the heart and soul of this fresh endeavour, but other fugitives from Berlin also participated, notably Ehrhardt, some of whose men followed him to Bavaria after the collapse of the putsch.[22] Another prominent conspirator was the peculiarly sinister figure of Major Franz von Stephani. The son of a general, Stephani had commanded one of the 'Free Corps' after the war and had been involved in bloody fighting in Berlin, where he participated in attacks on socialists. He was under official investigation for more than two years on no fewer than seven charges of murder, but never stood trial owing to lack of evidence. After joining in the Kapp putsch he fled to Bavaria. Although reputedly of Jewish origin, Stephani was recognized as an 'Ehrenarier' ('honorary Aryan') and later served as an extreme-right-wing member of the Reichstag.[23] Trebitsch was now moving into very dangerous company.

The new conspiracy was even more grandiose and fantastic in conception than the Kappist plot for a German revolution. Continental in scale, the new scheme was based on the notion of an international alliance of 'revisionists', all those dissatisfied with the post-war treaties. Using as their base the friendly environment of Bavaria, the plotters hoped to draw into their web north-German militarists and reactionaries, Bavarian and Austrian conservatives, 'White' Russian émigrés, and right-wing elements in other countries. The objective was nothing less than the creation of a 'White' International akin to the 'Red' International in Moscow: indeed, although the two movements were at opposite ends of the political spectrum, they were kindred in another sense (as the article by Radek at the time of the Kapp putsch had indicated) for both opposed Anglo-French dominance over central and eastern Europe.

The various 'Free Corps' forces scattered through Germany and Austria were seen by the plotters as the potential nucleus of this broad effort to overthrow the Weimar republic and the governments of the pro-Entente 'successor states' of what had formerly been Austria-Hungary. To this end, contact was established with another shady character, Georg Escherich, also a 'Free Corps' chieftain, who was at this time in the process of setting up in Bavaria his own private army, known as 'ORGESCH'. Appropriately, Stephani was designated by the Ludendorff circle to coordinate plans with Escherich. The recently-established right-wing Hungarian Government, with whose leaders Trebitsch had formed such amicable relations two months earlier, seemed natural allies in such a movement, and it was decided that Bauer and Trebitsch would travel to Budapest to sound them out.[24] On 28 April, thanks to the benign protection of the Munich police chief, Pöhner, the two men obtained travel documents in false names, Trebitsch as 'Karl Lamprecht' and Bauer as 'Dr Börner'.[25]

Before setting out for Hungary, Trebitsch made one further visit to Berlin. This was probably in search of financial support for the White International. But the trip also seems to have had a personal motive, for Trebitsch went to stay with his former secretary, Margaret Lenkeit, at her home in Trebbin, not far from Berlin. The suspicion inevitably arises that Trebitsch may again, as during his visit to the Hague in 1919, have been in the process of casting off one mistress for another. This impression is strengthened by the behaviour of Trebitsch's other woman-friend, Fräulein von Nägelein, with whom he had been observed so recently taking cab rides and promenading in the lobby of the Hotel Fürstenhof. On about 28 April she was questioned by the Berlin police — whether at her own initiative or theirs is unknown. In any event, she proved a most cooperative witness: she told the police all about Trebitsch's false identity document in the name of 'Wilhelm Ludwig'; she reported that Trebitsch was in close contact with Bauer; and she also stated that Trebitsch was planning to go abroad.[26]

Five days later Trebitsch was arrested at Trebbin. Mrs Lenkeit's house was raided by the police, and a number of highly incriminating documents were seized from Trebitsch's baggage. Among these were papers relating to Trebitsch's abortive plans to found a right-wing newspaper, a copy of his letter to Bauer of 29 January 1920 (announcing his 'withdrawal' from the Kappist conspiracy), and the unsigned appeal which he had read out to Ludendorff on the final day of the Kapp putsch.[27] These revealing documents were later to be laid in evidence in the trials of other participants in the coup. If Trebitsch had been tried in Germany on a charge of treason they would have been formidable weapons in the hands of the prosecution against him too. But no such trial ever took place, for almost miraculously Trebitsch managed to escape from police custody at Trebbin before he could be securely lodged in gaol.[28]

Highly embarrassed that they had allowed Trebitsch to slip through their fingers, the authorities belatedly invigorated their hitherto lethargic search for the fugitive Kappists. The investigating judge assigned to the case sent an urgent message to the chief of the Munich police requesting that a search be made for Trebitsch, 'who is said to be there under the name of an American, Ludwig, together with a Mrs Lenkeil [*sic*] from Trebbin'. The message continued: 'It is possible that Colonel (retd.) Max Bauer, wanted by me for High Treason, may be in his company. His arrest is also requested.'[29] This message was sent to Pöhner on 8 May. But by the time it reached him, the birds had already flown — thanks in large measure to Pöhner's own assistance. The last remaining impediments had in the meantime been removed. In order to resolve the financial problem, Trebitsch had arranged for his friend Wiegand to come to Rosenheim to interview Ludendorff. The representative of the Hearst Press paid a hefty fee for this exclusive opportunity — and the general unselfishly turned it over to his collaborators to cover their expenses.[30] The Hungarian consul in Munich arranged for sensitive documents, needed by Bauer and Trebitsch in their contacts with the Hungarians, to be sent to Budapest by diplomatic courier, thus precluding the possibility of their discovery on the persons of Bauer or Trebitsch as they crossed the German frontier.[31]

Accompanied only by Bauer's faithful secretary, Luise Engeler, the colonel and Trebitsch crossed the frontier into Austria on the afternoon of Saturday, 8 May. In order to reduce the risk of detection they travelled by slow local trains rather than on the main line, planning to change to the Vienna express when they reached Salzburg. Once on Austrian soil they breathed more freely, feeling safe from the attentions of policemen. But there were long delays on the local lines, and by the time they reached Salzburg it was after midnight, and the Vienna express had long gone. At that period the Austrian railway system did not operate at all on Sundays. The travellers were therefore compelled to spend two nights at a hotel in Salzburg. On the second night a stranger appeared at the hotel and inquired after them, and when they finally boarded the Vienna express on Monday morning they became aware that they were being followed. Austria at this time was ruled by a social democratic government, and they feared that the authorities might arrest them and hand them over to the Germans. Bauer and Trebitsch therefore jumped off the train at a small stop, continuing to Vienna by local trains.[32]

In order to try to shake off their pursuers, they decided to change their identities once again. The Hungarian minister in Vienna supplied them with fresh Hungarian passports. Bauer now became 'Dr Bürger' and Trebitsch 'Dr Tibor Lehotzky'. Trebitsch's latest passport, valid for eight days, gave his profession as lawyer and his domicile as Germany. According to the personal particulars Trebitsch's moustache was still shaven and he now wore spectacles.[33] As a further precaution, the journey to Budapest was resumed not by train but by a Hungarian river steamer sailing down the Danube.

In her unpublished memoirs, Bauer's secretary recalls the magical beauty of Budapest, as seen from the Danube upon their arrival.[34] The political situation in Hungary at the time was no less attractive from the point of view of the conspirators. The 'White Terror' directed against remnants of the Béla Kun régime (as well as leftists and Jews) was at its height. In March 1920 Admiral Horthy had been elected Regent for life, and, with the tacit acquiescence of the authorities, detachments of right-wing military officers, organized into semi-secret societies, went on a bloody rampage through the country. Since January a Hungarian delegation had been negotiating a peace treaty at the peace conference in Paris. But like the other defeated peoples, the Hungarians discovered that no genuine negotiation took place: the terms laid down by the victorious powers were in some respects even more far-reaching than those imposed on Germany. Hungary was compelled to yield vast territories to her neighbours and was reduced to a small Magyar rump; indeed, more than two million ethnic Hungarians were wrenched from Hungarian sovereignty and found themselves ruled by the newly-formed 'succession states' of Czechoslovakia and Yugoslavia as well as the enlarged Roumania.

The Hungarians protested bitterly against the dismemberment of their country, demanded recognition of the 'integrity of Hungary', and warned that the proposed territorial settlement would be 'the causes of eternal feuds, political disturbances, and, moreover, of cultural and economic decadence'.[35] But to no avail. As the awareness dawned that they had no choice but to accept the proposed treaty, a bitter seed of revanchism was planted in the Hungarian political consciousness. The demand for revision of the treaty dominated the country's foreign policy throughout the inter-war period; irredentism poisoned Hungary's relations with all its neighbours; and the process reached its natural culmination in Hungary's collusion with Hitler in redrawing the map of central Europe after 1938.

When Bauer and Trebitsch arrived in Budapest on 15 May 1920, the Hungarian Government was desperately casting around for any means of avoiding signature of the peace treaty. The Hungarians welcomed the visitors from Germany as the drowning man clutches a reed. They were lodged in a luxury hotel, and immediately entered into an intensive series of conferences with senior Hungarian officials, among them the head of the political department of the Foreign Ministry and the Chief of the General Staff. Two days after their arrival Bauer was received by the Regent, to whom he presented a letter from Ludendorff and outlined the German reactionaries' proposals for a 'white alliance'. Horthy did not give an immediate decision, but encouraged Bauer to continue the discussions with a view to formulating a more detailed plan of cooperation, whereupon the government would make up its mind.[36]

A period of almost continuous meetings ensued. The German conspirators were represented by Bauer and Trebitsch (at a later stage also by Stephani); the Hungarians by a trio of politicians who represented the most squalid elements of the extreme right — Tibor von Eckhardt, Gyula Gömbös, and Pál Prónay. Eckhardt (whom we have already met in his capacity as head of the press department of the Foreign Ministry) was the leader of a violently nationalist, anti-democratic, anti-socialist, anti-semitic organization of white terrorists known as the 'Awakening Hungarians'. Gömbös, a mystical Magyar nationalist (though he came of Swabian stock), was head of an ex-officers' society known as the 'MOVE', with similarly extremist aims. (Gömbös was to serve as the first fascist prime minister of Hungary from 1932 until his death in 1936.) The third member of the trio, Prónay, a former cavalry officer, had acquired a murderous reputation as a perpetrator of pogroms.[37] In spite of their quasi-criminal associations, all three men enjoyed the intimate confidence of Horthy. Their malignant fame was such that even Luise Engeler (who seems to have enjoyed their company) recalls that when Gömbös and Prónay joined the German delegates for dinner in restaurants a ring of empty tables always surrounded them.[38]

In his memoirs (published posthumously) Prónay recorded his first meeting with Trebitsch:

> Bauer and his group were living in the Pannonia Hotel and I visited them there. At that visit he introduced me to a fat, small, dark man, very Jewish in appearance, whom he presented as Mr Lincoln. As soon as the man started talking German it was clear to me that he was a Jew. Before we entered on confidential matters I called Bauer to one side and told him of my suspicions regarding Lincoln. I said to him: 'Colonel, you dark, fat friend is a Jew — I don't feel safe talking in front of him.' 'Oh, Lieutenant-Colonel!' he answered smilingly, 'I would put my hand in the fire for that man. You can talk in front of him without any fears.' I shook my head dubiously. 'You can't trust a Jew so long as there's breath in his body', I said, 'but if you believe in him, don't hold me responsible.'

Prónay relates that in spite of this warning Bauer brought Trebitsch with him to every meeting and that he 'learned everything'.[39]

By 26 May the conversations had progressed sufficiently for the two sides to reach tentative agreement. A document was drawn up detailing the proposed scheme of cooperation: a typescript copy survives among Bauer's private papers; it is headed 'Plan drawn up by Col. Bauer', but the colonel's biographer surmises that it may in fact have been composed by Trebitsch and merely signed by Bauer.[40] Whoever was the author, the document authentically reflects the unified political vision of the two men — and in large measure also of their Hungarian interlocutors.

The chief objectives of the plan were the annulment of the 'so-called' peace treaties and the liquidation of all revolutionary elements. A permanent central committee would direct the international movement, and a central press bureau (presumably to be presided over by Trebitsch) would handle all propaganda. All participants would be sworn to secrecy, and any who betrayed the oath would suffer the penalty of death. (In view of Trebitsch's own treachery a few months later, it is worth noting that he himself seems to have advocated the killing of traitors.) Arms were to be purchased secretly in Germany and distributed to other countries involved. As for money (since there was obviously a limit to the amounts that could be secured by means of interviews with the Hearst Press), it was proposed that 'White' Russian banknotes, known as 'Duma roubles', be manufactured on special printing presses. Once all these preliminary arrangements had been made, a time would be fixed — somewhere between autumn 1920 and the following spring — for unified action.[41] Although the plan did not specify the precise nature of this action, there can be little doubt that the plotters envisaged a concerted movement of all the anti-Entente forces in central and eastern Europe.

On 1 June 1920 the Hungarian Regent informed his German guests that he was in full agreement with the details of the proposed plan of action, and that preparations could now begin along the lines indicated.[42] Just four days later Hungarian representatives signed the peace treaty at Trianon, preceding their signature with an announcement that they did so 'owing to the pressure of political circumstances'.[43] Thus from the moment of its signature of the Trianon Treaty, the Hungarian Government (or at any rate the dominant elements within it) were taking simultaneous covert action to subvert what they regarded as an imposed and unjust settlement. For the next three months Budapest became the headquarters of the White International, and Bauer, Trebitsch and Stephani its moving spirits.

Trebitsch was throughout a vital link between the two main branches of the movement. This summer was perhaps the happiest of his life. He had always enjoyed luxury hotels and he could now savour to the full the delights of his home town from a charming hostelry on the Margaret Island in the Danube, looking out to Buda on one side and Pest on the other.[44] the atmosphere of high international intrigue exactly suited him, and with the support (and generous hospitality) of their hosts now assured, he and Bauer set about breathing life into their fantastic project, and seeking to draw further nationalities into the alliance.

As a third major element in the White International, their hopes focussed most particularly on the White Russians. Since the outbreak of the Russian revolution hundreds of thousands of opponents of the new order had fled Russia and found refuge throughout Europe. One of the largest concentrations of exiles had settled (temporarily, as they thought) in Germany, where they quickly developed a thriving political sub-culture. Quite apart from these voluntary émigrés, Germany also still held large numbers of Russian prisoners-of-war, many of whom refused repatriation to Soviet Russia under the agreement negotiated by Victor Kopp in April 1920. With the civil war still raging in Russia, these former soldiers of the Tsar were seen by the generals of the White armies as potential recruits to their cause. The advance of Polish armies deep into Russia in May had seemed for a moment to ring the death-knell of the Bolshevik régime. With its internal and external enemies still far from defeated, Soviet power seemed a Jacobin-style adventure tottering towards its Thermidor. Far-sighted men looked among the generals of the emigration for a Napoleonic figure who, with a whiff of grapeshot, might restore some semblance of order and unity to a divided and semi-anarchic land. Such a personality Trebitsch and Bauer persuaded themselves they had discovered in General Vasili Biskupski.

Among all the rotten apples of the White International Biskupski was perhaps the foulest of the lot. One historian has described him as 'a man of considerable cunning [and] a schemer in the grand style, always engaged in some major financial or political intrigue'.[45] Another has termed him 'undoubtedly one of the most universally disliked men of the Russian emigration'.[46] Biskupski claimed to incarnate Russian patriotism, but according to a journalist who knew him he 'cared no more about the fate of Russia than the future of Abyssinia'.[47] With these credentials it is hardly surprising that Biskupski was later to be taken up by the Nazis and appointed to nominal leadership of the Russian emigration in Germany. The memoirs of Luise Engeler give the impression that Biskupski was introduced to Bauer through their mutual friend Max Erwin von Scheubner-Richter, a similarly sleazy exotic of Baltic German extraction, who had served as German consul in Erzerum and occupied a key role in the links between the German and Russian right-wing extremists.[48] Bauer was greatly taken by Biskupski, calling him a 'clear and sober head with great political gifts', and a man who combined 'energy and the courage of a tiger'.[49]

Biskupski arrived in Budapest in late June 1920 and joined in the feverish conspiratorial discussions with the Germans and Hungarians[50] A memorandum, dated 8 July 1920, outlined the Russian monarchists' views on the proposed joint action. Written in execrable French, it has been ascribed to Biskupski.[51] Whether he or one of his assistants wrote it, the document certainly represented his opinions, and affords a frightening glimpse into the illusory political world of the émigrés. According to Biskupski, most of Russia's political ills could be ascribed to the malevolent influence of the Entente powers, above all Britain. The February revolution of 1917 he attributed to Britain's desire to ensure a pro-Entente government in Russia. Since then, he maintained, Britain had sought to turn Russia into a colony of the Entente. What was required to counter this was a secret alliance of all the conquered peoples with a view to recreating 'a great Russia, a great Germany and a great Hungary'. The memorandum indicated the stages by which such an international counter-revolution might be orchestrated. In passing, it demonstrated Biskupski's disdain for most of the leading White generals actively engaged in hostilities against the Red Army — with the exception of General Wrangel, whose cooperation he proposed to secure.

It may justly be asked how Bauer, who had so recently enjoyed friendly relations with the Bolshevik agent in Berlin, could now lurch to the opposite political extreme and embrace a man next to whom Rasputin would seem almost a moderate conservative. Part of the answer is given by Biskupski himself: for, strange to relate, this exponent of arch-reaction by no means excluded the possibility of cooperation with the Bolsheviks. On the contrary, his programme actually required it. No doubt realizing the power of the Red Army by comparison with the ramshackle and divided armies of the White generals, Biskupski's 'general plan' included, as step number one, an advance by the Red Army into Poland and the restoration of Russia's borders of 1914. During this initial phase the White and Red armies (he imagined) would arrange an 'entente' and fight together against the Poles. Once the Poles had been defeated, a putsch would be carried out within the Red Army and a military dictatorship established. A total 'cleaning-out' of communists in Russia would follow, paralleled in the other countries of the White alliance by a general 'purge of all non-monarchist elements'.[52]

With the triple alliance of Russians, Germans, and Hungarians thus assured, the conspirators devoted considerable efforts during the later part of the summer to broadening the membership of the White International to include other nationalities. In August, Bauer, Trebitsch, and Biskupski, accompanied by Luise Engeler, travelled to Villach on the Italian frontier, where they established contact with two Italian generals.[53] As a result of these discussions, it was proposed that Trebitsch go to Milan to meet an Italian nationalist politician at that time little known to the outside world — Benito Mussolini. Trebitsch was provided with the following letter to ease his path:

> We the undersigned, General W. Biskupsky and Colonel M. Bauer, give the carrier of this letter, Mr Theodor Lakatos [another

> of Trebitsch's pseudonyms at this period], full authority to go to Milan to Mr Mussolini, editor of the *Popolo d'Italia*, and to discuss with him or with his representative or with other persons there all political military and financial questions, and we authorise him to collect or receive money for our account.[54]

For reasons which are unknown, no such meeting between Trebitsch and the future Italian dictator ever took place. But the letter (and particularly its final clause) constitutes another powerful reminder of the total confidence which Bauer — and now also Biskupski — reposed in their collaborator.

In the hope of bolstering another flank of the alliance, Bauer and Trebitsch embarked a few days later on another journey, this time to Vienna. There they called on General Alfred Krauss, leader of an organization of German-Austrian army officers, and one of the foremost champions of pan-German nationalism. Bauer did not hide his identity from Krauss, but Trebitsch introduced himself as 'Dr Johann Lange'. (At Graz on 29 July he had somehow obtained an Austrian identity card in that name.[55]) The precaution was timely, for just a few weeks earlier Krauss had received a message from Germany warning him to beware of Trebitsch Lincoln, who was said to be an English spy masquerading as a German nationalist — no doubt an echo of Count Reventlow's invective against Trebitsch the previous spring. A little later, Bauer visited Krauss again, accompanied by Biskupski, but on this occasion without Trebitsch. Krauss asked Bauer the real identity of 'Dr Lange', whereupon Bauer admitted the truth. He added, however, that Trebitsch was an extremely capable politician, a tremendous enemy of England, and an absolutely trustworthy friend of the German people.[56]

These touching evidences of Bauer's faith in his closest political ally carry total conviction. Yet the first fissures in their friendship were already beginning to appear. The issue which disturbed the harmony of the relationship was the role of Ludendorff and the degree of independent political action to be accorded to the Bavarian (as distinct from the north German) plotters. All that summer Bauer had been pressing his political hero, Ludendorff, to come to Budapest to assume command of the White International. On one occasion Bauer even went to Bavaria to fetch the general — but he came back without him. Ludendorff's refusal may have stemmed from a reluctance to don the mantle of leadership without the full approval and involvement of his Bavarian hosts.[57] Instead of Ludendorff, a quasi-official delegation representing the Bavarian Government of Dr von Kahr arrived in Budapest. The Bavarians were well received by the Hungarians, who no doubt saw them as a valuable accession to the alliance. But Trebitsch was enraged, very likely sensing in these new arrivals competitors for the position of German representative that he felt he had built up for himself in Budapest.

In an undated letter that he wrote to Bauer, probably some time in July, Trebitsch expressed his feelings vehemently and revealingly. He began by announcing his 'decision' not to proceed 'even one step further' with Bauer unless Ludendorff came to Budapest within a week. He vented his irritation with the Bavarian role in the affair, declaring, 'Oh well, the whole grandiose matter will degenerate into a Bavarian party business'. He forecast that this would be a 'second Kapp affair in grand style'. A sign of the creeping onset of megalomania may be discerned in his use of the first person singular in the next passage:

> I, however, want to make world policy and not small-time Bavarian pettifoggery. But apart from all that, our programme, our promise when we came here, was that Ludendorff would come here for the laying of the foundation-stone. . . . My decision is made. If L. does not come, then the matter will not succeed. Neither you nor I can manage the Bavarians without Ludendorff. It will be a fiasco. One fiasco, because of my blind trust in you, was enough for me.[58]

Although Trebitsch did not at that stage sever his connection with Bauer, such a letter, particularly with its insulting reference to Bauer's role in the Kapp putsch, spelt trouble ahead.

Ludendorff made partial amends for his failure to go to Budapest by addressing a long letter to Horthy on 19 August. This explained that he could not travel to Hungary for fear of being recognized; the resultant publicity, he argued, 'might make the the work of order-loving elements in Germany more difficult'. He assured the Regent that Bauer enjoyed his complete confidence. For the rest, the letter merely restated Ludendorff's primitive political credo, affirming his 'warm sympathy' for Hungary and his belief in unified action against 'the red peril of the East.' He insisted that there was no danger of the Bavarians stepping out of line: 'I trust that they make German and not Bavarian politics'. And he declared his 'fervent desire also to support the "white" Russian organizations'. But he warned that armaments and money were required: in both regards, he suggested, 'Hungary may come to the rescue'.[59]

As Ludendorff's letter shows, the White International was dangerously dependent on the Hungarians, the one full-fledged government to give them support. The Bavarians, after all, represented only a province. And Biskupski in reality spoke only for himself and a few like-minded cronies. But in the course of the summer it became apparent that, in spite of the goodwill manifested towards them by Horthy and his friends, the conspirators could expect only limited material help from Hungary. While Horthy's commitment to the aims of the International is not open to doubt, he appears to have understood that all his purported 'allies' put together did not amount to very much, either politically or militarily. Increasingly, he seems to have run the White International less as the driving locomotive of his policy than as an auxiliary engine chugging along slowly on a side track to be used only in an emergency.

The Hungarian Government's reluctance to commit itself to the conspiracy was heightened by the failure of Bauer and his friends to keep their presence in Budapest secret. Prónay complains of Bauer's appearing around town in uniform, as a result of which 'the many spies in the city discovered him and the foreign Jewish press wrote about his plans'.[60] As early as 26 May, *The Times* reported that Bauer was in Budapest and 'engaged in reactionary intrigues'. Other papers printed similar reports, and on 4 June the Budapest newspaper *Szózat* confirmed that not only Bauer but also Stephani and Trebitsch were in the city. These press allegations stirred the British and other governments into action, and as a result of diplomatic pressure the Hungarians persuaded Bauer to withdraw temporarily from Budapest to the country estate of a hospitable right-wing nobleman.[61]

The faintheartedness of the Hungarian Government was perhaps the single most important reason for the eventual dissolution of the White International, but there were many others. In Russia the tide in the civil war began to turn; the value of the White Russian generals as potential allies was correspondingly reduced. There were quarrels among the conspirators both about tactics and about ultimate aims. General Krauss, for example, wanted Austria to be united in a greater Germany — but this was unacceptable to the Hungarians, who did not relish the prospect of such a super-power on their doorstep. The territorial dispute between Austria and Hungary over the border area known as the Burgenland rendered cooperation between the two groups of embittered nationalists even more difficult. In Germany the Social Democrats and their allies lost ground in the elections of June 1920, and in Austria too the political pendulum was swinging to the right. As a result, conservative elements who in other circumstances might have supported the extreme right began instead to reconcile themselves to working within the new republican institutions. In mid-August, Czechoslovakia, Yugoslavia, and Roumania, the three countries most directly menaced by Hungarian irredentism, formed a defensive alliance known as the 'Little Entente'. It soon became apparent that this arrangement enjoyed French protection. By the early autumn of 1920, therefore, both internal and international developments in central and eastern Europe were turning against the conspirators. The White International, still only half-formed, had had its day.

CHAPTER 11

Plots for Sale

In early September 1920 Trebitsch abruptly withdrew from the White International. To ascribe his exit to an appreciation of the absurd unrealism of the whole concept, or to an understanding of the powerful forces now moving against it, would probably be to credit him with too much insight. But Trebitsch does seem to have possessed some sort of rudimentary and instinctive political weathervane, and it may be that he began to discern the change in the wind by the end of the summer. His letter to Bauer concerning Ludendorff's failure to come to Budapest, as well as the arguments about the Bavarians, had already clouded his relations with the colonel. During August other irksome difficulties exacerbated Trebitsch's growing disillusionment. One problem was lack of money. A series of delays and technical hitches had prevented the initiation of the scheme for manufacturing 'Duma rouble' banknotes.[1] The limited resources available from the Hungarian Government became a bone of contention among the conspirators. Both Trebitsch and Bauer were at this time feeling the financial pinch; Trebitsch's natural response was (as on previous occasions) to blame his collaborators — and to seek other sources of pecuniary assistance.

Beyond the political and financial motives for Trebitsch's withdrawal, however, lay a more immediate personal one. By late August 1920 Trebitsch had begun to recognize some of his political allies for what they were — gangsters and killers. Even worse, he suddenly found good reason to fear that he himself might fall victim to their murderous attentions. The most reliable account of the incident which precipitated Trebitsch's panic is probably that given by Bauer's secretary, Luise Engeler, in her unpublished memoirs. She places the episode in Budapest; she does not date it, but from its position in her narrative it would appear to have occurred in the first half of August. At that time Captain Ehrhardt was visiting Budapest, and (as she relates it) one day he received a letter from

Major Stephani. Stephani wrote that Trebitsch was still in Budapest, and he advised Ehrhardt to see to it that this 'scoundrel' was eliminated; otherwise they would never be rid of him. The fact that Trebitsch was a Jew, Stephani added, rendered the matter easy to execute in Budapest (where the White Terror had not yet abated). Ehrhardt is said to have handed this letter, unsealed, to Trebitsch for him to pass on to Bauer — thus enabling Trebitsch to read his own death warrant.*[2]

Naturally shocked by this discovery, Trebitsch confronted Bauer, who reassured him that he would never allow his collaborator to suffer such a fate. A furious row ensued, in the course of which Trebitsch accused Bauer of being in league with his would-be murderers. Eventually the two men patched up an uneasy peace and continued their joint activities. But Trebitsch, it seems, was merely looking for a convenient opportunity to break off the relationship. The moment came in early September, when Trebitsch was staying at a hotel in Vienna, while Bauer returned to Budapest for another rendezvous with Biskupski. Luise Engeler, who was staying at the same hotel, reports that at first she paid little attention to Trebitsch, who seemed to be absent from the hotel most of the time. But one day the chambermaid came with a message that 'Dr Lehotzky' was asking for her. On going to his room, she found Trebitsch in bed with a high fever, moaning that he had been poisoned. Fräulein Engeler expressed some scepticism, but Trebitsch said that he had been at a 'French social occasion' the previous day, and that he must have been poisoned there; he added that the doctor had been to see him and had confirmed that he had indeed been poisoned.[4]

After a few days Trebitsch appeared to get better, but one morning, just before Bauer's return from Budapest, the hotel porter informed her that 'Dr Lehotzky' had left very early that day without giving any forwarding address. When Bauer arrived back from Vienna he was greatly upset by this news. His disappointment in his friend was magnified into a sense of betrayal and dread when he realized that Trebitsch had not gone empty-handed. According to Fräulein Engeler, it had been their practice, when the three went off on their travels, for Bauer and his secretary to carry only light hand-cases, whereas Trebitsch took with him a capacious suitcase. For this reason, Bauer had entrusted to Trebitsch, for packing in his case, virtually his entire archive of secret documents relating to the White International. Among them were records of the negotiations among the Hungarians, Germans, and White Russians, as well as other

* There exist two other versions of this curious episode — by Prónay and by Trebitsch himself.[3] While they differ at various points, all three agree that Stephani wrote a letter advocating Trebitsch's murder, and that Trebitsch found out about it.

valuable (and, in the wrong hands, potentially dangerous) papers. All these had now disappeared, as had a number of books belonging to Bauer, among them one of his most prized possessions, a copy of Ludendorff's war memoirs autographed by the author.[5]

Bauer was so alarmed by Trebitsch's precipitate departure with these incriminating materials that he went straight back to Budapest to enlist the help of Prónay and Gömbös in recapturing the fugitive. Prónay assigned two of his most trusted officers, György Giczey and Rezsó Faber, 'to try to bring this notorious criminal back'.[6] Giczey was certainly well qualified for such a mission: only a few weeks earlier he had invited Luise Engeler out to a celebratory dinner, remarking that he had an excellent appetite that evening as he had spent the afternoon roasting a Jew alive in a railway locomotive.[7] The two Hungarians succeeded in tracking Trebitsch down at the Archduke Charles Hotel in Vienna. They shrank from killing him on the soil of the Austrian republic, but invited him to accompany them back to Budapest, where it would be possible to dispose of him without any awkward legal consequences. (Or it may be that their instructions precluded Trebitsch's murder until he had disclosed the whereabouts of the stolen documents.) But Trebitsch must have relished Giczey's society somewhat less than did Fräulein Engeler, for he declined the invitation, saying that he was quite comfortable where he was. The two officers returned to Budapest emptyhanded.[8]

Trebitsch meanwhile took immediate measures to safeguard his security, both physical and financial. On 16 September he moved to another hotel, the Kaiserhof, where he stayed for the next month, registered under the name of 'Dr Johann Lange'. On the same date the Hungarian Legation in Vienna issued him with a travel document in the name of 'Thomas Lorincz'.[9] Possibly fearing lest the Legation officials might have recognized him, Trebitsch did not adopt his new identity at this stage, but kept the document for later use. With the flow of cash from the Hungarian Government now dried up, Trebitsch was, of course, in need of funds. He therefore set about trying to find a receiver for his hoard of stolen papers. His first call was on the military attaché of the French embassy in Vienna. He demanded a high price for the documents and was paid 50,000 Czech crowns on account while the matter was referred to Paris for a decision. But after a while Trebitsch became impatient (he may also have been frightened by the alleged 'poisoning' incident), and he broke off relations with the French.[10]

Trebitsch's second approach was to the British. As he had shown earlier in his career, he believed that, in the matter of sale of intelligence information, the best results could be obtained by negotiating with more than one potential buyer. On 21 September he called at the British embassy in Vienna, where he was received by the chargé d'affaires, Reginald Bridgeman. Trebitsch did not immediately broach the matter of the documents, apparently wishing to test the water first. He asked the diplomat to forward to the Home Secretary in London a petition expressing Trebitsch's 'readiness to make amendments [*sic*] for all his wrongs and mistakes if His Majesty's Government would extend [a] forgiving hand towards him'. Trebitsch admitted that while in Parkhurst Prison he had harboured 'vehement and vindictive feelings' towards Britain and a desire for revenge. He claimed, however, that it had only been the 'unjust action of Admiral Hall' that had driven him to behave as he did. Trebitsch declared that he was now 'leader of a very powerful political and military combination', adding: 'We are today on [the] eve of a big action on a much larger scale than [the] Kapp Putsch, but before I press [the] button and inaugurate in France [*sic*] a new period of bloodshed, I ask (the) British Government whether it is not possible to forgive and to forget.' Bridgeman refused to forward the petition without instructions from London; but he promised to cable the Foreign Office that day.[11]

Bridgeman's cable, of which a copy was sent also to the British embassy in Berlin, stirred up a hornet's nest in both Whitehall and the Wilhelmstrasse. Trebitsch's claim that he was the leader of the White International was treated with derision by the Director of Intelligence at Scotland Yard, Sir Basil Thomson, who commented that it was 'quite in accordance with the empty threats he is in the habit of using'.[12] Lord Kilmarnock, however, who had already made the mistake once of under-estimating Trebitsch's capacity for nuisance-mongering, took the matter a little more seriously, and discussed it with a senior official of the German Foreign Ministry. The official reassured him that, while the monarchist movement in Bavaria was 'chronic and serious', there was no expectation of imminent trouble.[13] Meanwhile in London the Home Secretary refused to entertain any petition from Trebitsch.[14] This reply was telegraphed to Bridgeman on 24 September, and what amounted to an official rebuke was administered to the diplomat. 'It would have been better if you had declined to receive this scoundrel and traitor and you should do so in future.'[15] Yet again the British Government tried to deal with Trebitsch by putting him out of sight and mind; but not for the first (or last) time he was to demonstrate that he could not be disposed of so simply.

Having failed to sell his documents to the French, and having merely aroused renewed hostility in the British, Trebitsch turned next to the Czechs. Of all the countries of central and eastern Europe, the new Czechoslovak state felt the most threatened by Hungarian (and Austrian) revisionism. It was this fear that had led the Czech Foreign Minister, Beneš, to take the leading part in the construction of the Little Entente in June 1920. The objectives of the White International clearly included the dismemberment of Czechoslovakia. As the foremost intended victims of the conspiracy, the Czechs were naturally interested in acquiring information which might help them to thwart it. They therefore welcomed Trebitsch's approach and expressed a readiness to consider what he had to offer.

In mid-October Trebitsch travelled from Vienna to Prague. He took with him a niece, Margaret, who came from Budapest 'at his express desire' to assist him in his work.[16] In the Czech capital he established contact with Jan Hajšman, a senior official in the propaganda department of the Interior Ministry. Within a short time of Trebitsch's arrival, a deal was struck. Trebitsch undertook to hand over virtually the entire archive of stolen documents on the White International; to this he added some papers of his own, as well as a long memorandum, specially prepared by himself, containing a commentary on the documents, a narrative history of the extreme-right movements in central Europe, and some unflattering remarks on the personal characteristics of his former fellow-conspirators. In return the Czechoslovak Government promised to pay him 200,000 Czech crowns immediately, and an additional 300,000 once they had had an opportunity to examine the documents and satisfy themselves as to their authenticity.[17] (The total of 500,000 crowns was then worth about £1,667 — equivalent to at least £25,000 in 1988 purchasing power.) On 23 October the exchange was effected: in return for about fifty documents, Trebitsch was handed a down payment of 200,000 crowns. The next day Hajšman issued Trebitsch with a special identity document in the name 'Thomas Lamprecht'. (Trebitsch's wife explains that he tended to select aliases with the initials 'T.L.' because his linen was marked with those letters.[18]) The document certified that 'Herr Lamprecht' had been 'invited to Prague on important official business'.[19] Thus armed with yet another identity and with a large sum in cash (plus the expectation of an even greater amount in the near future), Trebitsch could afford a generous gesture.

Drawing on his new-found fortune, he cabled £200 to London for the credit of his wife. He also sent her a telegram with a message, as from 'Mr Lamprecht', urging he to 'come as soon as possible with all boys to Prague'.[20] What induced in him this sudden access of family spirit we do not know. He had not lived with his wife since his rushed escape from Britain in early 1915; and, as we have seen, he had enjoyed intimate relations with several other women in the intervening period. Perhaps he dreamt of establishing at last a normal domestic life in a new environment; for at about the same time he approached American officials with an inquiry as to whether he would be allowed to enter the United States. He furnished the

Americans with a copy of his memorandum on the 'White International' and appears to have expected to receive a visa in return, for his mother in Budapest received a telegram from him announcing that he planned to leave for America within a few days.[21] His wife, who was still living in London in miserable circumstances, made the great mistake of risking a reunification. Towards the end of November Trebitsch was joined in Prague by Margaret and their sons. But hardly had they arrived when (for reasons quite beyond his control) Trebitsch's affairs once again began to go awry.

The Czechoslovak Government had had two objects in mind when they purchased Trebitsch's documents: the first was propagandistic (hence the role of Hajšman); the second, diplomatic. They had hoped to use Trebitsch's archive as the basis for a great publicity campaign designed to persuade international public opinion of the reality of the menace posed by the White International. At the same time they intended to utilise this proof of the reactionary threat as a cement to bind together the Little Entente and to solidify the support of their big-power patrons, the French and British. But both these aims encountered initial obstacles. Hajšman's propaganda office launched its campaign with great vigour: the story of the White International, together with the substantiating documentation, was offered to a dozen European newspapers. In almost every case the offer was rejected — probably because of suspicions that the fantastic tale was a factitious effort by the Czechs to profit from the spectre of a revisionist upsurge. Even Czech newspapers which supported the government were reported to have rejected the report (perhaps not surprising in a country whose founder-president, Thomas Masaryk, had first gained fame as a historian and statesman by the exposure of forged documents alleging an anti-Austrian conspiracy).[22] The only newspaper to print the report was an obscure Russian émigré daily in Prague, *Volia Rossii*, whence it was picked up by the Berlin Russian paper, *Rul'**, and a few other papers.[23] The publicity effort was thus a dismal flop.

The Czech diplomatic offensive was, if anything, an even greater fiasco. The Czechs placed Trebitsch's revelations (though not the actual documents) before the standing Conference of Ambassadors of the great powers in Paris. But the response of the British Ambassador, Lord Derby, was merely to pooh-pooh the whole affair, and

* *Rul'*, a 'non-party' paper edited by the Kadet V.D. Nabokov, had little sympathy with the intrigues of extremists such as Biskupski. Hence its readiness to publish the report. Biskupski was enraged by the exposure of his part in the conspiracy, and wrote a furious letter to the editor, declaring categorically that he knew nothing about any monarchist conspiracy, and asserting that the source must be either ignorant or 'an international provocateur'.[24]

to suggest to the Czechoslovak Government 'that the manoeuvres of this man should in no way alarm it'.[25]

Far from reassured, the Czechs resolved to persuade the British directly of the seriousness of their concern. The Czechoslovak Foreign Ministry passed on a copy of Trebitsch's accompanying memorandum to the British Minister in Prague, Sir George Clerk. Once again, however, they did not forward the documents themselves.* The envoy reported to London that he found it 'not surprising that the Czecho-Slovak Government were alarmed when they read this paper', given the 'direct menace to Czecho-Slovakia disclosed in the report.' Clerk added his own evaluation of its accuracy: 'After making all allowance for the unreliability of a confessed traitor, I should still be inclined to accept the report as an historical document of great value, since it is scarcely likely that Lincoln would have invented the whole of this connected narrative, which abounds in details that can be controlled.' With some insight Clerk commented: 'I feel that Lincoln's desertion of the cause for which he was working is somewhat weakly explained, and I should infer that something had happened in Hungary for which he meant to have his revenge. But even admitting exaggeration, the case against Admiral Horthy remains pretty black.'[26]

A fortnight later, Clerk passed the copy of Trebitsch's memorandum to the newly-arrived military attaché at the British Legation in Prague, and invited him to prepare an analysis of the document as he was 'specially qualified [presumably through experience in British intelligence] to judge of its accuracy.' The attaché, Colonel Sir T. Cunninghame, wrote a lengthy analysis within twenty-four hours of taking up his position. He shared the Minister's view that the report had to be taken seriously.

> I am of opinion that it is one that cannot be neglected, and that immediate action to prevent any further spread of mischief in Austria is imperative.... The whole plot — assuming that it is genuine — is fantastic in design, and little likely to succeed in its entirety, but that does not guarantee the state of Austria from a partial attempt of an embarrassing character at a critical time ... For the first time we have now in our hands the thread which

* But the British intelligence service may have obtained copies of some of the documents by other means. R.H. Bruce Lockhart, at that time serving at the British Legation in Prague, recalls (in his *Retreat from Glory*, New York 1934, p. 93): 'One of our intelligence officers ... called at Trebitsch's hotel. It was a cat-burglar call, carried out at considerable personal risk and during Trebitsch's absence. It consisted in a crawl along a third-floor ledge from a room specially hired to Trebitsch's quarters. The fruit of this unofficial visit was a series of documents revealing the ex-MP as a sworn enemy of the British empire and as an arch-plotter against the peace of Europe.'

> binds together certain isolated actions, whose common motive has previously been difficult to grasp. The report in this respect is remarkably circumstantial, and nobody could have written it, or concocted it — if that should prove to be the correct expression — without the most intimate acquaintance with the under currents of political action in the countries dealt with. The persons who are referred to fall naturally into their place, and there is no marked inconsistency in the narrative or anything in contradiction to known facts . . .

A detailed critique of specific points in Trebitsch's commentary followed: on some there was known to be corroborating evidence from other sources; in others the attaché cast doubt on Trebitsch's claims. He concluded:

> Thus as regards the genuineness of the report, judgement must be suspended until the whole matter can be thoroughly investigated, and the trail of the conspirators followed by the indications given by Mr Lincoln himself . . . It is not safe to conclude that there is no truth in the supposed plot or no danger of internal strife with or without it.

Although inclined to hedge his bets, Cunninghame evidently felt the whole matter merited speedy preventive measures to forestall any conspiracy. Clerk forwarded Cunninghame's report to London, mentioning in his attached letter that he intended to discuss the question the next day with the Czechoslovak president, Masaryk, 'who knows that Trebitsch Lincoln's confession has been given to me'.[27]

The reactions of both Clerk and Cunninghame as well as the involvement of the president of the republic, suggest that neither the Czechs nor the British Legation in Prague were (at first) inclined to regard Trebitsch's disclosures as false, his documents as forged, or his allegations of an international conspiracy as concoctions. Why then did the Czechs fail in their attempt to make diplomatic capital out of the unmasking of the White International?

The explanation can be found in the reaction of the Foreign Office in London. Trebitsch's reputation in Whitehall was not, of course, very high at this time. The Director of Intelligence had sneered at his 'empty threats' just a few weeks earlier. The Home Secretary had refused to entertain his petition for a pardon. And the Foreign Office had scoffed at his warnings of a second Kapp putsch. The dispatches from Clerk and Cunninghame were therefore read in London against a background of extreme scepticism about Trebitsch's claims and scorn for his person. The reaction was, indeed, predictable. Official after official read Trebitsch's memorandum and denounced it as a confection of untruths. One minuted: 'It is obviously impossible to believe a word that this man says, and I much doubt whether the paper is worth the time and trouble of translating.'[28] Perhaps the most damning indictment came from the head of the Foreign Office, Sir Eyre Crowe, whose antagonism to Trebitsch (dating back to Mr Lincoln MP's visit to Hungary in 1910) was of a mature and robust vintage. On 5 December 1920 Crowe wrote:

> I think this report is unmitigated rubbish and I am surprised that either Sir G. Clerk or the Czecho-Slovak government should attach to it any importance whatever. It reads like a tissue of inventions. The political 'plot' which it purports to reveal, is the invention of a fool: A Prusso-Bavarian army, supported by Russian reactionary forces, is to invade and conquer Austria, join with Hungary, and then with the support of Italy — who would as a reward receive Savoy with Nice, Corsica, Malta, Tunis *and* Trieste (sic) — declare war against the Entente. . . . I do not think the paper is worth translating. It might be circulated to the D[irector of] M[ilitary] I[ntelligence] and to Sir Basil Thomson who may be able to pick out a few crumbs of information.[29]

Nor was the Foreign Office any more convinced by the arguments presented in Cunninghame's analysis which reached London a few days later. On 13 December Alexander Cadogan minuted:

> Although Sir T. Cunninghame professes to find threads of truth running through Lincoln's story, he does not indicate them very clearly. Lincoln is a plausible rogue and has no doubt gained the confidence of persons connected with the backstairs politics of Central Europe. He has picked up enough to enable one of his ingenuity to piece together a story not demonstrably untrue. But the source is obviously so tainted as to be almost worthless.[30]

This last comment points to the sad paradox of Trebitsch's position. He had hoped to reestablish his credentials with the Entente powers by retailing to them information which he knew to be true and documents he felt he could show were genuine. But instead of the true information and genuine documents commending his character to the Entente governments, the reverse happened: his notorious personal reputation led the British (and French) and eventually also the Czechoslovak Governments to disbelieve everything he told them. The episode forms, indeed, an interesting case study in the genesis of a bureaucratic conventional wisdom.

A striking illustration of this is a further contribution to the debate by Cunninghame a few weeks after his initial comment. In his second memorandum he announced that he had been led to 'modify' his original opinion: although he still felt that Trebitsch's report proved the existence of 'a common impulse and central organising power for the counter-revolutionary associations of Bavaria, Austria, and Hungary', he too had decided that Trebitsch's known untrustworthiness cast doubt on the reliability of his information: 'The fact that Trebitsch Lincoln has received money for his disclosures from the French proves that his object is venal, and that no confidence can be placed in his word, that he concocted a saleable story and placed it where it found the best market'. Cunninghame adhered to his opinion that some of Trebitsch's allegations were true, but he now believed: 'It would be a pity if the growing hope of better relations between the states of Central Europe were endangered by the palpable misstatements of a swindler.[31]

Thus the Czechs, like Trebitsch himself, found that their supposed evidence backfired damagingly: far from convincing the British of their allegations, the 'tainted source' served only to cast doubt on the whole notion of a right-wing international conspiracy. In these circumstances the Czechs' connexion with Trebitsch was transformed from an asset to a liability. The 'tainted source', by a process of progressive contamination, was discrediting rather than verifying their claims. Trebitsch was in consequence struck from the Czechs' payroll. His applications for the 300,000 crowns still due to him as the residue of his payment were rejected by the Czechoslovak Government on the ground that, upon examination, the documens he had sold them had been proved to be forgeries.[32]

Perhaps the Czechs really believed this to be the case. Or perhaps they decided that this would be the best way to get rid of Trebitsch, who by now had become an embarrassment to them; if so, they, like so many other governments before and after, were to find that he could not be disposed of so simply. In any event, they repudiated Trebitsch personally and indicated that they believed his documents to be a fraud. But since they still remained vitally interested in proving the existence of the White International, they continued to make use of Trebitsch's materials in an underhand way. At the very time that they were telling Trebitsch that they placed no reliance on him or his documents, the Czechoslovak Government took renewed action, at the highest possible level, to secure maximum publicity in the world's press for the contents of Trebitsch's documents. On 17 December 1920, Sir George Clerk sent a 'secret' cable to the Foreign Office reporting that President Masaryk had given 'copies of the Trebitsch Lincoln papers' to a correspondent of the *Petit Parisien* and to Dr R.W. Seton-Watson 'to use as they may think fit'.[33] The renewed involvement of Masaryk suggests that the Czechoslovak Government, while wishing to avoid responsibility for proving the accuracy of Trebitsch's allegations, nevertheless remained determined to reap some propaganda advantage from the affair.

On this occasion, however, the Czechs chose their channel of communication with greater discrimination than before. Seton-Watson was the foremost British authority of the time on the history and politics of central and south-eastern Europe. A champion of Czechoslovak independence and a man of irreproachable integrity, he had often acted as Masaryk's main conduit to British public opinion. On 28 December *The Times* began publication of a three-part series of articles headed 'European Plot Divulged'. The series appeared in a very prominent position on the editorial page. No source or author was named, but there appeared an editorial note at the beginning; 'The record will show that it was written by one closely connected with every phase of the movement.' There followed long extracts from Trebitsch's memorandum and from the stolen documents concerning the White International. Although some connecting material had been added, as well as a few derogatory remarks about Trebitsch, the articles were essentially a condensation of everything that he had sold the Czechs.* The next day *Le Matin* in Paris printed long extracts from *The Times*'s first article, and over the following days the story was printed in a large number of newspapers throughout the world.

At one level this was Trebitsch's dream come true. He had always loved newspaper publicity. With the sudden success of the Czech propaganda campaign he now achieved international fame. Indeed, the screaming headlines and long articles in the world press in December 1920 and January 1921 marked a turning-point in Trebitsch's public life. Hitherto he had gained notoriety — thanks to his conduct during the war and his participation in the Kapp putsch — as a colourful but treacherous adventurer. From early 1921 onwards, thanks to the prominence given by the press (drawing on the materials originally supplied to the Czechs by Trebitsch himself) to his role in the White International, the name of Trebitsch Lincoln entered the realm of legend. For a generation he became a bogeyman, useful alike to right and left: the connexion in his life between reality and myth (which had always been tenuous) snapped; and in the hands of propagandists, particularly in Germany in the 1920s and 1930s, his reputation as a sinister influence in the shadows of inter-

* The motives of *The Times* in printing the story and giving it such prominence are uncertain. Neither its own archives nor the private papers of Dr Seton-Watson (both of which have been consulted) shed any light on this. Perhaps we need look no further than the paper's sagging circulation (114,000 in December 1920) and the fact that its proprietor, Lord Northcliffe, was at this time slowly going mad. The complete text of Trebitsch's memorandum as well as details of some of the documents he had stolen from Bauer were published in the French political weekly *L'Europe nouvelle* (with which Seton-Watson was closely connected) on 9, 16 and 23 April 1921.

national political intrigue soared aloft and acquired a self-perpetuating momentum.

All this might have served as grist to the mill of Trebitsch's massive egotism were it not for certain disagreeable features of this burst of publicity. *The Times* reports, while gratifying Trebitsch's vanity by according him a prominent role in the White International, insulted his dignity by printing a number of disobliging comments on his character. An editorial comment in the paper on 28 December expressed astonishment at the willingness of Prussian officers to accept a person such as Trebitsch into their embrace, but suggested that 'conspiracy, like poverty, makes strange bed-fellows'. In its description, on 30 December, of the quarrel between Bauer and Trebitsch concerning Ludendorff's non-appearance in Budapest, *The Times*, instead of depicting the incident as high political drama (as Trebitsch himself undoubtedly saw it), termed it a 'fit of violence' that 'must be taken, for the time being, as a lovers' quarrel'. (Perhaps the intention was to insinuate that there had been a homosexual element in the Bauer-Trebitsch relationship; if so, no evidence has come to light directly supporting such an allegation.)

Others were less oblique in their abusive attacks. Count Reventlow seized the opportunity to renew his vendetta, denouncing Trebitsch once more as an English *agent provocateur* — a charge echoed at the opposite end of the political spectrum by the German communist paper *Die Rote Fahne*.[34] The radical London weekly *The Nation* jeered that if Ludendorff and Bauer had given Trebitsch so much as an hour of their time that in itself showed they were not to be taken seriously as conspirators.[35] Most damagingly, reports began to appear in January 1921 alleging that the documents used by *The Times* were merely fabrications manufactured by Trebitsch himself.[36] All this was not the type of fame Trebitsch had sought — especially at a time when he was still trying to procure the remaining 300,000 crowns from the Czechoslovak Government.

Shortly after the reunification of his family in Prague, Trebitsch, sensing that the Czech capital no longer offered him a hospitable environment, decamped. In mid-December he surfaced in Vienna.[37] There he offered secret documents for sale to the Japanese minister and to a Bolshevik agent. He also called on the American Embassy. Over the next few weeks the Americans pumped him for information and documents; in return he received sympathy and perhaps some money — but no visa.[38] The American Minister subsequently told his British colleague that Trebitsch 'appeared to be a coward and in fear of his life'.[39]

Trebitsch had solid ground for his apprehensions. During the previous weeks his former comrades of the White International, now his bitter enemies, had not been inactive. Bauer, in particular, nursed harsh feelings of betrayal and vengefulness. Already in November painful letters were exchanged between Bauer and Reventlow in which the colonel had been obliged to admit his error in regard to Trebitsch. In an effort to minimise the embarrassment, Bauer informed Reventlow on 23 November that Trebitsch had not received any secret papers from him (Bauer), though he might have appropriated some documents in Budapest.[40] But this attempt to conceal his own stupidity boomeranged against Bauer himself as, with the publication of further details of the conspiracy, it became evident to all his right-wing collaborators that Trebitsch could only have obtained his archive of documents from Bauer. From his hiding-place near Munich, Bauer spent the month of December writing one draft after another of a tangled and self-contradictory statement trying to explain away his connexion with Trebitsch, his role in the White International, and his contacts with the extreme left before and during the Kapp putsch. Trebitsch's revelation of these contacts was, from the point of view of Bauer's more recent political company, the unkindest cut of all.[41]

Bauer's reply, which appeared in the form of a newspaper interview, was published in the Budapest daily *Szózat* on 28 December 1920. But hardly had Bauer, as he thought, rebutted Trebitsch's 'slander' when the *Times* articles inaugurated a much greater wave of unwelcome publicity. On 4 January Bauer issued another statement, complaining bitterly of attacks on him in both the left-wing and the rightist press. He admitted that his previous association with Trebitsch had been a 'Dummheit', but he again denied that he had given Trebitsch any documents, asserting that he would not have done so even if he had had any to give.[42]

The failure of the Czechs to pay Trebitsch the residue of his honorarium, coupled with the vindictive outrage expressed in public by his former collaborator, induced a rapid change in his mood. In late November, at the time of his family's arrival, he had, to all appearances, been on top of the world, looking forward to a further 300,000 crowns and a new life in America. By the end of the year this euphoria was transformed into virtual panic. The Czechs would not pay; the Americans refused a visa; and there was every likelihood that the murder gangs of the extreme right would be out for his blood.

Yet Trebitsch, like a hunted animal, was often at his most dangerous when cornered. In early January he engaged a lawyer in Vienna to press his claim against the Czechoslovak Government. On 12 January the lawyer, Dr Alexander Fuchs, addressed a stern letter to the Czech Minister in Vienna complaining that his client's residual fee of 300,000 crowns had not yet been paid and demanding a further 30,000 to cover Trebitsch's expenses. Fuchs warned the

Czechs: 'My client will not wait any longer, and he will not consent to lose 330,000 Czech crowns, but will, if payment is not made voluntarily, take all steps at his disposal to settle his claim without regard for any international consequences that might result therefrom'.[43] On 20 January Fuchs wrote to the Czechoslovak Foreign Minister, Beneš, again demanding 330,000 crowns, and declaring that if payment were not made within seven days he would seek redress for his client in court.[44] But the Czechs refused even to acknowledge these communications.

While Trebitsch thus sought to mobilize the resources of the law to obtain redress from the Czechs, he understood that legal processes could afford him scant protection against the danger of revenge from his former fellow-conspirators. He knew their murderous propensities, and realized that, with all his secrets already revealed to the world, the fear of disclosure would no longer deter his enemies. The shield that had protected him against Giczey and Faber when they had traced him to Vienna the previous autumn would now avail him nothing. In an effort to save himself Trebitsch changed his identity (making use at last of his document in the name 'Thomas Lorincz'), and moved with his family from hotel to hotel in Vienna.[45] At the same time he tried to head off any pursuers by spreading a rumour to the effect that he was already dead.

On 9 February 1921, Karl von Wiegand's secretary wrote to the Hearst correspondent from Berlin with the news that Major von Stephani had called: 'He wanted to warn you against Mrs Lenkeit. She came to him and told him of the supposed death of Lincoln, and how glad she would be if it was true. But Major St. is under the impression, he says, that she knows more of it and that she may be hiding him at Trebbin. Major St. says he did not value her acquaintance and would like to have nothing whatever to do with her.'[46] In a letter to Bauer at about the same time Stephani noted: 'About L's death nothing certain could be ascertained. One day la Lenkeit appeared and wanted to get information out of me, lied etc. Could it not be possible that L. is still alive and still in touch with the pretty lady?'.[47]

Stephani was plainly not convinced by the report of Trebitsch's demise; since he, after all, had been the originator of the threat to Trebitsch, the manoeuvre obviously failed of its central purpose. It is interesting to speculate on the significance of Mrs Lenkeit's sudden reappearance in his life (or death!). Was she consciously acting as a false witness when she appeared at Wiegand's office as a messenger of death? Was Trebitsch, so recently reunited with his wife, once again in touch with his former secretary? Or could it be that Trebitsch was trying to kill two birds with one stone? Having reemerged in the public eye he may have wished to persuade not only potential assassins but also former mistresses that he had disappeared for good. That would, after all, help avoid any awkward confrontations between former women friends and his wife. Stephani was right to suspect Mrs Lenkeit of not telling the truth. But he may well have been wrong to think that she *knew* she was telling a lie.

By the end of January Trebitsch's patience snapped. The longer he stayed in Vienna, the greater the danger to his life. But there seemed nowhere else for him to go. The Americans refused a renewed application for a visa.[48] There was a warrant out for his arrest in Germany. Hungary scarcely seemed inviting. Besides, if he left central Europe he would lose all hope of pursuing his claim against the Czechs. Trebitsch perforce remained where he was. But in an attempt to expedite his claim he made a long notarised statement recounting his relations with the Czechs; and he instructed his lawyer to issue a writ in Prague against the Czechoslovak Government demanding his money.[49]

This extraordinary action impelled the Czechs to take countermeasures against a man who was turning into a grave embarrassment for them. On 10 February 1921 a lawyer acting on behalf of the Czechoslovak Government lodged a formal complaint against Trebitsch at the Vienna police. He submitted copies of Trebitsch's lawyer's letters demanding 330,000 crowns, and, when asked what exactly he had against Trebitsch, he declared: 'Trebitsch Lincoln is a swindler!'[50] Neither the two letters nor this unsupported statement seemed to the police sufficient grounds for an immediate arrest. But the complaint was taken seriously enough for two police officers to be assigned to keep Trebitsch under surveillance.

At noon on 18 February Trebitsch was arrested at the Hotel Viktoria in Vienna. His sons Ignatius and John were present at the time of his arrest. Although registered at the hotel as 'Thomas Lorincz', Trebitsch immediately acknowledged his real identity.[51] A police search of his quarters at the time of his arrest yielded a brown suitcase, a yellow attaché case, these containing various items of correspondence, writings, and passports, as well as a five-barrel revolver with cartridges. Among the documents seized were notebooks, address books, a diary, a memorandum by Bauer as well as a copy of Bauer's pamphlet on the Kapp putsch, legal correspondence relating to Trebitsch's suit against the Czechoslovak Government, copies of three letters to the American Secretary of State concerning Trebitsch's application for entry to the USA, a large number of identity documents in different names, issued by the authorities of various countries, and (predictably) two packages of newspaper cuttings.[52] At the police station Trebitsch made a long statement, recounting his life history, his participation in the White

International, and his dispute with the Czechs.[53] He was then remanded in custody pending further inquiries.

There followed one of the strangest political trials in judicial history.[54] On 1 March Trebitsch appeared before Investigating Judge Ramsauer in the provincial court. He was charged with fraud and the court was notified that a further charge might be laid against him of high treason. The proceedings extended for more than two months. By contrast with his treatment at his trial in London in 1916, Trebitsch was granted a wide degree of latitude by the court, and he took full advantage of the opportunity thus offered. The bulk of the proceedings consisted of an almost endless monologue by Trebitsch. His evidence took up a full eighteen days of court hearings, spread out through March and April. On trial for his life (if the charge of high treason were made to stick), Trebitsch nevertheless seems to have enjoyed the proceedings. He was, after all, safe from the danger of a knife in his back. He was again the centre of attention. He could indulge to the full his taste for public speaking. And he was given free rein to talk about his favourite subject — himself.

Trebitsch's testimony began with a narrative of his early life, his election to parliament, his oil dealings in eastern Europe, and his visit to Rotterdam in December 1914. The latter he explained as a purely business journey with no political objectives. But on his return to London he had been called to the Admiralty for questioning. Falsely suspected by the British authorities, he had made his escape to America. He described his trial in London, claiming that he had been framed by the Admiralty for political reasons. He denied that he had been guilty on that occasion, and he pointed out that the fraud of which he had been wrongly accused in 1916 was in any case quite a different matter from his alleged forgery of political documents in the present case. The bulk of Trebitsch's testimony, however, consisted of a detailed account of his activities in German and European politics since his arrival at Rotterdam in August 1919. By and large it was an accurate description, although heavily larded with self-glorification and self-justification. On one or two points Trebitsch was caught out in a lie. For example, in recalling his visits to the Netherlands in the autumn of 1919, he asserted that he had been received in person by the German crown prince. This was roundly denied in a written submission sent to the court by 'authorised persons close to the Crown Prince' who insisted that Trebitsch had merely been met at the Wieringen railway station by the prince's adjutants and, after a brief conversation, sent packing. But Trebitsch stuck by his story and even added some picturesque details, such as a glass of madeira allegedly served to him at the Wieringen vicarage. (For good measure Trebitsch also claimed to have been received by the Dutch prince consort.) Although the point was in itself small, its rebuttal might have damaged Trebitsch's credibility in other matters and thus harmed his case. But fortunately for him the crown prince's own reputation was such that the court does not seem to have been swayed against Trebitsch by the denial.

The central issue facing the court was, of course, the status of the documents sold by Trebitsch to the Czechs. Were they or were they not forged? In its consideration of this question the court was hamstrung by its inability to call as witnesses many of the key persons involved. The Hungarian conspirators, of course, would not come from Budapest. Representatives of the French embassy in Vienna refused to give evidence concerning Trebitsch's relations with the French government. The Czechs, who had themselves lodged the complaint against Trebitsch, did not appear to give evidence in court. Indeed, apart from Trebitsch, only two other witnesses were called. The first was a representative of Bauer (at the time in hiding in Munich) who stated that the colonel denied ever having given Trebitsch documents. He also said that Major Stephani would come later to give evidence to the court — but Stephani never arrived. The other witness was General Krauss, whose testimony in large measure confirmed Trebitsch's claim that he had met him with Bauer — though Krauss strenuously denied any suggestion that he had somehow been involved in the conspiracy.

But the chief difficulty facing the court was not so much an absence of witnesses as the refusal of the Czechoslovak Government to hand over to the court as exhibits the documents sold to them by Trebitsch which they alleged were forged. Without an opportunity to examine the supposed forgeries, how could the court possibly reach a considered judgement as to whether Trebitsch had manufactured them? Both Trebitsch and his lawyer vociferously protested against the Czechs' failure to submit the documents in evidence. On this point the judge sided with Trebitsch, and on 6 April the attorney for the Czechoslovak Government was ordered by the court to submit all the documents within three days. Out of the fifty or so documents passed by Trebitsch to the Czechs, they eventually released to the court only sixteen.

Was Trebitsch in fact guilty of fraud? Before recording the judicial verdict, it is perhaps appropriate for the historian to state his own opinion. He is happily in a more fortunate position than the court, having at his disposal a great wealth of documentary evidence not available to the Austrian judge in 1921.

Let us consider first Trebitsch's long memorandum, sold to the Czechs, and made available by them to the British. (A copy had also been furnished by Trebitsch to the Americans.[55]) This is the memorandum that Sir George Clerk had termed 'an historical document of great value', but which the head of the Foreign Office had dismissed as 'unmitigated rubbish'. In the light of what is known today, from sources *other* than Trebitsch himself, there can be little doubt that Sir Eyre Crowe was completely misled by his decade-old loathing for Trebitsch into a mistaken assessment of this report. The account given therein of the origins of the White International, of the role of Admiral Horthy and the highest levels of the Hungarian Government, of the involvement of Ludendorff, of the intrigues of Biskupski and his White Russian sidekicks, of the central part played by Bauer, of the organization of the German, Austrian, and Hungarian secret military associations, of the travels to and fro of Stephani. Ehrhardt, Bauer, and Trebitsch himself, of the project for the manufacture of 'Duma rouble' banknotes, of the plans for the occupation of Vienna, the destruction of Czechoslovakia, the revision of the territorial provisions of the peace treaties — everything that Crowe had brushed aside as the 'invention of a fool' — was in fact (as we have seen) *true*.

Of course, Trebitsch gilded the lily. He greatly exaggerated his own role in the whole affair. He may occasionally have claimed to have been present at meetings of which he merely heard a later account. His understandable prejudice against his would-be murderers no doubt led him to portray the actions of men such as Stephani and Prónay in particularly harsh colours. His claim to have met the crown prince was a lie, and other such untruths may have been dispersed through his complex narrative.

But all this should not blind us (as it blinded Crowe) to the essence of the matter. The White International was not an invention but a reality. However impractical, absurd, anachronistic, disunited, half-baked, and melodramatic it may seem, it was not *grand guignol* but a genuine historical phenomenon. And the account given by Trebitsch of its origins, its development, its leadership, its organization, its aims, and its methods was, broadly speaking, correct.

If Trebitsch's own memorandum may, with these minor qualifications, be accepted as authentic, what of the fifty documents that he sold to the Czechs? The very reluctance of the Czechs to submit them for examination by the court is in itself suspicious — the more so given that the Czechoslovak Government, at the very time when it was complaining that the documents were forgeries, was urging them on a reluctant world press — and through no less a personage than President Masaryk. This, however, may be set aside as suggestive but circumstantial evidence.

Let us consider the nature of the documents themselves, beginning with the sixteen turned over to the court by the Czechoslovak Government. It is a reasonable presumption that the Czechs, who were, after all, the initiators of the prosecution for fraud, turned over those among the documents which they felt were most questionable.

At the very least, we may surely assume that they would not have turned over any documents which they thought might be genuine — for such a procedure would have undermined the very prosecution case that they wished to bolster. Yet among these was one document which we know for certain was genuine. Exhibit 11b was a letter in General Krauss's handwriting, dated 18 August 1920, arranging the meeting with Bauer in Vienna a few days later. In his testimony to the court on 20 April 1921 General Krauss confirmed the genuineness of the photographic copy of that letter shown to him as exhibit 11b. It should be remembered that Krauss was a prosecution witness, and was anxious to dissociate himself in every possible way from the conspiracy. Yet he nevertheless authenticated one of the sixteen supposedly forged documents selected by the Czechs themselves in order to prove the prosecution case.

Nor is this all. Apart from the fifty documents which Trebitsch turned over to the Czechs, there was one further document, apparently stolen from Bauer, which Trebitsch did not give to Hajšman on 23 October 1920. This was a memorandum, supposedly by Bauer, entitled 'Die Neue Taktik', containing some of the colonel's strategic ideas. Trebitsch claimed that he had kept this document in reserve pending the payment of the residual 300,000 crowns due to him from the Czechs. The document was discussed in a report prepared by the Vienna police and submitted to the prosecutor's office before the trial. The police had found a copy of 'Die Neue Taktik' during their search of Trebitsch's rooms at the time of his arrest. After examining the document the police concluded that it had been forged by Trebitsch; indeed, in the absence of any of the fifty other documents retained by the Czechs, this supposed forgery constituted the main item leading to a decision to prosecute. Satisfied that 'Die Neue Taktik' was a forgery, the Vienna police maintained that it served as 'an indication that Lincoln did commit forgeries' (in the case of the other fifty documents).[56]

Yet here too we have cast-iron evidence in favour of the accused. For in the testimony submitted to the court by Bauer's representative, the colonel explicitly admitted authorship of the memorandum, denying only that he had signed it on the front. Contrary to the view formed by the Vienna police before the trial, therefore, the court proceedings themselves proved the authenticity of this document — the single most important item in the prosecution case! Again we should bear in mind that Bauer was at this time fiercely hostile to Trebitsch (as the evidence presented in his name abundantly showed). Yet he could not bring himself to deny that he had written 'Die Neue Taktik'.

All this is not to argue the authenticity of the entire contents of Trebitsch's archive. As with his evidence in court, so too with his documents Trebitsch may well have sought to improve the shining hour. Such a procedure would accord with everything that we know of his character and previous history. But for our present purposes it is beside the point. The heart of the matter is that the very evidence adduced by the Czechoslovak plaintiffs and by the Vienna police as the supposedly strongest proof of his guilt rebounded on his accusers, and in itself goes far towards proving his innocence of the first charge against him.*

Given the prosecution's destruction of its own case, it is hardly surprising that the proceedings against Trebitsch on the charge of fraud were discontinued. As to the charge of high treason, however, Trebitsch's very success in vindicating the authenticity of the documents — and by extension the reality of the conspiracy — might have led to his rapid conviction. Trebitsch's defence against this charge consisted of the rather lame argument that, by disclosing the plot in advance, he had nipped it in the bud, thus meriting not condemnation for treason but on the contrary the grateful acknowledgement of the Austrian republic which he had helped to save. The effectiveness of such a line of defence was, of course, diminished by the facts, plain from the evidence Trebitsch himself submitted, that his exit from the White International had been prompted not by concern for the fate of the republic but rather by personal differences with his fellow-plotters, and in particular by fear for his life.

Any impartial examination of the historical evidence against Trebitsch on this count must lead to the conclusion that Trebitsch was deeply implicated in a conspiracy directed against the political institutions of Austria (and of other countries as well — most notably, Czechoslovakia). Yet on this charge too the judicial decision was in Trebitsch's favour. The reasons for this are to be sought less in the facts of the case than in the surrounding political conditions. The Austrian elections of October 1920 had confirmed in office the government headed by a Christian Social Party Chancellor, Dr Michael Mayr. The evidence offered in court during Trebitsch's trial had contained indications that earlier in 1920 some members of the (right-wing) Christian Social Party had been in contact with the White International with a view to cooperation in unseating their

* The above analysis is in large measure confirmed by a document which came to light shortly before this book went to press. On 10 June 1921 the Czechoslovak Government's legal representative in Vienna wrote to Prague reporting on the case. On the question of the 200,000 crowns, paid to Trebitsch by Hajšman the previous October in return for the documents, the lawyer remarked: 'We could not very well have asked for the money back, for after all the facts which he [Trebitsch] used in his presentation were, objectively, completely true, though they may in part have been ornamented in a novelistic manner.' In a book published in 1928, Jan Hajšman himself admitted: 'The material was true, which I verified by means of several tests.'[57]

predecessors, the socialist government of Karl Renner. To have proceeded against Trebitsch with the charge of high treason would have run the risk (in the eyes of the government) of opening a Pandora's box of further unedifying revelations deeply embarrassing to the Christian Social Party.

That political as well as purely judicial considerations were responsible for the dropping of this second charge is confirmed by an Austrian Justice Ministry memorandum dated 27 May 1921. Headed 'Pro Domo', this document summarised the failure of the prosecution to establish the accusation of fraud; as to the charge of treason it expressed the view that 'reopening a movement that belongs to the past would perhaps not be desirable from the point of view of foreign policy'. A note attached at the bottom of the memorandum states that the Austrian Foreign Ministry had examined the document and agreed that proceedings against Trebitsch on both counts should be discontinued.[58]

On 6 June 1921 Trebitsch was released from the jurisdiction of the Austrian provincial court. But he was not yet set free. Instead he was transferred to the jurisdiction of the lower district court, where he was charged with having registered in Vienna under a false identity. He was found guilty on this charge and sentenced to one week's imprisonment. But since he had already spent nearly four months in gaol in Vienna, the sentence was cancelled. Even now Trebitsch was not released, but was turned over to police custody pending deportation from Austria. He was deported in late June. Before leaving he managed to speak briefly to the press. 'My destination', he said, 'is a profound secret. I shall disappear as if the earth had swallowed me and shall reappear in an unexpected quarter within eight years. Meanwhile, I shall accomplish my task.'[59]

Trebitsch was alone again and on the run — not from the police but from his former political colleagues who, he feared, would now seek an opportunity to avenge his betrayal of their cause. He went, first, to Italy, travelling once again under an assumed name. On 16 July the British Ambassador in Rome, Sir George Buchanan, cabled to the Foreign Office: 'There is reason to believe that Trebitsch Lincoln has recently been in Rome under unknown alias, and has been trying to sell his experiences, especially in England to American journalist. I am endeavouring to ascertain his movements'.[60] The reply from the Foreign Office bore the indelible stamp of Sir Eyre Crowe: 'Please do not trouble to follow the movements of this impostor and scoundrel in whom we are not interested.'[61] This time, Crowe and his colleagues must surely have thought, they were well and truly rid of the pestilential nuisance. Again they were utterly wrong.

On 26 July an intelligence report, addressed to Mr J. Edgar Hoover at the Department of Justice in Washington, warned that reports had been received that Trebitsch seemed 'very desirous of coming to the United States, but that the American missions in Europe [had] been warned to refuse him a visa'.[62] On 14 September the American mission in Budapest informed the United States Consul in Trieste that it had learnt that Trebitsch was staying in Trieste, holding six passports (three Hungarian, the others Austrian and German), and hoping to obtain an American visa. The letter added:

> This man is a notorious international political crook, a radical, and open to disseminate any propaganda if well paid. He was arrested in London during the war because of pro-German activities and lodged in the Tower of London [*sic*], from which place he escaped, supposedly to Germany. He now desires to proceed to the United States for the purpose of realizing on some royalties supposed to be due him from a book he published entitled "Revelations of a British MP" [*sic*]. With the funds realized he hopes to go to Thibet to cause uprisings of the natives against England, I am informed.[63]

Inquiries by the American consul in Trieste confirmed Trebitsch's presence in the area, masquerading as 'Thomas Longford' and 'purporting to be a British colonial'.[64]

Thanks to the alertness of these American diplomats, Trebitsch failed to secure a visa for the United States. But he went there anyway. In the autumn of 1921 he crossed the Atlantic, again with a new alias — Patrick Keelan. By now Trebitsch was a veteran of the art of shipboard socializing. In the course of the ocean crossing he befriended an American millionaire, Albert Otto. He told Otto something of his doings in central European politics, and 'said that he had been forced to fly for his life to Rome where again the vengeance of his enemies had pursued him and he was now in flight to America'. When the boat docked at its destination, Otto was said to have noticed 'with some astonishment the ease with which Patrick Keelan entered America'. Otto had evidently been deeply impressed by his shipboard acquaintance: for he agreed to provide 'Keelan' with no less than £15,000, apparently as capital to finance a business scheme.[65]

For two months after his arrival in the USA, Trebitsch was kept under surveillance by the authorities without being apprehended.[66] But on 27 January 1922 he was arrested in New York on a charge of surreptitiously entering the United States. In a effort to earn leniency from the authorities Trebitsch handed over one of his last remaining assets — Bauer's strategic essay, 'Die Neue Taktik'. But when examined by the Military Intelligence Division of the War Department the document was pronounced to be 'of little value'.[67] Released on a bail bond of $1,000 (put up by Otto), Trebitsch was eventually sent for a hearing before the Immigration Commissioner at Ellis Island.[68] Instead of being deported, however, he was permitted to make his own travel arrangements and move across the continent to leave from the west coast.[69] A subsequent British intelligence report stated that 'at this time he was reported to be more violently Anglophobe than ever.' Then, in the autumn of 1922 [the report continued] 'it was ascertained that Lincoln was in Tokyo, apparently en route for China.'[70]

CHAPTER 12

China: The First Phase

When and how Trebitsch's fascination with China was first sparked we do not know. But it is certain that his fancy had begun to play with the notion of extending his activities to the Far East long before his arrival in the region towards the end of 1922. We have already noticed that, as early as April 1910, he had betrayed in public a surprising interest in the obscure diplomacy of railway politics in northern China, when he asked two parliamentary questions on the subject.* We have also seen how, in one of his press statements while on the run in New York in January 1916, Trebitsch claimed that he had earlier visited Central Asia disguised as a Buddhist monk for

* Among Trebitsch's Darlington constituents we have briefly encountered the Backhouse family. Sir Jonathan Backhouse, Bart., a Liberal Unionist, had taken the chair in January 1910 at the eve-of-poll meeting in favour of Trebitsch's opponent, H. Pike Pease. In the summer of 1910 Backhouse's son, Edmund, returned home from China for a long visit. The odd career of the younger Backhouse in many ways uncannily prefigured that of Trebitsch. Like Trebitsch, Backhouse had been a member of the National Liberal Club, but he was expelled following a financial scandal. In China he established himself as a writer and authority on oriental affairs. But supposedly valuable manuscripts which he claimed to have discovered are now widely believed to be forgeries. His unpublished memoirs contain a scatological and largely imaginary history of his relations with the most important figures in pre-revolutionary China (including the Dowager Empress). During the First World War he worked as a sales agent for the John Brown shipbuilding company. In these and other business dealings he appears to have been guilty of ingenious frauds. Like Trebitsch, he had shadowy connexions with British intelligence organs. Like Trebitsch, he infuriated the British diplomatic establishment in China. Like Trebitsch, he later adopted oriental habits of dress. Like Trebitsch, he remained in China during the Japanese occupation, with which he was outspokenly sympathetic. For the details of his life and a masterly analysis of its twists and turns, see Hugh Trevor-Roper, *Hermit of Peking: The Hidden Life of Sir Edmund Backhouse* (2nd rev. ed., London 1979). Did Trebitsch and Backhouse meet in Darlington in the summer of 1910? Given the intimacy of the narrow circle of the local Quakerocracy it is not improbable. It is a tempting speculation — but in the absence of evidence we shall not pursue it further.

espionage purposes, and announced that he planned to return there to raise the standard of revolt against British imperialism. The supposed earlier visit to Asia may safely be set aside as a figment of Trebitsch's roving imagination — set aside, but not dismissed, for we shall later discover the vital importance of this imaginary episode for an understanding of Trebitsch's psychological development.

Perhaps we should not look too far for the reason for Trebitsch's decision to go to China in 1922. It was, after all, one of the few places left for him to enter without fear of arrest. Britain and the entire British Empire were barred to him. In Germany he was still a wanted man. He could not be sure of a cordial reception in most of the other countries of western and central Europe. His recent experience in the USA did not suggest that he had much of a future there. The weakness of the central government of China and the anarchic condition of large parts of the country ensured that a visiting European would face little difficulty as regards the validity of his passport and no danger of extradition or deportation.

After travelling across the Pacific with false documents in the name of Patrick Keelan, Trebitsch landed briefly in Japan and then sailed on to China, where he arrived in the autumn of 1922.[1] The coastal cities of China, with their powerful foreign concesions and trading companies, were pervaded by European influence — nowhere more so than Shanghai. 'A stranger arriving in Shanghai by the P & O would scarcely realize that he was not on British territory', wrote one British diplomat.[2] Trebitsch had good reason to be wary of British officialdom and it may have been for this reason that he headed for the interior. He himself explained in an article published in 1925:

> I had never been to China; I knew nobody in China and I carried no letters of introduction; but I had a plan. My plan was to go to the Westernmost province of China, Szechwan, because that province adjoins Thibet and my purpose was to start trouble in Central Asia.[3]

Whatever may have been his motives (and he showed by his conduct in later years that he was obsessively preoccupied with the idea of getting to Tibet), he set off immediately on a remarkable journey up-country to the remote province of Szechwan.

The region had long been in the throes of civil war among rival warlords and its dangerous reputation among the Chinese had won it the sobriquet of 'the Devil's Cave'.[4] At the time of this arrival a major struggle was developing between two warlords for control of the largest city, Chungking. Hardly any Europeans ventured into this distant and inhospitable area. But Chungking seems to have held few terrors for Trebitsch, who succeeded with his usual garrulous affability in ingratiating himself both with the local authorities and with the tiny resident European community.

Writing in 1925 of his early days in China, Trebitsch alleged that he had even been entertained to a lunch, soon after his arrival in Chungking, by the commander of the British gunboat flotilla stationed on the River Yangtse, Captain Corlett. Another guest at the luncheon (so Trebitsch's account ran) had been the British Vice-Consul in Chungking, Mr Harry Steptoe*, with whom he had played bridge after lunch.[5] The tale has all the earmarks of a characteristic piece of Trebitsch bragging. We find, however, that when Trebitsch's story was reprinted in the *Peking Leader* in July 1925, Steptoe, by this time translated to the British Legation in Peking, admitted in an official minute: 'It is true that Lincoln was in Chungking & that he did lunch with Capt. Corlett & myself on board. He was then staying with an American whose name I have forgotten, but who was the local manager of a Chinese Bank. He was at the time posing as an Australian journalist.'[6]

According to Steptoe (who appears not to have realized Trebitsch's identity at the time), Captain Corlett was suspicious of his luncheon guest, and Trebitsch himself may have sensed this, for soon afterwards he disappeared from Chungking. He travelled down-river to Ichang, where he joined the entourage of the local warlord, General Yang Sen. If we are to believe Trebitsch, he secured appointment as adviser to Yang Sen, and persuaded him to form an alliance with another more powerful warlord, General Wu P'ei-fu, to whom he had formerly been opposed; with Yang Sen thus reinforced, Trebitsch successfully engineered his new master's seizure of Chungking. The events described did in fact take place, although we possess no independent corroboration of Trebitsch's claim to a major role in Yang Sen's victory. But there does exist evidence of Trebitsch's influence on the general — or at any rate of the hold over Yang Sen's mind which Trebitsch was believed to possess. Before we examine this evidence, however, it will be necessary to delve a little further into the political and military maelstrom into which Trebitsch now plunged.

In 1920 Yang Sen had been one of a group of military leaders, many of them like himself graduates of the Szechwan Short-Term Military Academy, who had declared the independence of the province. At this time Yang was appointed commander of the powerful Second Army. Ruthless, coarse and flamboyant, Yang developed a reputation for modernizing policies — although his

* According to one account, Steptoe was an agent of the British Secret Intelligence Service, MI6. See Nigel West [pseud.=Rupert Allason MP], *MI6* (New York and London 1983), p. 140. It is difficult to verify this or to know when (if at all) Steptoe joined the SIS.

16 General Yang Sen

reforms were often implemented with dictatorial inhumanity. In his study of the Szechwan militarists, Dr Robert A. Kapp writes of Yang Sen:

> To modernize the dress habits of his people, Yang at one time stationed soldiers at the gates of Chengtu with instructions to apprehend wearers of traditional lay gowns and shorten their garments with huge shears . . . At one point, during a campaign to emancipate women, he declared that women ought to learn to

> swim; when his wife bashfully refused his order to set the proper example, he dressed her in peasant clothes and forced her at gunpoint to splash in a river before fifteen thousand onlookers. After prohibiting the raising of pigs in the streets of Luchou, he had the city's police chief, holder of a *hsiu-ts'ai* degree, publicly beaten when he discovered hogs rooting in the road.[7]

Shortly before Trebitsch's arrival in the region, Yang Sen had suffered a serious military reverse at the hands of a coalition of enemies and had been forced out of the province altogether. When Trebitsch joined him he was regrouping the remnants of his forces at Ichang. We may doubt whether his decision to join ranks with Wu P'ei-fu owed much to the advice of the newly-arrived Trebitsch. But there seems little doubt that by the time Yang Sen's forces re-entered Chungking in triumph early in 1923, Trebitsch had inveigled himself sufficiently into the general's confidence to cause concern to local British commercial interests.

Among the European residents whom Trebitsch had met during his brief sojourn at Chungking was a British businessman named Davidson, the Secretary of a Chinese company, Young Brothers Trading Corporation, whose headquarters were at Chungking and who traded with British merchants at Shanghai and elsewhere. One of the marks of Yang Sen's régime, and one of his claims to be a progressive ruler, was his large-scale development of public works, particularly road-building projects. Under his administration a firm such as Young Brothers (which had ties with old-established British merchants exporting to the east) might have expected lucrative contracts. To his chagrin Davidson found not only that no such contracts were forthcoming, but that the government of Yang Sen seemed to be making it impossible for a firm with known British connections to operate in Szechwan. Davidson learnt that 'Patrick Keelan' was not only advising Yang Sen but was reported to be trying to float a company in Szechwan with a capital of fifteen million taels (at this time worth approximately £2,500,000). The British businessman feared that 'Keelan' was not only poisoning Yang Sen's mind against British commerce, but also planning to take advantage of the trading vacuum which he himself had helped to create, with the intention of cashing in on the rich pickings to be anticipated from Yang Sen's enlightened schemes of public expenditure.

So concerned was Davidson that he determined to inquire further into the antecedents of the troublesome newcomer. In the process of trying to launch his Szechwan development company Trebitsch had (as usual) sought to impress potential backers by dropping the names of wealthy persons supposedly already financing him. Not unjustifiably the name of Albert Otto featured prominently on this roll of honour. Davidson thereupon took the extraordinary step of travelling to the USA to question Otto about his relations with 'Keelan'. Otto narrated to Davidson the story of his meeting with Trebitsch and the £15,000 loan, and he added that he had lately received a communication from 'Keelan' demanding £2,000 more and hinting that if that were not forthcoming the original £15,000 could not be repaid. Otto said that he had initially been attracted to 'Keelan', 'but that subsequently Keelan had told him things which caused him to alter his opinion of the gentleman who had admitted his identity with Trebitsch Lincoln.'[8]

Armed with this information Davidson proceeded to London, where he communicated with his solicitors, and through them with Scotland Yard, the security services, and the Foreign Office. The resulting official documentation is almost our only source for Trebitsch's activities during these months and is thus particularly valuable. On 10 July 1923 the solicitors, Messrs Blyth, Dutton, Hartley & Blyth, submitted a letter to the Commissioner of Police at Scotland Yard, introducing Davidson, explaining his suspicions of 'Keelan', detailing his interview with Otto, and suggesting that Davidson might be allowed to inspect photographs of Trebitsch at Scotland Yard with a view to confirming his identity with the purported 'Keelan'. Davidson, of course, had no evidence of any criminal activity on the part of Trebitsch — who was in any case outside the jurisdiction even of the British municipal police who operated in some of the Chinese cities containing British concessions (but not Chungking, where there were no foreign concessions). It might be wondered, therefore, on what basis Davidson was approaching the British police at all. Perhaps for this reason he made his initial approach through the solicitors, who skated lightly over Davidson's own firm's interest in the matter, venturing more delicately and patriotically that 'if the identity of Mr Keelan with Lincoln is clear it may be important in the British interest in China to call the attention of the Foreign Office to the matter and endeavour to enlist their interest through the consular service'.[9]

Davidson visited Scotland Yard, was interviewed at length by the Special Branch, and from a photograph recognized Trebitsch as identical with 'Keelan'. According to the Special Branch report on the meeting, Davidson also expressed his fear 'that if Keelan retains his present post grave obstacles will be thrown in the way of British trade'.[10] Davidson's call led to a flurry of activity in police and government offices. The Special Branch compiled a comprehensive report on Trebitsch's life history. Davidson was invited to call on an official of the Far Eastern Department of the Foreign Office in order to explain his fears and his proposals for British consular action to secure the dismissal of Trebitsch from his apparently influential position in the Szechwan administration.[11] The businessman did obtain some reward for his long journey in the shape of British official action. On 8 August 1923 the Foreign Office sent a dispatch to the British Legation in Peking, with copies of the correspondence concerning Trebitsch. The dispatch stated that Davidson was 'of opinion that Mr Lincoln's activities are not likely to prove advantageous to British trade interests'. The Legation was instructed to 'communicate with the Consular officers concerned and take such other action as you may consider advisable'.[12]

But although Davidson's denunciation of Trebitsch (for the grave crime of interfering with the free flow of British trade) yielded the required action, it failed to produce the desired result. By the time the dispatch reached Peking and a further dispatch had been sent to the British Consulate in Chungking, Trebitsch had once again disappeared. The Acting Consul, Allan Archer (Steptoe, having moved on, was spared the humiliation of inquiring as to the whereabouts of his former bridge partner), reported that nobody in the city seemed to have heard of him. This news might seem welcome to Davidson, but it apparently arrived too late. Archer's dispatch was dated 6 June 1924, some eight months after the Legation's original inquiry. By then Trebitsch, as we shall shortly learn, was far away from Chungking. One apparent product of his visit to Szechwan endured: the destruction of Young Brothers' business in the province. This emerges from the final paragraph of Acting Consul Archer's dispatch, in which he explained:

> I had not replied earlier . . . because I had heard that Mr Davidson was shortly returning from England to resume his duties as secretary of the Young Brothers Trading Company, a Chinese firm of good repute in Chungking. I have now heard that owing to the heavy contributions required by the military authorities from this firm during recent years they are largely closing down in Chungking and transferring their main activities to Hankow, where it is believed that Mr Davidson is now stationed.[13]

Trebitsch's movements between the spring and autumn of 1923 remain obscure. He had certainly left the entourage of Yang Sen by April 1923, when the general had reinstated himself in control of Chungking.[14] He later claimed to have spent the next two years as adviser to Yang Sen's ally, Wu P'ei-fu, one of the leaders of the 'Chihli' faction among the Chinese militarists, and at this time in control of the greater part of north China. Trebitsch supported the claim with a wealth of circumstantial detail, even including complaints about the plumbing in the accommodation supplied by the general.[15] Unfortunately for Trebitsch, Wu issued a statement to the press in 1925 denying that 'Trebitsch Lincoln' had ever been his adviser, and asserting that he had never heard of him.[16] Wu's press statement evoked a fierce riposte from Trebitsch, who addressed a letter of complaint to the Shanghai manager of Reuters news agency, objecting to 'this stupid propaganda against me' and threatening darkly, 'I will deal with Marshal Wu myself.'[17] In fairness to all concerned it should be stated that Wu probably knew him under one of his several aliases. Moreover, by 1925 the general had suffered a severe military and political reverse, and he may well have had political reasons for repudiating any connection with a shady European adventurer, whatever name he went under. In the absence of firm evidence as to the nature of the relationship between the two men, the historian is obliged to suspend judgement.

But that Trebitsch remained in some degree of contact with the warlords of the Chihli faction is beyond doubt. For there exists definite evidence that in 1923 he returned to Europe in the company of a Chinese delegation headed by General Wu Hung Chiang, director of the port of Pukow. The mission had ill-defined purposes encompassing economic, political, and military affairs. One objective was the raising of a substantial loan — this at a time when the chaotic state of China's finances and her default on many foreign loans rendered the attraction of foreign capital very difficult. The mission appears also to have been authorised to hold conversations with friendly political and military figures. It was dispatched by an ally of Wu P'ei-fu, another leading Chihli warlord, General Ch'i Hsiehyuan, who held the imposing title of Inspector-General of Kiangsu, Kiangsi, and Anhwei. Ch'i had been appointed to this position as a reward for his support of Wu during the civil war of 1922. How Trebitsch came into contact with him is unknown. What is certain is that Trebitsch accompanied the mission as guide, dragoman and panjandrum.

The party reached Italy in September 1923. In Rome they endeavoured to obtain visas for onward travel to Austria, Hungary, and Germany. But Trebitsch was refused a Hungarian visa, and on that account the Chinese too decided to forgo a visit to Budapest.[18] They were able to continue on the remainder of their itinerary thanks to the help they received from an old friend of Trebitsch — Colonel Max Bauer. In her memoirs Luise Engeler recalls the amazement with which Bauer, living in exile in Austria, one day received a letter bearing Chinese postage stamps. This was his first communication from Trebitsch since their painful breach two year earlier. In the letter Trebitsch announced his imminent arrival in Europe with the Chinese delegation, and informed Bauer that General Ch'i Hsiehyuan wished to engage the colonel's services as a military adviser. By the time Bauer received the letter Trebitsch was already en route, and no reply could be sent. Soon afterwards, in response to a telegraphic summons from his former collaborator, Bauer travelled to Genoa to meet the party. His secretary reports that he was greatly impressed by the Chinese and by their plans, and undertook to do what he could to help them. The delegation and Trebitsch went to Vienna with Bauer, and during the remainder of their stay in Europe Bauer used his extensive connexions throughout central Europe on their behalf. Trebitsch, of course, was still under a ban in Austria, but Bauer used his contacts in high places to secure permission for his friend to stay in Vienna for a few days. After that Trebitsch moved to Zurich, where he remained for the next two months while the delegation travelled round Austria, Germany and Switzerland trying to raise a loan, inspecting industrial plants, and meeting important people to whom they were introduced by Bauer.[19]

The attempt to secure a loan met at first with little success: an application to the right-wing German industrialist Hugo Stinnes (with whom Bauer had been in touch for several years) was rejected.[20] But Bauer succeeded in arranging for the delegation to meet another old friend, General Ludendorff. On 2 November 1923 General Wu and his two Chinese colleagues went to see Ludendorff at his house near Munich. Trebitsch did not accompany them — there was still a price on his head in Germany. On 8 November the British Consul-General in Munich reported to the Foreign Office a 'curious story' he had heard from the Hungarian consul the previous evening:

> That arch-rogue and impostor, Trebitsch Lincoln, ex-MP, last heard of in the Kapp putsch, who is apparently 'wanted' in two or three continental countries, is said to have got into touch with the said Chinese delegation — where, it is not known, possibly in Shanghai, possibly in Rome. His whereabouts anyhow have not been definitely known for the past year and he is supposed to have no less than seven passports. Lincoln is said to be on very friendly terms with a Colonel Bauer who was himself intimate with Ludendorff. Lincoln, as ever wanting money, bargained with the Chinese for his requirements against an introduction to and the obtaining of a signed photograph of Ludendorff, which they wanted doubtless to prove their activity and justify a prodigious bill for expenses. The interview was arranged through the offices of Colonel Bauer. The Chinese had nothing to say but compliments. Ludendorff was bored to death with the whole thing, but after the interview . . . sent back a formal message of thanks with his photograph. The Chinese are now going on to Zurich where, it is said, they will again meet Lincoln.[21]

A Munich police report confirms these details and adds the interesting information that the meeting between the Chinese and

17 General Ludendorff on the steps of his villa, 1924

Ludendorff was organized by Max Erwin von Scheubner-Richter, who was himself present at the occasion.[22] Scheubner-Richter, it will be recalled, had introduced Bauer to the White Russian General Biskupski in 1920. Since then he had come to occupy a key role in the affairs of the fledgeling Nazi Party. He was killed just one week later, standing immediately next to Hitler in the course of the Nazi attempt (in which Ludendorff too participated) to seize power in Munich.

The question arises why Bauer, who had already been badly burned once by his relationship with Trebitsch, should so readily have entered into renewed political, financial, and personal intercourse with him. A partial explanation is provided by a letter written by Bauer to his mentor, Ludendorff, on 7 November 1923. The letter was sent from Zurich, where Bauer had arrived in order to hold further discussions with the Chinese. Among other things Bauer wished to discuss his own future, for he was (as his secretary confirms) greatly attracted by the invitation to work in China. To Ludendorff he wrote that he foresaw great possibilities in China, and that he was seriously considering devoting himself entirely to Chinese affairs. He saw no useful role for himself in German politics at that time. Of course, he declared, he would follow Ludendorff anywhere, but he was critical of other rightist leaders, among them Reinhold Wulle and Adolf Hitler, who, he wrote, were 'ineducable'. In view of all this he was unable to accede to an urgent message he had just received from Ludendorff pressing him to come to Munich immediately.[23]

Two days later Ludendorff joined Hitler in the streets of Munich in their abortive 'beerhall putsch'. Bauer was absent, and the results of the attempted coup seemed to confirm his negative evaluation of the political capacity of Hitler and his ilk. By remaining in Switzerland Bauer — and Trebitsch — avoided entanglement in another revolutionary fiasco.

After several days of discussion in Zurich, the primary object of the mission seemed to have been achieved on 17 November 1923, when a preliminary agreement was reached between the Chinese and a company headed by a business acquaintance of Bauer, an Austrian furniture manufacturer named Knoll. Other friends of Bauer who participated in the negotiations included Gustav Ritter von Kreitner, a lawyer and doctor who had worked for the Chinese Government before the world war and claimed some expertise in oriental affairs, and a certain Professor Otte. The agreement (apparently a draft which was to be ratified later by representatives of General Ch'i Hsieh-yuan and the Knoll company) provided for the raising of a loan of $25,000,000 'in American currency', the grant to the Knoll company of vast concessions for the exploitation of minerals and the right to operate transport and other monopolies, and the exclusive control by the Knoll company of all governmental orders from abroad for imports into the provinces controlled by the general. It was agreed that the first loan instalment would be paid as soon as the final contract had been ratified by General Ch'i.[24] In addition, Bauer undertook to go to China early in the following year (accompanied by Fräulein Engeler) in order to take up service under the general. Bauer was promised a high salary, payable in US dollars. The Chinese indeed pressed the colonel to return with them to China immediately. But Bauer was already committed to visit Russia as a guest of the Soviet government, and he explained that his journey to China would therefore have to be postponed.[25]

With his mission to all appearances happily concluded, Trebitsch once again summoned his family to join him. His wife, who was living in her native Germany, was ever-ready to believe that at last their lives would be restored to an even keel; she turned up in Zurich with their youngest son, Clifford, then aged twelve. (Julius Lincoln was at the time serving in the Criminal Investigation Department of the British army of occupation in Germany. Ignatius junior had also joined the British army, but was stationed in Britain. Edward, then aged thirteen, was living with a sympathetic Quaker family in England who adopted him and gave him their surname). John Lincoln, just turned nineteen, arrived from London, where he had been working in an estate agent's office. At first he refused to go to China, but Trebitsch (as his son later described it) 'urged, in fact commanded me to accompany him back there and help him in his work. I finally agreed.'[26] The Trebitsch family, thus partly reunited, together with the three Chinese, left for China on 4 December, arriving at Shanghai in January 1924. Trebitsch travelled on an Austrian passport issued at Sauerbrunn on 22 November 1923 in the name of 'Trautwein'.

After a short stay at the Oriental Hotel in Shanghai, the family moved to Nanking, where General Ch'i's headquarters were situated. Shortly afterwards the local English-language press carried an announcement:

> Mr H. Trautwein, accompanied by his wife and two sons, has recently come to Nanking as tutor to the son of General Wu, Chi Tuchun [i.e. Ch'i Hsieh-yuan]'s advisor. They are living at Chen Hsien Chai; the youngest son, Clifford, will attend Hillcrest.[27]

General Ch'i ratified the agreements concluded in Zurich, and the arrival of the first instalment of the loan and of Colonel Bauer seemed imminent.

On 19 January 1924 Trebitsch dispatched the following cable to Europe. The addressee is unknown but was probably one of Bauer's shady business contacts:

> Have received your wire of 17th. Tuchun Chi Yan [Ch'i Hsieh-yuan] has been advanced to Field Marshal and General Inspector of the provinces Kiangsu, Anwei, Kiangsi. My personal influence is great. If the loan cannot be taken up in the amount originally desired, try to get a part of it very quickly and come immediately with it and with technical experts. Act as quickly as possible. When can Dr [i.e. Colonel] Bauer come? We will pay what is necessary as soon as we hear from you. Can you immediately on receipt of order send 100 aeroplanes on account of loan? The loan can also be secured by the best anthracite coal. The mine is being worked. Its production is estimated at several hundred millions. It is favourably situated on a railway quite near the coast. Answer as soon as possible.[28]

The cable reached the eyes of the Special Branch, i.e. the political department, of the Shanghai Municipal Police, the British-controlled force in the International Settlement of Shanghai. Operatives of this agency, which worked, in effect, as an information-gathering arm of British intelligence in the Far East, kept a close eye on Trebitsch whenever he set foot in Shanghai throughout the next sixteen years. Their reports constituted a prime source for the British Government on Trebitsch's activities during that period in Shanghai, and indeed in China in general.

The cable seems to have elicited no response, and after several weeks of anxious waiting it became evident that some hitch must have arisen, for there was no sign of the money and no word from Bauer or his friends.

Trebitsch decided to return to Europe to find out what had gone wrong. Before leaving, he sent his son John to the British consulate in Nanking to present the 'Trautwein' passport for a 'chop' or endorsement to enable Trebitsch to travel to Vienna via either Canada or Suez. The Consul-General, noticing that the passport had been issued in Austria just two months earlier, pressed John for reasons why 'Trautwein' should be returning to Austria so soon. John's answer struck the consul as unsatisfactory, and his suspicions were aroused. He therefore refused to grant the necessary visa to travel via British territory unless the applicant appeared in person. When 'Trautwein' failed to come to the consulate himself, although he sent John twice more, the consul became even more suspicious — but did not at this time identify 'Trautwein' with Trebitsch.

Trebitsch was not, however, one to allow a minor technicality such as lack of a visa to upset his travel plans. Having failed at the Nanking consulate, he addressed himself to the British Consul-General's office in Shanghai, where on 11 February his Austrian passport was stamped with the required 'chop'.[29] Trebitsch seems to have been particularly fortunate on this occasion not to run into another old acquaintance — his former fellow luncheon guest and bridge partner on the Yangtse, Mr Steptoe, who was now working at the Shanghai consulate. It was only a few weeks later, after Steptoe had exchanged notes with the suspicious consul in Nanking, that he realized that Trebitsch had once again slipped past him unawares.

Trebitsch's renewed trip to Europe was not a success. In Zurich he was briefly detained for travelling with false papers.[30] As for the projected loan, it seemed to have dissolved into thin air. Colonel Bauer was conveniently delayed in Moscow, and evinced no desire, for the time being, to embark on the long journey to China. Was this Bauer's revenge for betrayal by Trebitsch two years earlier? We cannot be sure — nor for that matter could Trebitsch. But at least as regards his own proposed service in China Bauer may be acquitted of duplicity — for there seems little doubt that Bauer was genuinely interested in the idea. That is confirmed not only by Bauer's letter to Ludendorff already quoted, but also by the fact that Bauer did, in fact, go out to China in 1927 as military adviser to General Chiang Kai-shek — recommended on that occasion not by Trebitsch but by Karl von Wiegand.* The most likely explanation for the collapse of the loan appears to be the shady character of Bauer's commercial contacts. Luise Engeler points an accusing finger at Professor Otte. But the Knoll concern too was probably implicated. The catastrophe was perhaps less a product of the colonel's bad faith than of his poor judgement of men (of which we have already seen ample evidence in his relations with Trebitsch).

Trebitsch returned to Nanking in July 1924 to face the awkward task of explaining to General Ch'i the evaporation of his grandiose plans. We do not know the general's reaction — but it comes as little surprise to learn that Trebitsch soon afterwards disappeared from his entourage. This untoward episode, in fact, marked the termination of Trebitsch's career as an associate of Chinese warlords. He now decided to leave China, perhaps fearful of retribution from his former employers, who, it seems, had doled out large sums of money towards the expenses of Trebitsch's two European trips without seeing any return on their investment.

There was, in any case, a second pressing reason for him to move the base of his operations from China as soon as possible. The discouraging telegrams sent back from Europe by Trebitsch to his

* Trebitsch claims in his *Autobiography* (pp. 287–8) that he met Bauer in the Far East in 1928, and that the colonel pressed Trebitsch to take up a position in the Chinese government service. No confirmation of the story has been found in the Bauer papers, although it is corroborated by a Shanghai police report dated 24 April 1928. Bauer died of smallpox in Shanghai in 1929.[31]

family in Nanking had kindled in John Lincoln a desire to break away from his father. Even the long-suffering Margaret Trebitsch, abandoned for months in a strange country just a few weeks after their arrival, now tried to return to Europe with her youngest son. John Lincoln booked a passage on a ship due to sail from Shanghai for Vancouver. As a British passport-holder he would not require a visa to enter Canada. But his mother held no valid travel documents, and his brother too lacked a passport.

John therefore went to the British consulate in Shanghai, where he asked for the renewal of his own passport and for travel documents which would enable his mother and Clifford to return to Germany. Perhaps, like his father a little earlier, John reckoned that the Shanghai consulate would prove more lax in such matters than the suspicious British consul in Nanking. But John had the misfortune to appear before Vice-Consul Steptoe, who, as we have seen, had by this time worked out, with the aid of his Nanking colleague, that Trebitsch had duped him for a second time. The documents presented by John in support of his applications demonstrated even to the slow-witted Steptoe that he was in the presence of the son of his former bridge-partner. The consul's irritation at having twice been outsmarted found an outlet in the ill-treatment of John. The poor youth, caught unawares, became the whipping-boy for his father's misdemeanours. Steptoe told him that he knew who his father was, and that his various applications would have to await a decision from London. In the meantime he impounded John's (perfectly valid) passport on the dubious pretext that it held 'no endorsement of registration as a British subject', and he threatened to take proceedings against him for 'masquerading' in China under an assumed name.[32]

Without his passport John Lincoln was unable to leave for Vancouver. On his father's return he was obliged to confess to his attempt to escape (though it appears that he remained tactfully silent about his mother's effort to return to Germany). Trebitsch was enraged to discover not only that his son had notions of making his own way in life, but that he had betrayed Trebitsch's whereabouts to the British authorities in China, whom the former MP had so studiously sought to keep in ignorance of his presence in the country. He immediately addressed a furious letter of complaint to the British Consul-General in Nanking, declaring:

> I have just returned from Europe and my son, John, has informed me of all the circumstances and developments in connection with his passport. I beg leave to make the following observations:
>
> 1. My son is a minor, and as such must necessarily obey my orders.

2. In my capacity as his father, I brought him out to China last Dec.
3. He did not know, and I did not tell him, the nature of my work here.
4. He came out under his own name and was introduced to everybody in Shanghai as Mr Lincoln.
5. I have been living in Nanking under the name of Trautwein and as he lives in my house, by inference, and only by inference, he was taken to be Mr Trautwein. But he never assumed this name.[33]

Trebitsch demanded the return of John's passport and also a passport for Clifford. Since he now planned to leave China with his family he urgently required such documents.

But the British authorities were in no hurry to facilitate the travel arrangements of any member of the Lincoln family. John Lincoln's original request for a new passport had been referred to the Home Office, which recommended that since Margaret Trebitsch's naturalisation had not been revoked at the same time as her husband's in 1918, she and her British-born sons should be granted 'emergency certificates' valid only for travel to Britain.[34] Even this was regarded as too generous by the Foreign Office, where one official commented: 'I should say the whole family are a bad lot and it is a matter for regret that the HO did not revoke the British nationality of them all.'[35] But after consultation with MI5, the Home Office proposal was approved. On 6 August a printed circular to all British consuls and passport control officers throughout the world was issued by the Foreign Office.* This instructed that 'no facilities whatever' were to be granted to 'Ignatius Timothy Tribich-Lincoln (or Trebitsch-Lincoln), alias Trautwein, alias Patrick Keehan' [*sic*]. Margaret Trebitsch and her British-born sons were to be granted only the 'emergency certificates' valid for a single journey to the United Kingdom.[36]

The British Consul-General in Nanking did not deign to reply to Trebitsch's letter of complaint, though he informed John Lincoln of the Foreign Office's decision about his passport. Yet again Trebitsch resorted to the old tactic of lodging an application at the Shanghai consulate for travel documents for John, Clifford, and Margaret — as usual through the intermediary of John. But on this occasion the same answer was received as at Nanking.[37] On 15 October 1924 John Lincoln wrote again to the British Consul-General in Shanghai:

* Agents of the Secret Intelligence Service generally operated in the guise of Passport Control Officers attached to British missions overseas.

Sir,

Referring to my visits to the Consulate-General today in connection with an emergency certificate, I beg to say that I cannot accept a document with humiliating conditions attached to it. In consequence I must remain in China against my will until such time as I can obtain a passport like any other natural born British subject.[38]

The hand was that of John, but one suspects that the voice was that of his father; the letter appears to have been designed to deceive the British officials into thinking that Trebitsch intended to remain in China with his family. In fact, almost immediately after the dispatch of this letter, Trebitsch, his wife and his two sons, left Shanghai and (for the time being) disappeared from China and from the active files of British officialdom there.

We shall in a moment follow Trebitsch on his voyage, but at this point it may be well to reflect briefly on this first stage of his career in China. During the previous two years he seems to have served as adviser to at least three Chinese generals, Yang Sen, Ch'i Hsieh-yuan, and Wu Hung Chiang — and possibly to a fourth, Wu P'ei-fu. Of course the nature of his advice and the seriousness with which it was received are open to question. Trebitsch's claims to have been the *éminence grise* masterminding the political and military victories of his employers are self-evidently absurd. But that he occupied some political role beyond his public position as 'tutor' to the children of Wu Hung Chiang is certain, particularly given what we know of his travels to Europe in this period. The British authorities in China, while they were apt (like their mistaken predecessors elsewhere) to regard Trebitsch merely as a troublesome nuisance, accepted that he occupied some advisory position — although its exact nature was obscure. Steptoe, for example, who in some sense was in a better position than most to judge, wrote in 1926 that, while he believed that Wu P'ei-fu's denial of any connection with Trebitsch was correct, he knew for fact that 'Lincoln was adviser to & arms merchant for Ch'i Hsieh Yuan'.[39]

If we try to sift the fantasy from the reality of Trebitsch's dealings with the warlords, there remains a kernel of truth to his self-glorifying claims. The question therefore remains how a European, without any knowledge of China, its language, or its people, could arrive in the country and, within a matter of weeks, insinuate himself into a position of (albeit minor) political significance. Trebitsch had, it is true, already inserted himself into the political establishments of both

England and Germany — but the political circumstances of China seem so radically different that his feat here requires some explanation beyond the resourcefulness of his character.

Trebitsch's early career in China, the idiosyncrasies of his personality aside, in fact falls into a familiar category in modern Chinese history — that of the European adviser. Ranging along a spectrum from hyper-respectability to the verge of criminality, and often beyond, the European in China performed many of the functions, which might now be termed those of 'informal imperialism', that were elsewhere fulfilled by officials of colonial empires. Thus (to take a famous example), the Inspector-General and senior staff of the Chinese Maritime Customs were almost all Europeans, mainly British citizens. British, American, Japanese, French, Dutch, German and Swedish advisers were to be found in virtually every department of Chinese government. Indeed, the 1920s and 1930s were the heyday of the European adventurer in China. Figures such as the Italian Amadeo Vespa, the Australian 'Donald of China', the American Gordon B. Enders, or the Briton 'One-Arm' Sutton, were the stuff of legend. Moreover, in spite of nationalist resentment of European influences, the disintegration of the country into rival fiefdoms under the control of shifting coalitions of warlords accentuated the importance of the foreigners. For the general or politician who could secure external diplomatic support, foreign loans, supplies of modern weaponry, or advanced technical assistance might hope by these means to steal a march on his opponents.

In his study of the role of European and American advisers in China, Professor Jonathan Spence writes that most of them 'had a character that thrived on risk and yearned for radical solutions, a pattern generally exacerbated by feared or experienced frustrations at home. China seemed to offer them freedom of maneuver, a chance to influence history by the force of personality, and thus to prove their own significance'.[40] Trebitsch fits into this mould — albeit at its farthest edge where it merges into the *condottiere* and the confidence trickster. During the late twenties the British Legation in Peking (as well as certain British consular posts in China) opened 'bad hats' or 'sundry suspects' files.[41] Trebitsch figures prominently here in the company of other examples of this type. These included such dangerous agitators as Mr Bertrand Russell (regarded by British officials as a bad influence on Chinese youth), Lieutenant-Colonel Cecil L'Estrange Malone, a former RAF officer, Liberal MP, and member of the British Delegation at the Supreme War Council in Versailles in 1918 (described in a confidential consular circular as 'a well-known British Communist')[42], and the colourful character who perhaps most resembles Trebitsch, Morris 'Two-Gun' Cohen.* Studied in this ill-assorted society, Trebitsch, in spite of his increasingly virulent psychosis and aberrant behaviour, may be said to blend into the chaotic backcloth of the place and the time.

Trebitsch, his wife and their two sons sailed from Shanghai, probably in late October 1924. Trebitsch held an Austrian passport under the name 'Tandler' and the others accompanied him on the same document. They went to Batavia in the Dutch East Indies, where Trebitsch registered (as 'Tandler') at the Austrian consulate. Clifford, now aged thirteen, was put into a boarding-school (his education had so far been spread over at least four countries), and John found work as an apprentice on an estate belonging to the Austrian consul. Trebitsch had ideas of buying a plantation and setting down permanently in Java. But having no money or means of raising enough to buy an estate, he decided after a short time to return to Europe in order to try to obtain the necessary capital.

Clifford and John were left behind in Java when Trebitsch set off once again for Europe, this time accompanied by his wife. The couple's intention seems to have been to return to Java as soon as sufficient cash had been found to buy a plantation. But the weeks lengthened into months, and eventually into years, without their reappearance in Batavia. The two boys, bewildered at having been thus abandoned in this exotic spot, made do as best they could. John obtained a permanent position on the Austrian consul's estate, struggling against increasing odds to reduce the mountain of debt incurred in respect of Clifford's unpaid school fees. With great difficulty he borrowed money to pay for Clifford's passage back to Europe. John ultimately went to the British Consul-General in

* Morris A. Cohen, born in London in 1887, lived in Canada from the age of sixteen, working as a ranchhand, gambler and political operative. In 1922 he was appointed aide to the President of China, Sun Yat-sen; later he worked for Chiang Kai-shek. Awarded the rank of general in the Kuomintang government's army, he carried out arms-purchasing missions in Europe. He participated in fighting against the Chinese communists and the Japanese, and in 1941 was captured by the Japanese, later being repatriated to Canada. After his retirement to Manchester, he lectured to enthralled audiences of English public-schoolboys on his adventures in China, and he travelled to Taiwan as an honoured guest. Cohen was a well-known and much-disliked figure among British officials in China. H.N. Steptoe gave no credence to his alleged employment by Sun Yat-sen, writing in 1925: 'He is a pure adventurer with an unsavoury record and is believed to be an active member of the IWW [International Workers of the World].' Another official minuted: 'Mr Cohen struck me as being of the type known in America as a "saloon bum", offensive both in appearance & manner.'[43]

Batavia, confessed to his real identity and, after months of waiting, was issued with a travel document permitting him to return to England.*

On the long voyage back to Europe Trebitsch practised what he told his wife was an 'infallible system of winning money at baccarat'. Margaret Trebitsch recalled that 'he got so far as to convince himself that his new method, if systematically carried out, could not fail'.[44] Upon their arrival in France Trebitsch put his 'system' to the test in casinos at Monte Carlo and Nice. After initial successes the results were disastrous. Trebitsch was once again utterly ruined.

In March 1925 Trebitsch reached The Hague, whence he addressed letters to the British Home and Foreign Secretaries pleading for permission to return to England. The themes of these letters were to become constant refrains of their author over the next decade. He stressed his desire to see his sons in England (Ignatius, who was serving as a bombardier in the Royal Horse Artillery, and the fourteen-year-old Edward), without, of course, drawing attention to the abandonment of his two others sons on an antipodean island. He declared that his activities in China, while not pro-British, had not been anti-British either. And he announced: 'I shall willingly submit to any conditions that may be imposed upon me subject, however, that no indignities be (inadvertently, of course), imposed upon me, and that the British Government will kindly grant me an unconditional safe conduct for a return journey.'[45] The Foreign Office decided not to dignify the application with a reply. Although Trebitsch did not know it, he had lost his last opportunity of seeing his eldest son, Ignatius, the terrible culmination of whose short existence we shall shortly witness.

This indeed was the end of what remained of Trebitsch's life as a family man. In the spring of 1925 he left Margaret in Hamburg and somehow made his way to America. He probably thought of this as merely another one of his trips in search of good fortune, at the end of which he would send for his wife and sons to join him. But Trebitsch never reached the end of the rainbow.

For Margaret Trebitsch, life had, in a tragic way, turned full circle. Back in her birthplace she succeeded, after much difficulty, in being reunited with her youngest son, Clifford. Trebitsch thus left her, as he had found her, with a son to support — but having in the

* But he did not return. When the Japanese occupied the Dutch East Indies, after the outbreak of the Pacific War, John Lincoln was still there. Interned by the Japanese, he was subjected to appalling maltreatment. After the war he moved to Australia, where he started a restaurant. The business failed. John Lincoln suffered a nervous breakdown, and then committed suicide.

meantime dissipated her father's legacy, grossly abused her trust, and in effect ruined her life. On any reckoning she was well rid of him. And yet even her husband's spurious and self-centred affection might have been some comfort to her in the agonizing trial which was shortly to confront her.

CHAPTER 13

Out of The Lunatic Asylum

Trebitsch, now aged forty-six, was again alone. The remainder of his life was spent trying to adjust to this fact as he swayed between bouts of extreme withdrawal, depression and introspection, and periods when he seemed to recover, sometimes in an almost frenzied way, the gregariousness, desire for publicity, and effort to impress and dominate others that had been such marked features of his earlier life. The hitherto gradual change in his personality now accelerated, freed from the restraining brake of family responsibility. Trebitsch's mind careered wildly onwards, much of the time along familiar grooves, but occasionally colliding with reality and veering perilously beyond the edge of reason.

On his arrival in New York in the spring of 1925 Trebitsch seemed initially to be trying to re-enact the events of the stay, ten years earlier, which had first turned him into a figure of international notoriety. Once again he lodged at first with his brother Joseph Schlesinger, still living in New York. In desperate need of ready money, and obviously hoping to repeat his earlier journalistic success, Trebitsch wrote a series of sensational articles on his experiences in China. On five successive Sundays, beginning on 7 June 1925, the magazine section of the New York *World*, which had published Trebitsch's 'Revelations' in 1915, serialised a version of his latest exploits. Under the headline, 'Lincoln, World War Spy, Plotted to Control China', the series began with the statement: 'For three years I have been political adviser to Marshal Wu Pei Fu in China.' What followed was, as in the case of the 1915 articles, a palace of fantasy constructed out of a few bricks of reality. Trebitsch, it seemed, had been the master-mind pulling the strings of warlord puppets throughout China: graphic depiction of genuine incidents (as of the famous luncheon with Captain Corlett and Consul Steptoe on the River Yangtse), in themselves utterly trivial, was skilfully woven into the narrative, possibly with assistance from a ghost-writer. The result was to leave the impression (at any rate on the impressionable) that Trebitsch had been right at the heart of a struggle for the destiny of China. Trebitsch did not, of course, recount the ignominious circumstances of his hasty departure from Shanghai. He concluded his celebration of his achievements in oriental politics on a strange note of bathos:

> It has been my misfortune all through life to have been associated with fools, who spoiled and nullified all my efforts. And so it was in China. I have been successful there far beyond anything ever achieved by a foreigner. But when war broke out Wu Pei Fu would not listen to me.

As for his future, he wrote:

> I am once more at the parting of the ways. . . . Could I do what I want I would retire to some peaceful corner of the earth and, gathering my scattered family around me, end my days in serene contemplation. But I have debts in many parts of the world, which must be paid. Hence I may go on.

Where or what he would 'go on' doing was not explained. But that he still deludedly dreamed of returning to England was indicated by his acknowledgement of his 'supreme mistake' in placing himself 'in open opposition to the British Empire'. Now, 'having seen the British Empire at close quarters' (a curious claim since he had been banned from entry to British territory since 1919), he announced his opinion that it was 'the greatest political institution that has ever existed on this earth'.

Trebitsch must have thought that these fair words might butter some parsnips in British official quarters, for he sent along a copy of this last article to the British Consul-General in New York, together with yet another plea to return to England to see his two sons. Trebitsch further explained:

> Complying with the repeated entreaties of my Chinese friends, I am returning to China. Before doing so, I should like to go to London and place certain projects before the responsible Permanent Officials with a view to ensure their speedy and complete success.[1]

A few days after sending this letter Trebitsch called on the Consul-General and repeated his offer to render services to the British in China in the hope of securing reinstatement as a British citizen. The Consul-General agreed to forward his request to London, at Trebitsch's expense, and a long cable was forthwith dispatched to London.

Although the reaction in Whitehall was dusty, the news that he planned to return to China stirred up a few official hornets. 'I think

Lincoln is a little mad, and it seems to me that efforts should be made to prevent his return to China', wrote one official.[2] The statement was, of course, something of a non sequitur: if he was mad, why worry about his possible influence on events in China — or anywhere else? This inconsistency in fact characterised Foreign Office reactions to Trebitsch throughout his career. An oscillation was apparent in instructions to British representatives abroad, who were told alternately to keep a close eye on Trebitsch and to ignore him studiously. On this occasion the warning of his impending reappearance in the Far East led the Foreign Office to issue an instruction that British consuls in China should be reminded not to grant Trebitsch any facilities, and that they should inform the British Legation in Peking 'of any of his activities which may come to their notice'.[3]

Trebitsch arrived back in China in August 1925. His exact movements during the next few months remained obscure to the British authorities, although the British Consul-General in Shanghai and the Shanghai Municipal Police made considerable efforts to locate him. On 23 August he left an address with the Consul-General, asking that any response to the application he had made in New York be forwarded to him. The next day the (predictably negative) reply arrived. But it was found that the address he had given, that of a Mr W.F. Wong, was merely that of a forwarding agent. Any mail arriving for him there was sent on to Young Brothers Banking Corporation in Hankow. Had Trebitsch somehow become reconciled with Mr Davidson, who so recently had pursued him half-way round the world? It is difficult to believe. This remains one of the minor mysteries of Trebitsch's biography. What is clear is that he received the Consul-General's message addressed to him at Hankow, for he acknowledged it with a note dated 'In China, September 25th'.[4]

The autumn of 1925, which Trebitsch apparently spent wandering aimlessly around China, marked another turning-point in his life. In his last letter to his wife before his return to the Far East, he had given evidence of being plunged into deep depression:

> I am sick of life. I have experienced too great adversities. My power of resistance, my persistence, my pleasure in work, are all of the past. My life has been a failure. Nature did not equip me with the qualifications I was in need of. . . . But what is the use of lamenting? I am engulfed in an impenetrable darkness.[5]

From this trough Trebitsch ascended, after about two months in China, to a dizzy height of religious experience. In a book published in Shanghai seven years later Trebitsch recalled the date and place of this transcendent event.

On 27 October 1925, he wrote, in the Astor House Hotel in

Tientsin, 'I made the great renunciation, I quitted the world.... I forced the doors of the lunatic asylum open and — walked out.'[6]

Trebitsch's mystical experience in Tientsin determined him to take up the study of eastern religion as refracted through the ideas of the Theosophist movement. The Theosophical Society, founded in New York in 1875 by Mrs Helena Blavatsky, drew on Buddhist writings, Egyptain hieroglyphics, and the Kabbalah for its eclectic 'science of ancient and proved Magic.'[7] The Theosophists divided into warring sects following the death of Mrs Blavatsky in 1891 — and we shall shortly meet one of the claimants to the apostolic mantle of the founder. What precisely attracted Trebitsch to Theosophism is hard to know. Possibly the role of the movement as a conduit of eastern religious ideas to the west persuaded him that he might play some part in the society's propaganda work. The Buddhist and occult elements in its teachings certainly struck a chord which resonated in his mind. We have already noticed that as early as 1916 he had talked of having travelled in Central Asia disguised as a Buddhist monk. His exact words at that time merit recall:

> The British Government knows that they are not done with me. They know of my schemes to foment trouble against them in Central Asia. I will devote ten years, if necessary, to the carrying-out of this far-reaching scheme, but I must and will get even with them'. I will! It cannot, of course, be expected that I should divulge the details of this scheme. Its purpose, however, is to inaugurate à la Billy Sunday*, a great religious revival in the East, particularly in Central Asia, and, with the unified Mohammedans, to make an end of British rule in Egypt and the whole of Asia. You will do well to watch the East, and when you hear of a great religious revival there, think of I.T.T. Lincoln. A similar revival will be engineered among the Buddhists and the blundering British Government shall remember me.[8]

Trebitsch's mystical experience in Tientsin occurred just under ten years after he wrote these words of bombastic prophecy.

In Tientsin Trebitsch decided to travel to the headquarters of the Theosophist movement at Adyar near Madras in south India. En route he stopped in Shanghai, where he found a letter awaiting him from the British Consul-General, Sidney Barton, requesting refund

* Revd. Billy Sunday, the 'Baseball Evangelist', was one of the great revivalist preachers of the time.

of the cost of the telegram sent at Trebitsch's request by the Consul-General in New York. Barton's letter provoked a savage riposte from Trebitsch. He began by disputing the charge for the cable. Then he complained that a detective of the municipal police in Shanghai had tried to 'browbeat and bully' Mr Wong into revealing Trebitsch's whereabouts. Next he rebutted the allegation made by the detective to Wong that he (Trebitsch) was a dealer in munitions. He continued:

> This leads me to another question, ever uppermost in my mind. My relation to the British Government and their attitude to me. Shall this conflict go on for ever? Is a reconciliation impossible? ... I do not complain if the British Government does not trust me. I have to blame myself. But they go too far when they pass final judgement upon me ... And after all, was it not an act of Capt. Hall ... an act unjust to me that started the ball rolling?

After emphasizing his 'heart's desire' for a 'complete reconciliation' Trebitsch stressed his benevolent feelings towards the British Empire, adding:

> There are great things happening at present and greater things are in preparation of which most people know nothing, and would scoff at if they would. A new epoch is being ushered in, because the old order of things has become bankrupt. We shall presently be living in momentous days. I am speaking of quite different things than would be surmised. I have been privileged to get a glimpse and intimation of things to come.[9]

The excited tone of this letter suggests that Trebitsch's mood had now changed from the utter depression evidenced in his last letter to his wife to one of exuberant elation and confidence in his prophetic powers.

Immediately after writing to Barton, Trebitsch disappeared once again. The British authorities remained in total ignorance of his movements for the next three months until, in bizarre circumstances shortly to be explained, Trebitsch himself was forced to lift the veil of secrecy and reveal his whereabouts. *The Times* of 3 March 1926 published a report from Colombo which provides the most reliable account of Trebitsch's actions after he left Shanghai in November 1925:

> Buddhists in Ceylon are surprised at the suggestion that Dr Leo Tandler, who for some time past has been staying at a small Buddhist monastery not far from here, is really Trebitsch Lincoln, but all the evidence points to its being true. Tandler, who stated he was an Austrian, came to Ceylon from Manila, with the approval

of the local police, who had previously been in communication on the subject with the British consul at Manila.

Tandler's original intention was to proceed to the South Indian headquarters of the Theosophical Society, but when he reached Ceylon he abandoned the idea, intimating that he did so because he was out of sympathy with the recent trend of Theosophical thought. He obtained the permission of the police to take up his residence at a small Buddhist monastery five miles from Colombo, where he lived the simple life in a cell, his one meal a day being part of the food gathered by the monks during their daily begging expeditions. Leading Colombo Buddhists visited him there and persuaded him to accept a rather more liberal diet.

In the course of a few weeks he acquired a sufficient smattering of Pali to enable him, as he said, to pursue his studies privately. He impressed all who met him with his sincerity, his remarkable grasp of the fundamental principles of the Buddhist religion, and the rapidity with which he acquired a knowledge of Sinhalese and Pali. He told one monk that he had had serious trouble with a son, and referred to some recent trouble in a conversation with others, but he refused to confide further in them.

At a lecture in Colombo at the end of January he referred to the fact that the newspapers were full of crime. Why was this? he asked. Because people did not realize the full worth of life. He went on to explain that when a man committed a crime he might escape the consequences in this life, but not after his re-birth.

Trebitsch's contemplative existence in Ceylon was rudely interrupted around the end of January by shocking news from England. His eldest son, Ignatius, had been convicted of murder and sentenced to death on 21 January. The crime had been committed on 23 December: Ignatius (who at this time went by the name John*), in the company of a fellow soldier from Trowbridge Barracks, had broken into a nearby house in a state of drunkenness and with the intention of committing robbery. Discovered in the act, Lincoln fired his revolver and shot dead Edward Richards, a twenty-five-year-old brewer's traveller who lived in the house. The two men were arrested within hours. At their trial a few weeks later, Lincoln's accomplice was, on the direction of the judge, acquitted by the jury of the charge of murder. Lincoln's defending counsel faced an almost impossible task owing to the discovery of a letter, written by Lincoln while in prison awaiting trial, in which he confessed to having fired the fatal shot. The judge rejected the defence counsel's contention that Lincoln's drunken state at the time should be re-

* 'John' [Ignatius] Lincoln should not be confused with his younger brother, John Lincoln, who was still marooned on the island of Java.

garded as a mitigating factor: drunkenness was irrelevant, he said, and he felt bound to say that this was a case of wilful murder. Thus instructed, the jury took a quarter of an hour to decide on its verdict. An appeal was heard by a three-man panel of judges headed by the Lord Chief Justice: the decision of the lower court was confirmed: Ignatius Lincoln was sentenced to death.[10]

This terrible series of events brought parts of Trebitsch's scattered family together again. Margaret Trebitsch was given permission to travel on an 'emergency certificate' from Hamburg to England to say goodbye to her son. Ignatius's half-brother, Julius, who was still serving in the Criminal Investigation Department of the British Army in Germany, also returned to England, and raised funds to pay for the appeal. The fact that Lincoln's accomplice had gone scot-free on the murder charge (although later convicted on a lesser count), as well as a feeling that to have a father such as Trebitsch was in itself a mitigating factor, may have been responsible for the wave of public sympathy which burst forth in favour of the condemned man. On 24 February a demonstration in Trafalgar Square, attended by his mother, gathered signatures on a petition urging a reprieve. By 25 February fifty thousand people had signed the petition which was presented to the Home Secretary (whose constitutional function it was to advise the King whether to exercise the prerogative of mercy).

Meanwhile Trebitsch had somehow learned that Ignatius faced imminent execution. On 5 February he left Ceylon by sea, hoping to be allowed to visit his son before the execution was carried out. On 26 February it was announced that the Home Secretary had declined to advise the sovereign to interfere with the sentence of the court. Execution was set for the morning of 2 March. In response to Trebitsch's plea it was decided to allow him into Britain to see his son, provided he could reach an English port in time before the execution. There would, however, be no delay in the execution, and if Trebitsch arrived too late he would not be admitted.[11]

In the event Trebitsch did not arrive in time. Ignatius Lincoln, aged twenty-three, was executed at dawn on 2 March 1926. All reports indicated that he met his fate with resigned stoicism:

> Ignatius walked to the scaffold without visible emotion, standing rigidly at attention as the noose was adjusted. Until late last night he had waited in the death cell for his father's promised visit, and when told that it was impossible for him to arrive he broke down and wept ... Fearful that he would not be able to bid farewell to his father he left a letter for him ... Filled with remorse he [Trebitsch] is reported to have written to the son: 'My sins seem to have been visited on your head, and I pray you will forgive me

before you die. If I had been a better father, this might not have happened, and I am filled with a terrible regret for my past.'[12]

The depth of Trebitsch's remorse is, in fact, open to question. When he arrived at Amsterdam his first words to waiting reporters were 'How did my poor son die?' But his further comments suggest that this horrific event, far from inducing a return to the plane of reality, had propelled his mind with renewed impetus towards a state of heightened consciousness, a reinforced faith in his own extraordinary powers, now even including extra-sensory perception, and a further intensification of his utterly solipsistic view of the world. Thus in speaking to the press of the consolation he had derived from Buddhism, Trebitsch said:

> 'It brought my son and I together. I even held conversations with him by telepathy. He told me he died on Tuesday. I think the telepathy of Buddhism supported us so that when that terrible Tuesday came I could bow before the inevitable.'

Within a few minutes, however, Trebitsch stopped talking about his hanged son, and returned to his favourite theme — himself:

> 'My one aim is to get back to England. I have written to Home Secretary Hicks [Sir William Joynson-Hicks], who is a very fair-minded man, and I am going to the Hague to submit my case to the British representative. Let us bury the past. I was not a spy. I emphatically deny the accusation. I would like to reopen the matter.'[13]

It would seem, therefore, that Trebitsch regarded the execution of his son and the public sympathy this had engendered as a potential lever which might be used to apply pressure on the British Government to forgive and forget his own past offences.

On arrival at The Hague he duly applied for permission to enter England, allegedly for the purpose of visiting his son's grave.[14] When this was refused he remained in Europe for a while, and then, repeating the by now familiar pattern, he crossed to America and stayed for a time with his brother in New York. Once again he called on the British Consul-General in the city, who reported on 26 October that he 'presented a pitiable appearance, depressed, shabby and without, apparently, any monetary resources'.[15] He told the Consul-General that he had decided to give up politics and intended to enter a Buddhist monastery in Tibet. To this end he submitted a letter requesting permission to travel to Tibet by way of British India.[16] 'Every move this man makes is more amazing than the last', was the reaction of one Foreign Office official on receipt of a copy of Trebitsch's letter — which was forwarded to the India Office for an opinion.[17]

Before we follow Trebitsch in his peregrinations, it may be well to pause briefly to consider Trebitsch's obsession with the idea of travelling to Tibet — a haunting preoccupation which was to drive him ultimately to rarefied heights of self-delusion and almost grotesque fantasy. In Trebitsch's mind the notion appears at times to have been associated with the idea of withdrawal to a serene, contemplative existence, and at other times to have been bound up with his dreams of stirring up a religious whirlwind which would gust out of Central Asia and destroy the British Empire. Probably it was the very capacity of Tibet, as conceived by Trebitsch, to stir up *both* these alternating associations in his mind, as it swung with increasing violence from depression to exaltation, that rendered this mysterious region so irresistibly attractive.

For the British Government, Trebitsch's retirement to some remote Himalayan monastery might be thought an appealing prospect. Britain had no resident diplomatic representation in Lhasa, where communications with the outside world were difficult and infrequent. Trebitsch's tiresome nagging of British representatives around the world would perforce cease and considerable nuisance to government departments and cost to the public purse might therefore be obviated. Such reasoning, however, conformed neither to the realities of power in the monastic republic nor to the appreciation in Whitehall of Trebitsch's capacity for stirring up trouble. Tibet in this period, in practice more or less independent, formed a buffer between the competing imperialisms of Russia, China and British India. The external rivalries of her neighbours were frequently reflected in the internal politics of different parties among the ruling lamassariat. (One instance of this will impinge on our narrative a little later.) In these circumstances the British authorities in India traditionally pursued a policy of forbidding access through India to Tibet by any Europeans (save occasional British officers) who might disturb the delicate political balance in the country. Even explorers and mountaineers found that their political credentials were subject to intense scrutiny and that they were often refused access.*

* The greatest explorer of Tibet of the age, the Swede Sven Hedin, affords an interesting example of such British official suspicion. In his case there was ample justification for British hostility: during the First World War Hedin had been outspokenly pro-German and had even visited Ludendorff at the front. In the inter-war period Hedin's expeditions to Central Asia (via China) and his employment in the service of the government of China were followed with close attention by political intelligence officers of the Government of India.[18] During World War II Hedin lived for a time in Berlin and was strongly pro-Nazi.

Trebitsch's application was thus foredoomed — and was in fact rejected in a letter from the India Office dated 24 November 1926.[19]

Soon after his interview with the British Consul-General in New York in October 1926, Trebitsch once again disappeared from sight. He had entered the USA bearing a forged passport in the name of H. Ruh. Proceeding under this pseudonym he headed west, hoping somehow to reach Tibet. In a letter to the US Secretary of State in May 1927 Trebitsch described his activities during the early months of 1927:

> On the 11th of January this year I arrived in San Francisco under the name of Ruh, which in German means 'rest'. I lived under this name in the Japanese Hotel Ebisu, 1645 Buchanan Street. On the day of my arrival I met Mr Nyogen Senzaki, a former Buddhist Monk in Japan and who came to this country some 20 years ago.... He invited me to speak at his monthly meeting on Buddhism and which happened to fall on the 15th of January, a few days after my arrival there. I, of course, consented. As a result of my address there, I was invited to address other meetings in private houses. I never intended to remain in San Francisco. I and those who invited me to speak to them on Buddhism merely asked me to defer my departure a few days. The first few days became another few days and still another few days. Out of such beginnings there grew up spontaneously and without any planning or intention a Buddhist Center in San Francisco, the first of its kind in the Western Hemisphere. Three times halls, which had to be hired to accommodate the hearers, had to be changed for larger ones, such interest was manifested in my Lectures, which were solely on Buddhism. On the 24th of March this year we moved into hired permanent quarters in 234 Haight Street, San Francisco.[20]

Perhaps Trebitsch might have spent the rest of his life as the leader of an eastern cult — already at that time a fashionable occupation in California. The avowed purpose of his letter to the State Department was indeed to request permission to remain legally in the USA for a further six months in order to pursue his Buddhist evangelizing. But even before it was dispatched Trebitsch had already set off on renewed wanderings.[21] His roving urge took him first to the east coast of the USA, then back to the west, and then north into Canada, where he stayed for two months at Naramata, British Columbia, on a fruit farm belonging to a Buddhist, Carroll Aikens. From Aikens he borrowed $500 and booked a second-class passage on the *Empress of Canada*, which left Vancouver for Hong Kong on 1 September

1927. He had confused ideas of going to Burma, to India, to Ceylon, and to Siam. But (as he told the Hong Kong police on his arrival there in late September) he could not enter any of these territories legally — as for doing so by other means, he declared: 'I could easily have forged a passport but all this lying is against the principles of Buddhism.' The letter accompanying this declaration was signed 'I.T.T. Lincoln (at present H. Ruh under which name I am sailing)'.[22]

Trebitsch was permitted to stay in the British colony only until the next boat sailed for north China. On 27 September he left Hong Kong aboard the s.s. *Coblenz*, bound for Tientsin. A police report circulated to the British intelligence services stated that he took with him six trunks, three of which were filled with papers and books on Buddhism. The Director of the CID at Hong Kong, who had interviewed him before his departure, remarked that 'he seemed very chastened'.[23] On his arrival in Tientsin the British Municipal Police there continued to keep a watch on him.[24] From Tientsin on 26 October he wrote yet again to the British Consul-General in New York, applying (as he put it) '*for the last time*' to be allowed to travel to Tibet through India.[25]

On 28 October Trebitsch turned up in Peking. He called at the British Legation, where he was interviewed by a senior official. The visitor announced that he had been invited to give a public lecture on Buddhism in Peking the following week. He was staying, he said, at the Hotel du Nord under the name H. Ruh, but he also went by the Buddhist name Anagarika Pukkusati — Anagarika meaning, he explained, 'the homeless one, which I am even in a non-Buddhist sense'. He was on his way to Tibet, but his road through China was barred by the conditions of civil war still prevailing, and he was obliged to wait in Peking until the spring. At that time he would either travel to Tibet via India (if permission arrived in the interim) or embark on the hazardous journey overland from China. In reply Trebitsch was informed that the British Legation had no legal right to prevent him giving lectures in Peking if he wished. He was told to present any further requests in writing.[26]

Trebitsch's unexpected descent on the Chinese capital evoked considerable interest both among British officials and (as will shortly be seen) in broader circles of society. One Legation official commented: 'He ought to have been hanged years ago, instead of merely being deported as a traitor.' (The signature on this minute is indecipherable, but the handwriting is similar to that of Trebitsch's old antagonist Harry Steptoe, employed as 'local Vice-Consul' in Peking at this time.) After further consideration the British Minister, Sir Miles Lampson, gave instructions that Trebitsch was not to be received again at the Legation.[27]

In spite of the fact that Trebitsch was now masquerading under two aliases simultaneously, he made little secret of his true identity. On 29 October a report appeared on the front page of the London newspaper, the *Westminster Gazette*, to the effect that Trebitsch was now a Buddhist monk in Peking. The report added that he was trying to get to Tibet and that to this end he had contacted the senior Tibetan dignitary, the Panchen Lama, at that time resident in China. The report was brought to the attention of the Foreign Office on 1 November in a remarkable (although somewhat garbled) telegram from Sir Miles Lampson:

> Local British journalist has been informed by one of the Panshen Lama's suite here that Trebitsch Lincoln is endeavouring to get into touch with Panshen who is still in inner Mongolia in connection with Soviet intrigue with Dalai Lama who is alleged to be plotting for elimination of Panshen Lama in order that he may be left in unfettered control over Tibet when he will make treaty with Russians in return for their assistance in ridding him of Panshen Lama. I pass on this story for what it may be worth. Panshen's agent has been warned by the same journalist of Lincoln's reputation.[28]

These reports, fantastic though they appeared, in fact marked an important new stage in Trebitsch's Buddhist activity. Hitherto it seemed that his Buddhism consisted of alternating phases of passive reflexion and study and active propagandising and missionary work (not unlike his proselytism a quarter of a century earlier in Montreal). Now suddenly there intruded a political dimension — heralded, it is true, by Trebitsch's vague threats as early as 1916, but until this point to all appearances merely a figment of his frequently overheated imagination.

The Panchen (or Tashi) Lama was one of the two senior figures in the monkish hierarchy of Tibet, the other being the Dalai Lama. For centuries the relationship between the holders of the two offices had been uneasy, and in recent decades the Dalai Lama had tended to be associated with Russian and British Indian interests while the Panchen Lama was regarded as closer to the Chinese. Relations between the two rival monks degenerated in the early 1920s, and in February 1924 the Panchen Lama fled into exile in China, where he was accorded a State welcome in Peking in February 1925. At the time of Trebitsch's arrival in Peking he was reported to be in Mongolia, where he seems to have indulged in various shadowy intrigues with a view to reinstating himself in his homeland.[29]

On 4 November a police report, relayed to the British Legation, stated that Trebitsch had moved from the Hotel du Nord to rooms

18 The Panchen Lama

over a shop belonging to one E. Lee. The next day a British resident in Peking wrote to a friend at the Legation:

> Three times when my wife and I have been on the wall, we have met a man taking a walk, who, we feel sure from the photograph, is Lincoln, quite well dressed in foreign clothes, about 5 ft 9 in high, stoutly built, side view showed that he has a "Roman" nose. He was walking alone each time, and, evidently, like ourselves, taking fresh air and exercize.[30]

A handwritten note on the letter suggested that Trebitsch was now seeking to disguise his so easily recognized physiognomy: 'Russian beard his most prominent feature.' Soon after this sighting of Trebitsch taking his constitutional, he once again disappeared from town — without even delivering his lecture on Buddhism. The next official report on him arrived a month later, on 7 December 1927, and stated that British military forces at Tientsin* had received information that Trebitsch had arrived at Mukden in Manchuria and was trying to reach the Panchen Lama.[31]

We know, of course, that Trebitsch was keen to meet the Lama in order to secure permission to enter Tibet, but why did he so precipitately abandon his plan to wait until the spring before moving off, leaving Peking in such a hurry that he did not even afford himself the pleasure of appearing once again on a public platform? The answer seems to lie in a squalid little intrigue, of which Trebitsch was for once the victim rather than the initiator.

Shortly after his arrival in Peking, Trebitsch, as was his practice wherever he went at this period, had sought out local European Buddhists, partly no doubt in order to exchange views with like minds, but also, we may be sure, in the hope of obtaining more than merely spiritual nourishment from such new acquaintances.

The little group of European Buddhists in Peking was headed by a strangely-matched duumvirate of British expatriates — Mr Basil Crump and Mrs Alice Leighton Cleather, who were both staying (together with Mrs Cleather's son) at the Wagons-Lits Hotel. Crump was the former editor of the *Law Times* in London, but in 1912 he had been compelled to retire on account of what Mrs Cleather later described as 'a nervous breakdown through over-work'.[32] Long interested in psychic research, Crump had first met Mrs Cleather in 1892, the two being drawn together by their mutual attraction to Theosophism. Mrs Cleather had been an associate of the founder of the Theosophical Society, Mrs Blavatsky. After the latter's death she had refused to accept the leadership of Mrs Annie Besant, the socialist, educationalist, politician, and mystic who now headed the main body of the movement. Denouncing Mrs Besant, who, she wrote, was involved with a known 'sex pervert', and repudiating also a rival leader, Mrs Tingley, she promoted her own claims to the true succession to the movement's founder.[33]

In 1918 Mrs Cleather, by now a wealthy widow, travelled to India accompanied by her son and by Crump. According to her account, all three of them were initiated into the 'exoteric Buddhist order of 'Yellow Caps'' in India in 1920.[34] In the course of the next few years they made a number of expeditions towards Tibet, and in the spring of 1926 they moved on to Peking. In the Chinese capital they sought to establish themselves as exponents of Buddhism among the local

* A garrison of 1,631 British troops was at this time stationed at Tientsin (H.G. Woodhead, ed. *The China Year Book 1928* (Tientsin 1928), p. 1298).

European community. With a view to confirming their Buddhist credentials they established contact with another recent arrival in Peking, the Panchen Lama. By chance the Tibetan potentate shared with Crump an enthusiasm for fast motor-cars, and it may have been this common interest that secured the group admission to the exiled Lama's entourage. From the Panchen Lama Mrs Cleather claimed to have received 'ratification' of her membership of the 'Yellow Caps'. She, Crump, and other members of the group were received at Buddhist temples in Peking: a photograph taken at the Kwang Tze Temple in March 1926 shows the British Buddhists posing with the Panchen Lama and members of his suite.[35] When the Lama moved to Manchuria Mrs Cleather and Crump remained in touch with his representatives in Peking. Crump later wrote sympathetically of the political aims of the Panchen Lama: 'At the end of 1926, after an anti-Bolshevik government had been established in Peking, the Tashi [Panchen] Lama went to Mukden and later to Inner Mongolia, where his immense moral and religious influence as the Spiritual Head of Asiatic Buddhism was continually directed against the anti-religious power of Bolshevism.'[36]

Then, in the autumn of 1927, just as the Cleather-Crump group had settled down happily in Peking, Trebitsch arrived. His sporting of a Buddhist name, his disapproval of Theosophism, his announcement that he intended to deliver a Buddhist lecture, his efforts to contact the Panchen Lama, his desire to travel to Tibet — all this represented, in the eyes of Crump and Mrs Cleather, a direct challenge to their own pre-eminent position as the local leaders of European Buddhism. Their previous careers of vicious sectarian controversy with Mrs Besant, Mrs Tingley, Mrs Bailey, Mr and Mrs Sinnett and other supposed deviates from the path laid down by Mrs Blavatsky demonstrated their utter lack of scruple when faced with such challenges. To Trebitsch they showed no quarter, but in his case they resorted not to frontal assault but to more underhand methods.

A letter written by Crump on 20 November 1927 to a friend in England describes the opening of their campaign:

> Many thanks for yours of Oct. 28 with cutting [from the *Westminster Gazette* of 29 October: evidently the letter was misdated] re Lincoln. We were very glad to have this, as he called on us here, on his arrival, and wanted us to give him an introduction to the Panshen [Tashi] Lama's people here. We found he had all the theosophical and Buddhist talk pat, but Mrs Cleather did not like him and wrote putting him off. This led him to write an angry reply, which showed his hand, and soon after a friend of ours on the Press identified him and at once wired the Westminster Gazette, from whom Reuters repeated it here, whereupon he soon

> departed for 'parts unknown'. Of course, the Tashi Lama's people were duly warned. Mrs Henderson [another member of the Crump-Cleather party] reports his lecturing on Buddhism at Victoria [BC] on the way here, and he was going to lecture here if he had been able to conceal his identity. He had grown a beard and long moustache, but we at once recognised the picture you sent.... After he left, a letter arrived for him from a certain power advising 'immediate action', but it was intercepted by the Chinese, and reached our friend's ears, who again warned the parties concerned.[37]

Crump did not rest content with chasing Trebitsch out of Peking. Alarmed at the news that Trebitsch had been seen in Mukden trying to get in touch with the Panchen Lama, to whom the Cleather-Crump group felt they had exclusive entrée, Crump wrote again to his friend in England. The recipient of Crump's letters, G.D. Whiteman, a bank manager in South Croydon, acting no doubt at Crump's behest, forwarded extracts from them to the Foreign Office. Whiteman added his own commendation of the Cleather-Crump group: 'You may be assured that they are all good patriots, and satisfactory in every way. The only thing is that they seem to need warning about people like Lincoln.'

The reader will no doubt detect a curious logical inconsistency here. It was, after all, the Cleather-Crump group who were doing the warning in the first place; why then should the proposed result of their own representations (through Mr Whiteman) be another 'warning' directed back to themselves? The answer (as well as the motive of Crump) is, of course, transparent: Trebitsch had not been detected doing anything illegal; the British Legation, after all, had assured him that he was free to lecture in Peking if he wished; Crump could not actually show that Trebitsch was working against British interests. True, he was trying to contact the Panchen Lama — but in view of Crump's own record of intimacy with the Tibetan monk that could not be complained of directly; hence the confused story of intrigues involving the Bolsheviks and the Dalai Lama. Crump could not openly avow his (and Mrs Cleather's) fear that Trebitsch might subvert their leadership of European Buddhism in Peking; hence the oblique approaches through local journalists, unnamed friends in official quarters, and the Croydon bank manager.

This indirect method of attack calls to mind an earlier incident. Had not Mr Davidson, Trebitsch's former commercial rival in Chungking, adopted a strikingly similar form of aggression in 1923? He too contacted the Foreign Office through intermediaries; he too identified Trebitsch from photographs; he too claimed to act solely out of disinterested patriotism; and he too concealed behind this public-spirited front a desire to expunge a formidable competitor from the Chinese arena. One might almost feel sorry for Trebitsch — were it not that such roundabout conspiracies had so often in the past been his own favoured form of battle. Unlike Davidson, Crump swept Trebitsch from the field. Although he paid occasional visits to Peking after this, he never stayed long and he took care to keep well clear of the British Buddhists.

Trebitsch later told a journalist that he had not succeeded in gaining an audience with the Panchen Lama at Mukden.[38] In any case, he did not stay long in Manchuria, for by early January 1928 he was back in Peking. In March he popped up in Hong Kong.[39] British intelligence agents appear to have followed him to Shanghai, from where it was reported in June that he had evaded surveillance, having recently adopted a new alias, 'Jack Fisher'.[40] Only in August was it learnt at the British Legation that Trebitsch had settled down in Tientsin, where he had been living since mid-May at the Pension Bourgeoise in the French Concession.[41] Here he succeeded once again in turning tables, if not on Crump, at least on British officialdom in China who had banned him from entering their offices and had set their detectives to trail after him around north China.

On 16 August 1928 Trebitsch was the guest speaker at a luncheon 'tiffin' of the Tientsin Rotary Club. Appropriately (perhaps) the occasion took place in the Astor House Hotel in the British Concession, where, three years earlier, he had experienced the mystical revelation that enabled him to 'walk out of the lunatic asylum — the world'. A reporter for the local English-language newspaper wrote a long and enthusiastic description of the meeting which was attended by 'a more than usually large' audience. Trebitsch 'wore a neat suit of Tussore silk with a bow, and looked (according to our amanuensis) much younger than his 59 years' — not all that surprising, since Trebitsch was in fact only 49 years old at the time. Trebitsch was 'somewhat bald and with a keen intellectual face' which was said to show 'few outward signs of the stress of a life which is one of the most extraordinary and romantic that a man has ever lived'. The greater part of Trebitsch's address was devoted to an exposition of the teachings of Buddha; for us the most interesting passage in his speech was, however, that in which he declared that he had 'finished with all political work, directly and indirectly', and yet again offered the hand of reconciliation to the British Government: 'It is my intention and my desire to let byegones by byegones and if the British Government will make one step towards me I will make two towards them.' Trebitsch's speech was warmly applauded and extensively publicised.[42] All in all, he had every right to be pleased with this, his first public lecture in China.

If the British Government had been fortunate enough to have at

19 Trebitsch Lincoln in 1928

this time in Tientsin consular officers who (a) knew how to obey instructions or (b) possessed at least a modicum of common sense, this trivial incident might have passed by as an ephemeral irritation. Unfortunately both obedience and intelligence seem to have been in short supply at the Tientsin Consulate-General, as the embarrassing sequel indicates. Trebitsch, evidently on the crest of a wave of euphoria after his oratorical triumph, walked out of the Astor House Hotel after the meeting, and decided, while things were apparently going his way, to beard the local British authorities in their den. He called first on the Superintendent of the British Muncipal Police and asked for police protection. The police chief told him that this was a matter for the Consulate-General and handed him a card to take round to the Consulate. Armed with this introduction, Trebitsch arrived at the consular office, where, after an initial fracas with the constable at the door, he was interviewed by the Vice-Consul, A.H.

George. The consul's report, submitted the same day, failed to discern any very clear purpose behind the unexpected call:

> I asked why in particular he wanted police protection, as I was not aware that he was being molested or threatened. He admitted that this was so. I asked him where he was living. He evaded the question . . . He kept repeating his desire for 'reconciliation'. I said I was pleased to take note of his assurances. . . . People who have met him in Tientsin have derived the impression that he is tending towards insanity. He did not give me any such impression. He struck me as just what one would expect a person of his birth and antecedents to be, intelligent, but without any personal charm or magnetism that I could discover, in fact the reverse.[43]

Consul George had, of course, disobeyed standing instructions not to receive Trebitsch at any British mission — but a more serious error was made by his superior, the Consul-General, Sir James Jamieson. 'J.J.', as he was familiarly known (also, less familiarly, 'Monkey'), was an old-fashioned, somewhat pompous proconsular type who believed that his main task was to uphold British imperial prestige. Morris 'Two-Gun' Cohen, who liked and respected him, though they came into conflict more than once, remembered him as 'stiff and dignified and pretty peppery, too, when things happened to go wrong'.[44] The sensible course would have been to ignore the entire affair. Instead, Jamieson took the absurd step of picking a quarrel with the Rotary Club. In a dispatch to the British Minister in Peking, Jamieson explained:

> It was . . . the American element, by far the most considerable in the Club, which was responsible for the invitation. I understand the incident has given much offence to some of the British members, and has therefore added nothing to the Club's avowed object of international comity. I have seized upon it as an opportunity to withdraw from honorary membership of the Club, with which I was never very much in sympathy.[45]

The Minister himself, Sir Miles Lampson, was equally irritated. Even before receiving Jamieson's dispatch he had noted: 'I see this man has been addressing the Tientsin Rotary Club. How came they to ask such a creature to speak? It really is the limit.'[46]

Trebitsch could hardly have wished for more satisfying consequences of his first appearance on a Chinese public platform: not only had he secured widespread favourable publicity and impressed an audience of expatriate businessmen; he had also infuriated two senior British diplomats, and induced one of them to take a step which could not but cause bad blood between British and American residents in Tientsin — after Shanghai the most important foreign settlement in north China. In short, Trebitsch had demonstrated once again, albeit at a local level, his unique capacity for stirring up trouble wherever he went.

Trebitsch remained utterly obsessed with the idea of reaching Tibet;[47] but once again, it seems, he was foiled. He was next heard of in June 1929, when he was reported to be living at the Holländisch Restaurant in the French Concession at Shanghai.[48] Later that month he embarked on the ss *Trier*, bound for Hamburg. The German consulate in Shanghai had refused him a visa, but he was in possession of an Italian visa. The purpose of his journey was, he said, to pay a call on the German Buddhist savant, Dr Georg Grimm, at his home in Munich.[49] Trebitsch had been corresponding with him for the previous two years, and in a letter to Grimm shortly before his departure from Shanghai stated that he had recently been issued with a Chinese passport, valid for one year, in his own name.[50]

As the ship proceeded towards Europe, the German Foreign Ministry sent cables to German consular posts at ports all along the route, warning them to refuse any application by Trebitsch for a visa.[51] When the *Trier* docked at Genoa Trebitsch got involved in a furious wrangle with the German consul there over the question of a visa.[52] Unable to land at Hamburg, Trebitsch continued to Rotterdam; from there he took a train across the Netherlands and Belgium to France.[53] From Paris he wrote to Grimm explaining that, because of the lack of a visa, he had been obliged to call off his projected visit to Munich.[54] In a letter to the German Foreign Ministry, Grimm reported that Trebitsch was much upset by the refusal of the visa, and had even threatened to commit suicide if he was not granted admission to Germany.[55] But the government would not alter its decision.

By May 1930 Trebitsch was back in Shanghai. But he did not stay in China for long. Two months later he set off again for Europe, this time in the company of Gustav Ritter von Kreitner, the friend of Colonel Bauer whom Trebitsch had met at the time of his negotiations for a Chinese loan in Zurich in the autumn of 1923.[56] Kreitner had returned to China in March 1928, and thanks to his connexion with Bauer was subsequently appointed to a governmental position in Nanking. Some years earlier Trebitsch had entrusted to Kreitner the task of compiling material for Trebitsch's autobiography.[57] One purpose of Trebitsch's renewed visit to Europe appears to have been the completion of arrangements for the publication of the book.

Trebitsch's memoirs were published in German by a Viennese firm in 1931. Subsequently an English translation appeared in London and New York. By far the most readable of Trebitsch's books, this presented a kaleidoscopic view of his life: highly coloured, bizarre images flashed before the reader's eye in rapidly revolving succession. Dramatised tableaux of the great scenes of his career (some of them, such as his visit to the German Crown Prince, inventions) alternated with intervals of reticence. Thus his relations with the British and German intelligence services during the Great War were passed over in three pages. The author of *Revelations of an International Spy* now denied that he had ever engaged in espionage; his visit to Rotterdam in December 1914, according to this revised account, had been actuated solely by anxiety as to the welfare of his mother-in-law (at that time in Hamburg). Much of the book consisted of typical posturing, self-glorification and tall stories. But he ended on a downbeat, lamenting his failure to reach Tibet, his treatment after the Tientsin Rotary Club lecture, the refusal of European governments to grant him entry visas, and what he termed the 'folly' of his own enmity to England, which he now acknowledged as the 'one real bulwark of civilisation'.[58]

The appearance of the book attracted considerable press interest, but Trebitsch, who was normally gratified by public attention, disowned the work. In a letter to a Buddhist acquaintance in Germany, he declared that the text had been so much altered that he hardly recognized it any more.[59] That Trebitsch's complaint was not altogether without foundation is proved by letters written at about this time by Kreitner to Bauer's former secretary, Luise Engeler. In one of these Kreitner complained that further changes had been made (apparently by the publishers) without *his* consent. But he admitted that he had made some changes to Trebitsch's text: 'In the first manuscript there were many libellous remarks. I deleted what I could. . . . I could not of course totally sabotage the will of the author.'[60]

The publication of Trebitsch's memoirs heightened interest in his activities and the legends that accreted round his name. Meanwhile Trebitsch took another step which increased still further the sense of exotic mystery attached to him. After returning to China in late 1930 he remained in Shanghai for a few months, and then set out for Pao-hua Shan, a monastery near Nanking.

There, in May 1931, he was ordained a Buddhist monk. At the same time he once again took on a new name — by which he was to be known for the rest of his life — Chao Kung, to which Trebitsch (as we shall continue to call him) prefixed the title, 'The Venerable'.

The lengthy initiation ceremonies required weeks of prayer, fasting, and ordeals. On one occasion, Trebitsch later recounted, he and his one hundred fellow-novices had to go through a process of kneeling, chanting, and standing up a total of 108 times.[61] In a letter to Walter Persian, his German Buddhist correspondent, he announced that he had been ordained a *Bikkhu* (monk) on 11 May. On 19 May he was raised to the rank of *Bodhisattva*. One day earlier

20 Ordination ceremonies at Pao-hua Shan, May 1931 (Trebitsch circled at top left.)

21 Trebitsch Lincoln (second from left) at his ordination as a Buddhist monk at Pao-hua Shan in May 1931. On his left is the explorer, J. Prip-Møller

he had had twelve little stars (representing the twelve *Nidanas*, spokes on the Wheel of Becoming) branded on his scalp.[62] In a press interview a few weeks afterwards Trebitsch gave an account of this final ordeal:

> The most arduous part was the burning which is done on the skull with 12 small candles. They are first dipped in India ink and when applied give forth suffocating fumes which can be withstood only by gripping the object in front, which are the legs of your Buddhist teacher, who has to do the burning. A shawl is wrapped around your head to protect the eyes. The intense pain lasts for 10 hours, and we had to keep on our feet all the time, not going to bed until midnight, because the fumes might prove poisonous to our minds or hearts. The burning is a symbol to show that we are dead to all sensations.[63]

The ordination rites were witnessed by the Danish authority on Chinese Buddhist monasticism, J. Prip-Møller, who took a photograph of him at the time of his initiation. Prip-Møller's detailed description of the ceremonies corroborates Trebitsch's account.[64]

Following this ordination Trebitsch went to Peking (perhaps with a view to flaunting his new dignity in the face of the Crump-Cleather clique). He delivered a number of public lectures, wrote enthusiastic letters to Persian (who appears to have developed into a disciple-by-correspondence) and spoke of retiring to a monastery in Tibet or returning to Europe to found 'an International Buddhist Centre' there.[65] He insisted that 'he had no desire whatsoever to engage in political work or propaganda of any kind'.[66]

Yet even as he professed to seek a new life of spiritual calm and tranquil reflexion, in retreat from the horrors of the material world, he continued his incessant harassment and importunate nagging of foreign diplomats, newspapermen, and indeed almost anybody who would listen. In embracing Buddhism, a part of Trebitsch no doubt genuinely aspired to attain that abolition of Self, that merging of the individual consciousness in a universal '*Bodhi-citta*, which is all-Love all-Wisdom and all else'[67] — the ideal of *Nirvana*. Few men needed such inner peace more desperately than Trebitsch, and his conversion and ordination represented, in some sense, a recognition of that need. But Trebitsch's personality was, to say the least, poorly equipped for the attainment of this state of self-forgoing perfection. Tantalised by the dim perception of this goal, and tormented by the impossibility of its achievement, his mind seesawed ever more violently between mania and depression.

CHAPTER 14

The Abbot of Shanghai

Trebitsch's ordination as a Buddhist monk at the age of fifty-two did not put a stop to the wanderings that had characterised his existence for more than a decade. Indeed, during his first three years as a *Bodhisattva*, the frequency, distance, and duration of his meanderings actually increased. But during this time also he displayed a tendency to return again and again to the same resting-place, as if to pause for breath and reflection. In so far as he could call anywhere home during the last dozen years of his life, it was Shanghai. For someone of Trebitsch's unusual disposition, capabilities, and requirements, the unique social and political configuration of this city in the decade before the outbreak of the Pacific war rendered it specially suitable as a base and stamping-ground.

China's largest industrial centre, her greatest port, and her most heavily and densely populated urban area, Shanghai was a bustling, vital, intellectually creative, semi-westernised metropolis whose cosmopolitan character had been reinforced in the 1920s by the arrival of thousands of anti-Bolshevik émigrés from Soviet Russia. From 1932 onwards the Japanese army tightened a vice-like grip around the city, squeezing ever closer to the little European enclaves of quasi-colonial dominion, the International Settlement and the French Concession. Notorious for its criminal underworld, its gambling, prostitution, and protection rackets, its swarms of deformed beggars, its opium dens, and its extremes of ostentatiously displayed wealth and abject destitution, Shanghai in this period retained its reputation as the most dynamic, but also the most dangerous, city in Asia.

Yet for 'the Venerable Chao Kung' these degenerate surroundings proved to be, at one level, a benign environment. Life (that is, the cost of living) was cheap, the political confusion afforded him outlets for his conspiratorial and propagandist urges, and the air of excitement and almost perpetual tension helped lift him out of his depressions and intensified his moments of euphoria. But at another level the environment was profoundly malignant for a man who was already suffering from mental illness. Voyeur-like we now turn to view the distressing spectacle of Trebitsch being slowly consumed by his psychosis with its alternating rhythms of morbid melancholia and mystic ecstasy.

In Shanghai Trebitsch rarely stayed at one address for long. In 1932 he was living on Route Amiral Courbet in the French Concession. In 1933 he was reported to have set up a 'Buddhist House' at 131 Great Western Road in the Chinese Municipality of Greater Shanghai. In 1934 he stayed first at the Astor House Hotel, then at the Burlington Hotel on the Bubbling Well Road in the International Settlement. In 1935 he moved to a boarding-house at 23 rue Corneille in the French Concession.

From the time of his ordination until his death Trebitsch was never again seen in public in European clothes. His normal attire was 'a black robe with close-fitting white trousers and carpet slippers, a skull-cap on his closely-shaven head, and a string of beads'.[1] The reformed sybarite's diet was now exclusively vegetarian. (Had his campaign in 1910 against the consumption of dog-flesh been an unconscious pointer towards this final repudiation of a carnivorous life?) In one of his letters to the German Buddhist Walter Persian Trebitsch gave some details of his day-to-day pattern of life in Shanghai:

> I get up very early, between 2 and 5 o'clock in the morning, and sit down cross-legged meditating on the four infinities. I then remind myself of my four vows and meditate on the sacred eightfold path. Then I exercise insight. At about seven o'clock I wash myself. At half past seven I take some food. During the forenoon I study the words of the Sublime One, for which purpose I have my own system. In the afternoon I again practise insight and visions. In the afternoons I also receive visitors. At half-past eleven I take lunch — a little something. In the evenings again exercise in concentration. At about ten o'clock to bed.[2]

Trebitsch seems to have maintained this frugal regimen for the rest of his life.

In early 1932 external events intruded on Shanghai and on Trebitsch's hermit-like existence in a manner which thrust him back into political activity. On 18 January a group of Japanese including two monks was attacked by Chinese in the Chapei district of Shanghai: one monk was killed in the affray. The Japanese, fresh from victories over the Chinese in Manchuria, seized on the incident as a pretext for presenting a series of demands for compensation. When the response was judged inadequate they exacted retribution. At the end of January large-scale hostilities broke out between Japanese and Chinese forces in the city. The fighting continued for several months: hundreds were killed and thousands made homeless. The Japanese occupied a large part of the Chinese section of the city, and for a time seemed to threaten even the International Settlement and the French Concession. The presence in Shanghai of American, British, and French (colonial) forces gave the crisis an added international dimension, and focused on the city the anxious attention of foreign ministries, the world press, and alarmed overseas investors.

Thus only a short time after Trebitsch had begun his new life of contemplation and meditation, he found himself back where he most yearned to be — at the eye of the storm. Perhaps it was the assault on a fellow-monk that precipitated his renewed political involvement. But whatever his motive he immediately plunged into action. In his letter to Persian on 5 February, he wrote: 'For the past two weeks I have been occupied with the rescue of China.' Four days later he wrote a letter to the editor of the leading English-language newspaper of Shanghai, the *North China Daily News*, in which he presented his proposals for a resolution of the crisis. The letter began:

> I will not apologize for intruding with some suggestions into this supreme national tragedy that is being enacted before our eyes and right in our midst; nor will I apologize for my outspokenness. My right to offer a few practical suggestions . . . rests on my intimate association with China during the past ten years; it rests on the fact that what is happening now has been foretold by me for years . . . it rests on the fact that I have gone further in associating myself with the Chinese People than any foreigner before; I have a Chinese name, I wear constantly Chinese Clothes; and am the first foreigner to have been admitted into the age-old Order of Buddhist Monks in China.[3]

'Can China be saved?' Trebitsch asked. His answer consisted of an elaborate twenty-one point scheme for national regeneration, involving such unexceptionable reforms as the rooting-out of corruption and the abolition of opium dens. Above all, he laid stress on the need for the employment of foreign advisers in key administrative positions. But the content of these proposals was less significant than their form. At the height of this new Sino-Japanese conflict a plan couched in twenty-one points inevitably called to mind the notorious 'Twenty-One Demands' presented to China by Japan in 1915, a cardinal event in the rise of modern Chinese nationalism. If Trebitsch had any hope of impressing the Chinese with his scheme, this fact alone must have damned it in the eyes of all those of a patriotic disposition who bothered to look at it.

It is more probable, however, that with the sound of Japanese gunfire audible from his lodgings in the French Concession, Trebitsch was seeking to gain credit with the rising rather than the setting sun. True, he wrote that 'Japan has got sinister designs upon and against China', but his insistence that 'a War against Japan is suicidal' might be regarded by the Japanese as useful defeatist propaganda. It should not be thought that Trebitsch was at this stage a paid agent of the Japanese in China. But this letter was the first hesitant indication of movement towards a new alignment in Trebitsch's personal diplomacy — cooperation with the dynamic power which would within a decade realize Trebitsch's long-proclaimed goal; the destruction of the British empire in east Asia.

Trebitsch followed his letter with a more substantial literary endeavour. In March 1932 he published a book in Shanghai entitled *Can War be Abolished?* The author's name was given on the title page as 'Chao Kung, Buddhist Monk, formerly known as I.T. Trebitsch-Lincoln'. The frontispiece showed a berobed Trebitsch, seated cross-legged on a large cushion in a state of contemplation. There followed eighty-nine pages of jumbled ruminations on Buddhism and international politics, interspersed with autobiographical musings. The epigraphs to some of the chapters point to the author's apparently depressed and lugubrious state of mind: 'Life is frightful' (attributed to Socrates), 'Life is Death and our Body is in truth our grave' (attrib. do.), 'Labour, sorrow, grief, sickness, want and woe are the sauces of life' (attrib. Sterne), and so forth. Trebitsch deployed the full resources of punctuation and typography in his text, which was garnished with lavish over-use of capital letters, italics, exclamation and question marks. He recounted the story of his life (with suitable omissions) culminating in his mystical vision at the Astor House Hotel in Tientsin in 1925. As for politics, which consisted exclusively of lies, brutality, hypocrisy, lunacy, and humbug, he declared (not for the first time): 'I am out of it. I have fled into the VOID.'

But as usual Trebitsch's exit was prematurely announced, for his final chapter was devoted almost entirely to a discussion of politics. What was required, he suggested, was that one government should 'clearly, openly, resolutely, fearlessly' embrace truth, justice, and kindness: that government would then become 'the Centre of attraction, irresistible attraction for the rest of the world.' Was there any such government? Those of the USA, France, Germany, and Italy were briefly considered, and ruled out. Russia too was rejected, given that 'the mad intoxication of blood lust of her degenerates is not yet over.' As for Japan: 'If Japan will not mend her ways, her rapid decline towards Absolute Evil will be arrested by submerging a large part of Japan in the ocean, carrying millions of beings into the Deep. This also is a prophecy.' Almost the only Power for which

Trebitsch seemed to have a good word to say was, curiously enough, Great Britain: the book was indeed dedicated to 'His Britannic Majesty's Several Prime Ministers'. Even now it seems that Trebitsch had still not abandoned hope of a 'reconciliation'.

In a letter to Persian, Trebitsch explained that he hoped to earn enough money from the sales of the book to enable him to travel to Europe to realize his ambition of founding a Buddhist monastery.[4] But in mid-April he received a letter from Persian which caused him to break off relations with his would-be disciple suddenly and definitively. The cause of the breach was Persian's announcement of the establishment in Hamburg of a Buddhist Society. Trebitsch was enraged by what he no doubt saw as a pre-emption of his own plans. His final letter to Persian demanded to know 'who or what entitles you, and what are your perfect qualifications, to do such a thing?' He informed Persian sternly that he was obliged to cease all contact with him. The letter ended not with the usual Buddhist salutations, but with a curt 'Mit Gruss, Chao Kung'.[5] This bitter conclusion to his pen-friendship with Persian was unfortunately characteristic of Trebitsch's inability, by this stage in his mental illness, to form any enduring relationship other than one in which he was totally dominant.

The rupture does not appear to have distressed Trebitsch unduly, for within a few days he was once again enjoying his favourite pastime, public speaking. The interruption of one of his Buddhist lectures in Shanghai by a Christian heckler in the audience was, of course, a welcome challenge to the seasoned veteran of the battle for souls in Montreal, Cardinal, Iroquois and Ogdensburg.[6] This was useful training for his last — and astonishingly successful — missionary campaign, which was now about to open.

In June 1932 Trebitsch again applied to the German consulate in Shanghai for a visa to visit Germany.[7] On this occasion he enjoyed the good fortune of gaining the support of the Consul, Baron Rüdt von Collenberg, who sent a long letter to Berlin in support of Trebitsch's application. The Consul confirmed that Trebitsch was no longer involved in politics (a curious assertion in view of his recent public pronouncements); his 'literary and other scholarly and religious activities' were said to have aroused the admiration of prominent members of the German community in Shanghai; and his recently published book, 'written in parts with touching urgency', was offered as further evidence that he had changed 'from a Saul to a Paul, from a politician to an unpolitical Buddhist'.[8] Trebitsch could hardly have wished for a more enthusiastic letter of recommendation had he written it himself.

Before a reply to his application arrived, Trebitsch left for Europe on 1 August aboard the ss *Trianon*, sailing to Antwerp. On 25

August, while he was still at sea, the German Interior Ministry agreed to grant him an entry visa.[9] The main reason given for the change of heart by the German Government was the assurance furnished by the Consul in Shanghai that Trebitsch had given up political activity. The price that had been placed on Trebitsch's head following his participation in the Kapp putsch had been set aside in 1925 when the newly-elected President Hindenburg had decreed an amnesty for all those still wanted in connection with the abortive coup.[10] Trebitsch was therefore free to enter Germany again without any fear of legal complications. Or so it seemed.

On 10 September the *Trianon* reached Marseilles. Trebitsch had intended to continue with the ship to Antwerp. But on the quay awaiting him he found a group of French Buddhists from Nice, whose acquaintance he had made during his visit to France in 1929. They pressed him to stay with them for a time. He happily accepted the invitation, and moved in as the guest of Madame Escoffier, a Buddhist whose home was in Nice.[11] Trebitsch spent three pleasant weeks on the Côte d'Azur with the French Buddhists. He received money from them for his onward journey, and at the beginning of October set off for Germany by train (third class). He went first to Munich in order to visit Grimm. From there he hoped to travel to Hungary, where he had thoughts of founding a Buddhist monastery. Perhaps he was encouraged in this direction by news of the appointment as Prime Minister of Hungary of his old associate in the White International, Gyula Gömbös.[12] Trebitsch's mother was by now dead, but he still had many relatives in Budapest whom he might have visited. He did not, however, go back to his native land.

Instead, Trebitsch went to Berlin, where he delivered a lecture at a meeting sponsored by a local Buddhist group, the 'Gemeinde um Buddha', in the Philharmonic hall.[13] From there he travelled to Brussels, apparently with the intention of going on to Sweden. But on the way from Berlin to Brussels he suspected he was being followed by a man he concluded was a British secret agent. At Liège there appeared two further men who he decided were French agents.[14] After three days in Brussels Trebitsch was arrested by the police and deported as an undesirable character.[15] He went back to Germany and continued to give public lectures. But on 3 November he was arrested again, this time in Cologne, shortly after speaking on the subject 'My Way to Buddha'.[16] This arrest took place at the request of an old enemy, Mrs Nieuwkamp, wife of the Dutch Consul in Cologne, to whom Trebitsch still owed the large sum of money he had borrowed at the time of his visit to the Hague in 1919.[17] After a few days in prison Trebitsch managed to secure his release by swearing a declaration of insolvency.[18] He stated that, apart from claims against the proprietors of several concert halls,

22 Abbot Chao Kung, leaving a vegetarian restaurant in Berlin, 1932

he had no assets, and as a poor Buddhist monk owned nothing but travelling and ritual articles.[19]

After this dispiriting experience Trebitsch returned to his Buddhist friends in Berlin for a short stay. From there he went again to Nice. After a few weeks he applied for a renewed entry visa to Germany. The application was strongly supported in a letter to the German Foreign Minister from eighteen members of the Berlin Buddhist community.[20] But their letter was dated 2 February 1933; three days earlier Adolf Hitler had assumed office as Chancellor and a new era had begun for Germany, for the world — and for Trebitsch. On 7 February a meeting of senior Foreign and Interior Ministry officials in Berlin decided against granting Trebitsch a further entry visa.[21] He never returned to Germany again — although, as we shall see, this was by no means the end of his contacts with the German authorities.

Trebitsch arrived back in Shanghai on 25 June. His first effort to establish a Buddhist monastery in Europe had failed. But in the course of his eleven months of travel he had accomplished something almost as impressive. The extent of his achievement was revealed on 25 July, when ten Europeans reached Shanghai and joined Trebitsch in residence at the 'Buddhist House' at 131 Great Western Road. A few days later three more arrived.[22] (A fourteenth recruit, a young German woman, committed suicide en route to China by jumping overboard near Singapore.) All had been recruited by Trebitsch during his visit to Europe. They ranged in age from twenty-one to fifty-two, and included at least six members of the Nice Buddhist group (among them Madame Escoffier) and several adherents of the Gemeinde um Buddha from Berlin, including their leader, Martin Steinke.[23] They came to China to study Buddhism as disciples of the Chao Kung and with a view to taking the monkish vows and spending the rest of their lives in contemplation and the effort to attain *Nirvana* under his supervision. From about this time, by virtue of his new role as father-figure to the group of thirteen novices, Trebitsch awarded himself the title of 'Abbot'.

Truly this was an astonishing success! Thirty years earlier, as a young and vigorous missionary in Montreal, with all the resources of the Presbyterian and Anglican Churches behind him, Trebitsch had failed to convert a single soul. Yet now, entirely alone, without any organization behind him, lacking enough money even to pay off old debts, Trebitsch had converted thirteen men and women to a strange religion which offered no material inducements, but on the contrary demanded (through the mouth of its interpreter, Trebitsch) that they hand over all their worldly possessions to the 'Abbot', and follow him to the other side of the world to settle in uncomfortable quarters in a dangerous, war-racked country. If we were to regard

Trebitsch merely as a confidence trickster, this was surely the greatest coup of his career. But that is the beginning, not the end, of an explanation. For Trebitsch was a great deal more than a successful con-man. Nor would it be fair to categorize him as an impostor: for there is no doubt that Trebitsch himself was utterly convinced that he was endowed with mystic and prophetic revelations and powers. Without such an inner conviction it would, in any case, have been impossible for him to function for several years as guru of this quasi-monastic sect.

For a full explanation of the phenomenon we must look beyond the individual psychology of the self-proclaimed prophet to the social and intellectual climate in which he operated. The onset of the great depression in Europe, the apparent decrepitude of the established Christian churches, the rise of the competing ideologies of Nazism and Communism, and the inability of political and economic liberalism to respond to the crisis which seemed to threaten the very survival of bourgeois society — all this provided fertile soil for the sprouting throughout western Europe of an interest in eastern religions in general, and Buddhism in particular. In England the Buddhist Society split off from the Theosophists in 1926; shortly afterwards the schismatics set up a Buddhist Shrine in Lancaster Gate north of Hyde Park in London. In France 'Les Amis du Bouddhisme', formed in 1929 by the American-born Miss Constant Lounsbery, attracted the cream of café society and prominent Sorbonne intellectuals to the study of eastern religion. In Germany, Dr Paul Dahlke opened the first western *Vihara* (Buddhist retreat or monastery) near Berlin; as we have seen, a similar establishment was founded by Persian in Hamburg.[24] A poisonous variant of the trend was the movement founded by General Ludendorff under the influence of his second wife: this blended anti-semitism, anti-Bolshevism, anti-Catholicism, and atavistic Teutonism in an intoxicating quasi-mystical brew.

Trebitsch thus launched his Buddhist ark on a flood-tide. But he tended to be critical of many of these similar (and therefore rival) conventicles of European enthusiasts for oriental mysticism. He was scathing in his contempt for the Paris group: 'From the standpoint of *Buddha-Dhamma* [Buddhist teaching], the Paris group is absolutely worthless!', he wrote to Persian in 1931.[25] He denounced those who sought to elucidate the wisdom of the Enlightened One through pedantic philological scholarship — Dahlke, Rhys Davids, and Sir Max Mueller all (according to Trebitsch) fell into this category.[26] We have already observed Trebitsch's falling-out with the Cleather-Crump clique in Peking. And as for the second Mrs Ludendorff, one of whose publications was sent to him by Persian for inspection, Trebitsch dismissed her scornfully: 'the less said the better!'

was his only comment on the book.*[27] Indeed, of all contemporary European Buddhists only Dr Grimm met with Trebitsch's unqualified approval.

There was more to this than the competitive sectarianism of what were, after all, numerically insignificant religious groups. Oddly (given his personal history of fraud, duplicity and imposture), what Trebitsch could offer to potential disciples more effectively than any of these rivals was a touch of authenticity. Most of his followers, after all, were not, strictly speaking, converts. The Nice group had originally been Theosophists; Trebitsch steered them towards Buddhism proper (if his own variety may thus be termed). The Berlin group were already Buddhists; their leader, Martin Steinke, edited a Buddhist periodical and had even published a little book on Buddhism.[31] To these seekers after a higher truth, Trebitsch appeared as a prophet from the East — the 'Master' as Steinke called him.[32] His Buddhism was not the sophisticated salon mysticism of Madame David-Neel and her Paris coterie, nor the etiolated eclecticism of the English Buddhists, nor yet the crankish Theosophism of Mrs Cleather in China. By comparison with these, the Abbot Chao Kung, freshly arrived from Shanghai, clad in his robe and slippers, with the twelve spokes of the Wheel of Becoming branded on his scalp as a constant reminder of his induction into a Chinese Buddhist order, seemed like a genuine whiff of the Orient next to pale European imitators. Only too late did Trebitsch's victims discover that the slow boat to China was not an ark of salvation but a slave-ship bearing them to a destination in the vicinity of Hell.

After a short stay in Shanghai, Trebitsch and twelve of his fol-

* The aversion was probably mutual. Her husband's attitude to Trebitsch at this period is on record. In a letter to Ernst Bauer (son of Colonel Max Bauer) in 1934, Ludendorff called Trebitsch 'a very evil man'.[28] During this later part of his life the increasingly senile general came more and more under the influence of his second wife, Mathilde von Kemnitz. Her hold over his mind spread (according to a recent biographer) 'like an evil stain'.[29] Thanks to her, Ludendorff himself wrote, he 'became aware of the fungi within the structure of our society . . . in the form of secret supranational forces, i.e. the Jewish people and Rome, along with their tools, the Freemasons, the Jesuit order, occult and satanistic structures'.[30] Two essays of Ludendorff's, published posthumously by his wife, open a window into his crazed personality: in these he quotes at length from the writings of his friend Sven Hedin concerning the Panchen Lama; he inveighs against lamaism; he attacks the Theosophists, the Jews, the Pope, Mrs Blavatsky, Mrs Besant, Rudolf Steiner, and Mr Eden. He even drags in the ten-year-old Princess Elizabeth of England! From this litany of hatred, Trebitsch, the closest thing to a lama that Ludendorff had ever met, is surprisingly absent. Perhaps the general did not wish to revive the unsettling memory of his own earlier connexions with Trebitsch in the days of the Kapp putsch and the White International! Perhaps he too felt that 'the less said the better'? For the Ludendorff essays, see E. and M. Ludendorff, *Europa den Asiatenpriestern?* (Munich 1941).

lowers (the thirteenth dropped out soon after their arrival) moved to Ch'i-hsia Shan, a monastery near Nanking. On 26 November 1933, 'a most eminent monk, Ch'ing-ch'üan, the retired abbot of Chin Shan'[33] presided, and a large crowd, including senior Chinese officials, the Soviet Ambassador to China, Dmitri Bogomolov, several journalists, and a French diplomat, witnessed the initiation ceremony during which the twelve Europeans, together with 150 Chinese, were consecrated and introduced to the first degree of holiness. Prior to the public rite Trebitsch delivered an interview, or harangue, to the press. He complained of persecution by British agents. He threatened darkly that if he were forbidden to move freely throughout Europe to propagate Buddhism 'then the time will come for all Christian missionaries in China, and later on in other parts of Asia, to get their luggage ready and go home'. The report in the *Peiping Chronicle** of 7 December continued:

> Asked whether he had ever met the Panchen Lama, Abbot Chao Kung replied that he had not, 'but I shall have the great honour and pleasure of meeting him soon'. The Panchen Lama, continued Abbot Chao Kung, is at present in Mongolia but sent a telegram to his personal representative in Nanking, ordering him to come here to this monastery, 'salute me in his name, and, as His Holiness kindly put it, "invite me in co-operation with him in the propagation of the doctrine of the Buddha, in the Western world"'. [*sic*] The representative of the Panchen Lama visited Abbot Chao Kung last Sunday and informed him that the former was coming to Nanking. 'I shall return to the Western world, his emissary, and thus start my missionary work under the most propitious auspices, for His Holiness is the highest spiritual authority of the Buddhist world.'

The occasion constituted a major publicity triumph for Trebitsch; the *New York Times* hailed it as evidence that 'Buddhism today is preparing to make its first important bid for a place in the heterodoxy of Europe' and described Trebitsch as the leader of the movement.[34]

A more jaundiced version of these events was produced by the British Consul at Nanking, A.P. Blunt, who had not been invited but had obtained a detailed description from the French representative, M. Baudet. In his report on the affair, Blunt speculated on what might lie behind Trebitsch's Buddhist missionary movement in Europe:

* Peking had been renamed 'Peiping' ('Northern Peace') in 1928, following its occupation by the nationalist Kuomintang forces of Chiang Kai-shek. During the decade from 1927 to 1937 the capital of China was at Nanking.

> Both M. Baudet and myself have the impression that the enterprise may have been deliberately conceived as a stick with which to beat foreign missions and missionary enterprises in this country. Trebitsch Lincoln was described to me as having the typical face of the traitor. M. Baudet was not allowed to speak with any of the disciples except one Frenchman, of whom Trebitsch Lincoln, as it struck him, felt sure. The Italians had the faces of primitive saints [Two Italians were reported to be among the novices.]: the remainder those of criminals.[35]

Saints or criminals, the newly consecrated acolytes followed their Abbot back to Shanghai in December 1933. Trebitsch immediately set about making plans for a new expedition to Europe, in the hope once again of establishing a monastery there. On 27 December he applied to the German Consulate in Shanghai for entry visas to Germany for himself and his disciples.[36] But the friendly baron who had so enthusiastically facilitated his last visit to Germany had been removed from the consulate and replaced by a pro-Nazi, Richard Behrend.[37] The new consul told Trebitsch on the telephone that the application would have to be referred to Berlin. In the letter which he sent to the German Foreign Ministry accompanying Trebitsch's application, Behrend stated that there was no local reason for refusing a visa — but he failed to repeat his predecessor's encomium for Trebitsch's intellectual and spiritual qualities.[38]

Perhaps conscious that support at a high level would be required if he were to gain permission to re-enter Germany, Trebitsch characteristically decided to go to the top. On 8 January 1934 he addressed a letter to the German Chancellor in which he sought in a grotesque fashion to flatter Hitler into granting him a visa. After paying tribute to the Führer as a man of vision and insight, he admitted that he had not always held the Nazi leader in such high esteem. But as a result of Hitler's most recent speeches (Trebitsch declared) he now realized that he had misjudged the Führer. Graeco-Roman civilisation, he opined, was doomed; in its place there would arise, nay must arise, 'Indo-Aryan Civilisation, of which the foundations [were] the universal truths of Buddhist teaching'.[39] Interestingly, the missive made no reference at all to the brief encounter between Trebitsch and Hitler in the closing moments of the Kapp putsch in March 1920. Possibly Trebitsch did not realize that Hitler had ever set eyes on him!

Trebitsch's letter reached the Reich Chancellery on 12 February 1934, but Hitler probably never knew of it. Presumably his advisers considered it best not to bother the Führer with the ravings of an oriental holy man. Hitler's private office forwarded the letter to the Foreign Ministry for handling in routine manner. A minute prepared in the Ministry some time later pointed out that Trebitsch was of Jewish extraction, and recommended that a reply would be inopportune.[40] Trebitsch's visa application was rejected.[41]

Meanwhile, however, Trebitsch had made progress in other quarters. On 12 February 1934 he was issued a Chinese passport in the name of Chao Kung. Armed with this, he applied at the Belgian Consulate in Shanghai for a Belgian visa. Perhaps the consular officials were unaware that he was the 'undesirable character' who had so recently been deported from their kingdom, for he was granted a visa, valid for a visit of five days. In spite of the setback with the Germans he decided to embark for Europe. On 25 March he left Shanghai aboard the ss *Empress of Russia*, bound for Vancouver. He was accompanied by ten disciples (two more, it seems, had abandoned him in the interim), of whom six were reported to be nuns and four monks.[42]

On docking at Vancouver, Trebitsch and his followers were detained by immigration officials. Questioned as to his intentions he explained that he proposed to found a Buddhist monastery on the shores of Lake Constance.[43] The arrival of the 'White Buddhists' in British Columbia created a minor local sensation, and presented local officials with an awkward dilemma. He was initially refused permission to enter Canada, but Trebitsch, true to his principles, appealed against the decision to the Prime Minister of Canada, R.B. Bennett. For once Trebitsch's method worked: the Prime Minister considered the matter personally, and swiftly granted Trebitsch permission to remain in Canada until 5 May.[44] Trebitsch took full advantage of the respite. He delivered interviews to the local press, had his photograph taken together with his disciples, and addressed public meetings in Vancouver. At the City Temple he was introduced to the congregation by the minister, Revd. Robertson Orr. Trebitsch told his several hundred listeners that life was 'a nightmare, a delusion, the promise of a thing that does not exist'. Buddhism, he announced somewhat impenetrably, was 'like geology'. A further lecture (to which an admission fee of up to fifty cents was charged) was entitled 'How I Killed Trebitsch Lincoln'.[45]

Soon afterwards the party left for the east coast. En route they halted at Ottawa, where they were received by the Prime Minister.[46] They crossed the Atlantic on the Canadian Pacific liner, *Duchess of York*. At last, on 6 May 1934, Trebitsch reached Liverpool — his first landing in England since his deportation in 1919. When the steamer arrived, Home Office officials went aboard and told Trebitsch that he would not be admitted to Britain. He was brought ashore under police escort, and taken to a nearby gaol to await deportation back to Canada on the same boat a few days later. His followers, now reported to consist of five men and five women,

23 Abbot Chao Kung (centre) with his disciples, Vancouver, 1934

were given the option of continuing their journey to the continent, but they refused and were lodged for the time being at a boarding-house in Liverpool.

The *Liverpool Post* reported the next day:

> They were all garbed, men and women alike, in grey kimonos with black skull caps over closely shaven heads. Aboard the Duchess of York they did not partake of the ordinary food. They had only one meal a day, at lunch time. Their diet excluded meat and fish, and consisted principally of vegetables . . . The actual object with which they were coming to Europe is veiled in mystery. 'Abbot Chao Kung' was not allowed by the Immigration officials at Liverpool to give any interviews to Pressmen. The 'Abbot', through a messenger, sent a card to the *Daily Post*, which contained the following:- 'To Newspapermen — Years of experience with journalists has now finally forced upon me the decision: Not to receive any more journalists; not to grant any more interviews. I am not at all interested in publicity. My work, to help suffering humanity through and with the doctrine of Buddha, will be carried on by Buddhist means in a Buddhist manner. You are all doomed by your wickedness and folly! You cannot help me

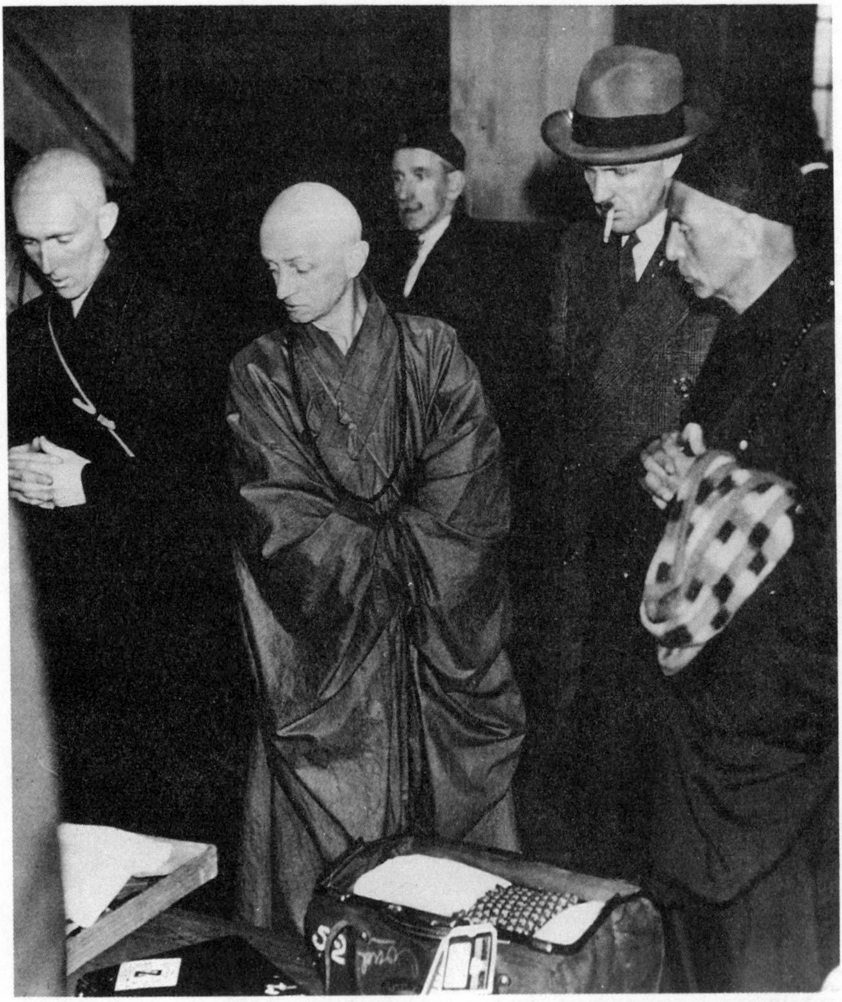

24 Trebitsch Lincoln and his followers attend customs examination, Liverpool 1934

and you shall certainly not hinder me. — Abbot Chao Kung.' From a reliable source it was learned that the authorities offered to give the 'abbot' and his party transit facilities to go through Liverpool to Antwerp to-night [7 May], but this Chao Kung indignantly refused, adding that if he could not go on to London, he would go back to the Far East. He demanded to be allowed to proceed to London, where he desired to remain for some months for the purpose of addressing meetings on religious subjects (presumably Buddhist). All efforts to induce him to accept the alternative of continuing his journey to Antwerp to-night proved futile and the authorities had no option but to order his return to Canada.[47]

While Trebitsch spent five days in a cell at Walton Prison, his followers were permitted a spell of unaccustomed liberty. By now they were so completely under the sway of their leader that they hardly knew what to do with freedom. Indeed, when Trebitsch was driven off to gaol one of his nuns clung to the vehicle weeping. The disciples were allowed to visit him in prison: they walked in procession through the city, their shaven heads and monkish habits attracting curious glances from the citizenry.[48] Apart from this outing the Buddhists remained in seclusion in their boarding-house until, on 11 May, they heard that the time for their departure had come.

Trebitsch was driven to the Gladstone Dock, and put aboard the *Duchess of York* for the return journey. He was shown the first-class cabins on the liner, but said that his religion forbade him to live luxuriously; he and his followers therefore travelled in the third-class section. A Buddhist sympathiser from Cannes had arrived to see him off and presented him with the sum of £118. His son Clifford, whom he had abandoned in Java nine years earlier, also came from London to say goodbye — almost certainly their final meeting. The publicity generated by his bizarre return to England mobilized a large crowd of onlookers who gathered on the quay to witness his departure. Perhaps Trebitsch hoped that, as at Harwich in 1919, a *deus ex machina* would intervene at the last moment to snatch him from the jaws of deportation. But on this occasion no Home Office telegram arrived. Just before the ship sailed, however, Trebitsch suffered a rude shock. One of his monks, the Berlin Buddhist, Martin Steinke, decided to desert him, came ashore with his bags, and headed back to his home in Germany.[49]

In spite of his contemptuous remarks about the press and his oft-proclaimed distaste for publicity. Trebitsch took care before his departure to issue a press release through the medium of his son. This pronouncement revealed his continuing obsession with a reconciliation with Britain, his growing megalomania, and his renewed desire to work for the British in the Far East. 'There is no doubt [he averred] but that my influence in the East would be of great value in face of certain events which may at any moment call for mediation ... my influence in the circles that would count in the event of trouble is no light thing.' Clifford Lincoln told a reporter: 'He has gone away, and I may never see him again, but he holds all my love.'[50]

Meanwhile Trebitsch and his remaining nine followers were returning whence they had come. Some of the disciples, still outwardly faithful, were by now beginning to harbour rebellious thoughts. Trebitsch himself brooded on the nugatory results of his mission: the ranks of his little sect had been further depleted, and there were dangerous rumblings of mutiny in the course of the return journey.

Moreover the philosophic acceptance of his fate in Liverpool was transmogrified in his retrospective imagination into a culminating instance of the vindictive persecution to which he had been unjustly subjected at the hands of the British Empire for the previous two decades. Once again Trebitsch and his entourage crossed Canada by train, and embarked for China from Vancouver. En route at Honolulu Trebitsch dispatched a verbose, rambling, almost incomprehensible telegram of protest to King George V, complaining of his 'wholly wanton imprisonment [at] Liverpool which is provocative insult challenge to China which sent me and to millions of Buddhists throughout Asia who are solidly behind me'.[51] His paranoia thus in a curious way fed his megalomania; he compensated for his humilation in Liverpool and the diminution of his monastic order by persuading himself that he was a representative of the people of China and a revered leader of Buddhists throughout the Asian land mass.

Before leaving England Trebitsch had spoken of going to live in a monastery in Japan. There, he said, 'my religion . . . is supreme, and I shall rule there as abbot'.[52] But instead of being welcomed in Japan as a light unto the millions, Trebitsch was interrogated by the Kobe police before being sent on with his followers to Shanghai. In the course of his interrogation it emerged that the admonitory thunder among his disciples had presaged a coming storm. Three of them had openly repudiated him: he had responded by excommunicating them, on the ground (so he told his police interrogators) that they were illiterate and unable to understand his teachings.[53] On 19 June 1934, their pointless and frustrating journey over, the unhappy Buddhists arrived back in Shanghai.

A week later one of the three excommunicands, a French citizen named Henri Chauve, was interviewed by British consular and police officers in Shanghai. The renegade Buddhist's story, as recounted to these officials, is of interest as one of the fullest accounts available to us of Trebitsch's methods of recruitment as a Buddhist missionary, his relationship with the members of his monkish order, and the economic basis of the little sect:

> He (M. Chauve) had, up to the year 1929, a prosperous perfumery business in Cannes. At the end of that year, he attended a lecture on Buddhism delivered by Trebitsch Lincoln at Cannes, and both he and his wife were very impressed with what was said, so much so that they decided to dispose of their business and seek seclusion from the toil and fret of the world by entering a monastery and devoting the rest of their lives to the study of Buddhism. They apprised Trebitsch Lincoln of their intention and he encouraged them to join him. Some time later . . . M. Chauve and his wife acted on their resolve and, having disposed of their business, came

to China where they handed over their money, linen (4 bales) and other personal effects to Trebitsch Lincoln who assumed responsibility for them until such time as the monastery was founded.[54]

Disillusionment set in soon after their arrival in Shanghai and installation in the Buddhist House in July 1933:

> Shortly after entering the novitiate stage, Mr Chauve realised that life under Chao Kung was nothing short of a terrible hardship, in no way similar to the picture that Chao Kung had painted whilst in the South of France. One meal per day, about sixteen hours of work out of twenty-four, rarely being permitted to speak aloud, and being tyrannically dominated all the while by the Abbot, were not conducive to happiness. After having seen Chao Kung in an embarrassing position with one of the younger nuns, Chauve decided that the time was ripe for him to leave.[55]

Matters came to a head on the voyage back from Europe and Chauve reported that the breach was now irreparable.

The Chauves' distress was compounded by the fact that they were now left destitute. When they wrote to Trebitsch asking him to return at least a portion of the money and linen which they had transferred to him, they received the following reply from one of Trebitsch's remaining monks:

> The Master has received your letter of yesterday evening and I am instructed to reply thus:- He is not a banker, he is simply the master of his disciples; the money which he has, he received from his friends and followers for the needs of himself and his disciples. You three have of your own free will chosen another way and, naturally, you must now submit to all the consequences of your decision. The Master has neither the time nor the inclination to have any further dealings with you three, who are disloyal, ungrateful, proud and wicked. He is interested and will solely interest himself in those who remain faithful to Buddha, Dhamma and Sangha and in those who remain loyal to him.[56]

The Chauves and their fellow excommunicand felt 'broken in health and spirit' and indignant against 'this cruel man' who thus condemned them to penury. They wisely decided to 'close this terrible chapter of our lives'; Chauve found a clerical position at the French Consulate-General, and they began the painful process of rebuilding their shattered existences.

Trebitsch's followers, although numbering millions in his imagination, were in reality now reduced from the original thirteen to a mere half-dozen. They stayed with him at the Astor House and then at the Burlington Hotel, while he engaged in arguments with the hotel management about unpaid bills and indulged in a flurry of letter-writing. The addressees included the British Consul-General, the British Minister in Peking, the Shanghai correspondent of Reuters, and the editor of the *North China Daily News*.[57]

The several letters, as well as a paid advertisement, from Chao Kung that appeared in the *News* all complained bitterly about the refusal of European governments to admit him to their territories, and again threatened retribution against Christian missionaries in China. Other correspondents, angered by his pronouncements, wrote back fierce rebuttals, in one case urging that death would be the most suitable reward for the abbot's earthly activities. The newspaper thereupon published an editorial under the heading 'Unwanted', which made it plain that, at any rate among the powerful British merchant community in Shanghai (of whom the *News* was the foremost mouthpiece), Trebitsch could count on little sympathy: 'If Chao Kung is being dealt with a little hardly by correspondents, it can but be said that he has indeed asked for it.' Rejecting Trebitsch's depiction of himself as a victim of anti-Buddhist prejudice, the editorial explained that the objection was not to his religion: 'The objection is to Chao Kung himself.'[58]

Yet even now Trebitsch succeeded in finding supporters among Shanghai residents of an eccentric or impressionable turn of mind. Among these were three who were reported to have provided him with financial assistance. The first was the Baroness Alexander de Soucanton, said to be an 'ardent admirer of the Abbot'. The second was Lo Chia-ling, the Chinese widow of Silas Hardoon, a Baghdadi Jew who, at his death in 1931, was reputed to be the richest foreigner in China. He left her $50,000,000 and his large estate near the Bubbling Well Road in Shanghai. Mrs Hardoon, herself a lay Buddhist initiate, contributed munificently to Buddhist causes, especially the upkeep of monks. Trebitsch's third source of support was Dr Walter Fuchs, a German who had at one time served as an official of the local German Consulate-General.* This last connexion aroused the suspicion of the Shanghai Police Special Branch, who speculated that Trebitsch might be 'working in some manner on behalf of the German authorities here'. But the evidence was inconclusive and the matter was left in abeyance.[59]

With financial underpinning from these sympathisers Trebitsch decided, shortly after his return to China, to set up a new organization to propagate his ideas — 'The League of Truth'. A bold

* Walter Fuchs (1888–1966), of Jewish origin, was dismissed from the German Foreign Service in 1933. He remained in Shanghai, practising as a lawyer. A Shanghai police report (D9969) in 1940 stated that he had served in Java, that he frequented the Park Hotel lounge, that he talked a lot, and that he was suspected of homosexuality.

letterhead on yellow writing-paper bore the League's symbol, a mirror-image swastika superimposed on two hemispheres. The League's objectives were declared to be '*for* TRUTH, JUSTICE, KINDNESS; against LIES, INJUSTICE, HATRED; EVERYWHERE AND IN EVERYTHING'.[60] An ambitious publication programme was launched under the imprint of the League: plans were announced for the establishment of two monthly journals, *Nirvana* and *Aurora*, each to appear in both English and French.

Trebitsch's pamphlets issued around this time suggest that he was passing through a mood of peevish depression. In *The Human Tragedy*, a short tract completed in August 1934, he opened with a universal wail —

> Suffering is the Great Human Tragedy. Suffering universal, perpetual, ceaseless suffering, that persists in spite of all our efforts to abolish it. . . . Life hurts, life is painful, life is suffering!

— before settling into the stride of his private moans:

> Is a humanity not mad, which allows Staviskys to travel about freely [that Trebitsch should himself invite the comparison with the discredited French financier is somewhat startling!] . . . but refuses me, a European, freedom of travel, to me, a Buddhist Abbot, carrying with me the noble message of the noblest and greatest Sage that ever lived, the Buddha? No wonder the whole world is suffering.

In this passage we may detect the essential link in his mind between his personal woes and the lunacy of the world around him.

That connexion was driven home in a horrifying manner in the late spring of 1935. Trebitsch and his disciples left Shanghai in April and moved south to stay at a Buddhist monastery, 'The Monk's Paradise' in Chekiang province. Here one of his nuns, a German known as Tao Ta (previously Hertha Henschel) committed suicide. According to a Chinese press report she took her life after being confined to a room by Trebitsch for a trivial offence. The report alleged that, following the suicide, the other monks and nuns went on hunger-strike in protest against their ill-treatment. Trebitsch (and his remaining followers) denied this version of events, but the incident left a sour taste, and perhaps for this reason Trebitsch resolved yet again to leave China.[61]

That autumn he began planning a journey to Europe, believing that he would be permitted to establish a monastery on the island of Madeira. But he was by now beginning to run out of money, and he encountered difficulties in securing credit from shipping companies as well as the customary obstruction from European consular officials. A confidential circular from the acting German Consul-General to other consuls in Shanghai, dated 2 October 1935, stated: 'I have the honour to inform you that as I learn from one of our honourable colleagues the abbot Chao Kung, alias Trebitsche-Lincoln [sic], falsely pretends that a visa will be granted to him to enter Germany on his impending voyage to Europe. This statement is untrue and apparently made by Trebitsche-Lincoln in order to get visaes from other countries.'[62]

Trebitsch nevertheless persisted in his scheme. A report by the Shanghai police in January 1936 narrated the sequel:

> He hit on the bright expedient of purchasing a sailing vessel of about 100 feet overall length and getting it converted into a floating monastery. With this sea-going ark he intended making a leisurely voyage to Madeira accompanied by the half dozen monks and nuns still willing to follow his leadership. A young adventurer named Reuben who has behind him considerable experience in piloting small vessels over thousands of miles of ocean was to act as Captain and provide a crew of three or four young dare-devils like himself to work the vessel. Many boats were inspected and it is believed that Trebitsch Lincoln would have gone forward with this scheme had he been able to furnish the few thousand dollars required for the undertaking. Unfortunately for the success of his plans, his credit in Shanghai being practically nil, he was unable to obtain sufficient money with which to purchase a boat; and so this project has had to be abandoned for the time being.[63]

Thus thwarted at every turn, Trebitsch fell back once more on his pen. In a pamphlet issued around this time he struck an apocalyptic note:

> The very elements are revolting and inflict all manner of sufferings on the human race: droughts, inundations, extreme heat, chase and succeed one another. And all the time there is in the offing the sombre and menacing shadow of the coming world war, which will surely sweep away a mad civilisation which artificially creates suffering and more suffering. In this general confusion and degeneracy the Evil has completely taken possession of the world. The governments, having lost (if they ever had) all moral considerations, willingly follow the pernicious ways of lies, injustice and hatred; violence, brutality, deception are their stock-in-trade . . . Their aberration is so vast, their blindness so dark, that they do not see the true causes of all the Evil which overpowers them.[64]

And so on. Trebitsch forwarded this pamphlet to the British Foreign Secretary, Sir Samuel Hoare, together with a bombastic letter complaining vehemently of the 'vindictive war which successive British

Governments have relentlessly waged against me, a single, peaceful individual, during twenty years!'.[65]

Trebitsch was by now in urgent need of money. Without new recruits his monastic order was costing him more than it brought in, a situation reminiscent of his expensive oil-drilling operations in Roumania in 1913. As we have seen, Trebitsch foresaw the imminent outbreak of a new world war. (In the disordered world of the late 1930s it required no prophetic powers to make such a forecast.) He response to this personal and international crisis followed to a remarkable degree the pattern of his reaction to that earlier private and public crisis in 1914. Then he had sought a way out of his difficulties by volunteering to work as a spy, preferably as a double agent. Spurned by the British, he had offered his services elsewhere, swearing vengeance on the National Liberal Club, where he had been snubbed, on Captain Hall, who had humiliated him, and on the British Empire in Asia, to the destruction of which he had announced he would devote his energies for the rest of his life. Now the situation was, in Trebitsch's eyes, remarkably similar. His repeated protestations of friendship to Britain has been ignored, his offers of reconciliation rejected. The British community in Shanghai ignored him, and its leading organ, the *Daily News*, insulted him. His letters to the Consul-General in Shanghai, the Minister in Peking, and the Foreign Secretary in London were not even accorded the courtesy of an acknowledgement.

His final letter to the British Government, written from Tientsin some time in mid-1937, was addressed to the Prime Minister, Neville Chamberlain: in it Trebitsch again wished Britain well, referred to himself as the victim of a 'diabolical vendetta' waged by the British Government by 'forms of open and secret machinations', and made a last demand for 'honorable amend for all the wrongs perpetrated against me'.[66] The letter was dismissed in London as the work of a crank. But as on previous occasions when Whitehall had tried to get rid of him by wiping him out of its collective sight and mind, the dismissal turned out to be premature. For the last time Trebitsch now bounced back to prove his sempiternal nuisance value.

CHAPTER 15

The Three Wise Men

By contrast with nearly every other period of his adult life Trebitsch's last years are sparsely documented and shrouded in secrecy. To reconstruct the patterns of his activity in the period from 1936 to 1943 we are compelled to rely on scattered jigsaw pieces of historical evidence. The resulting picture is at times fragmentary; but by drawing together isolated bits of information it is possible to build up a coherent, if not continuous, account of the final, and in many ways, most fantastic, period of his life.

Our first piece of evidence is a report by the Chief of Police of the British Municipal Council in Tientsin, addressed to the British Consulate in the city, and dated 30 November 1936. Trebitsch, it appears, had arrived in Tientsin some time before, accompanied by his disciples, and had there set up a 'Buddhist House' which attracted the attentions of the British police. Mr R.H. Dennis's report to the consulate presented the fruits of the ensuing investigation:

re: TREBITSCH LINCOLN

> Continuous observation has been kept on this man's house at the corner of Poppe Road and Romanoff Avenue in the 3rd S[pecial] A[rea]. All the inmates appear to be living a very quiet life, part of the morning is taken up with prayer, and at other times they are seen either quietly sitting on a bench near the Russian Ferry or on the Ex-Russian Bund. Occasionally they go for walks in the direction of the Jewish Cemetery. Some of them have been seen to visit the Post Office in Dickinson Road and at other times they have visited a Buddhist Temple in the Chinese City. When they first arrived here they received quite a number of visitors who used to call on them after 3 pm but these visitors have recently been considerably reduced owing to the publication of some very unfavourable remarks about them in the local Russian newspaper.
>
> A careful scrutiny has been made of all their visitors with a view

of ascertaining what Trebitsch-Lincoln's political activities are at this time, but most of his visitors appear to have visited him solely out of curiosity. All inmates, and Trebitsch-Lincoln himself, have declined every attempt on the part of visitors to discuss matters of a political nature.

Trebitsch-Lincoln has been observed to visit the Oriental Trading & Engineering Co. (Wostvag) 49 Taku Road on several occasions. It has been maintained in Russian political circles for many years that Mr Purpis, the head of this Trading firm in Tientsin, is a member of the Third International. It is well known as a fact that his firm has been engaged in trade with or for the Soviet Government in Mongolia for many years.

It is obvious that Lincoln is not short of funds, but the source of his supply is not known. It is most unlikely that his secret service for any Foreign Power could be of such an importance as to induce them to go to the great expense of maintaining his costly retinue. The Third International is probably the political concern interested in his services to this extent. As the activity of the Third International in China is confined to the North at present, the presence of Lincoln in Tientsin and his connection with 'Wostvag' is probably the solution to the problem.[1]

This report stirs memories of previous contacts between Trebitsch and Soviet officials — of Victor Kopp, who may have provided him with false papers at the conclusion of the Kapp putsch in Berlin in March 1920, and of the Soviet Ambassador to China, D. Bogomolov, who (somewhat remarkably) had attended the initiation of Trebitsch's disciples at Ch'i-hsia Shan in late 1933. These are suggestive but probably coincidental circumstances. These seems no reason to doubt that Trebitsch met the Comintern agent in Tientsin. But their discussions appear to have been inconclusive, for there is no further report of any connexion between Trebitsch and the Soviet Union.* Indeed, just a few months later he was once again to be found attacking communism (together, it is true, with almost all other contemporary political ideologies) in what turned out to be his last major publication.

Dawn or Doom of Humanity, published at Shanghai in 1937, was sent to the press from the 'Buddhist House' at Tientsin on 11 May.

* A report in 1925 by an intelligence agent working under the Department of State in New York City stated: 'The writer of this statement has been thoroughly convinced for some time that this Jewish individual [Trebitsch] is a part and parcel of the inner circle of the elements that control the Executive Committee of the Soviet Government of Russia, and that his passports and travel documents are furnished him through the agency of the usual mill which that element uses in its manufacture of false documents.' But the writer admitted that all this was 'merely a surmise'.[2]

Trebitsch seems to have been in an exceptionally depressed frame of mind while writing it, for the tone throughout is lugubrious and marked by contempt for most of his fellow men: 'It is really astonishing how stupid human beings are!' A little strangely for a man who claimed to have left politics behind him absolutely and definitively, much of the work was devoted to an exposition of his programme for the reform of political institutions the world over. Chapter VIII launched a violent attack on communism: 'The diagnosis of the Communists is wrong, their remedies are wrong and their methods are wrong.' Quoting Lao Tzu and Jesus, Trebitsch urged the pressing need for peace: 'Let the reconstruction of Humanity on ever-valid eternal principles begin here.'[3] At the front of the volume appeared a picture of Chao Kung, as usual wearing his robes, with his beard now starting to turn white. Overall Trebitsch's last book must be judged in every way a failure — long-winded, platitudinous, intellectually barren, without even the brazen audacity of his 1916 *Revelations* or the inventive flair of his 1931 *Autobiography*.

In July 1937 Trebitsch's apparently placid existence in Tientsin was rudely disturbed by the outbreak of full-scale war between Japan and China. Starting with the so-called 'Marco Polo Bridge Incident' near Peking, the fighting rapidly engulfed the whole of northern China. Tientsin was occupied by Japanese forces and the new rulers proceeded in every possible way to terrorise the local population and to trample on the prerogative of the British and other European concessions in the city. In early August they established a 'Peace Preservation Committee' composed of Chinese collaborators operating under the control of the local Japanese military.[4]

Trebitsch adapted to these new conditions with seeming alacrity. On 1 October he issued a pamphlet from Tientsin entitled *Anti-Japanese Propaganda*:

> The whole world is being inundated by untruthful anti-Japanese propaganda. All those who seek a better order of things on this earth than this occidental mess, chaos and suffering must counter all this cant and humbug about Japan. As a resident of Tientsin I declare: I have never seen a better behaved Army of Occupation than the Japanese Army. They molest nobody, interfere with no lawful occupation; they are kind and helpful to the people ...
>
> As a friend of China I declare: Free yourselves from the corrupting influence of the Kuomintang and Soviet; liberate yourselves from the selfish influence of Occidental Nations, and you will find that Japan is your true friend, ready to help you.
>
> As a buddhist Abbot I declare: Even if all the propaganda fabricated and disseminated against the Japanese were true (and they are not), those who conquered India, Burmah, Ceylon, etc. etc.

> etc.; those who hold in subjection Nations and Races all over the world; those who have, in turn, violently and unjustly interfered with the life and destiny of Portugal, Spain, Holland, Denmark, France, Germany, Italy, Russia, Persia, Afghanistan, Tibet, China, Ireland, etc. etc. etc.; those who deliberately broke their pledged world solemnly given to the Jews — those have no right to play the role of holy indignation against a chivalrous, well-intentioned and spiritually superior race like the Japanese.

The former British MP concluded:

> Be not deceived: A New Empire has arisen in the world — the Greater Japanese Empire. This New Empire will surely bring about more just, more tolerable, more peaceful conditions on this earth, than the Christians have done. Let China abandon this futile, suicidal and wholly mistaken enmity to Japan, and Peace and Prosperity will ensue.[5]

The British Embassy in Peking forwarded a transcription of the pamphlet to the Foreign Office in London with the comment: 'The most likely explanation for this recrudescence of Lincoln's political activity is probably lack of funds on his part combined with Japanese anxiety to enlist the services of a buddhist Abbot in their cultural campaign in North China, for which purpose Lincoln, with his anti-British proclivities and propagandist ability, must have appeared to them as eminently suitable.' The Foreign Office took no action on receipt of the dispatch, beyond circulating copies to other departments. A single official minute was recorded by Mr A. Scott, who wrote: 'I think the only comment I can make on this is ! ! !'[6] As it happens, this is the last notation concerning Trebitsch Lincoln that survives in the Foreign Office archives. Thus it was that after thirty-one years of trying to get rid of Trebitsch, and after hundreds of pages of official memoranda, telegrams, letters of recommendation, instructions to ambassadors and consuls, extradition documents, intelligence reports, infuriated comments by the head of the Foreign Office, exchanges of information with other departments and other governments, entries in 'suspicious persons' files, passport and visa applications, circulars, expense accounts, and official expressions of irritation, contempt, lofty dismissal, indignation, outrage, or resigned contemplation of each new twist and turn in the career of this utterly impossible, preposterous and disgusting man — after all this, the Foreign Office's last word was one of self-confessed speechlessness and reduction to Trebitsch's own level of extravagant punctuation.

Others, however, were less reticent. In an editorial comment, the *New York Times* mused:

> In Tientsin Chao Kung, a Buddhist abbot and associate of Kang Teh, Emperor of Manchukuo*, peers from the mist of history to assert that Japan has founded in North China a new empire which 'will bring about more peaceful conditions on earth than the Christians have done.' Those of us who remember can say with Hamlet in answer to his father's ghost: 'You hear this fellow in the cellarage? . . . Old mole! Canst work i' the earth so fast?' For Chao Kung is also a ghost. The benevolent Buddhist abbot is none other than I.T. Trebitsch Lincoln, the notorious international rogue.

Characterising Trebitsch as a 'human chameleon', the editorial writer concluded: 'Now he wears a Japanese coat. But he can turn it very quickly.'[7]

After that, little was heard of Trebitsch for some time. But the sincerity of his expression of satisfaction with life under Japanese rule was belied by his own action: on 12 December 1937 he addressed a letter to an old collaborator from his days in the White International, the Regent of Hungary, Admiral Horthy, appealing for permission to return to his country of birth and prophesying that 'people all over Asia, Europe and America' would be grateful to the Hungarian ruler for such an act of mercy.[8]

Trebitsch reinforced the message by dispatching to Hungary as his emissary one of his nuns, Margot Markuse, who had taken the Buddhist name of Tao Lo.[9] When Tao Lo reached Budapest in June 1938, she went to stay with relations of Trebitsch in Budapest.[10] The arrival of the shaven-headed nun in her Buddhist robes aroused considerable curiosity. Interviewed by a reporter, she said:

> My bald head may mislead you. I am not a monk. I am a nun, Tao L[o]. I was born in Latvia and became acquainted with Buddhism during university studies in Germany and decided to go to China to join a Buddhist religious order. There a monk of Hungarian origin initiated me into the mysteries of Buddhism. He was Chao Kung. After many years of voluntary exile he would like to return to his native country to visit the tomb of his parents. He is tired of the adventurous life of the last forty years and wishes to spend his last days in Hungary in pious contemplation.[11]

* A number of accounts of Trebitsch Lincoln's career repeat the allegation that he was an adviser to the Japanese puppet emperor of Manchukuo (Manchuria). It is even claimed by some that the relationship was a long standing and that Trebitsch played a significant role in the life of the emperor. These allegations are not borne out by any documentary evidence, nor by the memoirs of the ex-emperor: Paul Kramer, ed., *The last Manchu: The Autobiography of Henry Pu Yi, Last Emperor of China* (London 1967); nor by those of his tutor (who, for the earlier period, was in a position to know): Reginald Johnston, *Twilight in the Forbidden City* (London 1934).

25 Margot Markuse, 'Tao Lo', later known as 'Jhananandа', Trebitsch's most faithful nun, c. 1935; notice brandmarks on head

Tao Lo carried the following poignant message from Trebitsch to his native land: 'Tortured by nostalgia, broken of body and soul, a tired wanderer on this earth returns to his native soil. The path of glory and success is passed but with sorrow and grief until one rests at the place of his birth.' The precise meaning of this communication was perhaps less important than its tone — indicating that its originator had passed, between October and December 1937, from heady euphoria in the early weeks of the Japanese invasion of north China, to a mood of gloom and despair. The Hungarian Government's response to Trebitsch's application (announced only in December 1938) was negative.[12] As for Tao Lo, she did not return to China.*

Apart from the natural cycle of his moods of elation and depression, Trebitsch had another reason for feeling upset at this period. On 1 December 1937 the 'Pundit of Great Price', the Tashi or Panchen Lama, died near Jyekundo in western China. Although it is uncertain whether Trebitsch ever succeeded in gaining an audience with the Panchen Lama, he evidently regarded the Tibetan monk as his spiritual leader. The Panchen Lama's death left the world of Tibetan Buddhism in considerable disarray. Five years earlier his rival, the Dalai Lama, had died, and a replacement for that office had not yet been found. Both of the most senior lama offices were thus vacant at the same time — a simultaneous hiatus unprecedented in the annals of Tibetan history.[14]

The death of the Panchen Lama, coming as it did at a moment of high political and military crisis in China, not only left a vacuum in the Tibetan leadership: it also raised anew the issue of relations between the monkish republic and her powerful neighbours. At the time of his death the Panchen Lama had been poised near the Tibetan border, preparing for an imminent return to his homeland. He had been accompanied by a large body of Tibetan attendants and a substantial Chinese military retinue — the latter raising the eyebrows of fellow monks and British Indian officials alike. With the Lama's death questions arose about the fate of the valuable accumulation of treasure hoarded by the late Lama, the destination of his caravan of Tibetan followers, and the future role in Tibetan politics of his Chinese military guard stationed near the Tibetan border. But above all, the vacancies in the two great lama offices led to concern (not

* She spent the war years in France and then settled in England. Taking the name Jhanananda, she lived in north-west London, still with a bald head and Buddhist habiliment — causing heads to turn when she went shopping in John Barnes's deparment store on Finchley Road. She remained a Buddhist until her death in 1972.[13]

only among Buddhists) that the fragile internal stability and external security of the Tibetan state should be restored as rapidly as possible by the appointment of successors.

Traditionally, when one of the senior lamas died, a search was launched throughout Tibet for a child in whom the spirit of the late monk had been reincarnated. Teams of monks scoured the countryside in the hope of finding such an infant. But the signs were often ambiguous, and in truth the matter was as much prone to the vagaries of shifting political coalitions and alignments among influential lamas as, *mutatis mutandis*, the election of a new Pope. After four years of inquiry, and the rejection of several candidates, no reincarnation of the Dalai Lama had yet been found. With the further calamity in December 1937, the search was renewed with a sense of urgency, and a start was also made to the process of identifying the new Panchen Lama.

Against this background, in September 1938, the British Consul-General in Chungking, W. Stark Toller, dispatched a startling message to the British Embassy (temporarily located in Shanghai because of the war). Toller stated that he had been told by a 'Mr Cunningham of Tatsienlu' (not otherwise identified) of a report that 'Trebitsch Lincoln is proceeding towards Tibet and that he claims to be, by some extraordinary metempsychosis, a reincarnation of both the Dalai and the Tashi Lamas'. Toller was, however, plainly doubtful about the report, for he added: 'A man named Engler, who claims to be a citizen of the United States of America, and of whom little is known, has recently arrived at Tatsienlu after residing in Chengtu for two years, and Mr Cunningham is inclined to identify him with Trebitsch Lincoln, but such information as I have been able to secure does not seem to confirm this view.' A copy of Toller's message was forwarded to the Foreign Office in London, and thence (as was usual in all matters affecting Tibet) to the India Office.[15] Officials there shared Toller's scepticism about the report and scoffed at the alleged claim. One wrote whimsically: 'This report would be more useful if Mr Toller had given some indication of the trustworthiness of Mr Cunningham as a source of information. (Para. 5 [referring to Trebitsch] wd. present rather a theosophistical problem — 3 souls all occupying the same habitation — perhaps the original T. Lincoln has been cast out by the new occupants.)'[16]

In March 1938 Trebitsch, accompanied by his two remaining disciples, moved back from Tientsin to Shanghai.[17] Probably he thought of the shift as a temporary one, preparatory to renewed overseas travels, which he continued to plan with all his old restless wanderlust. But, in fact, Trebitsch's long career as a world traveller had at last drawn to a close. For the rest of his life he remained in Shanghai, living alternately in cheap lodgings or at the Foreign (ie

26 Abbot Chao Kung in 1938: notice brand-marks on head

non-Chinese) YMCA Meanwhile, the city, so long a haven of refuge, was slowly being transformed into a prison from which there was no escape.

Shanghai between 1938 and 1941 was a terrible place. These were the twilight years of the great international entrepôt, years of 'graveyard gaiety' in the night-clubs. While the war raged around them, the French Concession and the International Settlement maintained a precarious neutrality. Their European residents watched and waited, 'like a little Rome awaiting the barbarians'.[18] On 'Black Saturday', 14 August 1937, Chinese bombers dropped explosives intended for Japanese gunboats on the International Settlement. 'There were 2,000 deaths, 2,500 wounded, and blood flowed in the gutters of Edward VII Avenue.'[19] Penniless, starving refugees from the war in the interior flooded into the city in their hundreds of thousands. Unable to find anywhere to live, and with nowhere else to go, they lived and died on the streets. According to one (eminently sober and scholarly) historian, in the year 1938 the Shanghai Municipal Council picked up 100,000 dead bodies in the streets of the city.[20] Law and order collapsed as rival underworld gangs coalesced with the political underground of the Kuomintang or with the Japanese secret police in a submerged war of terror, reprisals, and counter-terror.

Yet somehow, amidst the convulsive agony of a city in its death throes, some semblance of ordinary life continued. Outside the Park Hotel 'hundreds of Eurasian bar-girls in ankle-length fur coats sat in the lines of rickshaws'. On the Bubbling Well Road 'crowds of gamblers pushed their way into the jai alai stadiums blocking the traffic'.[21] And for twenty thousand European Jews, refugees from the even greater horror of Nazi Europe, Shanghai, between 1938 and 1941, seemed to offer the prospect not of civilisation in torment and on the edge of an abyss, but of a relatively peaceful corner of a world gone mad. And so too it appears to have been for the Abbot Chao Kung.

Shortly before Christmas 1939 (the fortieth anniversary of his rebirth as a Christian in the Jerusalem chapel at Hamburg) Trebitsch issued an appeal for world peace. The announcement was couched in admonitory, not to say threatening, terms, for he demanded the simultaneous and immediate resignations of the British, French, German and Russian Governments. Only the Finns and Japanese were exempt from the decree. Trebitsch announced that new governments must be formed in all the countries at war, and a world-wide peace conference convened. The consequences of refusal, he declared, would be terrible: 'Otherwise, the Tibetan Buddhist Supreme Masters, without prejudice, pre-direction or favour will unchain forces and powers whose very existence are unknown to you and against whose operations you are consequently helpless.' Trebitsch did not identify the 'Supreme Masters' but he explained that whereas the world's statesmen were mere mortals subject to human limitations, the Buddhist masters 'by their unlimited and unbounded knowledge of nature's secrets and their ability to use certain powers have broken through those limitations'.[22] On 1 January 1940 Trebitsch announced his readiness to proceed immediately to Washington to discuss peace with President Roosevelt.[23] But a week later the United States Consulate-General in Shanghai indicated that Trebitsch would not be granted a visa for such a visit. The frustrated applicant denounced the rejection as proof that all governments were 'too stupid' to heed his call for international peace.[24] But by now even the world press who had hitherto regarded Trebitsch as good 'copy', were beginning to tire of what one magazine called 'his international vaudeville act'.[25]

The old stager performed his last turn without playing to any gallery. In a sense what happened next was a repetition of a familiar pattern — but with some grotesque twists. For more than year after his appeal for world peace, as the Japanese consolidated their position in north China and the Nazi stain spread across Europe, Trebitsch lay low in Shanghai. In the spring of 1940 he paid farewell visits to some of his acquaintances, and announced that he would soon be leaving for the USA.[26] But with no American visa and no money, he had no prospect of doing any such thing. In late October 1940 the Shanghai police produced its final report on him, stating merely that he had moved to a cheap lodging-house on the Peking Road.[27] Trebitsch was now sixty-one and his eventful life seemed to be drawing to a close with an uncharacteristic whimper. Then, in early 1941, he re-emerged in one of his old roles — that of international spy.

We do not know exactly how Trebitsch managed to insinuate himself into the counsels of the Nazi security apparatus in the Far East. Our only evidence on this point is contained in a statement published after the war by an acquaintance of Trebitsch's in Shanghai, Dr Hans Oberländer, who served in the Far East as a German secret service agent.[28] According to this account, Trebitsch was approached by the chief of the German wireless station in Shanghai*, who sought to persuade him to travel to Tibet in order to bring that country under German influence and to establish there a German broadcasting station which would beam propaganda to

* The German-controlled broadcasting station, XGRS, was the most powerful in Shanghai. Situated near the Kaiser Wilhelm School on the Great Western Road, XGRS broadcast on long and short waves in several languages to Asia and Australia. Among the broadcasters were American and other pro-Axis collaborators.

India.[29] Knowing as we do of Trebitsch's long-festering obsession with the idea of getting to Tibet, we may question whether the initiative for this strange proposal came from the Germans or from himself.

The scheme was, however, taken sufficiently seriously for Trebitsch to be introduced to the local office of the Abwehr, the German secret intelligence organization headed by Admiral Canaris. The Shanghai representative of the Abwehr at this time was Captain Louis Siefkin — hence the Abwehr's ring of local agents was known as 'Bureau Siefkin'.[30] In the early part of the war the Abwehr toyed with a number of far-fetched schemes for stirring up anti-British feeling in India. There was talk of installing a pro-German government in Afghanistan. Among those consulted about these schemes was the pro-Nazi Swedish explorer Sven Hedin.*[31] In the third week of January 1941 the Germans received a boost to these projects when an Indian nationalist politician, Subhas Chandra Bose, fled from Calcutta to Kabul. From there the Italian Embassy arranged for his onward journey via Moscow to Berlin, where he began a wartime career of pro-German and pro-Japanese propaganda activity. Among the followers of Chandra Bose was a pro-Japanese journalist, Anand Mohan Sahay, who, it appears, turned up in Shanghai in early 1941 to organize anti-British activity among the local Indian community.

It was against this background that, on 5 February 1941, a secret coded telegram was sent by the German Consul-General in Shanghai (apparently at the behest of the Bureau Siefkin) to Berlin:

> Trebitsch as Abbot Chaokung [has been] for many years [a] member [of the] Grand Council [of] Yellow Cap Lamas who [possess] special influence in Tibet and India. Whereas English influence is on the increase again in Lhasa [seat of the Dalai Lama], an anti-British tendency has the upper hand in Tashilumpo [seat of the Tashi or Panchen Lama], the spiritual centre of Buddhism. Chaokung wants to organise from Tashilumpo [an] Indian independence movement together with [the] Congress Party and nationalist leader Sahay, who [is] in Shanghai this week. Tibet, as a key position, is to be won for German influence. Advisory posts of military and aviation technical nature as well as ground organisation [are] to be created. Chaokung proposes that he be accompanied by a General Staff officer, an aviation expert, a wireless operator with transmitter, and a courier. Apart from [. . .] travel and living expense [he makes] no financial demands. He undertakes [the] mission out of a desire to make himself important, thirst for adventure, and hatred for England. Travel to Tibet is

* See above p. 227.

most easily arranged from Afghanistan. Chaokung could either meet the requested travel companions in Kabul or he could come to Berlin. About arranging the journey consult Sven Hedin. Necessary: passport of any nationality, but it must be in the name of Chaokung. This connection seems to offer at least a point of contact and travel possibility to Tibet for specialists.[32]

Unfortunately no reply to this communication has been traced in the German archives. We cannot therefore know the reaction of the chiefs of the Abwehr to Trebitsch's plan, which, while it may appear bone-headed to us, nevertheless chimed in perfectly with much that the Abwehr was conceiving at this period. In any case, if any reply was sent to Shanghai it was not communicated to Trebitsch — as becomes apparent from what followed.

In May 1941 the recently appointed 'police attaché' at the German Embassy in Tokyo, Police-Colonel Joseph Meisinger, paid a visit to Shanghai. Since 1937 such a 'police attaché' had been attached to the embassy supposedly to serve on a commission supervising the implementation of the Anti-Comintern Pact, concluded between Germany and Japan in November 1936. The real functions of the attaché included spying on members of the embassy staff to ensure their loyalty to National Socialism. Unlike other German diplomats, the police attaché was responsible not to the German Foreign Ministry, but to the Reichssicherheitshauptamt, or RSHA, headed by Reinhard Heydrich (who operated under the overall supervision of Heinrich Himmler).[33] Not surprisingly, friction developed between the police attaché and ordinary embassy staff, who did not relish being kept under surveillance by the Gestapo.

In mid-May 1941 Trebitsch somehow succeeded in gaining an interview with Meisinger in Shanghai. He told Meisinger of his previous contacts with two German organizations, and complained that he had not heard anything further about the proposals made to him the previous February. Further details of the conversation are given in a post-war article published by a senior German diplomat, H.G. Stahmer, who served in 1941–2 as ambassador in China to the pro-Japanese puppet régime of Wang Ching-wei. According to Stahmer, Trebitsch told Meisinger that the sages of Tibet, who represented a sort of unofficial world government, had formed the view that the time was now ripe for Germany to make peace. He claimed that he had been authorised by his Tibetan masters to take the necessary steps. He therefore wished to travel to Berlin by the swiftest possible means, for an interview with Hitler. Meisinger (Stahmer continues) inquired what evidence Trebitsch could offer for his assumptions, and what arguments he thought would be likely to convince Hitler. Whereupon Trebitsch replied that, the instant he was alone with the Fuehrer, three of the wise men of Tibet would appear out of the wall; this (Trebitsch allegedly said) would be the best proof of the supernatural powers at the disposal of the Supreme Initiates.[34]

One might perhaps be inclined to dismiss this as a colourful diplomatic anecdote — were it not that the essential elements in Stahmer's narrative are corroborated by Meisinger himself in contemporary official documents. On 15 May 1941 the German Consul-General in Shanghai, Martin Fischer, sent a secret and very urgent telegram to the German Foreign Office in Berlin, containing the following message from Meisinger:

> Following for Reichssicherheitshauptamt, Chief of Department IV [i.e. Gestapo] . . . I had a long talk today with the well-known Trebitsch-Lincoln. He has long held a leading position as a Buddhist Abbot under the name Chou [*sic*] Kung. In the conversation he developed plans and ideas concerning China, Tibet and India that are worthy of consideration. He would like to put these at the disposal of Germany. He offered to travel to Berlin for this purpose should this be desired there. I consider the authoritative influence of Trebitsch in Buddhist circles so important, and his personal qualifications such, that an order should be issued there [in Berlin] for his journey to Germany . . . Trebitsch requested a response to his offer by May 19th, since in the event of the rejection of his proposal he intends to travel to the interior of China — Tibet. I therefore ask for telegraphic instructions one way or another by the above-mentioned date via the Consulate-General, Shanghai.[35]

Trebitsch, it is now clear, had made his last — and most remarkable — convert. The power to impress strangers at a first meeting, so crucial in his relationships with men such as Burt, Rowntree, and Bauer, had evidently not deserted him.

Meisinger was depicted by one of his Gestapo colleagues as a 'frightening individual, a large, coarse-faced man with a bald head and an incredibly ugly face'. The Australian journalist Richard Hughes, who saw him in Tokyo, called him 'a grinning, swashbuckling, donkey-faced scoundrel'. Before the war Meisinger had been in charge of a Gestapo office specialising in the investigation of homosexuality and abortions. After the Nazi invasion of Poland he was sent to Warsaw, where he was said to have ordered the execution of sixteen thousand Jews, earning the title 'Butcher of Warsaw'. That such a hard-bitten Gestapo agent should have taken seriously the Jewish-born Buddhist's medley of geopolitics and mysticism might seem hard to credit. According to Hughes, Meisinger boasted that he trusted no-one: 'Sometimes I even have doubts about myself.'[36] Yet in reality he was supremely, almost laughably gullible.* In the case of Trebitsch, however, Meisinger's credulity was not shared by his diplomatic colleagues, and in the bureaucratic process to which Trebitsch's initiative was subjected we can see an illuminating example of the inter-agency jealousies characteristic of the Nazi régime — as well as of Trebitsch's inextinguishable knack for getting under the skin of senior officials of almost any government.

Unknown to Meisinger, Consul-General Fischer did more than merely forward the Gestapo agent's message to Berlin. Plainly annoyed by the secret policeman's descent on Shanghai, and by his encroachment on the Consul-General's diplomatic turf, Fischer decided to take full advantage of the opportunity to teach Meisinger a lesson.† Along with the telegram containing Meisinger's message, dispatched as cable no. 117, Fischer sent simultaneously another telegram, no. 118. Unlike the first cable, the second was marked 'secret' and 'only for the Foreign Ministry'. Fischer's commentary on Meisinger's message presented a rather different evaluation of the character and significance of the Abbot Chao Kung:

> Lincoln is a political adventurer. His connexions with Buddhist circles here, which are politically insignificant, do not permit the drawing of any conclusions as to his influence on lama circles. I know that Lincoln, out of a wish for political importance, has also tried to approach Roosevelt.[37]

Fischer's ploy achieved its purpose. When the two telegrams reached Berlin they were considered together. The German Foreign Minister, Ribbentrop, had long been a zealous defender of the prerogatives of his department, and these cables arrived at a time when he was engaged in a bitter struggle with Himmler and Heydrich over the control of foreign intelligence in general, and police attachés in particular. Just as Fischer, at the local level, had seen the matter as a stick with which to beat Meisinger, so Ribbentrop, in the jockeying for position at the centre of the Third Reich, sought to use the Tre-

* The best example of Meisinger's gullibility was his total bamboozlement by the famous Soviet double agent Richard Sorge. See F.W. Deakin and G.R. Storry, *The Case of Richard Sorge* (New York 1966). At the end of the war Meisinger was arrested by American forces in Japan and turned over to the Polish Government for trial as a war criminal. He was found guilty, and hanged in 1947.

† There may have been a personal element in Fischer's apparent antagonism to the police attaché: the Consul-General's wife was a Norwegian (i.e. an enemy national) and he is said to have been criticised for being only luke-warm in his enthusiasm for Nazism (Arch Carey, *The War Years at Shanghai 1941–45–48* (New York 1967) pp. 108–9).

bitsch-Meisinger proposal as ammunition in his private war against Himmler and Heydrich.

Ribbentrop was helped by a peculiar accident of timing which dashed the prospects for Trebitsch's scheme of mystic intervention in the high politics of Nazi Germany. On 10 May 1941, just a few days before Meisinger's message reached Berlin, the Deputy Führer, Rudolf Hess, abruptly flew on his abortive peace mission to Scotland. Police investigations after his departure revealed that Hess had been a 'silent adherent' of the doctrines of the 'anthroposophists', that he had had close associations with 'astrologers, seers, mediums, nature therapists and so forth', and that he had undertaken his flight on astrological advice. In consequence, a large number of such mystics found themselves under arrest; Hitler, who had previously shown a tolerance for astrology, turned against all such doctrines; and Himmler, who had a strong inclination towards superstition, and sympathised with these esoteric groups, was compelled, much against his wish, to show the utmost zeal in opposing all such mystical practices.[38]

A week earlier the Trebitsch-Meisinger proposal might actually have been considered by the credulous Himmler — at any rate seriously enough for Trebitsch to be sent off on a final trip to Berlin. The flight of Hess and the round-up of the mystics ensured that Trebitsch would be given no opportunity to conjure three wise men out of the wall for the benefit of Hitler. Moreover, in these circumstances Ribbentrop found a perfect lever to apply against Himmler and Heydrich.

On 17 May, even before Meisinger's message had been forwarded to the RSHA, Ribbentrop fired off an angry telegram to Fischer:

> Re telegrams 117 and 118 of 15.5. I ask you to inform Herr Meisinger at once that it is not part of his functions to hold discussions there with Trebitsch concerning his plans and ideas about China, Tibet and India and to report on these to Berlin. He [*ie* Meisinger] is to be informed that it was an implicit precondition of his attachment to the Tokyo Embassy that he was to deal exclusively with those police matters with which he is charged and not with reporting on foreign policy matters with which he is not entitled to deal. Meisinger's telegram will be transmitted to the RSHA, which will be informed in the same sense.[39]

Two days later, Meisinger's message (but not the accompanying cable from Fischer) was forwarded to Heydrich. At the same time a senior Foreign Ministry official, Martin Luther, sent a sternly worded letter to Heydrich setting out Ribbentrop's views 'at the explicit instruction of the Foreign Minister'. Luther added that Trebitsch Lincoln, 'by birth a Hungarian Jew', was an international adventurer whose influence in Buddhist circles was insignificant. He asked that the RSHA instruct Meisinger immediately to 'confine himself to police matters and refrain from reporting on matters of foreign policy'.[40]

Meanwhile, in Shanghai, Fischer had (no doubt with private glee) shown Ribbentrop's telegram of rebuke to Meisinger. The Gestapo agent seems to have been somewhat sobered by this. At any rate the ardour of his enthusiasm for Trebitsch's scheme cooled. Evidently in a defensive frame a mind, Meisinger sent back to Berlin a reply in which he sought to distance himself from what had turned out to be an unwise connexion:

> With reference to my telegram of 15 May, no. 117, concerning interview with Trebitsch Lincoln. . . . I declare that my discussion with Trebitsch did not, so far as I was concerned, touch on any matters of *foreign* policy. Subject of the discussion was exclusively receipt of a complaint by Trebitsch about 2 German authorities which some months ago approached him with 'requests' and who had not 'deigned to give him an answer' up to the time of the interview. As regards the declarations of Trebitsch, which were made on his own initiative, as well as his offer to take orders from me, I declared from the outset that I had no such authority, but that I was willing to transmit his proposal to go to Berlin himself. For this I chose the prescribed service channel.[41]

Meisinger's second message to Berlin was again sent through 'the prescribed service channel', namely the Consulate-General in Shanghai. And once again Fischer sent a shadow telegram of his own containing further valuable information. Fischer's cable explained that 'the expression "German authorities" who approached T. does not of course refer to the Consulate-General'. Having thus safeguarded his own flank, Fischer added a note, marked 'Confidential: In February this year there were discussions with T. by agents of the Abwehr bureau here.'[42]

This little inter-office squabble seemed to end in an outright victory for the Foreign Ministry, when, on 22 May, Heydrich wrote to the Foreign Ministry saying that he 'completely agree[d]' with Ribbentrop's view concerning the role and functions of the police attaché.[43] And indeed a formal, and apparently definitive, instruction was cabled to Meisinger by Heydrich (but through Foreign Ministry channels):

> As police liaison officer you are to deal exclusively with the police functions you are charged with. You are not authorised to report on foreign policy matters. In the matter of Trebitsch Lincoln, therefore, you are not to proceed. Surely you are aware that he is a Jew. Heydrich.[44]

Heydrich's apparently complaisant response to Luther (whom he detested) was probably nothing more than an outward display of deference while he planned his longer-term strategy for outmanoeuvring Ribbentrop.* Perhaps Heydrich was genuinely appalled by the notion of dealing with a man who was (by Nazi standards) a Jew. Yet, astonishingly, neither Trebitsch's Jewish origins nor this seemingly definitive rebuff from Berlin terminated the Buddhist abbot's wartime relations with German espionage agents in Shanghai.

On 8 December 1941, immediately after their attack on Pearl Harbor, the Japanese at last completed their conquest of Shanghai by occupying the International Settlement area of the city. Although they continued for a while to permit the (pro-Vichy) French Consul-General some limited degree of authority in the small French Concession, the event marked the effective end of a century of European power in the city.

The destruction, within sight of the population of Shanghai, of HMS *Petrel*, the last remaining British gunboat on the Yangtse, was the microcosm of a larger capitulation. By February 1942, with the surrender of Singapore, the entire British imperial house of cards in east Asia, hitherto so resplendent, self-confident, and apparently impregnable, had tumbled at the mere touch of the Japanese war machine. Trebitsch's prophecy had been fulfilled. Twenty-six years after his confrontation with Captain Hall, this cataclysmic revenge (to which Trebitsch no doubt deluded himself that his own actions had contributed) must have tasted sweet to the palate of the vegetarian abbot.

With occupation came a full assumption of the apparatus of power by the Japanese army and secret police. Allied nationals were subjected to various restrictions and eventually rounded up and placed in internment camps. Contacts between Shanghai and the outside world were almost entirely cut off. Bank assets were frozen. Pro-allied newspapers were closed. And a reign of terror was initiated against suspect persons of whatever nationality.

For information on Trebitsch's intelligence connexions after the outbreak of the Pacific war, we are restricted to one source — evidence given at a post-war trial before a US military court at Shanghai in a case involving members of a wartime German espionage organization in Shanghai. Among those presenting testimony was a former German agent in Shanghai, Dr Hermann

* Ribbentrop won the battle, but lost the war. On 11 June 1941 he sent Himmler a memorandum complaining again about Meisinger's conduct in relation to Trebitsch, and insisting that the police attachés be subordinated to Foreign Ministry authority.[45] But by August Ribbentrop had been checkmated by Heydrich, and found it necessary to concede the point.[46]

Erben.[47] A German-American who had qualified as a physician in Vienna, Erben arrived in Shanghai in March 1941. He met and became very friendly with the head of the Gestapo in Shanghai, Gerhardt Kahner. As a result, in May 1941, he was introduced to Siefkin, who recruited him to his intelligence organization. Erben remained a German agent until after the end of the war; he gave ample proof of his devotion to the German cause by spending more than two years as a prisoner in a Japanese internment camp spying on American fellow-internees.

In the course of his lengthy testimony Erben mentioned Trebitsch several times. He said that he had met him through his partner in medical practice in Shanghai, Dr Albert von Miorini. A shady character who had close relations with the German secret intelligence network in Shanghai, Miorini happened to be Trebitsch's doctor, and consulted Erben about some (unspecified) medical conditon of Trebitsch. As a result he met Trebitsch, who seems at the time to have been connected with the Bureau Siefkin and also with a Japanese secret police agent named Konishi. A former immigrant to the USA who had lived in Seattle for twenty-seven years, Konishi was employed in Shanghai by the *Kempeitai* (military police) organization. Unfortunately Erben did not specify the nature of Trebitsch's activities in connection with either German or Japanese intelligence, though he did say that Konishi had been assigned by the *Kempeitai* as 'liaison between Chow Kun [*sic*] and myself and various other agencies'. Asked when he had last seen 'Abbot Chow Kung', Erben replied that he could not be sure, but he guessed that it had been in 1942.

Since Erben was not interned until April 1943, this seems to indicate that Trebitsch's connection with the German intelligence organization had diminished or ended before the end of 1942. A possible explanation for this may be a change in the nature of the 'Bureau Siefkin' in December 1942. According to Erben, the change was connected with long-standing disputes between Siefkin and German diplomats in Shanghai, notably Consul-General Fischer and Ambassador Stahmer. The quarrel was yet another of those petty jurisdictional disputes typical of the Nazi régime. Siefkin, whose bureau was under the authority of the German High Command, reportedly saw no 'reason why he should submit his reports to the scrutiny and censorship . . . of the German Embassy . . . in Shanghai'. The diplomats, on this occasion, seem to have enjoyed the support of the local Gestapo official, Kahner, as well as of Meisinger, who denounced Siefkin as a homosexual.[48] Moreover, Siefkin's position may have been undermined by the discovery of contacts (of which we know from a different source) between him and an underground group of democratic, anti-Nazi Germans in Shanghai, as well as of secret help from him to Jewish refugees in the city.[49]

On 1 December 1942 Siefkin was summarily dismissed and replaced by Colonel Ludwig Ehrhardt, the name of the organization changing at the same time to 'Bureau Ehrhardt'. Henceforth all communications to Berlin were dispatched through the embassy. We have already noticed the Shanghai diplomatic establishment's hostility to Trebitsch at the time of the Meisinger affair. It may be, therefore, that, as on the earlier occasion, there was some connection between the diplomats' victory in their private war against the intelligence apparatus and the dismissal of Trebitsch. In any event, after this we hear no more about relations between Trebitsch and German (or Japanese) intelligence bodies, and we may tentatively conclude that the long career of the 'international spy' had finally run its course.

But before we retire Trebitsch altogether from his trade as a free-lance spy, mention must be made of a strange twist in the tail. Just as in World War I the British secret service had apprised themselves fully of Trebitsch's links with German intelligence, so in World War II his renewed activity in the German interest did not pass unnoticed. This is shown by the official reaction to a sudden rash of newspaper reports which appeared in Britain in 1942. The first was in the *Daily Herald* of 7 May, which, under the headline 'Japs Fight Radio War from Tibet' printed an absurd allegation that Trebitsch, together with other Japanese agents, was broadcasting 'a steady stream of lies and distortions aimed at creating suspicion and disquiet between India and Britain' from a secret short-wave radio station somewhere near Lhasa. In answer to an inquiry from the Foreign Office, a report was prepared by the Indian Political Intelligence department: this presented a brief history of Trebitsch's pro-Japanese propaganda activities, and ended with the statement: 'In May 1941 he was known to be living in Shanghai'.[50] After further (perhaps 'inspired') reports appeared in *The Scotsman* and other papers, an official minute pointed out that the alleged Tibetan radio station, 'Radio Himalaya', was in fact based in Rome; as for Trebitsch, it was stated that no later information was available than the May 1941 Shanghai report.[51]

How did the British know he was in Shanghai at that date? And where did the 'radio war' story originate? Here we are once again reduced to speculation. But the conjunction of the date and the story are suggestive. It was, after all, in May 1941 that Trebitsch approached Meisinger with his complaint that the scheme for a Tibet radio station, to be established by Trebitsch himself, had not been pursued. The conclusion seems inevitable that at least some garbled version of the Meisinger-Trebitsch episode had percolated through to the British — the most likely route being penetration by British signals intelligence of those very 'prescribed service channels' which

Meisinger and Siefkin so urgently (and, it appears, correctly) sought to circumvent.

Trebitsch's last months were spent as a resident of the 'Foreign' YMCA in Shanghai. He does not seem to have been in any way molested by the Japanese occupation authorities. Ambassador Stahmer recollected that he was to be seen every afternoon taking a stroll up the Bubbling Well and Nanking Roads. The contemplative life of the monk seems to have been relatively undisturbed by the great events in the outside world. Perhaps, during this last period, Trebitsch met his old friend Karl von Wiegand, who was under nominal internment at the Hotel Metropole.* In a letter written after Trebitsch's death, Wiegand says that he 'knew him as Trebitsch-Lincoln and also as Chao Kung'.[52] But unfortunately there is no further information as to whether the two survivors of the Kapp putsch and the White International met to exchange memories in these final months.

Our last glimpse of Trebitsch finds him, mercifully, at a moment of relative tranquillity. In July 1943, a small trilingual Russian-Yiddish-English newspaper, circulating among Jewish refugees in Shanghai, published an interview with him. A reporter, Anna Ginsbourg, visited him at the YMCA and was charmed by his 'brilliant and magnetic personality'. Trebitsch was 'clad in a black Buddhist robe, with soft Chinese shoes on bare feet, and a rosary around his neck'. He apparently spent most of his time 'in studies with his disciples'. The interview took place in the downstairs tea-room where Trebitsch acted as host, serving Miss Ginsbourg tea. For the last time he spun out the anecdotes about his early life, his election to Parliament, and his conversion to Buddhism. He presented his views on the Jewish problem, dismissing Zionism as 'a dangerous idea'. He told the reporter how he had devised schemes for settling Jewish refugees on a stretch of land near Shanghai belonging to the Buddhists, 'proposing to build there a Model Settlement, a Tel Aviv in miniature'. But like so many of Trebitsch's bright ideas, this had been rejected. He reiterated his faith in 'the doctrine of Buddha, THE TRUTH, the only exact scientific unravelling of the problem of life, of the problem of being and of the problem of the world'.[53]

Trebitsch died on 6 October 1943 following an operation for an

* Wiegand was in Shanghai in December 1941 and then went to the Philippines. When the Japanese attacked Manila, Wiegand was blinded by a Japanese bomb. Following the Japanese occupation of the Philippines, he was interned together with his companion, Lady Drummond Hay. In June 1942 they were transported to Shanghai, where, thanks to the intercession of a member of the Bureau Ehrhardt, the blind pro-Nazi was exempt from internment in a camp and permitted to stay at the Hotel Metropole. He was later 'repatriated' to the USA.

intestinal complaint at the Shanghai General Hospital.[54] But from the Buddhist standpoint, his death was merely an incidental event in a sequence leading to reincarnation. 'The cause of death', as the Buddhist saying goes, 'is not disease but birth.'[55]

Afterword

THE MANIC MESSIAH

He was born to a middle-class family in a small provincial town. His father was a merchant and a 'scrupulously observant Jew'. 'In his memoirs he makes much of the pranks and bold adventures of his childhood and adolescence.' After turning to religion he married the daughter of a respectable family. He later changed his religion twice and founded his own little sect. His life was characterised by incessant wanderings from country to country. 'A man of unbridled ambition, domineering to the point of despotism', he 'envisaged a great future for himself'. A supreme political opportunist, he transferred his loyalties without pause or scruple. He sought the protection of crowned heads and was mixed up in shady political activity or espionage for several governments. He 'spoke a great deal about a general revolution' and about conquests in the east. Adopting an oriental mode of dress, he 'put on a show of strange practices, deliberately "Eastern" in nature, in order to emphasize their exotic nature.' He 'revealed himself as the living embodiment of God's power'. His acolytes called him 'Master'. He was accused of sexual malpractices with his female followers. He warned in apocalyptic terms of the impending end of days. 'People were overcome and dominated by his powerful personality, which was compounded of limitless ambition and cunning, together with a facility of expression and marked imaginative faculty which even had a tinge of poetry.' His 'personality reveals clear signs of the adventurer, motivated by a blend of religious impulses and a lust for power'. 'Perhaps it can be said of [him] that he was a mixture of despotic ruler, popular prophet and cunning impostor.'[1]

This depiction of the eighteenth-century pseudo-messiah Jacob Frank might be applied without alteration to the subject of this book. Trebitsch, in fact, fits squarely into the tradition of false messiahs well known to historians of Judaism and Christianity — and also to contemporary psychiatrists. There can be little doubt that, towards the end, Trebitsch came to believe that he was in some sense a messiah. We may date the dawning of this idea from his first mystic illumination at the Astor House Hotel in Tientsin on 27 October 1925, when he made the 'great renunciation' and 'walked out of the lunatic asylum — the world'. From that moment Trebitsch gave repeated demonstrations of his conviction that he was the anointed herald of an era of redemption. In November 1925 he wrote of the 'new epoch' that was being ushered in: 'We shall presently be living in momentous days. I am speaking of quite different things than would be surmised. I have been privileged to get a glimpse and intimation of things to come.' Soon Trebitsch persuaded himself that he possessed extrasensory faculties. Over the plasticine minds of his disciples Trebitsch gained almost total intellectual, psychological and emotional dominance, such that (so long as they followed him) his authority seemed to them to carry divine sanction.

When Armageddon flamed forth all around him, Trebitsch issued his summons to universal peace, and, using images that recalled the book of Ezekiel and the Revelation of St John the Divine rather than the Buddhist scriptures, he forewarned of the vials of wrath that would pour like fire out of heaven, at the behest of his Supreme Masters, and devour the embattled forces of mankind. Even if we set aside as uncorroborated the suggestive accounts of his alleged claim to reincarnate the Dalai and Panchen Lamas (three souls in one), and his putative ability to conjure three wise men out of the wall, the evidence of Trebitsch's own words and actions in his last years affords clear proof of his delusion that there had come to reside within him a spark of the divine.

Trebitsch's conversion to Buddhism and his initiation as a *bodhisattva* (one who embraces 'self'-extinction in order to be a 'Saviour of Mankind')[2] drew out tendencies, long latent in his character, towards what we may call a 'messiah complex'. In this regard, his fascination with the Panchen Lama and his teachings was crucial. For during his exile in China the Panchen served as a foremost exponent of the Tibetan brand of Buddhism, of the Tantric doctrines of mysticism, and of the possibility of acquiring paranormal powers.[3] Trebitsch manifestly believed that he possessed such supernatural capabilities. He found in Tibetan Buddhism access to esoteric truths which endowed him with the power to save mankind, and the duty to take action on the basis of his unique awareness. From this source he plucked what he most needed, thus reinforcing his fundamental messianic urge.

Trebitsch was in no sense a *religious* impostor. All the evidence points to the vigour of his religious zeal, even if not to profundity of spiritual thought. It is difficult to conceive that an impostor would voluntarily undergo the excruciatingly painful head-branding that

Trebitsch endured at Pao-hua Shan in 1931. After his death Karl von Wiegand would sneer: 'I never was much impressed with his Buddhism, that is the spiritual side of him, for he could not renounce his interest in high politics.'[4] It is true that Trebitsch's persistent meddling in backstairs politics, his authoritarian treatment of his slave-like followers, and his arrogant denunciation of his supposed enemies seem alien to the spirit of his adopted faith. Nevertheless, strange to relate, a distinguished authority on Chinese Buddhism reports that in the 1950s and 1960s Chinese monks still spoke of Chao Kung 'with affection and pride'. In their eyes 'it was he who at the end of a century of Christian privilege had enabled them to turn the tables on the missionaries'.[5] This attitude was, of course, as much a simplification as Wiegand's. But it points us in the right direction.

For the trouble with Trebitsch's religion was not that it lacked sincerity but rather that it was rooted in a vast *folie de grandeur*. Trebitsch's Buddhist sect, at its height in 1933, numbered (including himself) fourteen souls. Yet he repeatedly spoke of the 'millions' of Buddhists throughout Asia whom he represented and who he deluded himself would heed his commands. 'Having saved myself [he wrote in 1935], and having already saved some other beings, I will now try to carry aid and rescue to the multitudes.'[6] This was the benign aspect of his vision. But more often, and increasingly towards the end, it was the malevolent side that was dominant. The 'multitudes' would be, not the object of his spiritual care, but the instrument of his revenge, rising up (in a most unBuddhist fashion) to wreak vengeance on Captain Hall and on the British Empire.

Trebitsch Lincoln's religion was in fact not really Buddhism at all, but a syncretistic combination whose primary function was to serve as the framework, both internally and externally, for his deep-seated messianic drive. The very elements that appear to us as inconsistencies or lapses from the high ideal of the *bodhisattva* were for Trebitsch evidence of his own supernatural authority, his capacity to override conventional morality, his power to transform a 'world in disequilibrium' and to 'save it from total destruction'.[7]

His delusions of grandeur were one symptom of the manic depressive psychosis which governed his thinking and his conduct during most of the later part of his life (though one can detect strong indications that it was already present much earlier). We have already observed the repetitive cycles of elation and despair to which he was subject, his threats of suicide (not to mention his lecture on 'How I Killed Trebitsch Lincoln'), his alternating states of gloom, pessimism, and paranoia on the one hand, and of supernal omnipotence, euphoria, gregariousness, and hyper-activity on the other. These are typical manic-depressive symptoms.[8]

In Trebitsch's desperate need to dominate others and to receive outward recognition of his authority, as well as in his confusion of his own depression with an imminent apocalypse, we discover the essential link between his medical and his spiritual condition. Here he may be compared with the most notorious of all pseudo-messiahs, the seventeenth-century mystic from Izmir, Sabbatai Tsvi, of whom Gershom Scholem has written: 'The sources suggest with almost absolute certainty that Sabbatai suffered from a manic-depressive psychosis, possibly combined with some paranoid traits.'[9] If the outward conditions of Trebitsch's life inevitably recall Jacob Frank, his inner condition seems closely to resemble that of Sabbatai Tsvi.

The messianic manic-depressive syndrome provides the key to an *explanation* of Trebitsch's life, and in particular of the link between his inner mental constructs and external reality. But what, if anything, was the *significance* of this disordered existence? Is Trebitsch simply to be dismissed (as he was so often in his lifetime) as a liar, a show-off, and a cheat, a promoter of crackpot ideas and jerry-built companies, an electoral freak, a fraud in commerce, an irritant in diplomacy, and a disaster in his family life?

Trebitsch earned a precarious foothold in political history by his election to parliament, his participation in the Kapp putsch, and his role in the White International. But he left nothing of enduring value in legislation, in the realm of political thought, or in international relations. In a real sense his political career was an imposture, in which he deceived and ultimately betrayed the Liberal electors of Darlington, the German, Hungarian and Russian reactionaries, and the victims of Japanese aggression. Such marginal political significance as he acquired arose less out of anything he himself said or did than out of the unscrupulous use made of his legend as a bogeyman by propagandists of right and left.

The trouble that Trebitsch caused lived after him most malignantly in the blight it cast on his family. His wife, who maintained her faith in him with such touching, simple-minded naïveté, was ruined financially and psychologically by his selfishness and unthinking cruelty towards her. She survived her husband (whom she never formally divorced) by sixteen years, but she never really recovered from the scars he left on her innocent and defenceless psyche. All of his family suffered in one way or another from his stain. It is a sobering reflection that the same world war in which Trebitsch worked with such enthusiasm for the Japanese and the Germans produced the maltreatment on Java of his son John and the death in Auschwitz of his brother Sándor. Trebitsch cannot, of course, be held accountable for their fates any more than for the hanging of his son Ignatius. But these personal tragedies highlight the reckless irresponsibility and purposelessness of Trebitsch's life as a whole.

And yet the story of Trebitsch Lincoln thrusts itself insistently on our imagination. I think it does so not because of its intrinsic importance (for it has none), nor merely because of its outlandish and picaresque qualities, but rather because it seems somehow to mirror, albeit in a grotesque and distorted fashion, the unquiet spirit of the age. His life as a whole offers us an unintended but revealing parody of the style and substance of politics, diplomacy and religion in a period of lost ideological, social and spiritual bearings. Trebitsch was an extreme, but in a sense a characteristic product of the era of political messianism when madness gained an ascendancy over large portions of humanity. He shared many of the manic attributes of the Great Dictators of the period, most notably the pseudo-messiah of the Third Reich. Indeed, it was a short walk from Trebitsch's buffoonery to their bombast — from the Kapp farrago to Hitler's Munich putsch.

There was 'something almost Olympian about this man's scoundrelism', wrote one of Trebitsch's enemies in March 1920, a couple of days after his brief encounter with Hitler.[10] It might have been written of either. The one kindled a great inferno; the other an empty pyrotechnic display. But Trebitsch's squib still casts a momentary illumination over the disturbed history of his time.

SOURCES

When Trebitsch passed through Hong Kong in September 1927, en route to Tientsin, he was reported to have with him six trunks, 'three of which were filled with papers and books on Buddhism'. It is a reasonable surmise, given Trebitsch's attachment to evidence of his own importance, that some, at least, of the contents of the three latter trunks remained with him in his quarters at the Shanghai YMCA until his death in 1943. Throughout my work on this book I was tantalised by the thought of those three trunks, and by the treasure trove of documentary materials they might contain. The chances of survival of any of Trebitsch's hoard of papers must be acknowledged to be extremely remote. Nevertheless, I thought it worth while to make inquiries in various parts of the world in the faint hope of locating some part of these documents. So far, alas, the search has been unsuccessful.

Notwithstanding this major (but hardly unexpected) disappointment, my efforts to find primary source material concerning Trebitsch met with remarkable success — thanks to the help I received from scholars and archivists in many countries. The great bulk of the unpublished documents used for this book are drawn from six major repositories; these, therefore, will be discussed first.

The single most important source has been the collection of British official records at the Public Record Office in Kew. Most of the relevant papers are contained in the Foreign Office general correspondence (FO 371) or in the related categories, Foreign Office treaty class (FO 372), commercial class (FO 368), or consular class (FO 369). Some material was also found in the records of the British Embassy in Peking (FO 228 and FO 676), the Brussels Embassy (FO 123), and the Paris Embassy (FO 146). The Foreign Office material, which covers the period 1906 to 1937, includes documents sent to the Foreign Office by Scotland Yard and the intelligence services. The MI5 file on Trebitsch Lincoln, reportedly very bulky, is, like all MI5 material, permanently closed. Naval intelligence records at the Public Record Office (ADM 137/3962 & 3963) do *not* include the texts of intercepted German cables concerning him (see below p. 306 n. 10), but valuable information may nevertheless be gleaned from the brief summaries of these intercepts. The voluminous Home Office records concerning Trebitsch Lincoln are lodged at the Public Record Office in a category closed to public inspection. I was exceptionally permitted by the Home Office to examine selected papers from relevant Home Office files. The Public Record Office holds files, formerly lodged at Companies House, concerning Trebitsch's business activities: BT 31/13861/121172 (Lincoln & Co.), BT 31/13387/111850 (Anglo-Austrian Petroleum Syndicate), BT 31/13595/115577 (Amalgamated Oil Pipe-Lines of Galicia), and BT 31/20641/121766 (Oil and Drilling Trust of Roumania).

The private papers of Colonel Max Bauer, now held by the Bundesarchiv in Koblenz, are of immense interest for the period 1919–23. This remarkable collection was invaluable for an understanding of Trebitsch's relations with Bauer. Its peculiar importance arises from the fact that it includes not merely correspondence between Trebitsch and Bauer, but Trebitsch's correspondence with other members of the Kapp conspiracy and of the White International. Among Bauer's papers are the Vienna court records concerning Trebitsch's trial in 1921: these provide vital evidence concerning Trebitsch's activities during 1920. They also include the text of an appointments diary kept by Trebitsch from May to December 1920. Unfortunately the original diary itself is not available; what we have is a transcription prepared for the court; it is an open question whether the diary is an authentic contemporary record or was constructed after the event by Trebitsch in order to give verisimilitude to his story and help sell his hoard of stolen documents to the Czechs. For this reason (and also in accordance with the general principle enunciated in the Foreword that documents originating with Trebitsch would not be regarded as authoritative) no reliance has been placed on this diary — nor on Trebitsch's testimony to the court. It is an interesting speculation how these court records arrived among Bauer's papers. Certain tell-tale clues suggest that Gustav Ritter von Kreitner may have obtained copies in connection with his work on Trebitsch's autobiography, and may thereafter have passed them on to Luise Engeler, the custodian of Bauer's papers. Miss Engeler's diary, also included in the Bauer collection, is of great significance, corroborating as it does information derived from sources which by themselves might be suspect.

The United States National Archives in Washington contain several large blocks of relevant material. The records of the Justice Department (record group 60) contain a large file (177263) concerning Trebitsch's arrest, imprisonment, escape, re-arrest, extradition, appeal to the Supreme Court, and deportation from the USA in 1915–16. A further file (181595) provides some supplementary information. Among State Department general records (record group 59), file 211.41T73 includes documentation on Trebitsch's extradition as well as material relating to his activity in Europe in 1920. A number of other State Department files furnish further evidence mainly about his political conspiracies in 1919 and 1920. The records of the Office of the Special Agent (record group 59), in effect the private intelligence service of the State Department in the 1920s, includes a voluminous file (862.2.898), lovingly built up by the Chief Special Agent, recording all available information on Trebitsch. The Modern Military Field Branch, Military Archives Division, holds the case records of US vs. Lothar Eisentraeger alias Ludwig Ehrhardt (Record Group 153, Case 58–137, Book 1), containing Hermann Erben's testimony on Trebitsch's connections with German and Japanese intelligence organs in Shanghai in World War II.

Several other record groups at the United States National Archives hold valuable material. The records of the Office of Strategic Services (record group 226), predecessor of the CIA, which have recently been transferred to the National Archives, include a number of files which provide valuable background information on Shanghai during World War II and on German intelligence activities in the Far East. US military intelligence records (record group 165) include many files concerning Trebitsch Lincoln, mainly dealing with the period 1919 to 1922. This record group also includes documents on the court-martial of poor Harry Trebitsch, and his pathetic hoard of family letters — useful for plotting Trebitsch's familial relationships. World War II war crimes interrogation records (record group 238) include a transcript of the post-war interrogation of Joseph Meisinger. The investigative case files of the Federal Bureau of Investigation (record group 65) include two files concerning Trebitsch: B[ureau] S[ection] file 202600–1356 and O[ld] G[erman] file 500. The latter runs to several hundred pages in length and provides voluminous, often hilarious, details of the Bureau's dealings with Trebitsch in 1915 and 1916. The FBI also holds other files concerning Trebitsch Lincoln which have not yet been transferred to the National Archives but which were made available to me under the admirable provisions of the US Freedom of Information Act (notably BS 61–257 and 65–813).

The most exotic, and in many ways most revealing, documents concerning Trebitsch held by the National Archives are the files of the Special Branch (i.e. political section) of the Shanghai Municipal Police, the British-controlled security agency active until 1941 in the Shanghai International Settlement. These records were transferred by the Nationalist Chinese Government to the CIA in 1949, just before the communist capture of Shanghai. They were loaded on to an American ship under communist bombardment — in the haste of the operation some of the papers fell into the Whangpoo river. Transported to the USA, they were held by the CIA until their recent transfer to the National Archives. They are of unique interest to modern historians, constituting as they do the only more-or-less complete block of records of a British security organization ever to become available to the public. (It has been officially announced in Britain that security and intelligence-related records 'are never released to the PRO') The Shanghai police records contain several files of interest to Trebitsch's biographer, of which the most important are three large files numbered I.O. 5607, I, II, and III. These contain scrupulously detailed reports by police officers who, from 1925 to 1940, kept track of Trebitsch's movements, his business dealings, his religious activities, and his dabbling in the murky waters of Chinese politics and international espionage.

The archives of the German Foreign Ministry in Bonn hold Trebitsch's Rotterdam memorandum of 30 December 1914 (AA PA Generalkonsulat Rotterdam Paket 80: Militärsachen 1914–15), which is unfortunately isolated and completely without any accompanying minutes, commentary, or material showing how it was regarded or dealt with by the German authorities; it is nevertheless of great importance, confirming as it does part of Trebitsch's claims as well as British suspicions of his connexions with the Germans. The Foreign Ministry's material for the early 1920s is disappointing, and contains little of importance concerning either the role of Trebitsch in the Kapp putsch (when he was briefly an employee of the Foreign Ministry) or its aftermath. Documents relating to this period are contained in AA PA Referat Deutschland 56/3 and 56/4 and 87/1 well as Gesandtschaft Budapest P46: Lincoln-Trebitsch. More useful is the large amount of material concerning Trebitsch's visits to Germany (abortive and actual) in the late 1920s and early 1930s, and reports from the German Consulate-General in Shanghai: AA PA Politische Abteilung IV — China, PO 11 Nr. 6, Bd. 1 and Bd. 2. The file on Trebitsch's meeting with Meisinger and his projected meeting with Hitler in 1941 is AA PA Inland IIg 522. Also important for this final period are files AA PA Inland IIg 17b and PA Pol. Im Mil. Po. 15g, Bd 18.

The Bodleian Library in Oxford holds on deposit the archive of the Church Ministry among the Jews, formerly the London Society for the Promotion of Christianity among the Jews. Papers concerning the Montreal Jewish mission are in file d 43/7; the minutes of the society's London committee are listed as c 34/1.

The British Library holds the thirteen letters written by Trebitsch to Walter Persian, between December 1930 and April 1932. Only Trebitsch's side of the correspondence appears to be extant. Nevertheless, these letters were a particularly happy discovery for Trebitsch's biographer, covering as they do the period of his initiation as a Buddhist monk and conveying something of his inner turmoil at that time. The authenticity of this set of documents is certain. But their origin is obscure. The letters held by the British Library are not originals but a typescript copy bound as a book. They form part not of the library's manuscript collection but of the division of printed books (call no. 4509. g. 1). The volume was donated to the library in 1954. A search of the library's records was kindly undertaken by its administration, but I am informed that there appears to be no record of the donor or origin of the correspondence.

A number of other institutions have supplied copies of documents in their possession. These include: the Amtsgericht of Hamburg (probate record of J.H. Kahlor); the Nordelbisches Missionszentrum (copy of entry no. 213b in the Breklum Seminary register kept by Dr Christian Jensen II and now held by Dr Hildegard Jensen); the Budapest Drama Academy (entries in its register for 1895 and 1896); the Canadian Public Archives, Ottawa (material from the private papers of Prime Minister R.B. Bennett concerning his meeting with Trebitsch in 1934, as well as records of the Secretary of State: record group 6, vol. 590, file 269–4; and vol. 540, file 203); Durham County Record Office, Darlington Branch (some material concerning the 1910 elections); the Haus-, Hof-, und Staatsarchiv, Vienna (some Austrian Government papers covering the period during and after the 1921 Vienna trial: Neues Politisches Archiv, vol. 451: alt 512); the Austrian State Archives (some Austrian Foreign Ministry papers covering the years 1910–15); the archives of the Hoover Institution, Stanford, California (four items in the Karl von Wiegand collection); the Hungarian State Archives (documents from the Horthy papers: K section 589–III. H. 22; and Interior Ministry file K 149 – 1938 – 4341); the Central State Archives, Prague (documents from the Ministry of Interior and the Prague police headquarters; cuttings from the Foreign Ministry press clippings archive); India Office records now held by the British Library (one file directly concerned with Trebitsch: L/P&S/11/286, dealing with his movements in the late twenties; three others holding some material about him for the period 1938 to 1942 — particularly useful since the Foreign Office records hold nothing on him for those years — L/P&S/12/487, 12/494 and 12/720; also other files cotaining background material on Tibet, the Panchen Lama, the Cleather-Crump clique, Radio Himalaya and related topics); the Royal Library, Copenhagen (diary of J. Prip-Møller); the Institut fuer Zeitgeschichte, Munich (material for 1920 and 1921: MA 804/1: 6647–8 and MA 616/4: 56441–56661); the Joseph Rowntree Memorial Trust, York (Joseph Rowntree's letter of 26 November 1910 to his son); Lambeth Palace Library, London (entries in Archbishop Davidson's Ordination Book and in the Ordinands Examination Book for 1904); Berlin Document Center (records relating to Joseph Meisinger); Quebec Superior Court, Prothonotary's Office, Montreal (Marriage certificate of Ignatius and Margarethe Trebitsch; birth and death certificates of Robert Trebitsch); Staatsarchiv, Munich (Munich police file on Trebitsch Lincoln, 1920–1949, Nr. 10166); St. Antony's College, Oxford (diary and private papers of General Sir Neill Malcolm); the archives of *The Times*, London (H.G. Daniels's letter of 14 March 1920); United Church of Canada Archives, Toronto (Montreal Jewish Mission papers, files, 26, 27, and 28).

The published sources for this study were voluminous and cannot all be listed here. A great deal of information (much of it to be taken with large pinches of salt) was derived from newspapers and periodicals. Several organizations and archives, particularly in Germany, supplied me with press cuttings concerning Trebitsch, mainly from the inter-war period.* Of particular importance for Trebitsch's period as parliamentary candidate and MP were the local Darlington newspapers, the *North Star* and the *Northern Echo*; the *Moniteur du Pétrole Roumain* provided fortnightly coverage of the progress — or regress — of Trebitsch's oil-drilling operations in 1912–13 (I was fortunate in finding an almost complete run of this rare newspaper in the library of the Haifa Institute of Technology); and for the China period the *North China Daily News* and its weekly edition, the *North China Weekly Herald.*

Works by Trebitsch himself fall into a special category. Again it should be emphasized that while all his published books and all available pamphlets and articles have been consulted, none has been used as a source — except, of course, as direct evidence of what he wrote. Since his main works are discussed in the course of the narrative, no further comment is required here, but they may be listed for convenience: *Revelations of an International Spy* (New York 1916); *The Autobiography of an Adventurer* (New York 1932) originally published as *Der grösste Abenteurer des XX. Jahrhunderts!?* (Vienna 1931) — there are minor variations between the German and English versions, but all references here are to the New York edition; *Can War Be Abolished?* (Shanghai 1932); *The Human Tragedy* (Shanghai 1934); *1,000 Questions to YOU!* (Shanghai 1935); and *Dawn or Doom of Humanity* (Shanghai 1937). Dwight Goddard's *Buddhist Bible* (2nd

* In this connection I wish especially to mention the help I received from the Buddhist Society, London, the Presbyterian College, Montreal, the Bayerisches Hauptstaatsarchiv, the Staatsarchiv München, the Zentrales Staatsarchiv, Potsdam, the British Library Newspaper Division, the Widener Library of Harvard University, Harvard Yen-Ching Library, the Library of Congress, the Staatsbibliothek Preussischer Kulturbesitz, Garrett Theological Seminary, the Hebrew University Library, Brandeis University Library, and Pacific Press, Ltd., Vancouver.

rev. ed. Thetford, Vt. 1938) includes a translation, supposedly by Trebitsch, of the '118th Discourse from the Collection of Middle Discourses'. Trebitsch published too many newspaper articles to be listed here. His last two articles, disquisitions on Buddhist philosophy, appeared posthumously in a pro-Japanese Buddhist journal published in Shanghai, *Buddhist China*, I (1943), 2, 12–19, and II, (1944), 1, 24–7. The first article was illustrated by photographs (alas, too blurred for reproduction) of Trebitsch's funeral ('attended by his many friends and acquaintances of different nations') in one of the Shanghai Municipal Council cemeteries.

Another special category is that of books previously published which deal wholly or mainly with Trebitsch's life. With one exception, none deserves to be taken seriously. The exception is the biography by David Lampe and Laszlo Szenasi, *The Self-Made Villain* (London 1961), but even this relies heavily on Trebitsch's own writings; moreover it was written without access to any of the major unpublished documentary materials listed above. Other biographies of Trebitsch include: László Frank, *Szélhámosok — Kalandorok* (Budapest 1957), in which Trebitch figures as one of four subjects; Imré Gyomaï, *Trebitsch Lincoln* (Paris 1939), which suggests that Trebitsch had designs on the Chinese imperial crown; Maurice Laporte, *Bouddha contre l' Intelligence Service* (Paris 1933), alleges that Trebitsch engineered the overthrow of the King of Afghanistan in 1929 — as well as many other entertaining absurdities; Joseph Nedava's *Trebitsch-Lincoln: Parashat Hayyim So'arim* (Tel Aviv 1956) is a novel, which includes some authentic data. Endre Gömöri, *Az igazi Trebitsch* (Budapest 1985), rehashes much of the previously published material.

Among other works used for this study, two stand out: Adolf Vogt's biography, *Oberst Max Bauer: Generalstaboffizier im Zwielicht 1869–1929* (Osnabrück, 1974); and Bruno Thoss, *Der Ludendorff-Kreis 1919–1923: München als Zentrum der mitteleuropäischen Gegenrevolution zwischen Revolution und Hitler-Putsch* (Munich 1978). Both these works have been drawn upon for material concerning the early twenties. But both authors rely, albeit with reservations, partly on documents written by Trebitsch himself. To that extent these works have been used with all due caution.

Only a limited selection of the very large number of other works consulted in the course of writing this book can be mentioned here. Max Bauer's *Der 13. März 1920* (Munich 1920), of which Trebitsch claimed to be part-author, does not mention him; nor does any other of Bauer's books. Karl Brammer, *Fünf Tage Militärdiktatur: Dokumente zur Gegenrevolution* (Berlin 1920), and the same author's *Verfassungsgrundlagen und Hochverrat* (Berlin 1922) provide important information on the Kapp putsch. Asa Briggs, *Social Thought and*

Political Action: A Study of the Work of Seebohm Rowntree 1871–1954 (London 1961), is the standard life of the Quaker philanthropist. Edward Corsi, *In the Shadow of Liberty: The Chronicle of Ellis Island* (New York 1935), by a former official of the US Immigration and Naturalization Service, contains a chapter on Trebitsch, and prints verbatim his long letter of 17 May 1927 to the US Secretary of State. Johannes Erger, *Der Kapp-Lüttwitz Putsch* (Düsseldorf 1967), is the best modern account of that episode, but contains disappointingly little about Trebitsch. Jan Hajšman recalls his complicated transactions with Trebitsch in *O špionáži: špioni špionky, špiclové, lidé podzemní zpravodajská a informační služba* (Prague 1928). Admiral Sir William James, *The Eyes of the Navy: A Biographical Study of Admiral Sir Reginald Hall* (London 1955), is helpful on Trebitsch's escapades in 1914–15. G.E. Miller [pseud.], *Shanghai, The Paradise of Adventurers* (New York 1937), gives a vivid picture of various scandalous characters, including Trebitsch; the author, Mauricio Fresco, Honorary Consul of Mexico in Shanghai, was shown some of the documents in the files of the Shanghai Municipal Police; shortly after the book's publication, the author's identity was disclosed in the local press: in the ensuing hullabaloo the diplomat decided to leave the city in a hurry. J. Prip-Møller, *Kina før og nu* (Copenhagen 1944), gives an eye-witness account of Trebtisch's Buddhist ordination at Paohua Shan in 1931. Martin Pörksen, *Pastoren für Amerika: Aus der Geschichte des Breklumer Martineums* (Breklum 1980), is a history of the Breklum Seminary which, a little surprisingly, devotes space to a celebration of the career of its most notorious alumnus. B. Seebohm Rowntree, *Land and Labour: Lessons from Belgium* (London 1911), contains the fruits of Trebitsch's investigations in Europe for Rowntree between 1906 and 1909. 'Spectator', *Die Geschichte der Berliner Fünftageregierung* (Leipzig 1920), provides a lively eye-witness account of the Kapp putsch. Agnes Szabó and Ervin Pamlényi, eds., *A határban a Halál kaszál . . . : Fejezetek Prónay Pál feljegyzéseiből* (Budapest 1963), is a memoir by Prónay written during World War II, but based on contemporary documentation. Basil Thomson, *Queer People* (London 1922) and *The Scene Changes* (London 1939), by the former Director of Intelligence at Scotland Yard, furnish an intelligent policeman's view of Trebitsch. Holmes Welch, *The Buddhist Revival in China* (Cambridge, Mass., 1968), accords Trebitsch respectful treatment and a remarkably large place in the Buddhist revival; this judgement, by an eminent authority on Chinese Buddhism, deserves to be weighed seriously.

I have left to the end information provided by members of Trebitsch's family. I obtained extremely useful material from interviews with his granddaughter, his nephew, a second nephew, his niece, and his great-niece. In addition I was sent a copy of a short essay about her family by another niece. Letters from that niece, one of his nephews, a grandson and a second granddaughter answered specific questions that arose in the course of my research. As for Margaret Trebitsch Lincoln's memoirs, published in the *Empire News* in 1934, I have not located the original manuscript (though I believe it still exists). But on the basis of information from family members I have satisfied myself completely as to the memoir's authenticity and (with reservations arising only from normal lapses of memory in a memoir written many years after the events it describes) its reliability.

At the time of writing I am still pursuing a few lines of inquiry in several parts of the world. But in all research, particularly in history, there comes a moment when it is necessary to release the guillotine. The amount and nature of the evidence already collected are such that it is most unlikely that any new material could radically change our picture of Trebitsch. Hence my decision to proceed with publication now. The only possible exception is, of course, those three trunks of Trebitsch's own books and papers. A small flame of hope still burns in the back of my mind that something of these may yet be found (perhaps in some basement in Shanghai).

NOTES

Abbreviations used in notes

AA PA	Politisches Archiv des Auswärtigen Amtes, Bonn
BAK	Bundesarchiv, Koblenz
BL IOLR	India Office Library and Records, British Library, London
BL TL	Trebitsch Lincoln letters to Walter Persian, British Library, London
CMJ	Papers of the Church Ministry among the Jews (formerly the London Society for the Promotion of Christianity among the Jews), Bodleian Library, Oxford
CSA	Central State Archives, Prague, Interior Ministry files
FBI	Federal Bureau of Investigation case files, Washington D.C.
HHSA	Österreichisches Haus-, Hof- und Staatsarchiv, Vienna
MOL	Magyar Országos Levéltár (Hungarian State Archives), Budapest
MPR	*Moniteur du Pétrole Roumain*
NCWH	*North China Weekly Herald*
NYT	*New York Times*
PRO	Public Record Office, Kew
SMP	Shanghai Municipal Police Special Branch files
USNA	United States National Archives, Washington, D.C.

FOREWORD

1 Hugh Trevor-Roper, *The Hermit of Peking: The Hidden Life of Sir Edmund Backhouse* (Penguin edition, Harmondsworth 1978), p. 17.

CHAPTER 1

1 Ruth Kestenberg-Gladstein, *Neuere Geschichte der Juden in den Böhmischen Ländern* (Tübingen 1969), discusses the impact of the law.

2 Birth certificate in MOL, K 149–1938–4341. His name is spelt thus on the certificate.

3 Most of the information concerning the Trebitsch family is derived from interviews with Mr Alexander Krausz (nephew of Trebitsch Lincoln), Mrs Rennie Rudas (niece), Mrs Martha Vandor (great-niece), and Mrs Bryony Heap (granddaughter), as well as from a short typescript memoir, 'Family History', written by Miss Elsie Tarcai (niece) in the late 1920s, a copy of which was kindly made available to the author. Miss Tarcai recalls her father speaking of sixteen children in the Trebitsch family; other sources give the number fourteen.

4 Elsie Tarcai, 'Family History'.

5 Extract from Paks Jewish elementary school register in MOL, K 149–1938 –4341. On the Bratislava episode, see *Northern Echo* (Darlington), 5 April 1909, and *Pester Lloyd*, 28 Jan. 1910; the source for these reports was probably Trebitsch himself, and they should therefore be treated with appropriate reserve — but in this instance we may probably suspend disbelief.

6 *Pester Lloyd*, 28 Jan. 1910; *Az Ujság*, 21 June 1921; Information from Hungarian police report contained in note from Hungarian Minister-President to Graf Aehrenthal (Austro-Hungarian Foreign Minister), 18 May 1910, HHSA PA XI/kart. 174.

7 Register of the Budapest Színház- és Filmművészeti Főiskola.

8 Elsie Tarcai, 'Family History'.

9 See details of report in note from Hungarian Minister-President to Graf Aehrenthal, 18 May 1910, HHSA PA XI/Kart. 174.

10 See e.g. J.T. Trebitsch-Lincoln, *The Autobiography of an Adventurer* (New York 1932), p. 9. Trebitsch repeated the story so often that if frequency of iteration were our criterion for belief there could be no room for doubt. But there is no other evidence.

11 Montreal Jewish Mission, draft memorandum (probably by Revd. A.F. Burt), 1903, CMJ d 43/7.

12 Copy of pamphlet in CMJ d 36/5.

13 *Ibid.*

14 *Ibid.*

15 *NYT*, 14 June 1915.

16 *The Glory of Israel*, ı, 3, March 1903, p. 61.

17 Note to Aehrenthal, 18 May 1910, HHSA PA XI/Kart. 174.

18 Montreal Jewish Mission, Report for 1900, CMJ d 43/7. On Frank's view of Trebitsch, see Robert Allen, *Arnold Frank of Hamburg* (Lodon 1966).

19 'My Life with Trebitsch Lincoln' by Mrs Trebitsch Lincoln, *Empire News*, 13 May 1934.

20 Report by Special Branch, Scotland Yard, 23 July 1923, PRO FO 371/9221/186–191.

21 Montreal Jewish Mission, Report for 1900, Statement of Superintendent, CMJ d 43/7.

22 Records of Breklum Theological Seminary, Jensen papers, register of Dr Christian Jensen II, entry 213 b.

23 Martin Pörksen, *Pastoren für Amerika: Aus der Geschichte des Breklumer Martineums* (Breklum 1980), p. 12.

24 'My Life with Trebitsch Lincoln' by Mrs Trebitsch Lincoln, *Empire News*, 13 May 1934.

25 Jensen papers, *loc. cit.*

26 Trebitsch-Lincoln, *Autobiography*, pp. 22–4.

27 'The Jewish Mission' by the Revd. J. McCarter, *The Dominion Presbyterian*, 16 April 1902, p. 246.

28 *Ibid.*

29 *Ibid.*

30 Quoted *ibid.*

31 *Ibid.*

32 Montreal Jewish Mission, handwritten draft memorandum (probably by Revd. A.F. Burt), 1903, CMJ d 43/7.

33 *The Glory of Israel*, I, 3, March 1903, p. 61.

34 I.T.T. Lincoln, *Revelations of an International Spy* (New York 1916), p. 6.

CHAPTER 2

1 Montreal Jewish Mission, Report for 1900, CMJ d 43/7.

2 *Ibid.*

3 'The Jewish Mission' by Revd. J. McCarter, *The Dominion Presbyterian*, 16 April 1902, p. 246.

4 See Revd. G. Osborne Troop to Revd. A.F. Burt, 13 Dec. 1901, CMJ d 43/7.

5 Presbyterian Church in Canada, *Acts and Proceedings*, 1902, pp. 210–11; *The Presbyterian College Journal*, XXI, 6 (April 1902), p. 430.

6 'My Life with Trebitsch Lincoln' by Mrs Trebitsch Lincoln, *Empire*

News, 13 May 1934. Marriage certificate, 15 July 1901, Quebec Superior Court.

7 Montreal Jewish Mission, Quarterly Statement, October 1901, CMJ d 43/7.

8 'My Life with Trebitsch Lincoln', *Empire News*, 13 May 1934.

9 *Dominion Presbyterian*, 16 April 1902.

10 Revd. John McCarter to Revd. A.F. Burt, 17 April 1902, CMJ d 43/7. See also numerous letters written by Revd. McCarter in the United Church of Canada Archives, Toronto: Montreal Jewish Mission papers, files 27 and 28.

11 Revd. A.F. Burt to the Secretaries, London Society for the Promotion of Christianity among the Jews (henceforward London Society), 23 Feb. 1901 (includes reference to letter from Revd. J.L. George, dated 13 Dec. 1900), CMJ d 43/7.

12 'Our Canadian Auxiliary', by Revd. A.F. Burt, *Jewish Missionary Intelligence*, Sept. 1901.

13 Revd. G. Osborne Troop to Revd. A.F. Burt, 13 Dec. 1901, CMJ d 43/7.

14 Burt to Secretaries, London Society, 28 Dec. 1901, CMJ d 43/7.

15 Burt to Secretaries, London Society, 21 April 1902 (includes reference to letter from Trebitsch), CMJ d 43/7.

16 *Ibid.*

17 Burt to 'Christianity, London' [cable address of London Society], 13 April 1902, CMJ d 43/7.

18 Burt to Secretaries, London Society, 21 April 1902, CMJ d 43/7. See also United Church of Canada Archives, Toronto: Montreal Jewish Mission papers, file 28.

19 Committee minutes, 16 May 1902, CMJ c 34/1.

20 *Ibid.* 30 May 1902.

21 Burt to Secretaries, London Society, CMJ d 43/7.

22 Robert Johann Naphthali Trebitsch, birth certificate, 25 April 1902, death certificate, 22 July 1902, Quebec Superior Court.

23 Committee minutes, 1 Aug. 1902, CMJ c 34/1.

24 *Jewish Missionary Intelligence*, November 1902.

25 Invitation and programme of proceedings, CMJ d 43/7; *Montreal Daily Witness*, 17 [?] Oct. 1902; *Jewish Missionary Intelligence*, Feb. 1903.

26 *Jewish Missionary Intelligence*, Feb. 1903.

27 'My Life with Trebitsch Lincoln' by Mrs Trebitsch Lincoln, *Empire News*, 13 May 1934.

28 See Spencer Ervin, *The Political and Ecclesiastical History of the Anglican Church of Canada* (Ambler, Pennsylvania 1967)

29 *Halifax Herald*, 21 and 23 Jan. 1903.

30 *London Society ... Report for 1902–3* (London 1903), pp. 104–5.

31 Information from Mr Alexander Krausz and Mrs Rennie Rudas.

32 General Committee minutes, 20 Feb. 1903, CMJ c 34/1.

33 *Canadian Churchman*, 26 Feb, 1903.

34 General Committee minutes, 20 Feb. 1903, CMJ c 34/1.

35 'My Life with Trebitsch Lincoln', *Empire News*, 13 May 1934.

36 General Committee minutes, 20 March 1903, CMJ c 34/1.

CHAPTER 3

1 *NYT*, 14 June 1915.

2 Minutes of Correspondence Committee, 3 April 1903, CMJ c 34/1.

3 General Committee minutes, 3 April 1903, *ibid.*

4 General Committee minutes, 17 July 1903, *ibid.*

5 General Committee minutes, 25 Sept. 1903, *ibid.*

6 General Committee minutes, 20 Nov. 1903, *ibid.*

7 *NYT*, 14 June 1915.

8 Archbishop Davidson's Ordination Book, 1902–1914, p. 114, Lambeth Palace Library.

9 'My Life with Trebitsch Lincoln' by Mrs Trebitsch Lincoln, *Empire News*, 13 May 1934.
10 Archbishop Davidson's Ordination Book, pp. 113–4, Lambeth Palace Library.
11 *Empire News*, 13 May 1934.
12 *Ibid.*
13 Deed poll dated 11 Oct. 1904, Home Office papers.
14 Statement by B. Seebohm Rowntree, June 1916, PRO FO 372/900.
15 *Empire News*, 13 May 1934.
16 Asa Briggs, *Social Thought and Political Action: A Study of the Work of Seebohm Rowntree 1871–1954* (London 1961), p. 62.
17 Statement by B. Seebohm Rowntree, June 1916, PRO FO 372/900.
18 Unsigned minute, 21 March 1906, PRO FO 369/52.
19 Hardinge (Brussels) to Foreign Office, 23 March 1906, *ibid.*
20 *Ibid.*
21 C.H. Funch to H. Chilton, 12 Sept. 1906, *ibid.* Chilton was Acting Chargé d' Affaires at the Copenhagen Legation; Funch's letter was fowarded by him to the Foreign Office with an accompanying letter from Chilton dated 13 Sept. 1906, *ibid.*
22 J.T. Tribich Lincoln to Lord Edmund Fitzmaurice, 17 June 1907, PRO FO 369/115.
23 Minute, intialled 'R.S', 18 June 1907, *ibid.*
24 Cynthia Gladwyn, *The Paris Embassy* (London 1976), pp. 160–7.
25 R. Lister (Paris) to W. Tyrrell, 15 Aug. 1907, PRO FO 371/256; Lister to A. Ponsonby, 15 Aug. 1907, PRO FO 146/3989; J.T. Tribich Lincoln to Sir H. Lee, 12 Aug. 1907, PRO FO 146/3986.
26 Ponsonby to Tyrrell, 16 Aug. 1907, PRO FO 371/256.
27 P. Alden M.P. to W. Tyrrell, 18 Sept. 1907, *ibid.*
28 W. Langley, for Secretary of State for Foreign Affairs, to Sir Francis Bertie, 1 Oct. 1907, *ibid.*
29 Copy of draft letter [from Tyrrell ?] to Lister, 1 Oct. 1907, *ibid.*
30 S. Pichon to Sir F. Bertie, 3 Dec. 1907, *ibid.*
31 G. Grahame to G.S. Spicer, 6 Dec. 1907, *ibid.*
32 *Empire News*, 13 May 1934.
33 Statement by B. Seebohm Rowntree, June 1916, PRO FO 372/900.

CHAPTER 4

1 *North Star*, 23, 24, & 25 Nov. 1909.
2 See the excellent B.A. thesis (Huddersfield Polytechnic 1979) by Alistair John Andrew McCulloch, 'One Election, One Constituency, and One Challenger', p. 19.
3 See M.W. Kirby, *Men of Business and Politics: The Rise and Fall of the Quaker Pease Dynasty of North-East England, 1700–1943* (London 1984) and H. Pelling, *Social Geography of British Elections 1885 — 1910* (London 1967), pp. 328–9.
4 *Northern Echo*, 9 Sept. 1909.
5 'When Trebitsch Lincoln Became a British MP' by Mrs Trebitsch Lincoln, *Empire News*, 20 May 1934.
6 L. Mallet to E. Howard (Budapest), 2 Sept. 1909, PRO FO 368/374.
7 E. Howard to Sir E. Grey, 28 Sept. 1909, PRO FO 368/374.
8 E. Howard to L. Mallet, 23 Sept. 1909, PRO FO 368/374.
9 Sir J.B. Whitehead (Belgrade) to Sir E. Grey, 18 Oct. 1909, PRO FO 368/374.
10 Unsigned minute dated 30 Sept. 1909, PRO FO 368/374; and subsequent minutes, *ibid.*
11 I.T.T. Lincoln to Sir E. Grey, 13 Oct. 1909, PRO FO 368/374.
12 Minute by A. Law [?], undated [probably 14 Oct. 1909], PRO FO 368/374.
13 *North Star*, 16 Nov. 1909.
14 A copy is in Durham County Record Office, Darlington Branch.
15 Churchill to Lincoln, 7 Jan. 1910, printed in *Lincoln's Election Special*, *ibid.*
16 Lloyd George to I.T.T. Lincoln, 11 Jan. 1910, reproduced in Lincoln,

Revelations, p. 11. Not surprisingly perhaps, the Lloyd George papers at the House of Lords Record Office retain no trace of any communication between Lloyd George and Trebitsch. (See also *supra*, p. 97)
17 *Northern Echo*, 23 Dec. 1909.
18 *Northern Echo*, 14 Jan. 1910.
19 'When Trebitsch Lincoln Became a British M.P.' by Mrs Trebitsch Lincoln, *Empire News*, 20 May 1934.
20 *Ibid.*
21 Grey to Lincoln, 16 Jan. 1910, reproduced in New York *World*, 23 May 1915.
22 E. Howard (Budapest) to A. Law (Foreign Office), 19 Jan. 1910, PRO FO 368/374.
23 Howard to Sir E. Grey, 8 Feb. 1910, PRO FO 368/384.
24 Howard to Grey, 8 Feb. 1910, PRO FO 371/826/448.
25 Minute dated 21 Feb. 1910, PRO FO 371/826/447.
26 'When Trebitsch Lincoln Became a British M.P.', *Empire News*, 20 May 1934.
27 *Manchester Guardian*, 15 Dec. 1928. See also *supra*, p. 67.
28 *House of Commons Debates*, 5th Series, vol. 14, cols. 277–84.
29 Loc. cit., vol. 14, cols. 896–7.
30 *The Times*, 7 March 1910.
31 *House of Commons Debates*, 5th Series, vol. 17, cols. 1135–6.
32 Loc. cit., vol. 17, cols. 1137–9.
33 Loc. cit., vol. 16, cols. 421 and 864–5.
34 Loc. cit., vol. 16, cols. 878–9.
35 Loc. cit., vol. 16, cols. 2286–7.
36 I.T.T. Lincoln to Revd. Lypshytz, 11 Dec. 1909, Durham County Record Office, Darlington Branch.
37 *Darlington and Stockton Times*, 27 Aug. 1910. See also *Life and Labour in Belgium* 'by a party of Darlington Working Men' (Darlington 1910).
38 Certificate of incorporation, 26 Sept. 1910, PRO BT 31/13387/111850.
39 Miss Elsie Tarcai, 'Family History'; information from Mr Alexander Krausz; US military intelligence report on Harry Trebitsch, Feb. 1918, USNA RG 165/9605/23.
40 'When Trebitsch Lincoln Became a British MP', *Empire News*, 20 May 1934.
41 Rowntree papers, Joseph Rowntree Memorial Trust, York.
42 Lincoln, *Autobiography*, p. 74.
43 Mensdorff to Aehrenthal, 24 June 1910, HHSA PA VIII/Kart. 145.
44 *North Star*, 5 Dec. 1910.
45 Statement 'on solemn affirmation' by Benjamin Seebohm Rowntree, June 1916, PRO FO 372/900. See also *The Times*, 14 June 1915.

CHAPTER 5

1 *The Times* and *NYT*, 14 June 1915.
2 'When Trebitsch Lincoln Became a British MP' by Mrs Lincoln, *Empire News*, 20 May 1934; and information from Mr Alexander Krausz.
3 Leon Rymar, *Galicyjski przemysł naftowy* (Kraków 1915), pp. 115–6; *The Times*, 3 Feb, 17 March 1911.
4 Certificate of incorporation, 29 March 1912, PRO BT 31/13861/121172.
5 Return of allotments from 24 to 25 May 1911, PRO BT 31/13595/115577.
6 *The Times*, 22 May 1911.
7 *The Times*, 10 July 1911.
8 *MPR*, 1 (14) April 1912.
9 *The Times*, 28 March 1911.
10 W.H. MacGarvey to the editor, *The Times*, 7 April 1911.
11 *The Times*, 28 Sept. 1911.
12 Return of Allotments, 26 May to 31 Oct. 1911, PRO BT 31/13595/115577.
13 Return of Allotments, 29 May 1912, *ibid.*
14 *The Times*, 15 June 1912.
15 See Lincoln, *Autobiography*, pp. 83–4; and *Empire News*, 20 May 1934.
16 Agreement dated 16 Oct. 1912, PRO BT 31/13595/115577.
17 *The Times*, 27 Sept. 1924.
18 Certificate of incorporation, 29

March 1912, and related documents, PRO BT 31/13861/121172.
19 *MPR*, 1 (14) May 1912.
20 *MPR*, 1 (14) June 1912.
21 *MPR*, 10 (23) May 1912.
22 Oil and Drilling Trust of Roumania Ltd., Report, 12 Aug. 1912, PRO BT 31/20641/121766.
23 *MPR*, 10 (23) Aug. 1912.
24 *MPR*, 20 Oct. (2 Nov.) 1912.
25 Information from Mr Alexander Krausz and from Mrs Bryony Heap.
26 *Empire News*, 27 May 1934.
27 *MPR*, 10 (23) Nov. and 20 Nov. (3 Dec.) 1912; appointment of Ladenburg as 'additional director', 16 Dec. 1912, PRO BT 31/20641/121766.
28 *MPR*, 1 (14) Feb. 1913.
29 *MPR*, 10 (23) Feb. and 20 Feb. (5 March) 1913.
30 See e.g. *MPR*, 1 (14) March 1913.
31 See map, PRP BT 31/20641/121766.
32 *MPR*, 1912–13, *passim*.
33 Balance sheet dated 10 Sept. 1913, PRO BT 31/20641/121766.
34 Statement by Rowntree, June 1916, PRO FO 372/900.
35 Return of allotments, 7 and 13 March, 15 April, and 11 June 1913, PRO BT 31/20641/121766.
36 Statement on oath by John Goldstein, June 1916, PRO FO 372/900.
37 Mortgage form dated 21 July 1913, PRO BT 31/20641/121766.
38 Notice dated 6 Sept. 1913, *ibid.*
39 Report by Deloitte, Pender, Griffiths and Co. on balance sheet dated 10 Sept. 1913, *ibid.*
40 Gilbert Samuel to Registrar of Joint Stock Companies, 29 Sept. 1913, *ibid.*
41 *MPR*, 20 Nov. (3 Dec.) 1913.
42 Register of Directors, 23 Dec. 1913, PRO BT 31/20641/121766.
43 Dissolution recorded, 24 Feb. 1922, *ibid.*
44 *Empire News*, 27 May 1934.
45 Statement by Goldstein, June 1916, PRO FO 372/900.
46 Report by Special Branch, Scotland Yard, 23 July 1923, PRO FO 371/9221/186–191.
47 Statement by Goldstein, June 1916, PRO FO 372/900.
48 Statements by Goldstein, Rowntree, and an employee of the National Liberal Club, *ibid.* Copies of correspondence between Goldstein and Rowntree, 10–11 July 1914, as well as further statements by Goldstein and Rowntree, in USNA, RG 59, State Dept. Decimal File 211.41T73.

CHAPTER 6

1 'Ruined by Oil Gambles' by Mrs Trebitsch Lincoln, *Empire News*, 27 May 1934; Report by Special Branch, Scotland Yard, 23 July 1923, PRO FO 371/9221/186–191.
2 'Revelations of I.T.T. Lincoln', New York *World*, 23 May 1915.
3 Report by Special Branch, Scotland Yard, 23 July 1923, PRO FO 371/9221/186–191.
4 *House of Commons Debates*, 5th series, vol. 83, col. 715 (27 June 1916) and col. 1030 (29 June 1916).
5 *Ibid.*
6 Sworn statements by Farmer and Finklestone, June 1916, PRO FO 372/900. Copies of letters in USNA, RG 59, State Dept. Decimal File 211.41T73.
7 Sworn statement by Goldstein and statement 'on solemn affirmation' by Rowntree, June 1916, PRO FO 372/900. Copies of letters in USNA, RG 59, State Dept. Decimal File 211.41T73.
8 'Ruined by Oil Gambles' by Mrs Trebitsch Lincoln, *Empire News*, 27 May 1934.
9 Copy of letter, dated 2 December 1914, in USNA, RG 59, State Dept. Decimal File 211.41T73. See also related documents in this file.
10 Statement by Goldstein, June 1916, PRO FO 372/900.
11 Report by Special Branch, Scotland Yard, 23 July 1923, PRO FO 371/9221/186–191.

12 See Basil Thomson, *Queer People*, London 1922, pp. 152–3. Thomson served (after these events) as Director of Intelligence at Scotland Yard. His account corroborates these (although not other) essentials of Trebitsch's story as set forth in the New York *World*, 23 and 30 May 1915.
13 New York *World*, 23 May 1915.
14 AA PA Generalkonsulat Rotterdam Paket 80: Militärsachen 1914–15.
15 Dispatch dated 21 June 1915, HHSA PA XXIII/Kart. 33.
16 Thomson *Queer People*, pp. 152–3; Admiral Sir William James, *The Eyes of the Navy: A Biographical Study of Admiral Sir Reginald Hall*, London 1955, p. 37; *The Times* and *NYT*, 20 June 1916; and USNA, RG 59, State Dept. Decimal File 211.41T73.
17 'Ex-MP as German Spy' by Sir Henry Dalziel, *Reynolds's Newspaper*, 13 June 1915.
18 E. Marsh (Admiralty) to I.T.T. Lincoln, 27 Jan. 1915 (copy: authenticity attested by Addison S. Pratt, Attorney, sworn before a notary public, New York, 16 October 1915), USNA, RG 59, State Dept. Decimal File 211.41T73.
19 *Reynolds's Newspaper*, 13 June 1915; *Daily Mail*, 14 June 1915.
20 Director of Intelligence, Admiralty, to Lincoln, 28 Jan. 1915 (copy: authenticity attested by Addison S. Pratt, Attorney, sworn before a notary public, New York, 16 Oct. 1915), USNA, RG, 59, State Dept. Decimal File 211.41T73. 'Ruined by Oil Gambles' by Mrs Trebitsch Lincoln, *Empire News*, 27 May 1934.
21 James, *Eyes of the Navy*, p. 37; Hugh Cleland Hoy, *40 O. B. or How the War was Won*, London 1932, pp. 121–8.
22 *Reynolds's Newspaper*, 13 June 1915.
23 *Empire News*, 27 May 1934.
24 Report by Special Branch, Scotland Yard, 23 July 1923, PRO FO 371/9221/186–191.

CHAPTER 7

1 Foreign Office to Maxse (Rotterdam), 16 Feb. 1915, PRO FO 371/9221/186–91.
2 Maxse to Foreign Office, 18 Feb. 1915, *ibid.*
3 Report by Agent Scully dated 21 Jan. 1916; reports by Agent Adams, 24 Jan. and 1 March 1916, FBI OG 500.
4 Passenger manifest of s.s. *Philadelphia*, New York, Feb. 1915, USNA.
5 Trebitsch's letter to Harry, dated 14 Feb. 1915, was one of a number of documents seized together with Harry's belongings at the time of his arrest. US military intelligence compiled a lengthy report on Harry, based on these documents and on interviews with him. The report, the documents seized (which include correspondence between Harry and family members in Hungary), as well as details of the court martial verdict and Harry's subsequent imprisonment, are all in a dossier in USNA RG 165/9605–23. The report by the British Consul-General in New York, dated 9 Aug. 1933, with related documents, is in PRO FO 371/16618/115 ff.
6 Statement by Charles Jundt, 24 Feb. 1916, FBI OG 500.
7 Statement by Mrs Anna Jundt, 23 Feb. 1916, *ibid.*
8 Report by Agent Adams, 28 Jan. 1916, *ibid.*
9 *The Times*, 6 Aug, 1915. See also report by Agent Benham, 7 Dec. 1915, FBI OG 500.
10 Summaries of the cables are available in PRO ADM 137/3962 (no. 256) and 137/3963 (nos. 248 & 313) but the texts of these cables have been removed from the volumes. A note in volume 3962 states that cable no. 256 was removed in 1975 by 'DS 16' on what are described as 'personal sensitivity grounds.'

H.W. Blood-Ryan, *Franz von Papen: His Life and Times* (London 1940) alleges that Trebitsch was detailed to von Papen's ring of agents and saboteurs in the USA by the German Ambassador, acting on instructions from Berlin. (pp. 49–51). No such instruction has been found in the German archives. On the evidence of these intercepted cables this story must be adjudged a romance. Papen, who in his *Memoirs* (London 1952) discusses his activities in the USA at this period with considerable candour, does not mention Trebitsch.

11 New York *World*, 23 May 1915.
12 Statements by Rowntree, Goldstein, Farmer and Finklestone, June 1916, PRO FO 372/900; *The Times*, 20 June 1916.
13 H.B. Simpson (Home Office) to Under-Secretary, Foreign Office, 15 July 1915, PRO FO 372/741.
14 Court documents, USNA, RG 60/177263; *The Times* and *NYT*, 6 Aug. 1915.
15 Foreign Office minute [signature not identified], 6 Aug. 1915, PRO FO 372/741.
16 *NYT*, 1 Sept. 1915.
17 *NYT*, 4 Sept. 1915.
18 *The Times*, 11 Sept. 1915; and court documents, USNA, RG 60/177263.
19 Report by Chief Inspector Ward, 19 Nov. 1915, PRO FO 372/900.
20 Report by Ward, 19 Jan. 1916, *ibid.*
21 Ignatius Lincoln to Sir Edward Grey, 8 Nov. 1915, PRO FO 372/741.
22 Foreign Office minute [signature not identified], 8 Nov. 1915, *ibid.*
23 *NYT*, 22 Feb. 1916. The letter was held up by Trebitsch's former colleagues in the British postal censorship, and returned to the USA.
24 Agents' reports, 21 Jan. 1916, FBI OG 500.
25 *NYT*, 21 Nov. 1915.
26 Letter dated 21 Nov. 1915, FBI OG 500.
27 Copy of letter dated 2 Dec. 1915 in report by Agent Benham, FBI OG 500.
28 Report by Agent Benham (incorporating memorandum by Trebitsch), 8 Dec. 1915, FBI OG 500.
29 Report by Agent Benham, 9 Dec. 1915, FBI OG 500.
30 Report by Agent Benham (quoting the Admiralty cable as read out to him by Captain Gaunt), 14 Dec. 1915, FBI OG 500.
31 Report by Agent Benham, 15 Dec. 1915, FBI OG 500.
32 Report by Agent Underhill, 20 April 1916, *ibid.*
33 Report by Agent Benham, 17 Dec. 1915, *ibid.*
34 Report by Agent Benham, 20 Dec. 1915, *ibid.*
35 Report by Agent Benham, 21 Dec. 1915, *ibid.*
36 Report by Agent Benham, 22 Dec. 1915, *ibid.*
37 Report by Agent Benham (with memorandum by Trebitsch appended), 24 December 1915, FBI OG 500.
38 Letters dated 10 and 15 January 1916, FBI OG 500.
39 Report by Agent W.B. Matthews, 1 July 1918, FBI BS 61–257.
40 *NYT*, 19 and 20 Jan. 1916; statement by Deputy Marshal Johnson, 17 Jan. 1916, USNA RG 60/177263; note by acting Attorney General Wallace, 19 Jan. 1916, *ibid.*; Marshal James Power to Attorney General, Washington, D.C., 25 Jan. 1916, *ibid.*
41 *NYT*, 20 Jan. 1916; Foreign Office minute (signature not identified), 19 Jan. 1916, PRO FO 372/900.
42 Report by Special Branch, Scotland Yard, 23 July 1923, PRO FO 371/9221/186–91. Home Office papers.
43 H.B. Simpson (Home Office) to Under-Secretary, Foreign Office, 31 Jan., 16 and 23 Feb. 1916, PRO FO 372/900.
44 Agents' reports, Jan.–Feb. 1916, FBI OG 500 *passim.*
45 Statement by Mrs Jundt reported by Agent Adams, 1 March 1916,

FBI OG 500. Statement by Charles Jundt reported by Agent Adams, 25 Feb. 1916, *ibid.*

46 *The Times* and *NYT*, 21 Jan. 1916.

47 Agents' reports, Feb. 1916, FBI OG 500 *passim*.

48 Agent Perkins to Chief of Bureau of Investigation, 20 Feb. 1916, FBI OG 500.

49 *NYT*, 20 Feb. 1916; *The Times*, 21 Feb. 1916.

50 *NYT*, 9 May 1916; court documents, USNA, RG 60/177263.

51 *NYT*, 27 May 1916.

52 *The Times*, 6 June 1916; *Glasgow Herald*, 7 and 14 June 1916.

53 *The Times*, 14 June 1916.

54 *The Times* and *NYT*, 20 June 1916.

55 *The Times* and *Glasgow Herald*, 5 July 1916.

56 British Consul-General, New York, to Foreign Office, 2 June 1916, PRO FO 372/900.

57 *NYT*, 17 June 1915.

CHAPTER 8

1 Home Office papers.

2 *Ibid.* See also Lincoln, *Autobiography*, pp. 139–42; interview with Trebitsch in *Trans-Pacific* (Tokyo), 1 Jan. 1927.

3 Home Office papers; and *The Times*, 14 Dec. 1918.

4 *House of Commons Debates*, 5th Series, vol. 118, col. 558, 17 July 1919.

5 Thomson to Sir E. Troup, 3 July 1919, Home Office papers.

6 Letter dated 4 April 1918, quoted in Rudolf L. Tőkés, *Béla Kun and the Hungarian Soviet Republic* (New York 1967), p. 232. See also Miss Elsie Tarcai, 'Family History'; Susan M. Papp, *Hungarian Americans and their Communities of Cleveland* (Cleveland 1981), p. 246; E. Howard to Foreign Office, 8 Feb. 1910, PRO FO 371/826/448.

7 See J.M. Henderson to Registrar of Joint Stock Companies, 19 Sept. 1919, PRO BT 31/20641/121766.

8 Reports by General Malcolm (Berlin) to Director of Military Intelligence, 22 and 28 Aug. 1919, Malcolm Papers, St Antony's College, Oxford.

9 See Bruno Thoss, *Der Ludendorff-Kreis 1919–1923* (Munich 1978) pp. 242 and 245–8.

10 Wulle to Trebitsch, 4 Sept. 1919, BAK Bauer 27/8.

11 Trebitsch to Wulle [copy or draft in Trebitsch's handwriting], n.d. BAK Bauer 27/6.

12 See Sally Marks, '"My Name is Ozymandias": The Kaiser in Exile', *Central European History*, XVI, 2, June 1983, pp. 122–70.

13 See Sir R. Graham (The Hague) to Foreign Office, 17 Dec. 1919, PRO FO 371/4272/151–2.

14 *Daily Graphic*, 23 Sept. 1919. See also Percy Brown, *Germany in Dissolution* (London 1920), pp. 209–16.

15 *NYT*, 22 Sept. 1919.

16 See report forwarded to the State Department in Washington by U. Grant Smith (Budapest), 8 Jan. 1921, USNA, RG 60/177263/41.

17 Max Bauer, *Konnten Wir den Krieg vermeiden, gewinnen, abbrechen?* (Berlin 1919).

18 See the unpublished reminiscences of Bauer's secretary, Luise Engeler, BAK Bauer 69. See also Martin Kitchen, 'Militarism and the Development of Fascist Ideology, — The Political Ideas of Colonel Max Bauer 1916–1918', *Central European History*, VIII, 3, Sept. 1975.

19 See Adolf Vogt, *Oberst Max Bauer 1869–1929* (Osnabrück 1974), pp. 227–31; also Otto-Ernst Schüddekopf, *Linke Leute von rechts* (Stuttgart 1960), p. 90; and Marie-Luise Goldbach, *Karl Radek und die deutsch-sowjetischen Beziehungen 1918–1923* (Bonn 1973), pp. 47 and 50.

20 Malcolm (Berlin) to Director of Military Intelligence, 30 July 1919, PRO FO 371/3777; and Malcolm diary, 29 July 1919, St Antony's College, Oxford.

21 Max Bauer to Adolf Hitler, 25 April 1923, BAK Bauer 30b/211.
22 Trebitsch to Bauer, 1 Oct. 1919, BAK Bauer 26/1.
23 See Robert G.L. Waite, *Vanguard of Nazism: The Free Corps Movement in Postwar Germany 1918–1923* (Cambridge, Mass. 1952), pp. 145 ff.
24 Trebitsch to Bauer, 6 Oct. 1919, BAK Bauer 26/3.
25 See Max Bauer, *Der grosse Krieg in Feld und Heimat* (Tübingen 1921), esp. pp. 213 ff.
26 Bauer to Trebitsch, 8 Oct. 1921, BAK Bauer 26/5.
27 *Memoirs of the Crown Prince of Germany* (New York 1922); Georg Freiherr von Eppstein, *Der deutsche Kronprinz* (Leipzig 1926); Marks, 'Ozymandias', p. 128.
28 See e.g. *The Times*, 28 July 1919.
29 Memorandum dated 24 Oct. 1919, BAK Bauer 26/23; see also Lincoln, *Autobiography*, pp. 153–5; Johannes Erger, *Der Kapp-Lüttwitz Putsch* (Düsseldorf 1967), p. 103; D. Lampe and L. Szenasi, *The Self-Made Villain* (London 1961), p. 112.
30 Gunther (The Hague) to State Department, 10 Oct. 1919, USNA, State Dept. Post Files (RG 84), 'General Correspondence: The Hague', file 801.
31 Trebitsch to Kummer (copy), 17 Oct. 1919, BAK Bauer 26/9–15.
32 Memorandum by Hünefeld, n.d. [Oct. 1919], BAK Bauer 26/17.
33 Kummer to Bauer, 27 Oct. 1919, BAK Bauer 26/7.
34 J.G. Berlott (The Hague) to Police-President, Vienna, 22 March 1921, BAK Bauer 27/75; testimony by Trebitsch to Landesgericht, Vienna, 23 April 1921 [transcript mistakenly dated 23 Feb. 1921], BAK Bauer 27/141–2; Berlin police report, 28 April 1920, BAK Bauer 27/85.
35 Memorandum dated 11 Nov. 1919, BAK Bauer 26/41.
36 Sir R. Graham (The Hague) to Foreign Office, 17 Dec. 1919, PRO FO 371/4272/151–2.
37 Memorandum by Captain R.C. Davies, n.d. [Aug. 1920], PRO FO 371/4869/75–8; memorandum forwarded to State Department, Washington, by U. Grant Smith (Budapest), 8 Jan. 1921, USNA, RG 60/177263/41.
38 Quoted in Robert C. Williams, *Culture in Exile: Russian Emigrés in Germany, 1881–1941* (Ithaca, N.Y. 1972), p. 205; see also Walter Laqueur, *Russia and Germany: A Century of Conflict* (London 1965), pp. 52, 56, 147, 155, and 157.
39 Bauer to Trebitsch, 8 Oct. 1919, BAK Bauer 26/5; Wulle to Trebitsch, 14 Oct. 1919, BAK Bauer 26/4.
40 Bauer to Reventlow (copy), 15 Nov. 1919, BAK Bauer 73/153.
41 Reventlow to Bauer, 17 Nov. 1919, BAK Bauer 22/387.
42 See correspondence of lawyers with Trebitsch, Reventlow and Mrs Lenkeit, Dec. 1919, BAK Bauer 26/55–65.
43 'Note from short-hand pad': Bauer to Herr von Kreckwitz, Bureau Officer of Nationale Vereinigung, n.d. BAK Bauer 26/67; Bauer to Helfferich [sim.], n.d. [6 Dec. 1919], *ibid.*
44 Helfferich to Bauer, 8 Dec. 1919, BAK Bauer 22/417; Bauer to Helfferich (copy), 10 Dec. 1919, BAK Bauer 73/209.
45 See memorandum (unsigned) by Trebitsch, 15 Dec. 1919, BAK Bauer 26/59.
46 Memorandum by Captain R.C. Davies, n.d. [Aug. 1920], PRO FO 371/4869/75–8.
47 Memorandum forwarded to State Department, Washington, by U. Grant Smith (Budapest), 8 Jan. 1921, USNA, RG 60/177263/41.
48 Typed copy of passport [from Vienna court records, 1921], BAK Bauer 27/173.
49 Trebitsch to Bauer (copy), 29 Jan. 1920, BAK Bauer 26/69.
50 Bauer to the Crown Prince Wilhelm, 1 Feb. 1920, BAK Bauer 20/93.
51 Kaufmann to Fürstenberg (copy),

27 Jan. 1920, BAK Bauer 27/15.
52 Fürstenberg to Foreign Office, Berlin, 24 Dec. 1920, AA PA Referat Deutschland 56/4.
53 Eckhardt to Trebitsch, n.d. [19 Feb. 1920], enclosing printed invitation card, BAK Bauer 27/13–14.

CHAPTER 9

1 Malcolm (Berlin) to Director of Military Intelligence (London), 25 March 1920, PRO FO 371/3783/528–31.
2 Marks, 'Ozymandias', p. 157.
3 Secret Intelligence Service report, 23 February 1920, PRO FO 371/3780/183–7.
4 Erger, *Kapp-Lüttwitz Putsch*, pp. 102–3.
5 John W. Wheeler-Bennett, *The Nemesis of Power: The German Army in Politics 1918–1945* (London 1953), p. 71.
6 Malcolm to D.M.I., 25 March 1920, PRO FO 371/3783/528–31.
7 Erger, *Kapp-Lüttwitz Putsch*, p. 115; Harold J. Gordon Jr., *The Reichswehr and the German Republic 1919–1926* (Princeton 1957), p. 105.
8 Erger, pp. 115–6.
9 Margarethe Ludendorff, *Als ich Ludendorffs Frau war* (Munich 1929), pp. 272–6.
10 Malcolm to D.M.I., 25 March 1920, PRO FO 371/3783/528–31.
11 Memorandum forwarded to State Department, Washington, by U. Grant Smith (Budapest), 8 Jan. 1921, USNA, RG 60/177263/41.
12 Gordon, p. 107.
13 Erger, p. 121.
14 Wheeler-Bennett, pp. 73–4.
15 Gordon, p. 109.
16 Memorandum forwarded to State Department, Washington, by U. Grant Smith (Budapest), 8 Jan. 1921, USNA, RG 60/177263/41.
17 Lieutenant-General Jenö von Egan-Krieger to J. Erger, 2 July 1958, in Erger, pp. 319–20.
18 Vogt, pp. 261–2.
19 Memorandum forwarded to State Department, Washington, by U. Grant Smith (Budapest), 8 Jan. 1921, USNA, RG 60/177263/41.
20 Gordon, p. 115.
21 Wheeler-Bennett, p. 77.
22 *NYT*, 16 March 1920.
23 Vogt, p. 263.
24 Karl Brammer, *Fünf Tage Militärdiktatur: Dokumente zur Gegenrevolution* (Berlin 1920), pp. 31–5.
25 Memorandum forwarded to State Department, Washington, by U. Grant Smith (Budapest), 8 Jan. 1921, USNA, RG 60/177263/41.
26 Declaration by Lensch to Reichsgericht, Leipzig, 15 June 1920, Institut für Zeitgeschichte, Munich, MA 616/4, Akten Luetgebrune 156509–12.
27 Karl Brammer, ed., *Verfassungsgrundlagen und Hochverrat: Nach stenographischen Verhandlungsberichten und amtlichen Urkunden des Jagow-Prozesses* (Berlin 1922), pp. 37–8.
28 W. Zechlin, *Pressechef bei Ebert, Hindenburg and Kopf* (Hannover 1956), p. 35.
29 Testimony of Legionsrat Schmidt-Elskop, quoted in Brammer, *Verfassungsgrundlagen*, pp. 58–9.
30 Brammer, *Fünf Tage*, pp. 31–5.
31 Report dated 'Saturday night' [13 March], *Daily Telegraph*, 17 March 1920.
32 *The Times*, 17 March 1920.
33 *Daily Chronicle*, 17 March 1920.
34 Daniels to Mcgregor, 14 March 1920, Archives of *The Times*, London.
35 Kilmarnock to Foreign Office, 13 March 1920, PRO FO 371/3780/232.
36 Kilmarnock to Foreign Office, 13 March 1920, PRO FO 371/3780/230.
37 Text of message in Foreign Office minute, 15 March 1920, PRO FO 371/3780/331.
38 *Daily News*, 17 March 1920.
39 Erger, p. 168.

40 'Spectator', *Die Geschichte der Berliner Fünftageregierung* (Leipzig 1920), p. 61.
41 Erger, pp. 225–6.
42 Report dated 'Sunday' [14 March], *Daily Telegraph*, 18 March 1920.
43 *Daily News*, 17 March 1920.
44 *Ibid.*
45 *Daily Telegraph*, 18 March 1920.
46 *NYT*, 16 March 1920.
47 Testimony of Reichsbank President Havenstein, quoted in Erger, pp. 334–5. See also Erger, pp. 210–11; and Friedrich Freksa, ed., *Kapitän Ehrhardt: Abenteuer und Schicksale* (Berlin 1924), p. 184.
48 See Berlin report dated 14 March, *The Times*, 17 March 1920.
49 Kilmarnock to Foreign Office, 16 March 1920, PRO FO 371/3780/364; and Stewart Roddie, *Peace Patrol* (London 1932), p. 146.
50 See Intercepted Political Report from the (German) Army of the Rhine, 25 March 1920, PRO FO 371/3784/35 ff.; Malcolm diary, 27 March and 5 April 1920, St Antony's College, Oxford; and Wheeler-Bennett, *Nemesis*, p. 79.
51 Memorandum forwarded to State Department, Washington, by U. Grant Smith (Budapest), 8 Jan. 1921, USNA, RG 60/177263/41.
52 'Spectator', *Geschichte*, pp. 58–9.
53 See Vogt, p. 269.
54 *Daily Chronicle*, 18 March 1920.
55 Lampe and Szenasi, *Self-Made Villain*, p. 136.
56 Text of statement in Brammer, *Verfassungsgrundlagen*, p. 78; see also pp. 82–3.
57 Erger, p. 267.
58 *Daily Telegraph*, 22 March 1920.
59 See e.g. Werner Maser, *Die Frühgeschichte der NSDAP: Hitlers Weg bis 1924* (Frankfurt-am-Main 1965), p. 217; Richard Hanser, *Putsch: How Hitler Made Revolution* (New York 1970), p. 230; Konrad Heiden, *Hitler* (Zurich 1936), pp. 138–9.
60 Otto Dietrich, *The Hitler I Knew* (London 1957), p. 163.
61 Otto Dietrich, *Mit Hitler in die Macht: Persönliche Erlebnisse mit meinem Führer* (Munich 1934), pp. 83–4.
62 See Albrecht Tyrell, *Vom "Trommler" zum "Führer"* (Munich 1975), pp. 110 and 255.

CHAPTER 10

1 Memorandum to State Department, Washington, by U. Grant Smith (Budapest), 8 Jan. 1921, USNA, RG 60/177263.
2 Aide-mémoire forwarded to German Foreign Office by Hungarian Legation, Berlin, 24 Oct. 1923, AA PA Referat Deutschland 87/1; memorandum by Captain R.C. Davies, n.d. [Aug. 1920], PRO FO 371/4869/75–8.
3 Vienna police report, 22 Feb. 1921, BAK Bauer 27/48–51.
4 Berlin police report, 28 April 1921, BAK Bauer 27/85–7.
5 *NYT*, 29 March 1920.
6 Memorandum by Captain R.C. Davies, n.d. [Aug. 1920], PRO FO 371/4869/75–8; memoranda by U. Grant Smith (Budapest), 17 Dec. 1920 and 10 Feb. 1921, USNA, RG 59/211.41T73, and 8 Jan. 1921, USNA, RG 60/177263.
7 Erger, p. 105.
8 See Thoss, p. 379; and Abraham Ascher, 'Russian Marxism and the German Revolution 1917–1920', *Archiv für Sozialgeschichte*, VI/VII, 391–439.
9 Engeler memoirs, BAK Bauer 69/15.
10 Adolf Hitler, *Mein Kampf* (New York 1939), pp. 508–9.
11 Vienna police report, 22 Feb. 1921, BAK Bauer 48–51.
12 Typewritten copy of passport (from Vienna court records), BAK Bauer 27/174.
13 Engeler memoirs, BAK Bauer 69/10.
14 [Max] Bauer, *Der 13 März 1920* (Munich 1920).

15 Bauer to Bartram, 6 April 1920, BAK Bauer 29/37.
16 Berlin police report, 28 April 1920, BAK Bauer 27/85–7.
17 Malcolm diary, St Antony's College, Oxford.
18 Malcolm to his wife, 2 April 1920, *ibid.*; Kilmarnock to Foreign Office, 15 April 1920, PRO FO 371/3784/138.
19 *The Times*, 12 April 1920.
20 Berlin police report, 28 April 1920, BAK Bauer, 27/85–7.
21 J.T. Lincoln to K. von Wiegand, Hoover Institution Archives, Wiegand Collection, Box 21, file 'Trebitsch-Lincoln'.
22 Engeler memoirs, BAK Bauer 69/24; also Thoss and Vogt, *passim.*
23 Thoss, p. 64; Horst G.W. Nusser, *Konservative Wehrverbände in Bayern, Preussen und Österreich 1918–1933*, Bd. I (Munich 1973), p. 176.
24 Engeler memoirs, BAK Bauer 69/14 ff. See also Thoss, p. 395; Vogt, pp. 296 ff.; and Nusser, p. 162.
25 Vienna police report, 22 Feb. 1921, BAK Bauer 27/48–51; Engeler memoirs, BAK Bauer 69/15.
26 Berlin police report, 28 April 1920, BAK Bauer 27/85–7.
27 Indictment vs. Traugott von Jagow and Konrad Freiherr von Wangenheim, Leipzig Oberreichsanwalt, 11 July 1921, Akten Luetgebrune, Institut für Zeitgeschichte, Munich, MA 616/4/156663–83; undated copy of Berlin police report [May 1920], BAK Bauer 27/88; Brammer, *Verfassungsgrundlagen*, pp. 78 and 82–3.
28 Undated copy of Berlin police report [May 1920], BAK Bauer 27/88.
29 Memorandum signed by Oelschläger, 8 May 1920, Akten Luetgebrune, Institut für Zeitgeschichte, Munich, MA 616/4/156456.
30 Engeler memoirs, BAK Bauer 69/14.
31 *Ibid.*, 69/16–17.
32 *Ibid.*, 69/17–21.
33 *Ibid.*; and typewritten copy of 'Lehotzky' passport (from Vienna police records), BAK Bauer 27/175.
34 Engeler memoirs, BAK Bauer 69/22–3.
35 Robert Machray. *The Little Entente* (London 1929), p. 104. See also Nicholas M. Nagy-Talavera, *The Green Shirts and Others: A History of Fascism in Hungary and Rumania* (Stanford 1970), esp. pp. 51–5.
36 See Bauer to T. von Eckhardt and G. Gömbös, 30 May 1920, BAK Bauer 27/32; see also M. Szinai and L. Szücs, eds., *The Confidential Papers of Admiral Horthy* (Budapest 1965), p. 26; also Thoss, p. 396; and Vogt, p. 304.
37 See Vogt, pp. 302–4; Thoss, p. 386; and Nagy-Talavera, pp. 51–5.
38 Engeler memoirs, BAK Bauer 69/24.
39 Agnes Szabó and Ervin Pamlényi, eds., *A határban a Halál Kaszál . . .: Fejezetek Prónay Pál feljegyzéseiből* (Budapest 1963), pp. 200–1.
40 Vogt, p. 664.
41 Memorandum dated 26 May 1920, BAK Bauer 27/33.
42 See Szinai and Szücs, *Horthy Papers*, p. 26.
43 Quoted in Machray, *Little Entente*, p. 108.
44 Engeler memoirs, BAK Bauer 69/23; memorandum by Captain R.C. Davies, n.d. [Aug. 1920], PRO FO 371/4869/75–8.
45 Laqueur, *Russia and Germany*, p. 108.
46 Williams, *Culture in Exile*, p. 93.
47 Quoted in Laqueur, p. 109.
48 Engeler memoirs, BAK Bauer 69/26; see also Laqueur, pp. 58–68.
49 Quoted in Vogt, p. 374.
50 Memorandum by Captain R.C. Davies, n.d. [Aug. 1920], PRO FO 371/4869/75–8; also Engeler memoirs BAK Bauer 69/26 ff.
51 By Vogt, p. 376.
52 Typescript copy of memorandum, BAK Bauer 27/38.
53 Engeler memoirs, BAK Bauer 69/39–40.
54 Photographic copy showing original signatures of Bauer and Biskup-

ski (from Vienna court records), BAK Bauer 27/248.
55 Typescript copy (from Vienna court records), BAK Bauer 27/183.
56 Testimony of General Krauss to Landesgericht, Vienna, 20 April 1921, BAK Bauer 27/79; Krauss to 'Dr Lange' [Trebitsch], 18 Aug. 1920, BAK Bauer 27/248.
57 See Vogt, p. 313.
58 Trebitsch to Bauer (copy), n.d., BAK Bauer 27/34.
59 Ludendorff to Horthy, 19 Aug. 1920, in Szinai and Szűcs, *Horthy Papers*, pp. 26–9.
60 Szabó and Pamlényi, *Prónay*, p. 202.
61 Engeler memoirs, BAK Bauer 69/27–8; Foreign Office to Hohler (Budapest), 5 June 1920, PRO FO 371/3561.

CHAPTER 11

1 Engeler memoirs, BAK Bauer 69/26–7.
2 *Ibid.*, 69/35–6.
3 Szabó and Pamlényi, *Prónay*, pp. 204–5; testimony by Trebitsch before Landesgericht, Vienna, 5 April 1921, BAK Bauer 27/121–5.
4 Engeler memoirs, BAK Bauer 69–42.
5 *Ibid.*, 69/42–3; statement to Landesgericht, Vienna, 21 March 1921, by Rolf Krause, speaking on behalf of Max Bauer, BAK Bauer 27/71.
6 Szabó and Pamlényi, *Prónay*, p. 205.
7 Engeler memoirs, BAK Bauer 69/33.
8 Szabó and Pamlényi, *Prónay*, p. 205.
9 Vienna police report, 22 Feb. 1921, BAK Bauer 27/48.
10 See Fürstenberg (Budapest) to German Foreign Office, 24 Dec. 1920, AA PA Referat Deutschland 56/4; also U. Grant Smith (Budapest) to State Dept., Washington, 10 Feb. 1921, USNA, RG 59/211.41T73.
11 Bridgeman (Vienna) to Foreign Office, 21 Sept. 1920, PRO FO 371/4716/127.
12 Sir Basil Thomson to Under-Secretary of State, Foreign Office, 23 Sept. 1920, PRO FO 371/4716/131.
13 Kilmarnock to Foreign Office, 23 Sept. 1920, PRO FO 371/4798/149; see also German Foreign Ministry memorandum, 23 Sept. 1920, Institut für Zeitgeschichte, MA 804/1, Bl. 676647–8; and German Foreign Ministry to Ambassador in London and Chargé d'Affaires in Munich, 25 Sept. 1920, AA PA Referat Deutschland 56/3; and German Ambassador in London to German Foreign Ministry, 25 Sept. 1920, *ibid.*
14 Under-Secretary, Home Office, to Under-Secretary, Foreign Office, 24 Sept. 1920, PRO FO 371/4716/133.
15 Lord Curzon to Bridgeman, 24 Sept. 1920, *Documents on British Foreign Policy*, First Series, vol. XII, p. 272.
16 Letter to the author from Mr A. Krausz, 7 March 1985; Fürstenberg (Budapest) to German Foreign Ministry, 24 Dec. 1920, AA PA Referat Deutschland 56/4.
17 Memorandum (probably from Justice Ministry) to Austrian Foreign Ministry, 19 Feb. 1921, HHSA 451/512. A copy of Trebitsch's memorandum is in US Military Intelligence files, USNA, RG 165/124–501.
18 'Disguises and Passports' by Mrs Trebitsch Lincoln, *Empire News*, 3 June 1934.
19 Notarised typescript copy (from Vienna court records), BAK Bauer 26/67.
20 *Empire News*, 3 June 1934.
21 U. Grant Smith (Budapest) to State Dept., Washington, 17 Dec. 1920, USNA State Dept. Decimal File 211.41T73. See also telegrams from U.S. representatives in Vienna to State Dept., 23 Sept., 8 and 13 Nov. 1920, USNA, RG 84, 1920

Gen. Corr. Vienna 810.8.

22 *Daily Herald*, 13 Jan. 1921; *Az Est* (Budapest), 28 Jan. 1921. (The latter report was severely mauled by Hungarian censors.) For Hajšman's retrospective (and selective) account of his relations with Trebitsch, see *A-Zet Pondělaík*, 24 Oct. 1932.

23 *Rul'*, 20 Nov. 1920; *Der Kampf*, 14 Dec. 1920, See also *Le Petit Parisien*, 15 Nov. 1920, and *České Slovo*, 14 Dec. 1920.

24 Biskupski to editor, *Rul'* (copy), n.d. [Nov./Dec. 1920], BAK Bauer 74/10.

25 Minutes of meetings on 8 and 18 Nov. 1920, USNA, RG 256/180.03301/91–3 (microfilm M820 reels 77–8).

26 Clerk to Foreign Office, 19 Nov. 1920, PRO FO 371/4841/120.

27 Clerk to Foreign Office, 3 Dec. 1920, enclosing Cunninghame to Clerk, 1 Dec. 1920, PRO FO 371/4841/131–8.

28 Minute dated 24 Nov. 1920 [signature not deciphered], PRO FO 371/4841/117.

29 Crowe minute, 5 Dec. 1920, PRO FO 371/4841/118–9.

30 Cadogan minute, 13 Dec. 1920, PRO FO 371/4841/130.

31 Cunninghame to British Minister, Vienna, 24 Dec. 1920, PRO FO 371/5836/55–9.

32 Vienna police report, 22 Feb. 1921, BAK Bauer 27/48 ff.

33 Clerk to Foreign Office, 17 Dec. 1920, PRO FO 371/4841/143.

34 *Der Reichswart*, Jan. 1921; *Die Rote Fahne*, 14 Jan. 1921.

35 *The Nation*, 1 Jan. 1921.

36 *Daily Herald*, 13 Jan. 1921; *Az Est* (Budapest), 28 Jan. 1921.

37 Lindley (Vienna) to Foreign Office, 17 Dec. 1920, PRO FO 371/4841/145–6.

38 State Department to Vienna mission, 1 Dec. 1920, USNA State Dept. Central Decimal Files Card Index (original document lost; card index summary only available), 811.111 Lincoln; Vienna mission to State Dept., 10, 15, and 27 Dec. 1920, State Dept. to Vienna mission, 21 Dec. 1920, and Johnson (Rome) to Vienna Mission, 3 Jan. 1921, USNA, RG 84, 1920 Gen. Corr. Vienna 810.8.

39 Lindley to Foreign Office, 28 Dec. 1920, PRO FO 371/5836/66–7. Memorandum forwarded to State Department by U. Grant Smith (Budapest), USNA State Dept. Decimal File 211.41T73.

40 Bauer to Reventlow, 23 Nov. 1920 (copy), BAK Bauer 74/16.

41 Successive drafts, Dec. 1920, in BAK Bauer 30.

42 Copy of statement, BAK Bauer 30/125.

43 Fuchs to Fiedler, 12 Jan. 1921, BAK Bauer 27/17–18.

44 Fuchs to Beneš, 20 Jan. 1921, BAK Bauer 27/19–20.

45 Vienna police report, 22 Feb. 1921, BAK Bauer 27/48–51.

46 Miss Kerr [?] to K. von Wiegand, 9 Feb. 1921, Hoover Institution Archives, Wiegand Collection, Box 21, file 'Trebitsch Lincoln'.

47 Stephani to Bauer (copy), n.d. [early Feb. 1921?], BAK Bauer 75/11.

48 Clerk to Foreign Office, 14 Jan. 1921, PRO FO 371/5836/74.

49 See Hajšman to Zeifart, 10 Feb. 1921, BAK Bauer 27/149. Trebitsch's statement is in CSA č.j. 12266/1921.

50 Minute by Vienna police department, 10 Feb. 1921, BAK Bauer 27/52–3; see also copy of letter from Dr Z. Zeifart to Prague, CSA č.j. 6301/1921.

51 'Amtsvermerk', 18 Feb. 1921, BAK Bauer 27/55.

52 'Protokoll', 18 Feb. 1921, BAK Bauer 27/56–7.

53 'Protokoll', 18 Feb. 1921, BAK Bauer 27/56–61 (pages out of sequence).

54 Trebitsch's testimony and other trial documents (from Vienna court records) in BAK Bauer 27 *passim*.

See also CSA č.j. 6301/1921, 8754/1921, 12266/1921, and 13310/1921.
55 USNA, RG 165/124–501.
56 Vienna police to prosecutor's office, 22 Feb. 1921, BAK Bauer 27/48–51.
57 CSA č.j. 15416/1921. Jan Hajšman, *O špionáži: špioni, špionky, špiclové, lidé podzemní zpravodajská a informační služba* (Prague 1928), pp. 238–251.
58 HHSA 451/512.
59 *NYT*, 26 June 1921. *The Times*, 10 June 1921; Vienna Police Dept. to Austrian Foreign Ministry, 16 June 1921, HHSA 451/512.
60 Buchanan to Foreign Office, 16 July 1921, PRO FO 371/5836/78.
61 Foreign Office to Kennard (Rome), 19 July 1921, PRO FO 371/5836/80.
62 Col. Mathew C. Smith, Chief, Negative Branch, Military Intelligence Division, War Department, to J. Edgar Hoover, Special Assistant to the Attorney General, Department of Justice, 26 July 1921, USNA, RG 60/177263–43. See also Gunther (Rome) to State Dept., 14 July 1921, USNA State Dept. Decimal File 862.20/42 and attached note, 16 July 1921.
63 Digby A. Willson (Budapest) to Joseph Haven (Trieste), 14 Sept. 1921 [copy enclosed with dispatch from German Embassy, Rome, to German Foreign Ministry, 10 Oct. 1921], AA PA Referat Deutschland 87/1.
64 US Consul, Trieste, to German Consul, Trieste, 26 Sept. 1921, *ibid.*
65 Report by Special Branch, Scotland Yard, 23 July 1923, PRO FO 371/9221/186–91.
66 *NYT*, 28 Jan. 1922.
67 USNA, RG 165/10058–313.
68 *NYT*, 29 Jan. 1922; *The Times*, 30 Jan. 1922. Agents' reports in FBI BS 61–257.
69 Record of hearing (and related documents) in USNA, RG 59, 862.2.898.
70 Memorandum dated 26 July 1923, PRO FO 371/9221/183.

CHAPTER 12

1 Memorandum dated 26 July 1923, PRO FO 371/9221; Report by Special Branch, Scotland Yard, 23 July 1923, *ibid.*
2 Eric Teichman (Chinese Secretary at the British Legation in Peking), quoted in Nicholas R. Clifford, *Shanghai 1925: Urban Nationalism and the Defense of Foreign Privilege* (Ann Arbor 1979), p. 5.
3 'Lincoln, World Spy, Plotted to Control China', New York *World*, 7 June 1925.
4 Robert A. Kapp, *Szechwan and the Chinese Republic: Provincial Militarism and Central Power 1911–1938* (New Haven 1973), p. 69.
5 New York *World*, 7 June 1925.
6 Minute by H.N. Steptoe, Peking Legation, 13 July 1925, PRO FO 228/2952; *Peking Leader*, 11 July 1925.
7 Kapp, *Szechwan*, pp. 28–9.
8 Blyth, Dutton, Hartley & Blyth to Chief Commissioner, Metropolitan Police, 10 July 1923, PRO FO 371/9221.
9 *Idem.*
10 Special Branch report, 23 July 1923, *ibid.*
11 Memorandum dated 26 July 1923, *ibid.*
12 Victor Wellesley (for Secretary of State for Foreign Affairs) to Sir J.W.R. Macleay, Peking, 8 Aug. 1923, *ibid.*
13 Archer (Chungking) to Macleay (Peking), 6 June 1924, PRO. FO 372/2101.
14 *Ibid.*
15 'Lincoln, Spy, Becomes Confidential Adviser of General Wu Pei Fu', New York *World*, 21 June 1925.
16 *The Times*, 14 Sept. 1925.
17 I.T.T. Lincoln to Manager, Reuters

Ltd., Shanghai, 22 Oct. 1925, PRO FO 372/2252.

18 Aide-mémoire forwarded by Hungarian Legation, Berlin, to German Foreign Ministry, 24 Oct. 1923, AA PA Referat Deutschland 87/1.

19 Engeler memoirs, BAK Bauer 69/99 ff. Polizeikommando des Kantons Zürich to Prague Police, 3 Dec. 1923, Central State Archives, Prague, Police Headquarters, Prague 1921–30, T 927/7.

20 See Bauer to Ludendorff, 7 Nov. 1923, BAK Bauer 30b/447.

21 Consul-General Clive (Munich) to V. Wellesley (Foreign Office), 8 Nov. 1923, PRO FO 371/8820/6.

22 Munich police reports dated 5 Nov. 1923 and 18 June 1924, Staatsarchiv, Munich, Pol. Dir. 10166.

23 Bauer to Ludendorff, 7 Nov. 1923, BAK Bauer 30b/447.

24 Copy of agreement, dated 17 Nov. 1923, in BAK Bauer 43/1–5.

25 Engeler memoirs, BAK Bauer 69/106 ff.

26 John Lincoln to British Consul-General, Batavia, 1 March 1927, PRO FO 372/2388/174 ff.

27 Quoted in Fitzmaurice (Nanking) to Steptoe (Shanghai), 28 April 1924, enclosed in Peking dispatch to Foreign Office, 26 June 1924, PRO FO 372/2101.

28 S. Barton (British Consulate-General, Shanghai) to Commissioner of Police, Shanghai Municipal Council, 18 Sept. 1925, SMP I.O. 5607.

29 Barton (Shanghai) to Macleay (Peking), 16 June 1924, enclosed in Peking dispatch to Foreign Office, 26 June 1924, PRO FO 372/2101.

30 Munich police reports, 16 and 25 June 1924, Staatsarchiv, Munich, Pol. Dir. 10166.

31 See Vogt, p. 685; and H.G. Woodhead, ed., *The China Year Book 1929–30* (Tientsin 1929), p. 1192. Police report, 24 April 1928, in SMP I.O. 5607.

32 Barton to Macleay, 16 June 1924, enclosed in Peking dispatch to Foreign Office, 26 June 1924, PRO FO 372/2101; also minute by H.N. Steptoe 13 July 1925, PRO FO 228/2952; and John Lincoln to British Consul-General, Batavia, 1 March 1927, PRO FO 372/2388/174 ff.

33 J.T.T. Lincoln to British Consul-General, Nanking, 24 July 1924, PRO FO 372/2101/33.

34 John Pedder (Home Office) to Under-Secretary of State, Foreign Office, 23 July 1924, PRO FO 372/2101/12.

35 Minute by H. Ritchie [?], 24 July 1924, PRO FO 372/2101/11.

36 Passport Office circular, 6 Aug. 1924, PRO FO 372/2388/169.

37 J.T. Pratt (Shanghai) to Sir R. Macleay (Peking), 31 Oct. 1924, PRO FO 372/2101/39.

38 John Lincoln to British Consul-General, Shanghai, 15 Oct. 1924, PRO FO 372/2101/41.

39 Minute dated 6 Jan. 1926, PRO FO 228/2953.

40 See Jonathan Spence, *To Change China: Western Advisers in China, 1620–1960* (2nd. rev. ed., New York 1980), pp. 291–2.

41 PRO FO 228/3667; FO 228/3872; FO 228/2952; FO 228/2953.

42 Circular dated 13 April 1926, PRO FO 228/2953.

43 Minute by Steptoe, 24 July 1925, PRO FO 228/2952; minute dated 29 Sept. 1925 [signature unidentified], *ibid.*; see also Charles Drage, *Two-Gun Cohen*, London 1954.

44 'Lincoln's "System"' by Mrs Trebitsch Lincoln, *Empire News*, 10 June 1934.

45 I.T.T. Lincoln to Home Secretary, 29 March 1925; I.T.T. Lincoln to Foreign Secretary, 29 March 1925, PRO FO 372/2150/130–3.

CHAPTER 13

1 I.T.T. Lincoln to Sir Harry Armstrong, 9 July 1925, PRO FO 372/2150/151.

2 Undated minute [signature not identified], PRO FO 372/2150/139.
3 Foreign Office to M. Palairet (Peking), 28 Aug. 1925, PRO FO 228/2953.
4 See Barton (Shanghai) to British Minister, Peking, 11 Dec. 1925, PRO FO 372/2252/98.
5 Quoted in 'Lincoln's "System"' by Mrs Trebitsch Lincoln, *Empire News*, 10 June 1934.
6 Chao Kung [I.T.T. Lincoln], *Can War Be Abolished?* (Shanghai 1932), pp. 64–5. See also *The Trans-Pacific* (Tokyo), 1 Jan. 1927.
7 Josephine Ransom, *A Short History of the Theosophical Society 1875–1937* (Adyar 1938), p. 76.
8 Trebitsch letter of Jan. 1916 quoted in editors' preface to his article in New York *World*, 7 June 1925.
9 I.T.T. Lincoln to British Consul-General, Shanghai, 11 Nov. 1925, PRO FO 372/2252/103.
10 *The Times*, 28 Dec. 1925, 21, 22 Jan., 6 Feb. 1926.
11 Foreign Office to Marling (The Hague), 26 Feb. 1926, PRO FO 372/2252/90. *The Times* and *NYT*, 27 Feb. 1926.
12 Associated Press report in *NYT*, 3 March 1926.
13 *NYT*, 6 March 1926.
14 *The Times*, 8 March 1926.
15 Armstrong (New York) to Foreign Office, 26 Oct. 1926, PRO FO 372/2252/118.
16 I.T.T. Lincoln to Armstrong, 19 Oct. 1926, PRO FO 372/2252/119–20.
17 Minute [signature and date unclear], PRO FO 372/2252/117.
18 See BL IOLR L/P&S/12/4282: 'Central Asia — Dr Sven Hedin'.
19 E.G. Turner (India Office) to Under-Secretary, Foreign Office, 24 November 1926, PRO FO 372/2252/126.
20 I.T. Trebitsch Lincoln to United States Secretary of State, 17 May 1927 (copy), PRO FO 372/2388/196–210.
21 See postscript to previously cited letter in version published in Edward Corsi, *In the Shadow of Liberty* (New York 1935), p. 280.
22 I.T.T. Lincoln to T. King, C.I.D. Police Headquarters, Hong Kong, 26 Sept. 1927. See also Trebitsch to Daniel Cahn, 22 Aug. 1927, and related documents in USNA, RG 59/862.2.898.
23 New Scotland Yard [signature indecipherable] to Secret Intelligence Service, Foreign Office, Home Office, M.I.5, Indian Political Intelligence, and Colonial Office, 16 November 1927, PRO FO 371/12513/81.
24 See W.P.W. Turner to W.P. Thomas, 26 Oct. 1927, PRO FO 228/3667.
25 I.T. Trebitsch Lincoln to Sir Harry Armstrong, 26 Oct. 1927, PRO FO 371/12513/96.
26 I.T. Trebitsch-Lincoln to Secretary, British Legation, Peking, 28 Oct. 1927, PRO FO 228/3667 and attached minutes.
27 Lampson (Peking) to Foreign Office, 2 November 1927, PRO FO 371/12513/70.
28 Lampson to Foreign Office, 1 Nov. 1927, PRO FO 371/12513/66.
29 H.G. Woodhead, ed., *The China Year Book 1928* (Tientsin 1928), p. 396; also BL IOLR L/P&S/12/4181; and *North China Daily News*, 27 Sept. 1927.
30 W.P. Thomas to W.P.W. Turner, 5 Nov. 1927, PRO FO 228/3667.
31 See Lampson to Foreign Office, 7 Dec. 1927, PRO FO 371/12513/87; also V.R. Burckhardt (Tientsin) report, 2 Nov. 1927, SMP I.O. 5607.
32 Alice Leighton Cleather, *H.P. Blavatsky: Her Life and Work for Humanity* (Calcutta 1922), p. 4.
33 Alice Leighton Cleather, *H.P. Blavatsky: The Great Betrayal* (Calcutta 1922).
34 Alice Leighton Cleather, *Buddhism: The Science of Life: Two Monographs* (Peking 1928), p. 2: see also Alice Leighton Cleather and Basil Crump, *The Pseudo-Occultation of Mrs A. Bailey* (Manila 1929), intro-

ductory note; *The China Weekly Review*, 20 June 1931; memorandum by F. Williamson (of Political Dept. of Government of India, on leave), 21 March 1927, BL IOLR L/P & S/12/4174, and other papers in this file; and minute by H.N. Steptoe, 1 March 1928, PRO FO 228/3872.

35 Cleather, *Buddhism*, opp. p. 139.

36 Basil Crump, 'Tibetan Initiates on the Buddha', in Cleather, *Buddhism*, p. 62.

37 B. Crump to G.D. Whiteman, 20 Nov. 1927, quoted in G.D. Whiteman to Foreign Office, 6 Dec. 1927, PRO FO 371/12513/90–1.

38 *Peiping Chronicle*, 7 Dec. 1933.

39 I.T. Trebitsch-Lincoln (Peking) to Sir Harry Armstrong, 14 Jan. 1928, PRO FO 371/13174/124; *South China Morning Post*, 30 March 1928.

40 Deputy Secretary, Government of India, Foreign and Political Department, to Political Officer in Gangtok, 5 June 1928, BL IOLR L/P & S/11/286.

41 Minute by H.N. Steptoe, 21 Aug. 1928, PRO FO 228/3872.

42 *Peking & Tientsin Times*, 17 Aug. 1928; see also dispatch from Sir James W. Jamieson (Tientsin) to Sir Miles Lampson (Peking), 17 Aug. 1928, PRO FO 228/3872.

43 Memorandum by A.H. George, 16 Aug. 1928, enclosed *ibid.*

44 Drage, *Cohen*, p. 122.

45 Jamieson to Lampson, 17 Aug. 1928, PRO FO 228/3872.

46 Minute by Lampson, 18 Aug. 1928, PRO FO 228/3872.

47 Charles J. Fox to British Consul-General, Tientsin, 11 Aug. 1928, PRO FO 371/13174/132; Deputy Secretary, Government of India, Foreign and Political Department, to Political Officer in Gangtok, 28 Aug. 1928, BL IOLR L/P & S/11/286.

48 Shanghai police report, 25 June 1929, SMP I.O. 5607.

49 German consul, Shanghai, to German Foreign Ministry, 24, 25 and 27 June 1929, AA PA Politische Abteilung IV — China, PO 11 Nr. 6, Bd. 1.

50 See Grimm to German Foreign Ministry, 10 Sept. 1929, *ibid.*

51 *Ibid.*

52 I.T. Trebitsch-Lincoln to German Consulate, Genoa, 4 Aug. 1929; German Consul, Genoa, to German Foreign Ministry, 5 Aug. 1929, *ibid.*

53 German Consul, Rotterdam, to German Foreign Ministry, 14 Aug. 1929, *ibid.*

54 See Munich police department to Bavarian Ministry of the Interior, 27 Aug. 1929 (copy), *ibid.*

55 Grimm to German Foreign Ministry, 10 Sept. 1929, *ibid.*

56 Shanghai police report, 7 July 1930, SMP I.O. 5607; Deputy Commissioner, Shanghai Police, to British Consul General, 11 July 1930, *ibid.*

57 See I.T. Trebitsch Lincoln to US Secretary of State, 17 May 1927 (copy), PRO FO 372/2388/196–210.

58 Lincoln, *Autobiography*, p. 291.

59 Trebitsch to Persian, 27 Aug. 1931, BL TL.

60 Kreitner to Engeler, 2 Feb. 1931, BAK Bauer 70/154.

61 *The China Weekly Review*, 20 June 1931.

62 Trebitsch to Persian, 19 June 1931, BL TL.

63 *The China Weekly Review*, 20 June 1931.

64 See Holmes Welch, *The Buddhist Revival in China* (Cambridge, Mass. 1968), pp. 188–9; J. Prip-Møller, *Chinese Buddhist Monasteries* (2nd. ed., Hong Kong 1967), pp. 317–23.; J. Prip-Møller, *Kina før og Nu* (Copenhagen 1944), pp. 98–108; and Prip-Møller Diary, Royal Library, Copenhagen.

65 Trebitsch to British Consul-General, Shanghai, 21 July 1931 (copy), PRO FO 371/15513/354; see also W. Stark Toller (Chungking) to Sir M. Lampson (Peking), 1 Oct. 1931, PRO FO 371/15513/357–8; and the Trebitsch-Persian correspondence, BL TL, *passim*.

66 J.F. Brenan (British Consul-General, Shanghai) to Sir M. Lampson, 23 July 1931, PRO FO 371/15513/352–3.

67 Christmas Humphreys, *Buddhism* (3rd. ed., Harmondsworth 1983), p. 157.

CHAPTER 14

1 *The Times*, 7 May 1934.

2 Chao Kung to Persian, 5 Feb. 1932, BL TL.

3 Chao Kung to editor, *North China Daily News*, letter dated 9 Feb. 1932. reprinted in *NCWH*, 16 Feb. 1932.

4 Chao Kung to Persian, 9 March 1932, BL TL.

5 Chao Kung to Persian, 21 April 1932, BL TL.

6 *NCWH*, 3 May 1932.

7 Chao Kung to German Consulate-General, Shanghai, 23 June 1932, AA PA Politische Abteilung IV — China PO 11 Nr. 6 Bd. 1.

8 German Consul-General, Shanghai, to German Foreign Ministry, 27 June 1932, *ibid.*

9 German Ministry of Interior to Foreign Ministry, 25 Aug. 1932, *ibid.*

10 *The Times*, 10 Sept. 1925.

11 Ven. Chao Kung to German Consulate-General, Antwerp, 14 Sept. 1932, AA PA Politische Abteilung IV — China PO 11 Nr. 6 Bd. 1; and Mme B. Bonnamy to M. Steinke, 12 Nov. 1932, with enclosure, *ibid.*

12 *NYT*, 9 Oct. 1932.

13 Berlin police report dated 25 Oct. 1932, AA PA Politische Abteilung IV — China PO 11 Nr. 6 Bd. 1.

14 Chao Kung to unnamed German official, 18 Oct. 1932, *ibid.*

15 *The Times*, 20 Oct. 1932.

16 *The Times*, 5 Nov. 1932.

17 Rechtsanwalt Dr Josef Schoemann (Cologne) to German Foreign Ministry, 22 Nov. 1932, AA PA Politische Abteilung IV — China PO 11 Nr. 6 Bd. 1.

18 *The Times*, 12 Nov. 1932.

19 According to one account, Trebitsch's defence counsel in Cologne was Dr Robert Servatius (later a defence counsel at the Nuremberg war crimes trials, and counsel for Adolf Eichmann in the trial held in the District Court of Jerusalem in 1961). See 'Trebitsch-Lincoln' by Abba Ahimeir in *Encyclopaedia Hebraica*, vol. 18 (Tel Aviv 1964), cols, 896–7. Efforts to obtain confirmation of this report have been inconclusive.

20 Gemeinde um Buddha to German Foreign Minister, 2 Feb. 1933, AA PA Politische Abteilung IV China PO 11 Nr. 6 Bd. 1.

21 Minute to Reichsminister des Innern, 13 Feb. 1933, *ibid.*

22 Shanghai police reports, 27 and 31 July 1933, SMP I.O. 5607.

23 See list of Chao Kung's disciples sent as enclosure 2 with dispatch from German Consulate-General, Shanghai to German Foreign Ministry, 3 Jan. 1934, AA PA Politische Abteilung IV — China PO 11 Nr. 6 Bd. 2; and *The Trans-Pacific* (Tokyo), 3 Aug. 1933.

24 See Humphreys, *Buddhism*, pp. 223–9.

25 Chao Kung to Persian, 23 May 1931, BL TL.

26 Chao Kung to Persian, 9 July 1931, BL TL.

27 Chao Kung to Persian, 13 April 1932, BL TL.

28 Ludendorff to Ernst Bauer, 28 June 1934, BAK Bauer 66/107.

29 Roger Parkinson, *Tormented Warrior* (London 1978), p. 203.

30 Quoted *ibid.*

31 Martin Steinke, *Praktische Wege zum Übersinnlichen in der Buddha-Lehre* (Berlin 1926). See also the periodical *Der Buddhaweg und Wir Buddhisten*, vol. 5 (1932–3).

32 Steinke to Mme Bonnamy, 8 Nov. 1932, AA PA Politische Abteilung IV — China PO 11 Nr. 6 Bd. 1.

33 Welch, *Buddhist Revival*, p. 188.

34 *NYT*, 31 Dec. 1933.

35 A.P. Blunt (Nanking) to Chargé d'Affaires, Peiping, 20 Dec. 1933, PRO FO 371/18135/100 ff.
36 Chao Kung to German Consulate-General, Shanghai, 27 Dec. 1933, AA PA Politische Abteilung IV — China PO 11 Nr. 6 Bd. 2.
37 See Donald M. McKale, 'The Nazi Party in the Far East, 1931–45', *Journal of Contemporary History*, 12 (1977), pp. 291–311.
38 Behrend to German Foreign Ministry, 3 Jan. 1934, AA PA Politische Abteilung IV — China PO 11 Nr. 6 Bd 2.
39 Chao Kung to Adolf Hitler, 8 Jan. 1934, *ibid.*
40 Minute by Erdmannsdorff, 4 April 1934, *ibid.*
41 German Foreign Ministry to Consulate-General, Shanghai, 16 March 1934, *ibid.*
42 J.F. Brenan (Shanghai) to British Minister, Peking, 10 April 1934, PRO FO 676/191.
43 *The Times*, 12 April 1934.
44 *Vancouver Sun*, 11 April 1934; *NYT*, 7 May 1934.
45 *Vancouver Sun*, 10, 11, 12, and 14 April 1934.
46 *Evening Citizen* (Ottawa), 23 April 1934.
47 *Liverpool Post and Mercury*, 7 May 1934.
48 *Liverpool Post and Mercury*, 8 May 1934.
49 Home Office papers; *Liverpool Post and Mercury* and *The Times*, 12 May 1934; *Empire News*, 13 May 1934.
50 *Empire News*, 13 May 1934.
51 Abbot Chao Kung to King George V, 7 June 1934, PRO FO 676/191.
52 *Empire News*, 13 May 1934.
53 Shanghai police report, 18 Jan. 1936, SMP I.O. 5607.
54 Minute by R.S. Heaney, 27 June 1934, PRO FO 676/191.
55 Shanghai police report, 14 July 1934, SMP I.O. 5607.
56 Quoted *ibid.*
57 Chao Kung to British Consul-General, Shanghai, 28 June 1934 (copy), PRO FO 676/191; Chao Kung, Abbot, to Sir Alexander Cadogan, Peking, 12 Dec. 1934 (copy), PRO FO 371/19319/379; Chao Kung, Abbot, to C.J. Chancellor (Reuters Ltd.), 12 Dec. 1934 (copy), PRO FO 371/19319/380: *North China Daily News*, 11 July 1934.
58 *NCWH*, 11 and 18 July 1934.
59 Shanghai police reports, Sept. 1934 to Jan. 1935, SMP I.O. 5607.
60 See Chao Kung to Sir Samuel Hoare, 5 Nov. 1935, PRO FO 371/19319/388–90.
61 Shanghai police report, 13 July 1935, SMP I.O. 5607; *China Press*, 31 July 1935.
62 Behrend to Senior Consul, Shanghai, 2 Oct. 1935 (copy), PRO FO 371/19319/386.
63 Shanghai police report, 18 Jan. 1936, SMP I.O. 5607.
64 *The League of Truth* [Shanghai? 1935?]: copy in PRO FO 371/19319/391.
65 Chao Kung to Sir S. Hoare, 5 Nov. 1935, PRO FO 371/19319/388–90.
66 Chao Kung to Neville Chamberlain, n.d. [summer 1937], PRO FO 371/20995/9–11.

CHAPTER 15

1 R.H. Dennis to H.C. Rabbetts, 30 Nov. 1936 (copy), PRO FO 371/20995/7–8.
2 Report by Agent Sharp, 20 Aug. 1925, USNA RG 59/862.2.898.
3 Quotations from pp. 9, 116, and 247 respectively.
4 John Boyle, *China and Japan at War 1937–1945: The Politics of Collaboration* (Stanford 1972), p. 85.
5 Transcription of text in PRO FO 371/20995/14–15.
6 Young (Peking) to Foreign Office, 14 Oct. 1937, and minute dated 21 Dec. 1937, PRO FO 371/20995/12.
7 *NYT*, 18 Oct. 1937.
8 MOL, Horthy Papers, K section 589 — III. H. 22.
9 List of Trebitsch's followers (giv-

ing original and Buddhist names), enclosure 2 to dispatch from German Consul-General, Shanghai, to Foreign Ministry, Berlin, 3 Jan. 1934, AA PA Politische Abteilung IV — China: PO 11 Nr. 6, Bd. 2.

10 Information from Mrs Martha Vandor; documents in MOL, K 149-1938-4341.

11 *NYT*, 18 July 1938.

12 *Shanghai Times*, 27 Dec. 1938; documents in MOL, K section.

13 Information from Mrs Martha Vandor, Miss S. Carmen, Mr M.O.C. Walshe, and Mr Burt Taylor.

14 *The Times*, 4 Dec. 1937; *NCWH*, 26 Jan. 1938.

15 Toller to Sir A. Clark Kerr (Shanghai), 16 Sept. 1938, BL IOLR, L/P & S/12/487. No copy survives in the Foreign Office archives.

16 Minute dated 16 November 1938, signature indecipherable, *ibid.*

17 Shanghai police report, 22 March 1938, SMP I.O. 5607.

18 George Woodcock, *The British in the Far East* (London 1969), p. 223.

19 Marie-Claire Bergère, '"The Other China": Shanghai from 1919 to 1949' in Christopher Howe, ed., *Shanghai: Revolution and Development in an Asian Metropolis* (Cambridge 1981), pp. 22–3.

20 *Ibid.*, p. 25

21 J.G. Ballard, *Empire of the Sun* (London 1984), p. 23. The author of this evocative, semi-autobiographical novel was born in Shanghai in 1930 and lived there until 1945.

22 *NYT*, 20 Dec. 1939; see also *Time* and *Newsweek*, 1 Jan. 1940.

23 *NYT*, 1 Jan. 1940.

24 *NYT*, 7 Jan. 1940.

25 *Living Age*, vol. 357, no. 4481, Feb. 1940, p. 537.

26 Shanghai police report, 8 April 1940, SMP I.O. 5607.

27 Shanghai police report, 30 Oct. 1940, *ibid.*

28 See US Naval Intelligence report, 19 Nov. 1945, USNA RG 226 (O.S.S. files) XL 39875.

29 *Heim und Welt*, 5 Nov. 1950.

30 Evidence of Hermann Erben to Military Commission, Shanghai, 31 July 1946, in case of US versus Lothar Eisentraeger, alias Ludwig Ehrhardt, et al., USNA RG 153, Case 58–137, Book 1, pp. 105–70.

31 See Lahousen Tagebuch (Lahousen was a senior Abwehr officer), Institut für Zeitgeschichte, Munich, F 23/1, *passim*.

32 Fischer (Shanghai) to German Foreign Ministry, 5 Feb. 1941, AA PA Pol. IM, Mil. Po. 15g, Band 18.

33 See McKale, 'Nazi Party', p. 302; and David Kahn, *Hitler's Spies: German Military Intelligence in World War II* (London 1978), pp. 60–1.

34 Fischer to German Foreign Ministry, 19 May 1941, forwarding message from Meisinger to RSHA, Amtschef IV, AA PA Inland IIg 522; H.G. Stahmer, 'Hitler und die drei weisen Tibetaner', *Der Volkswille* (Schweinfurt), 11 Nov. 1949; see also H.G. Stahmer, 'Diplomaten, Spione und böse Geister', *Lübecker Nachrichten*, 9 March 1952.

35 Fischer to German Foreign Ministry, 15 May 1941 [No. 117], AA PA Inland IIg 522.

36 Walter Schellenberg, *The Labyrinth: Memoirs of Walter Schellenberg* (New York 1956), pp. 14–15, 160–1; Richard Hughes, *Foreign Devil: Thirty Years of Reporting from the Far East* (London 1984), pp. 34–5; records relating to Joseph Meisinger held at the Berlin Document Center; O.S.S. file on Joseph Meisinger: report dated 15 November 1945, USNA, RG 226/XL 30046; *NYT*, 10 Sept., 16 Nov. 1945, 8 March 1947.

37 Fischer to German Foreign Ministry, 15 May 1941 [No. 118], AA PA Inland IIg 522.

38 On the flight of Hess and the astrologers' round-up, see Schellenberg, *Labyrinth*, pp. 184–5; on the Ribbentrop-Heydrich conflict, see Kahn, *Hitler's Spies*, pp. 61 and 70; and Christopher R. Browning, '*Unterstaatssekretaer* Martin Luther

and the Ribbentrop Foreign Office', *Journal of Contemporary History*, 12 (1977), pp. 313–344.
39 Ribbentrop to Fischer, 17 May 1941, AA PA Inland IIg 522.
40 Luther to Heydrich, 19 May 1941, *ibid.*
41 Fischer to German Foreign Ministry, forwarding message from Meisinger for RSHA, 19 May 1941 [no. 121], *ibid.*
42 Fischer to German Foreign Ministry, 19 May 1941 [no. 122], *ibid.*
43 Heydrich to Foreign Ministry, 22 May 1941, AA PA Inland IIg 522.
44 Luther to Consulate-General, Shanghai, forwarding message from Heydrich for Meisinger, 26 May 1941, *ibid.*
45 Ribbentrop to Himmler, 11 June 1941, AA PA Inland IIg 17b.
46 See Karl Wolff to Heydrich, 4 Aug. 1941, BAK 58/859; and Kahn, *Hitler's Spies*, p. 61.
47 Evidence of Hermann Erben to Military Commission, Shanghai, 31 July 1946, in case of USA versus Lothar Eisentraeger, alias Ludwig Ehrhardt et al, USNA, RG 153, Case 58–137, Book 1, pp. 105–70.
48 Interrogation record of Joseph Meisinger, USNA RG 238, microfilm M1270, roll 25.
49 David Kranzler, *Japanese, Nazis and Jews: The Jewish Refugee Community of Shanghai 1938–1945* (New York 1976), pp. 531–2.
50 Note prepared for C.H. Silver, India Office, June 1942, BL IOLR L/P & S/12/494; see also A.L. Scott (Foreign Office) to Miss C.I. Rolfe (India Office), 16 May 1942, *ibid.*
51 H.A.F. Rumbold (India Office) to C.H. Silver, 23 July 1942, *ibid.* See also comments on article in *Review of the Foreign Press* (unsigned but by G.F. Hudson), no. 139, June 1942, BL IOLR L/P & S/12/720.
52 Wiegand to Cyril Benson, 4 March 1944, Hoover Institution Archives, Wiegand collection, Box 21, file 'Trebitsch Lincoln'.
53 *Unzer Lebn* (Shanghai), 9 July 1943.
54 *Unzer Lebn* (Shanghai), 15 Oct. 1943; see also report in another Shanghai paper, *Novaya Zhizn*, 9 Oct. 1943.
55 Humphreys, *Buddhism*, p. 105.

AFTERWORD

1 Gershom Scholem, 'Jacob Frank', *Encyclopaedia Judaica* (Jerusalem 1972), vol. 7, cols. 55–72.
2 Humphreys, *Buddhism*, p. 49; see also Edward Conze, 'Buddhist Saviours' in *Thirty Years of Buddhist Studies* (Oxford 1967), pp. 33–47.
3 Welch, *Buddhist Revival*, p. 175.
4 Wiegand to Cyril Benson, 4 March 1944, Hoover Institution Archives, Wiegand collection, Box 21, file 'Trebitsch Lincoln'.
5 Welch, *Buddhist Revival*, pp. 188–90.
6 Chao Kung, *La Tragédie Humaine* (Shanghai 1935), pp. 18–19.
7 *Ibid.*, pp. 16–17.
8 See Dinshah D. Gagrat and Herzl R. Spiro, 'Social, Cultural and Epidemiologic Aspects of Mania' in Robert H. Belmaker and H.M. van Praag, eds., *Mania: An Evolving Concept* (New York 1980); and Mortimer Ostow, 'The Hypomanic Personality in History', *ibid.*
9 Gershom Scholem, *Sabbatai Sevi: The Mystical Messiah* (Princeton 1973), p. 126.
10 See above p. 157.

INDEX